REVOLUTION UNENDING

The CERI series in Comparative Politics and International Studies

Series editor CHRISTOPHE JAFFRELOT

This series consists of translations of noteworthy publications in the social sciences emanating from the foremost French research centre in international studies, the Paris-based Centre d'Etudes et de Recherches Internationales (CERI), part of Sciences Po and associated with the CNRS (Centre National de la Recherche Scientifique).

The focus of the series is the transformation of politics and society by international and domestic factors—globalisation, migration and the post-bipolar balance of power on the one hand, and societal dynamics, ethnicity and religion on the other. States are more permeable to external influence than ever before and this phenomenon is accelerating processes of social and political change the world over. In seeking to understand and interpret these transformations, this series give priority to social trends from below as much as the interventions of state and non-state actors.

Founded in 1952, CERI has fifty full-time fellows drawn from different disciplines conducting research on comparative political analysis, international relations, regionalism, transnational flows, political sociology, political economy and on individual states.

GILLES DORRONSORO

Revolution Unending

Afghanistan: 1979 to the Present

TRANSLATED FROM THE FRENCH BY JOHN KING

Columbia University Press
New York
*in association with the Centre d'Etudes et de
Recherches Internationales, Paris*

Columbia University Press
Publishers Since 1893
New York
Copyright © 2005 Gilles Dorronsoro

Library of Congress Cataloging-in-Publication Data
Dorronsoro, Gilles.
  [Révolution afghane. English]
  Revolution unending: Afghanistan: 1979 to present/by Gilles
Dorronsoro; translated
  from the French by John King.
      p. cm.
  Includes bibliographical references and index.
  ISBN 0-231-13626-9 (cloth: alk. paper)
1. Afghanistan—History—Soviet occupation, 1979-1989.
2. Afghanistan—History—1989-2001. 3. Afghanistan—History—2001-
I. Title.

  DS371.2.D69313 2005
  958.104'5—dc22

                                        2004057131

Columbia University Press books are printed on permanent and durable
acid-free paper.

c 10 9 8 7 6 5 4 3 2 1

Printed in India

Contents

Maps

Tables

Foreword

This book on the Afghan war emerged from a sequence of research visits undertaken from 1988 onwards. In contrast to an ethnological approach, I opted to travel from one province to another, seldom staying more than a few weeks in the same place. A drawback of this approach was that it restricted my knowledge of any particular region, although the periods I spent in Herat were more substantial, but it did give me a basis for comparison between different local situations. Perhaps more important, I was able to escape from the stifling routine of daily life in a village and, bit by bit, to discover this wonderful country.

Travelling in Afghanistan during a war, often alone, was not always easy, particularly with a linguistic ability which was, at the outset, limited; and throughout with restricted financial resources. Each trip, even though it lasted only a few weeks, became a battle against physical fatigue and the consequent lowering of spirits. The task of observing guerrilla warfare necessitates a Spartan existence, with long periods of inactivity interspersed with infrequent bursts of combat. Being fired on in an ambush, then being shelled several times, I was left—whatever idea I might have had that I was immortal—with a fear of being wounded possibly even greater than the fear of death.

These things serve to show that the researcher is not untouched by the landscape in which he works and that much of the effort one makes goes into the mastery of one's own emotions. The consciously detached tone of the analyses which follow is no more than the calm reconstruction of a sometimes far from calm reality.

Desperately clutching his notebooks, which—especially towards the end of the trip—he is terrified of losing, the researcher himself becomes the object of sociological interest on the part of those whom he observes. The same questions are repeatedly put to him

about his religion,[1] his salary, his food, the existence and status of
Muslim communities in Europe—all matters which enable Afghan
interlocutors to make their own estimations of the researcher. The
traveller's host derives prestige from his presence, so that he is himself instrumentalised in the politics of local power. In particular he is
appealed to as an 'exterior' or 'neutral' witness regarding the claims
of one party or another, and is asked to make these claims known in
the outside world. A stranger is also viewed as a potential source of
aid for the community, which conditions attitudes towards him. Confusion between journalists, humanitarian aid workers and researchers brings with it an ambiguous situation. This is not the fault of the
Afghans alone: the journalists have often worked with NGOs (non-
governmental organisations), as have the researchers, with the risk
that the ground-rules governing each of these separate activities may
become confused.

In the villages the polite formalities are calculated to minimise the
potential disruption of which the traveller may be the cause. He will
be greeted in a room set aside for guests, he will have no contact
with the women of the household, and he is rarely allowed to move
about alone.[2] The researcher will therefore be obliged to take any
excuse to go out, in order to widen his contacts and to maintain a
wider perspective on the situation. In the bazaars the visitor may stay
at the hotel, and thus be more free in his movements. In spite of
these circumstances, the Afghans on the whole showed much pa-
tience when I asked silly questions; walked on the table linen (since
one ate sitting on the ground); or made appalling *faux pas*, such as being understood to ask in a bazaar where there had just been a bloody
settling of scores 'where the treachery is' (the words for 'treachery'
and 'tailor' are very similar). I was particularly startled by the freedom with which Afghans commented on the political situation.
Inaccurate information, on an issue of no direct personal concern,
was often to be taken as no more than a well-meant wish to tell the

---

[1] In Islam, Christians are seen as 'people of the Book', who as such benefit from
protection, or at the very least enjoy a recognised status.
[2] For an analysis of the rules of hospitality, see Julian Pitt-Rivers, *Anthropologie de
l'honneur*, Paris: Hachette, 1998, and in the Afghan context *Encyclopaedia Iranica*
IX (1), New York: Bibliotheca Iranica, 1998, pp. 53 ff.

researcher what should be the case rather than what it was in fact; this did not indicate any intention to deceive him.

Interviews were my primary source concerning local issues, which were rarely covered by the press or the radio. My preferred informants were often people on the fringes of power.[3] Those who had been through the process of education before the war, often ill at ease in the rural context, were especially valuable; as also were the *khans*[4] (notables) who had been pushed aside by political developments; as well as transport professionals, such as truck drivers and merchants, who were well acquainted with the local political realities. There was a constant falling-short in perceptions of national politics in comparison with local analyses, which were fascinating in their precision and insight. Through the opportunities afforded to him by his position of externality, a foreigner enjoys a privileged status, especially if he is able to stay aloof from the stereotypes of various groups. However, certain foreigners—whether journalists, researchers or humanitarian aid workers—have on occasion succumbed to the temptation to side with some particular political group, and sometimes even to propagate accounts which are virtually mythological.

My first two journeys benefited from the presence of Stéphane Thiollier, who was a superb guide, translator and friend. The present text owes much to his influence and is dedicated to him. I also offer my thanks to Hélène Arnaud, Anne-Françoise Basquin and Alain Besançon, who supervised the thesis on which this book is based; to Amélie Blom, Philippe Bonhoure, Hamit Bozarslan, Pierre Cent-livres, who agreed to read the first draft; and to Micheline Centlivres-Demont, Gérard Chaliand, Marie-Odile Clerc, Sylvie and Jean Dol-beault, Nathalie Fustier, Marc Gaborieau, Delphine Hery, Mirwais Jâlil, Bertrand Labaux, Cristina L'Homme, Régis Lansade, Chantal Lobato, Sophie Mousset, Mathilde Pinon, Jean-José Puig, Nicolas Rageau, Rémi Reymann and Alexandre Toumarkine. My research was funded in part by assistance from Marc Gaborieau and Alexandre

---

[3] It may be somewhat misleading to speak of a process of selection, since it was later that I became aware of common characteristics among my informants. A degree of correspondence between the social position of the researcher and that of the informant was often a source of rapport.

[4] Expressions in italics are defined in the glossary on pp. xvi ff.

Popovic's 'Groupe de recherche sur la transmission du savoir dans le monde musulman périphérique' based at EHESS, as well as by a grant from the Goodbooks foundation and through a contract with DAS (Délégation aux affaires stratégiques). Nicolas Rageau kindly drew the maps on the basis of information I provided. For obvious reasons I do not name those in Pakistan and Afghanistan who agreed to answer my questions, but they should count themselves the recipients of my sincere thanks.

The Anglophone reader will find here a somewhat different version of the text from that which appeared in French in 2000. This has been dictated both by the need for factual corrections, and because a reassessment was necessitated by the new phase of the civil war which began with the American intervention.

Le Couderchet,   G. D.
March 2004

Chronology

1747	Foundation of Durrani Empire by Ahmad Shah. At its maximum, after the battle of Panipat in 1759, this stretched to the River Indus.
1818–5	Partition of Afghanistan into three separate principalities (Kabul, Kandahar, Herat).
1835–9	Dost Muhammad on the throne.
1839–42	First Afghan-British war. The British puts Shah Shuja in power.
1842–63	Dost Muhammad restored to power.
1863–78	Sher Ali (a son of Dost Muhammad) comes to power after civil conflict.
1878–80	Second Afghan-British war. Britain puts on the throne Yaqub Khan (Sher Ali's son).
1880	Beginning of reign of Abdul Rahman Khan (a grandson of Dost Muhammad). Earliest foundations of the modern state. Abdul Rahman unifies Afghanistan after bloody campaigns.
1887	Northern frontier of Afghanistan defined.
1893	Eastern frontier defined by the 'Durand Line'.
1919	Assassination of Habibullah. His son Amanullah succeeds. Third Afghan–British war leads to Afghan independence.
1919–29	Reign of Amanullah who attempted to modernise Afghanistan. First Constitution promulgated in 1923.
1929–30	Rebellion against Amanullah, who goes into exile. Interlude of government by self-styled Habibullah II (Bacha-yi Saqao).
1930–3	Nadir Shah comes to power as king, installing a new dynasty and a conservative regime.
1931	Afghanistan's second constitution comes into effect.
1933–73	Zahir Shah on throne, after succeeding aged nineteen following his father's assassination.
1953–63	Daud (Sardar Muhammad Daud Khan) Prime Minister.
1964	Afghanistan's first liberal constitution announced, with two elected houses of parliament.
1973	Coup by Daud establishing the Afghan republic. Ex-King Zahir goes into exile in Rome.

1978   (27–28 April) Communist coup brings Taraki and Amin to power. Daud and his family put to death.

1978–9   Following the communist coup the countryside rises in rebellion; 'parties in exile' formed in Peshawar.

1979   (March) Rebellion in Herat when defecting army units fought government troops, Soviet advisers arrive in April to assist the communist government.

1979   (27 December) Soviet invasion. Babrak Karmal installed in power by the Soviets.

1986   (4 May) Karmal resigns, replaced by Najibullah under policy of 'National Reconciliation'.

1988   (April) Geneva Accords.

1989   (January) The Soviet retreat proceeds according to plan.

1992   (20 April) Fall of Najibullah regime. The *mujahidin* enter Kabul. War between the victorious parties begins immediately.

1994   (November) Kandahar captured by newly-formed Taliban movement.

1995   (5 September) Taliban takes Herat.

1996   (27 September) Taliban takes Kabul; Najibullah executed.

1998   Taliban takes Mazar-i Sharif.

2001   (9 September) Masud murdered.

            (11 September) Twin Towers of the World Trade Center in New York destroyed by Al-Qa'ida-linked guerrillas flying hijacked aircraft.

            (20 September) A council of Afghan *ulema* rules that Osama Bin Laden should leave the country.

            (5 October) The first contingent of US troops arrives in neighbouring Uzbekistan.

            (7 October) Operation 'Enduring Freedom' begins; US bombs Taliban and Al-Qa'ida positions; US special forces assist Shura-yi Nazar.

            (9 November) Dostum's forces and his allies take Mazar-i Sharif.

            (12 November) Kabul falls to Shura-yi Nazar.

            (25 November) Hundreds of Taliban prisoners killed at Mazar-i Sharif.

            (5 December) Schloss Petersberg agreements provide for setting up of Afghanistan Interim Authority.

            (9 December) Fall of last Taliban stronghold at Kandahar.

            (22–23 December) Afghanistan Interim Authority established. Hamid Karzai becomes chairman.

2002   (21–22 January) Afghanistan Reconstruction Steering Group holds international conference in Tokyo for aid donors to Afghanistan.

(28 January) Joint statement by President George W. Bush and Hamid Karzai on new partnership between United States and Afghanistan.

(11 June) *Loya Jirga* inaugurated by ex-King Zahir Shah.

(24 June) Government formed under presidency of Hamid Karzai.

(30 June) United States kills forty-two Afghan civilians in bombing raids on villages.

2003 (22–23 April) President Karzai visits Pakistan.

(4 June) Major battle between Taliban and government troops indicates strength of Taliban resurgence.

(11 August) NATO takes over command of ISAF.

2004 (4 January) *Loya Jirga* concludes with adoption of new constitution, conferring strong presidential powers on Hamid Karzai.

Glossary

asabiyya	solidarity based on belonging to the same group
agha	'sir', a term of respect
akhund	theologian, master of a school
alaqadari	sub-district administered by an *alaqadar*
alem	religious scholar or teacher (pl: *ulema*)
amir	prince/ruler
amir al-mu'minin	commander of the faithful
arbab	village leader: also has the sense of *khan* in Hazarajat
barakat	blessedness or holiness, which brings personal benefits
bey/beg	major landowner
chador	woman's veil
dari	Persian dialect spoken in Afghanistan
dawa	religious preaching
daulat	state, government
deqhan	peasant, sharecropper
faqih	religious scholar
farsi	Persian language
farsiwan	Persian speaker
fatwa	juridical opinion given by an *alem* (pl. *fatavi*)
fiqh	Islamic jurisprudence
gholam bacha	slave in the *amir*'s administration
ghund	regiment
hadith	reported sayings of the Prophet Muhammad (pl. *ahadith*)
hazrat	Excellency/Highness
hajj	pilgrimage to Mecca
haji	one who undertakes the *hajj*
hamsaya	client
hasht nafari	system of conscription where one man in eight is called
hijra	The Prophet Muhammad's migration from Mecca to Medina
hukumat	government
ijaza	certificate granted by an *alem* to a pupil, authorising him to teach

imam	one who leads the prayers; more generally the head of an Islamic community
imarat	principality
jamiyat	society, party
jerib	one-fifth of a hectare
jihad	holy war
jirga	tribal council
jombesh	movement
kafir	unbeliever, sinner
khan	man of influence, notable
khanaqah	Sufi center for meeting and meditation
khutba	Friday prayers
khwaja	master, a descendant of the Caliph Abu Bakr
kuchi	nomad
kundak	battalion
Loya Jirga	Great Council: an institution from the monarchical period, recently revived
madrasa	religious school
maktab	Quranic school: in Afghanistan a state school
malang	wandering mystic; beggar
malek	proprietor; village chieftain chosen by the elders
mamur	government employee
markaz	centre; base used by *mujahidin*
masjid	mosque
mawlawi	spiritual master; *alem*
maulana	spiritual master
mehman khana	guest house
mellat	nation
mir	equivalent to *amir*: a chief or lord
mirab	person responsible for water supplies
mubaraz	fighter
mudarris	teacher in a *madrasa*
muhajir	religious refugee (pl. *muhajjirin*): a Quranic expression
muhallim	elementary teacher (pl. *muhallimin*) equivalent to Arabic *mu'allim*
mujahid	fighter in the holy war (pl. *mujahidin*)
Muslim	Muslim (pl. *Muslimin*)
mulgerey	associate of a *khan* (Pushtun)
mullah	religious official of a small community
murid	disciple of a *pir*
namaz	prayer
namus	honor

pushtunwali	Pushtun tribal law
pishkhedmat	a particular rank of state employee under Abdul Rahman Khan
pir	master Sufi, a Sufi saint
qanun	non-religious law
qarargah	military base used by *mujahidin*
qowm	a solidarity group (pl. *aqwam*)
qadi	Islamic judge
rowhani	man of religion (senior cleric in Iran) (pl. *rowhanihun*)
sarluchi	literally 'bare-head': an opponent of Islam
sayyed	descendant of the Prophet Muhammad (pl. *sadat*)
shabname	tract
shahadat	Muslim profession of faith
shah	sovereign, ruler
shahid	martyr, one who dies in the *jihad* (pl. *shuhada*)
shaikh	man of religion, head of a brotherhood (pl. *shuyukh*)
Shaikh ul-Islam	title of a major religious figure
shariat	Islamic law
shahrwal	mayor
shura	consultative council: an Islamic concept
silsila	chain of masters deriving their authority from a given *pir*
tabligh	preaching, teaching
takfir	excommunication: declaring a person to be an apostate
takhie khana	place of retreat for Sufis; place of worship for Shi'ites where the tragic stories of Hassan and Hussein are re-enacted
talib	student of religion (pl. *tullab* Arabic; *taliban* Persian)
tariqat	Sufi order or brotherhood
tawiz	talisman
ulema	plural of *alem* (religious scholars, referred to as a group)
uluswali	district administered by a local official (*uluswal*)
ushur	an Islamic tax (a tithe)
wakil	deputy
wali	provincial governor
waqf	religious foundation or endowment (pl. *awqaf*)
watan	fatherland, nation
wilayat	province
wilayat-i faqih	authority exercise by a *faqih*
zakat	an Islamic tax
zikr	Sufi practice consisting of the repetition of the name of God (literally 'remembrance')
ziyarat	pilgrimage to the tomb of a saint
zulm	oppression

Regional context.

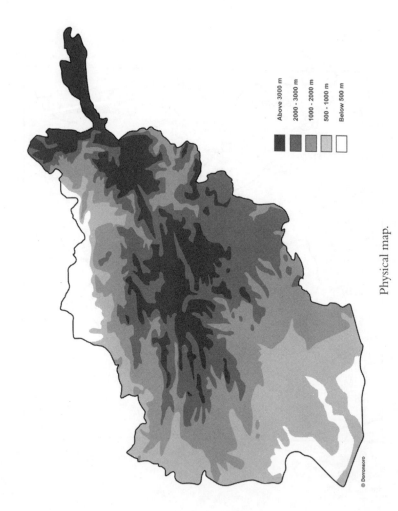

Physical map.

Above 3000 m
2000 - 3000 m
1000 - 2000 m
500 - 1000 m
Below 500 m

© Domanisoro

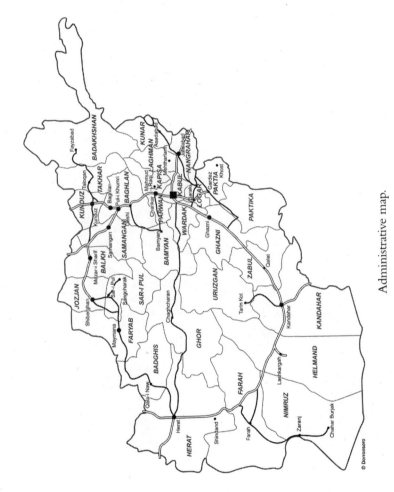

Administrative map.

Introduction

In the 1970s nothing indicated that Afghanistan was soon to be plunged into interminable war. The country had enjoyed an unexpected tourist boom, with more than 60,000 visitors in 1969, and was the obligatory route between Iran and the Indian subcontinent. Travel books and novels such as *Les cavaliers* by Joseph Kessel, translated into English and other western languages, had disseminated the image of a kingdom with pristine lands where proud tribesmen practised *buzkashi* and the vendetta.[1] Even the coup of 1973 and the establishment of a republic did not occasion undue concern either inside or outside the country. The monarchy had been on a constitutional basis since 1964, and its transformation into a republic was undertaken bloodlessly: King Zahir remained in Italy, from where he did not return until the spring of 2002. The personality of President Daud, who was a cousin of the king and had already played a role as Prime Minister between 1953 and 1963, conveyed the impression that the country would be able to summon up the energy it had lacked.

In April 1978, however, international attention was focused on the coup by the Hezb-i Demokratik-i Khalq-i Afghanistan (Afghan People's Democratic Party), carried out with the assistance of the Soviets. For a time there was a debate over whether the government was truly 'communist' or merely 'progressive', but the rapid breaking off of ties with the western countries and the uprising in the countryside made this an increasingly academic question. Under the momentum of the revolution the new regime went on to conduct bloody purges within its ranks, and in September 1979 Hafizullah

[1] Joseph Kessel, *Les cavaliers*, Paris: Gallimard, 1967. The brilliant photographic essays of Roland and Sabrina Michaud bring into play, in an almost mystical perspective, the notion of continuity between the past and the present: see *Mémoire de l'Afghanistan*, Paris: Chêne, 1980.

1

Amin rose to the leadership of the country after eliminating his predecessor Nur Muhammad Taraqi, who had been more moderate and was more highly regarded in Moscow. Meanwhile, as the rebellious countryside became impossible to control, the regime appeared on the point of collapse, until it was rescued by the arrival of Soviet troops on 27 December 1979. Commando forces installed in power a new leader, Babrak Karmal, after killing Hafizullah Amin. Against all the evidence, the Soviet Union claimed that Amin had—though only orally—asked for their intervention. The Soviet contingent rapidly settled down at about 100,000 men, and the process of integrating the country into the Soviet bloc gathered momentum.

In the months which followed the invasion, historical parallels multiplied, but also contradicted each other. According to a proverb, 'Experience is a light which shines only backwards.' Could armed Afghans overcome the invaders from the north, in the same way as their ancestors wiped out the British expeditionary force in 1842, or would Afghanistan end up after a few decades as a dismal Central Asian colony? Some predicted failure for the Soviets, basing their arguments on the disastrous outcome of the 19th-century British campaigns, while others expected the rebels to be defeated, as they had been in Central Asia in the 1920s when the Basmachis were overcome by the Red Army.[2]

Whatever might be the case, western opinion was outraged at such a blatant violation of the sovereignty of an independent country, and the invasion of Afghanistan signified the end of the period of détente. President Jimmy Carter, who said that in the space of a few days he had learned much about the Soviets, launched a rearmament programme which Ronald Reagan would in due course continue.[3] He also took reprisal measures, such as the boycott of the Moscow Olympics and halting grain exports, which—contrary to the general view—caused considerably inconvenience to the Soviet Union. The director of the CIA, William Casey, had the job of coordinating assistance to 'freedom fighters', whether Afghans, Angolans or Nicaraguans. These were sometimes put in contact with each other, and

[2] Hélène Carrère d'Encausse, 'Les Soviétiques en Afghanistan. Un nouveau Cuba?', *Politique internationale* 6, winter 1979/80.

[3] The US administration, which had already begun to finance anti-governmental movements, was in fact warned of the invasion when it was imminent and allowed the Soviet Union to make the mistake of entering Afghanistan.

soon realised that they had little in common except an enemy and a provider of funds.

After the initial crisis, the Afghan war settled down for the long haul. Over the years the world began to be familiar with the images of the fighters, wearing their *pakols* (Nuristani caps) or turbans, with a willingness to fight which was hard to explain in view of the trying conditions of their lives and the disproportionate odds they faced. Badly armed, deeply divided into competing groups, operating in an informal style which took observers aback, the Afghan resistance—perhaps even because of all these factors—could not be overcome. A number of heroic figures emerged, such as Masud, the young and photogenic commander of Panjshir, a valley to the north of Kabul, who displayed a strategic mastery in his resistance to the most massive Soviet onslaughts. These attacks, increasingly violent, created hundreds of thousands of refugees each year: of 12 million Afghans, 3 million would soon have migrated to Pakistan and 2 million to Iran, making up the largest refugee population of modern times.

In spite of the violence of the fighting, the resistance did not give way, with the result that the war became too costly for the Soviets, who in the summer of 1986 decided to withdraw. The Soviet Union, which had been in difficulties since the first oil crisis, had failed to make economic adjustments, and this had implications for its external policies. For Gorbachev *perestroika* and *glasnost* were no substitute for western cooperation, and the settlement of the Afghan issue, as an earnest of good faith, became a priority. It was also the first step towards the abandonment of an empire which had finally become too expensive, although Angolan oil financed the Cubans and Afghan gas was bought cheaply. In addition, the pointless deaths of young conscripts were viewed increasingly badly by Soviet public opinion. Gorbachev's speech of 13 January 1988 was a fundamental break with the 'Brezhnev doctrine': the Soviet Union announced its withdrawal from Afghanistan with no conditions as to who would constitute the successor government. This was the end of proletarian internationalism. The communist bloc began to break up. In the spring of 1988 the Geneva accords formalised the Soviet withdrawal, which was completed by 15 January 1989. The accords also envisaged—with some hesitations on the American side—what was called a 'positive symmetry', where the two superpowers would each remain free to arm their own allies.

The United States hoped, in fact, to bring about the downfall of the pro-Soviet regime within months of the withdrawal. The Americans may, have entertained the fantasy that the humiliation of Vietnam might be avenged by the evacuation of the Soviet ambassador by helicopter from the rooftops of Kabul. Urgent in their pursuit of victory, the United States and Pakistan adopted an ill-thought-out and ill-executed strategy of frontal attack against Jalalabad, a town whose capture presented particular difficulties. The failure of the resistance fighters, who were unprepared for conventional warfare, led to US disengagement. In contrast to most forecasts, the Kabul regime, even in its weakened condition, survived the withdrawal and became the linchpin of the unsuccessful negotiations undertaken by the United Nations. It was not till the spring of 1992 that the regime collapsed for lack of external support, some months after the coup against Gorbachev and the dissolution of the Soviet Union. At this point a new phase of the war began, as the victors fought among themselves in rapidly fluctuating coalitions. In 1994, just as Masud seemed definitively to have taken control of the capital, the appearance of a fundamentalist movement, the Taliban, radically altered the political balance. The Taliban were supported by a part of the population and received substantial assistance from Pakistan, and they conquered the southern regions of Afghanistan over the space of a few months. The capture of Herat in 1995 and of Kabul in 1996 marked the point when the movement broadened out, and with their completion of the conquest of the north during the summer of 1998 they controlled 90 per cent of the Afghan people. Only Masud continued to resist in his mountain fastness in the northeast, with help from the Russians, from Iran and from the West, especially France.

On 9 September 2001 the death of Masud in a suicide attack organised by Al-Qa'ida appeared definitively to mark the success of the Taliban, but the events of 11 September were to bring about its downfall. *Mullah* Omar refused to hand over Bin Laden to the United States, which launched a military onslaught on 7 October, largely from the air, leading to the fall of Kabul and the principal towns in November. The Petersberg accords of 5 December paved the way for the later formation of a provisional government led by Hamid Karzai, but dominated by Masud's successors. Several thousand western soldiers of the ISAF (International Security Assistance

Force) secured the capital within the framework of a UN operation. The meeting in June 2002 of a *Loya Jirga* (traditional assembly) gave a legal framework to the Afghan government, still under Hamid Karzai's leadership, but it also endorsed the return of the regional powers, who sometimes became involved in military clashes with each other, as well as the domination of the Panjshiris in the capital. The American forces, based mainly in Kandahar, continued to pursue the Taliban and the Al-Qa'ida militants. Once the initial shock was over, the Taliban effectively regrouped in the southeast and south-ern regions, relying on the help of the tribes of the Afghanistan-Pakistan frontier to escape from the Americans. In the absence of a clear victory, *mullah* Omar and Bin Laden for the time being disap-peared from view, leaving the Kabul government without authority over the country. The American military presence persists, bringing with it growing resentment in the Pushtun south, the sole theatre of western military operations.

Reference points

Over the last twenty years the events briefly summarised above have been the object of changing points of view which have revealed the assumptions of experts and journalists as much as the internal devel-opment of the conflict. In reality the way in which alien societies are viewed, infiltrated by our own agendas, has a tendency to create imaginary countries. In another context this has been illustrated by Lucette Valensi's analysis of how from the 17th century onwards the image of the Turk has been constructed in the light of the entirely European criterion of despotism, with a resulting distortion of the Ottomans' own concerns.[4] In interpretations of the Afghan war two biases can be singled out, which may be described as the geopolitical and the essentialist.

During the Soviet occupation from 1980 to 1989 the war was analysed broadly in terms of the East-West confrontation, and the local actors and their strategies were interpreted largely in terms of global issues relevant to American-Soviet rivalry. In this perspective all actions were decoded as if they had some bearing on the global struggle. Analyses took little account of random factors, of the auto-

---

[4] Lucette Valensi, *Venise et la Sublime Porte*, Paris: Hachette, 1989.

nomy of local actors, or of bureaucratic considerations. The Soviet invasion, in particular, was positioned in the context of an overall strategy directed at the domination of warm-water seas, in a continuation of the objectives of the pre-1917 Russian Empire. Geopolitics was fashionable, and there was much talk of a continuation of the 'Great Game', the period of confrontation between the British and Russian Empires in the 19th century when the aim of the Russians was to secure a route to the Indian Ocean.[5] By the same token the Taliban are often represented as no more than tools of Pakistan's its anti-Indian strategy and pursuit of influence in Central Asia.[6] The geopolitical interpretation here suggests dubious geographical determinisms and invalid historical analogies which a more precise analysis does not confirm.

After the Soviet withdrawal in 1989 the Afghan crisis, once more reduced to regional dimensions, invited attempts to discover the 'real nature' of the conflict. After 1992, when the fall of the regime in Kabul opened the way to a new war between the victorious parties, there were many such attempts, which followed fashionably on the heels of the return to 'realism'. Once the Afghan conflict could no longer be understood in terms of global imperatives, it became part of what the language of international relations refers to as an example of 'disorder'. Thus the war in Afghanistan was described as a 'Hobbesian' situation,[7] a special case where the war of all against all fails in reality to provide a foothold for political analysis. Meanwhile 'culturalist' analyses, which had been put forward since the start of the conflict, proposed a non-political understanding of the war. This then became a curiosity, to be interpreted in terms of the exotic and sub-political aspect of ethnicity, and to be viewed as springing from factors of a 'cultural' nature, almost in a genetic sense of the term. The war was seen simply as a return to the natural state of wickedness of the savage; so that that virtually nothing needed to be explained. It only remained to deplore the propensity of the Afghans to internecine struggle.

---

[5] See Mike Barry, *Le royaume de l'insolence*, Paris: Flammarion, 1984.
[6] Ahmed Rashid, *Taliban, Islam, Oil and the New Great Game in Central Asia*, London: I. B. Tauris, 2000.
[7] See Mohammad Tarzi, 'Afghanistan in 1992: a Hobbesian state of nature', *Asian Survey* 33 (2), 1992.

In those of its versions which deserve analysis, the culturalist approach reduced actions to unconscious cultural patterns, denying the capacity of the actors to act independently, and repudiating the observation of practice in favour of a number of basic texts which, like all written texts, are capable of an infinite variety of interpretation.[8] For instance, the supposed policy of equilibrium between East and West followed by Muslim statesmen was to be explained in part by the position of children within the harem: a hypothesis which is unverifiable to say the least.[9] Although they did succeed in expressing western social fears, such explanations failed to include any consideration of the causes of political violence. Three types of explanation—tribalism, ethnicity and Islam—belong at least in part to this deceptive system of observation.

A tribal revolt? Afghan political life has sometimes been represented as being a 'recurrent process of fission and fusion', where the integrating tendency of the state is opposed to the centrifugal force of the tribes: the present war is presumed to be the most recent expression of this tendency.[10] Afghanistan actually came into being in the 18th century as the result of the disintegration of the Persian and Moghul empires, which the Ghilzai and later the Durrani Pushtun tribal confederations were able to exploit in order to impose their own will on neighbouring populations. The political domination of the Pushtun tribes over the other ethnicities did not, however, obstruct close relations with the modern state which took shape progressively from the 1880s onwards. In fact, the tribes were organised in a manner which was characterised by the absence of political institutions. Oppositions at the segmentary level of clan and tribe normally impeded the emergence of a central power, other than at moments of crisis. The tribe could therefore be defined as the largest unit able to unify in the face of an external attack. Tribal identity also makes reference to a common ancestor, as well as to a code of conduct

---

[8] For a critique of these 'culturalist' theses see Jean-François Bayart, *L'illusion identitaire*, Paris: Fayard, 1997.

[9] Louis Duprée, *Afghanistan*, Princeton University Press, 1980, p. 193.

[10] See Louis Duprée, *New York Times*, 6 June 1989. This concept describes in theory the politics of segmentary societies.

predicated upon a method of settling conflicts by means of actual or threatened vendettas, within a system of collective responsibility.[11]

Tribal revolts against the state were frequent throughout the entire first half of the 20th century, but the most notorious—of which more will be said—was that of 1929. In that year the Pushtun tribes overthrew King Amanullah, who had embarked on a rapid modernisation of society on the Turkish model, though without the necessary military resources. The government was undermined by clashes with the *ulema*, as well as the cost of the programme of modernisation envisaged by Amanullah. An initially small-scale tribal revolt was able to spread because of the weakness of the armed forces and the support of the *ulema*, who issued a call to *jihad* (holy war) against King Amanullah, the king who was routed and went into exile. Subsequently, to widespread surprise, a Tajik bandit, Habibullah, known as 'Bacha-yi Saqao' (son of the water-carrier), was able to take advantage of the interregnum to capture Kabul, where for some months he ran a fundamentalist regime.[12] Only when Nadir, a cousin of the king, came back was it possible, with difficulty, to restore a coalition of all the Pushtuns and with the discreet help of the British to establish the Pushtun dynasty which reigned up to 1973.

Can the events of the present day be interpreted in the light of 1929? In 1978 the modernising reforms of the communists precipitated a tribal revolt, followed by the overthrow of the central authority and the occupation of Kabul by Masud—who, like Habibullah, was a Tajik—before the reconquest undertaken by the Taliban, who were mainly Pushtuns. This analogy, attractive as it may be, does not explain a fundamental novelty: the emergence of political parties,

---

[11] The expression 'tribe' has many definitions. Here we concentrate on those characteristics which are relevant to the Afghan situation, laying particular stress on segmentarisation. See Pierre Bonté, Michel Izard, *Dictionnaire d'ethnologie*, Paris: PUF, 1980, p. 720. This theoretical model does not exclude the occasional exploitation of segmentarisation by the most powerful elements to create a central authority. See Jean-Pierre Digard, 'Une contribution équivoque du droit coutoumier Baxtiari à la théorie de la segmentalité' in Jean-Pierre Digard (ed.), *Le cuisinier et le philosophe*, Paris: Maisonneuve et Larose, 1982. In Afghanistan there sometimes exists a division at the level of tribes, clans and families into two *bast* or factions: *spin* (white) and *tor* (black). These correspond to voluntary groupings, or fraternities, a phenomenon encountered in many segmentary societies.

[12] See Leon Poullada, *Reform and Rebellion in Afghanistan, 1919–1929: King Amanullah's failure to transform a tribal society,* Ithaca, NY: Cornell University Press, 1973.

which were far from being representative of the tribes. Further, it was not the tribes who took the initiative in the rebellion but the urban and rural population as a whole. The non-tribal communities, which are in the majority, were involved in the fighting to the same extent as the rest. It should finally be pointed out that it was broadly forbidden to bear arms in Afghanistan—with the exception of a number of eastern Pashtun tribes attached to the state—and that the tribes were in decline and had not for some decades represented any threat to the central authority.

An ethnic war? If an explanation based on tribalism finds too little foundation in fact, the appeal to ethnicity recapitulates in an apparently more convincing style some aspects of the same argument. Do ethnic antagonisms, or at least the hierarchy among the principal ethnicities present in Afghanistan (the Pushtuns, the Tajiks, the Uzbeks and the Hazaras), contribute to an understanding of the dynamics of the conflict? Before reaching a conclusion, prudence dictates that the concept of ethnicity, which has been the subject of a number of controversies in recent decades, should be more precisely defined.

Up to 1978 a significant part of the literature on Afghanistan was of an ethnological or anthropological nature, reflecting the interest of western researchers in a pre-industrial society which appeared to be a rich repository of cultures and languages. Much discussion concerning the concept of ethnicity was therefore based on the Afghan situation. Up to the 1950s, in the tradition of colonial ethnographic literature, an 'essentialist' idea of ethnicity prevailed. At that stage the concept of 'ethnogenesis' occupied a central position, since ethnic affiliation appeared to entail characteristics, which were virtually inflexible as well as culturally and biologically defined, as for example in the case of the 'warrior races' beloved of the British officers.[13] A catalogue of objective criteria—language, history, community, religion, material interests—constituted the definition of an ethnicity, in a theoretical approach which was carried over into Soviet ethnography. Later, by contrast, Afghanistan became one of the prime fields for a new approach to ethnicity, viewed now in terms of a social rela-

---

[13] Nirad C. Chaudhuri, 'The 'Martial Races' of India', *Modern Review* 68 (41–51), 1931, pp. 295–307.

tionship, in a departure from the illusory supposition that communities are natural objects. Henceforth the accent would be on the construction of communal identity in its relation with other groups, hence the interest in the concept of an ethnic 'frontier', implying an altogether more subjective and relational idea of ethnicity.[14]

In Afghanistan the identity of each individual is defined by a series of affiliations, from the most general—to the *umma* (the Muslim community as a whole)—to the narrowest, the close family. A sense of identity may be based on a shared geographical origin, or on a common affiliation—professional, religious, family, ethnic etc. In the tribal context, the extended family, the clan, the tribe and then the tribal confederation appear as a series of concentric circles, which they are not in a non-tribal context. The idea of a *qowm* specifies precisely these identities when they are mobilised within a solidarity network.[15] According to context, different identities are mobilised, exemplifying 'the jostling and pluralism of collective identities'.[16] For example a solidarity among Shi'ites arises out of their confrontation with a largely Sunni society.

Each individual has a place within the networks of solidarity (*qowms*) based on obligations which are more or less extended and defined. The *qowm* leans towards the nature of a system of exchanges which expands on the model of the extended family, although its actual basis may be different, e.g. professional, political or confessional. Affiliation to the same *qowm* may in particular imply an extended co-responsibility in the case of a vendetta. This follows the conclusions of Jean Leca and Yves Schemeil relating to the Arab world, where interpersonal relations are conceived on the pattern of family relationship.[17] The concept of *qowm* is also close to that of *asabiyya*,

[14] Fredrik Barth (ed.), *Ethnic Groups and Boundaries: the Social Organisation of Culture Difference*, Boston, MA: Little, Brown. See also Jean-Pierre Digard (ed.), *Le fait ethnique en Iran et en Afghanistan*, Paris: Ed. du CNRS, 1988.

[15] In the first instance this Arabic term signified a patrilineal group, but today it is the word for 'fatherland' used in the Arab world. The Afghans use it in a more generalised sense for any solidarity group.

[16] 'Le chevauchement et la pluralisme des identités collectives', Pierre Centlivres, Micheline Centlivres-Demont, *Et si on parlait de l'Afghanistan*, Paris, Neuchâtel: Editions de l'Institut d'Ethnologie de Neuchâtel et la Maison des Sciences de l'Homme, 1988, p. 37.

[17] Jean Leca, Yves Schemeil, "Clientélisme et néo-patrimonialisme dans le monde musulman," *International Political Science Review*, December 1983.

introduced by Ibn Khaldun, which designates the 'fellow feeling' which results from 'agnatic solidarity, or something similar to it'.[18]

According to its context, the word *qowm* may signify solidarities of a very different kind, within communities of variable size. A solidarity group emerges, for example, through the necessity to maintain relations with the state via the intermediary of the administrative official at the village level (the *malek*). Ecological conditions are also sometimes a factor conducive to cooperation at the village level. The election of a person to oversee the distribution of water, namely the *mirab*, who organises the irrigation system, defines a solidarity group.[19] A phenomenon revealed by the war was the significance of solidarities of place. This was often defined by attachment to the same administrative division (province, district or sub-district), a phenomenon that illustrates the capacity of the state to redefine the framework within which networks of solidarity operate, rather than to challenge the structural principle.

A further factor is that a *qowm* does not necessarily correspond to a contiguous area. For example, the inhabitants of a valley may be divided into two non-territorial groups due to a religious difference, with the two *qowms* so defined enjoying no spatial coherence. Since the reign of Abdul Rahman Khan (1880–1901) the majority of the villages in the south and centre of Afghanistan had lost the homogeneity which dictated that clan solidarities should have a territorial basis,[20] although this continued to be partly the case in the east of the country. Thus the village did not necessarily represent a *qowm* and cooperation is sometimes confined to the upkeep of the mosque.

Classifications by macro-ethnic groups (see table, page 15), which almost correspond to linguistic groups, therefore constitute only one level of communal affiliation among others and do not necessarily

---

[18] Olivier Carré, 'Note critique à propos de la sociologie politique d'Ibn Khaldoun', *Revue française de sociologie* 14 (1), 1973. Ibn Khaldun, *Al-Muqaddimah: An Introduction to History*, tr. Franz Rosenthal, 3 vols, London: Routledge and Kegan Paul, 1958.

[19] Barthélémy Amat, 'L'organisation paysanne pour la distribution de l'eau pour l'irrigation dans les villages de la steppe, l'institution du mirab', *Afghanistan Journal*, 1977. See also R. and M. Poulton, 'Coopération spontanée autour d'une mosquée afghane', *Revue des études coopératives* 4, 1979.

[20] Louis Duprée, 'The changing character of South Central Afghanistan villages', *Human Organization* 14 (4) 1956.

imply the existence of operational solidarities. The case of the Tajiks clarifies this issue. According to some estimates, there were before the war around 3.6 million Tajiks in a total Afghan population of 12 million, who were therefore numerically the second largest ethnic group after the Pushtuns. In Afghanistan any settled, Sunni, non-tribalised Persian speaker will be described as a Tajik—a definition which therefore emerges from a combination of linguistic, religious and sociological criteria, and so lacks 'both homogeneity and precision'.[21] Thus the Aymaqs, who are both tribalised and nomads, are not designated as Tajiks even though they are also Persian speakers and Sunnis, and do not describe themselves as such;[22] the same applies to the Ismailis, who are distinguishable from the Tajiks only by their religious affiliation.[23] The differences between identity as claimed and that as attributed by other groups, as well as apparently anomalous cases such as those of Tajiks who speak Pushtu or Baluchi, relate to the value attached to classification, a dynamic and conflictual social process in which context influences the choice of declared identity.

Tajik identity relates to and is weakened by the ambient situation, since affiliation to Persian culture transcends the Afghan context and is also linked to Iran and Tajikistan. The linguistic criterion does not by itself permit a simple differentiation of the Tajik population, since the Persian language is also used by the Hazaras, the Aymaqs and numerous other communities (sedentarised nomads, some of the Arabs, and so on).

In addition, Tajik identity competes with other strongly—held local identities which are linked to more substantial solidarity rela-

---

[21] 'à la fois d'homogénéité et de précision', Pierre Centlivres, *Un bazar d'Asie Central. Forme et organisation du bazar de Tashqurghan (Afghanistan)*, Wiesbaden: Ludwig Riechert Verlag, 1970, p. 155. It should be added that the category of Tajik is partly the outcome of administrative classification. During the 1970s, in fact, the State included on its identity cards an indication of linguistic (and hence indirectly ethnic) affiliation of a highly simplistic nature, classifying individuals as Turkmens, Pushtuns or Tajiks.

[22] Alfred Janata, 'On the origin of the Firuzkuhis in Western Afghanistan', *Archiv für Völkerkunde* 25, 1971, pp. 57–65.

[23] Another issue is that Louis Duprée, *Afghanistan, op. cit.*, p. 59, classifies the *farsiwan* (Persian-speakers) as an entirely separate ethnic group, defined by their spoken language (Persian) and their affiliation to the Imamite Shi'ite sect. For a critique of the ideas of Louis Duprée, which derive from an objective approach to the issue of ethnic identity, relying on ethnogenesis, see Jean-Pierre Digard (ed.), *op. cit.*

tionships. People refer to themselves, for example, as Herati, Kabuli, Badakhshi, Panjshiri, Andarabi or Munjani. These identities have more mobilising power than the more abstract affiliation to a Tajik group which depends primarily on the linguistic criterion. These populations do not view themselves subjectively as belonging to a community: there is no feeling of solidarity with the outside world nor are there common values, although this statement should probably be qualified in the case of the mountain Tajiks in the north-east, who are a more homogeneous and self-conscious group.

Finally, the Tajiks are dispersed throughout Afghanistan, and although they are in a majority in the north, the ethnic distribution here is also especially complex. In contrast to the other ethnicities— the Hazaras, Pushtuns and Uzbeks—the Tajiks are not mainly concentrated in any one region. In this sense there is no Tajik diaspora, since they have no heartland from which they might be supposed to have migrated. In fact the Tajiks belong to two distinct groups according to their geographical locality and their way of life. In Afghanistan the geographical distribution of the communities is to an extent regulated by the ecological opportunities afforded by economic occupations. The Tajiks live in the towns, or more properly in the bazaars, and occupy an important position in trade, but the term Tajik also applies to the long-standing Iranian populations who farm in the high valleys of the Hindu Kush. Another factor is that a person is deemed to have become a Tajik when he takes up the urban way of life and adopts Persian as his everyday language, especially in such towns as Herat and Kabul. In this case the category Tajik has 'least to do with ethnicity'[24] and can hardly be viewed as a positive affiliation with the capacity to produce real effects.

Despite the complexity of communal affiliations, however, the course of the war after the Soviet withdrawal tended towards the notion of an 'ethnic conflict' as the criterion of analysis, sometimes as an alternative paradigm to that presented by Islamism.[25] The proliferation of texts in which macro-ethnicities are posited as collective actors has entailed frequent confusion between the two ideas, with

[24] 'représente le degré zéro de l'ethnicité', Pierre Centlivres, Micheline Centlivres-Demont, *op. cit.*, p. 47.
[25] For an instance of this change of paradigm see Olivier Roy, 'La guerre d'Afghanistan. De la guerre idéologique à la guerre ethnique', *L'Homme et la Société*, 1993, no. 107–8.

Introduction

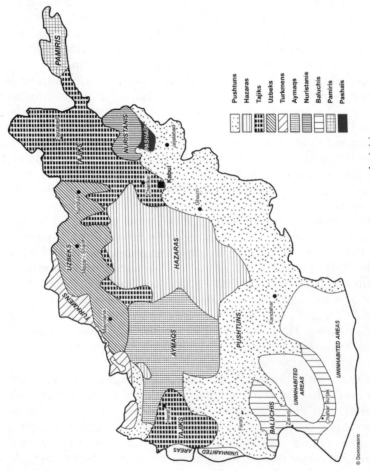

Simplified distribution of macro-ethnicities.

MACRO-ETHNIC GROUPS IN AFGHANISTAN (1978)[26]

		%
Pushtun	4,800,000	40
Tajik	3,600,000	30
Uzbek	1,200,000	10
Hazara	1,000,000	8.3
Aymaq	500,000	4.2
Turkmen	400,000	3.3
Baluchi	200,000	1.7
Nuristani	70,000	0.6
Pashaï	60,000	0.5
Other	170,000	1.4
Total	12,000,000	

Pushtun being equated with Taliban. At this point the war was viewed as a clash between communities, of a type liable to recur. With the ideological dimension left out of account, the identity of a political leader is reduced to his communal aspect alone, especially by the media. In reality the employment of the category of 'ethnic warfare' to describe the Afghan conflict is far from being neutral, and is in itself an ideological position. In the case of external observers, the use of such terminology tends to erect this category as in some way scientific or meaningful, when it is actually part of what is at stake in the conflict. The antithesis between 'ethnic' war and 'ideological' war is not appropriate, since nothing could be more political than the mobilisation of community identities.

However, it was not 'ethnicities' that made war, but political organisations with ideological objectives and particular institutional practices. Furthermore, the initial mobilisation took place in the context

[26] Table from A. Janata, 'Notizen zur Bevölkeringskarte Afghanistan', *Afghanistan Journal* 8 (3), 1981, pp. 94–5, quoted by Pierre Centlivres, *Les Nouvelles d'Afghanistan* 47, April 1990, p. 4. According to other sources, the number of inhabitants may have been as many as 14 million (it is noteworthy that this is the figure accepted by the World Bank). The percentages of the various macro-ethnicities are uncertain, due to the lack of reliable sources. Pierre Gentelle estimates the number of Pushtuns at 35–37 per cent, putting them on a par with the Tajiks (*Encyclopaedia Universalis*, supplement, Afghanistan, 1980), while Leon B. Poullada estimates the percentage of Pushtuns to be double that of the Tajiks, see *The Pushtun role in the Afghan political system*, Occasional Paper no. 1, the Afghanistan Council of the Asia Society, 1970.

of local *qowms* and not macro-ethnicities. It is also because of this specificity that, especially at the beginning of the war, it was impossible to discern the disposition of forces on the ground since *qowms* were not necessarily territorially based, with different parties often represented within the same village. Subsequently some parties actually did make use of communal affiliations to mobilise support, since—especially at times of crisis—identities are up to a point susceptible to manipulation. The appearance of nationalist ideology within certain communities was a political development which sprang from the strategies of the parties and the history of particular groups. The political role of the Panjshiris, who exercised a political influence disproportionate to their demographic weight, may perhaps have redefined them as an ethnic group separate from the Tajiks, thus indicating the plasticity of identities and their political origin.

After the Soviet withdrawal events moved in the direction of an alignment of the distribution of ethnicities and political affiliations on the ground. It should be understood, however, that the ethnicisation of the parties was a consequence of the war. Finally, the focus on ethnicity excluded the consideration of other dynamics, both social and ideological, which were equally significant. The new political equilibrium which had its origin in the American intervention tended to favour a new interpretation of the war as 'ethnic', since this was the only language which the foreign powers understood without difficulty.

A blend of religion and politics? The interpretation of the Afghan war also hangs on a tendentious question: what is the relationship between politics and religion in Afghanistan?—or, to take up a familiar theme, does Islam necessarily identify these two fields? Within the term 'Islam' a distinction must be drawn between a system of belief which gives a direction to action, and a theological system, although an excessive focus on the latter aspect, neglecting social practices, is to be avoided. For instance it is difficult to argue, as Bernard Lewis does,[27] that in a Muslim society political and religious power are identical, argu-

---

[27] Especially in *Le retour de l'islam*, Paris: Gallimard, 1985, p. 375. Bernard Lewis is sympathetic to the theories of Samuel Huntington, for whom the 'clash of civilisations' is the key to present developments.

ing from the absence of a word for 'laicity'. In the first place the Arab-Persian vocabulary distinguishes religious concepts (*ulema, jihad* and so on) from those of politics (such as *hukumat* or *qanun*), which is some basis for the supposition that the two domains are distinct. Secondly, when the *ulema* reject the Christian doctrine of the separation of religion and politics,[28] their claim is that it is their prerogative to provide politics with its moral standards, rather than appealing for a somewhat improbable fusion of the two domains.

Above all, throughout the entire Muslim world the separation of the religious and political functions has historically been the norm: few *ulema* have exercised political power other than in situations of crisis which have been viewed as exceptions to the norm.[29] In Afghan history the *amirs* (rulers), or those who aspired to power, were always members of the tribal aristocracy, and were never *ulema*. This practical and theoretical separation dates from an early era, in the 9th and 10th centuries, with the emergence of the *ulema*, a body of men of religion,[30] who constituted a relatively autonomous social group, identifiable principally through their knowledge of the Quran and its exegesis, acquired by means of recognised processes.

If the fields of politics and religion are not the same, what is their relation to each other? Such relationships as exist in the West in modern times—for example laicity in France and secularism in the Anglo-Saxon world—do not exist in the Muslim countries. A further factor is that the frontier between the religious and the political spheres constantly fluctuate: just as in the West the meaning of the idea of laicity is not the same at different epochs and in different

---

[28] For example in 1939 al-Maraghi, *shaikh* al-Azhar, cf. Gustav von Grünebaum, *L'identité culturelle de l'islam*, Paris: Gallimard, 1973, p. 56.

[29] From the historical standpoint, the proposition that politics and religion are one is in part vindicated by the nature of the community surrounding the Prophet Muhammad, where, significantly, the building where the Prophet lived served as both a place of worship and the seat of government. The practice of the first caliphs showed the same lack of distinction between religious and temporal authority. However, at that time there was no state as such, though a minimal institutionalisation of power, and the tribal power struggle, were always basic. Even in this case, the identification is not total, since the politico-religious power was obliged constantly to compromise with the tribes, whose source of legitimacy lay outside religion. See Maxime Rodinson, *Mahomet*, Paris: Fayard, 1961.

[30] Olivier Carré, *Islam laïque ou le retour à la grande tradition*, Paris: Colin, 1993.

countries, so the language of the religious establishment in Islam tends to vary in response to historical circumstances.[31]

In the context of relations between the state and the *ulema*, the central question is that of the legitimacy of political power. The state needs the backing of the *ulema* to persuade individual citizens of the religious legitimacy of state domination, since it was scarcely able to exercise a monopoly over security. The recourse to solidarity in the private sphere to guarantee the protection of individuals here relates to anthropological realities preceding Islam, which obstruct or delay the formation of a central state. Without exception the *ulema* have legitimated the political order, while quietism amongst the religious establishment tends to be prevalent in the Islamic world.

It would be difficult, especially in the case of Afghanistan, to argue that actors who reject the separation of the political and the religious spheres embody the 'essential principles'[32] of Islamic culture, or that such a 'return' belongs to 'the great tradition of Muslim history'.[33] Other authors, such as Olivier Carré, correctly stress the 'marginal and unusual' aspect of these tendencies over the long historical perspective.[34] In any case, unless one accepts the ideology of certain political groups, Islam does not connote a genetic predisposition to a unique mode of interaction between religion and politics.

On the other hand, initiatives do emerge from time to time which are aimed at a religious repositioning of the political order. Shah Walihullah in India and Ibn Abdul Wahhab in the Arabian Peninsula are the outstanding examples, both from the 18th century; in addition to the variegated ensemble of contemporary Islamist and funda-

---

[31] In the case of the Shi'ite clergy Pierre-Jean Luizard has shown how the political claims of religious figures have in the past been linked to particular historical situations, and in particular their relationship with the Safavid state (1501–1786). In fact the language of the Shi'ite *ulema* has been notably variable, and includes a substantial element of tactical positioning. The imperative to assume the powers of the Imam, and thus to lead the community, has never met with unanimity, even among the Shi'ite clergy themselves. See Pierre-Jean Luizard, *La formation de l'Irak contemporain*, Paris: Editions du CNRS, 1991, p. 126.

[32] 'les principes essentiels', Bertrand Badie, *Les deux Etats*, Paris: Fayard, 1988, p. 103.

[33] 'la grande tradition de l'histoire musulmane', Jean-Paul Charnay, *Sociologie religieuse de l'Islam*, Paris, Hachette, 1994, p. 39.

[34] 'marginal et déviant', Olivier Carré, *L'utopie islamiste dans l'Orient arabe*, Paris: Presses de la Fondation nationale des sciences politicques, 1991 p. 10 and p. 31. The constant danger is of supposing there exists a *homo islamicus*, an idea discredited by Maxime Rodinson in *La fascination de l'Islam*, Paris: Presses Pocket, 1993, p. 82.

mentalist movements.[35] The narrative of the origins of the Muslim community does duty as a utopia which can be turned to whenever social conditions are propitious. What distinguishes Islam is therefore not the absence of separation between politics and religion, whether in the theoretical or the practical sphere, but the availability of a utopian religious model to contest the political authority. In practice, however, the sociology of contending groups, *ulema* or students, provides an explanation of such social mobilisations. From this viewpoint the Afghan Islamist movements were represented at the onset of the war as a privileged route towards political modernity.[36] However, although this analysis may well illuminate some aspects of Afghan political movements, it has led to excessive simplification. In the first place, identifying a social group—in this case young people who have emerged from the educational system— with a political tendency is misleading, since the Islamists never attracted more than a minority of students. Secondly, the focus on the Islamists has resulted in an underestimation of the role of the traditional élites, sometimes themselves modernisers, and particularly of the *ulema*, who played a central part in the Afghan resistance.

Issues and hypotheses

The present study makes no claim to cover all aspects of the Afghan crisis. For example, the military, diplomatic and economic dimensions lie largely outside the selected field of study, and are touched on only to the extent that they explain more strictly political phenomena.[37] A number of questions are crucial to an understanding of developments since the 1980s.

First, how can the origin of this state of political violence be accounted for? In the 1960s a revolutionary situation had developed as

[35] On these movements, see particularly Gilles Kepel, Yann Richard (eds), *Intellectuels et militants de l'islam contemporain*, Paris: Seuil, 1990, and Olivier Carré, *L'utopie islamiste dans l'Orient arabe, op. cit.*

[36] Olivier Roy, *Afghanistan, Islam et modernité politique*, Paris: Seuil-Esprit, 1985.

[37] For more complete biographical resources the interested reader should consult the thesis which I successfully presented at EHESS in December 1995. The section of the thesis devoted to economic issues in the war is partly reproduced in 'Afghanistan: from solidarity networks to region' in François Jean, Jean-Christophe Rufin (eds), *Economies des guerres civiles*, Paris: Hachette, 1996.

a result of changes in the educational system.[38] The emergence of a group of politicised educated persons in a developing country is clearly not peculiar to Afghanistan,[39] but the parliamentary regime which was belatedly installed was unable to respond to social demands and gradually forfeited all support. Nevertheless, the communist coup of 1978 was in no way inevitable, and did not bring about any significant degree of social mobilisation—in contrast, for example, to the Iranian revolution.[40] In particular, nothing points to a profound rejection of the state for cultural or other reasons.

After 1978 how did mobilisation against the state take place? The origin of the civil war lay much more with the violence of the state than in the reforms implemented by the new authorities. In contrast to the situation of most guerrilla movements of the 20th century, the rural masses were not led by a modernising and revolutionary élite. With a few exceptions uprisings were spontaneous, and the political parties were formed after the event or independently of the popular rebellion. This was initially a counter-revolution, a rejection of atheism and of foreign occupation. The *jihad* (holy war) was the moral basis of the individuals engaged in the war, and militated against a political view of the conflict. Mobilisation took place in practice within the context of local networks of solidarity, under 'commanders'. The dichotomy between the commanders and the parties in exile explains why the parties had great difficulty in maintaining a monopoly over political representation and over the disposition of resources, and also why the parties disappeared after the fall of the regime in Kabul.

In what areas did the Afghan war result in revolutionary social changes? Political ideology and the politics of the ruling class were

[38] Charles Tilly draws the distinction between a revolutionary situation—the emergence of a group mobilised in the defence of its interests, and the revolutionary process itself, cf. Charles Tilly, *From Mobilisation to Revolution*, Reading, MA: Addison-Wesley, 1978.

[39] See Maurice Martin, "Egypte, les modes informels du changement," *Etudes*, April 1980, pp. 435–52.

[40] Which contradicts the postulation of a relationship between 'massive' effects such as civil war, and 'profound' causes. On these issues, see Michel Dobry, *Sociologie des crises politiques*, Paris: Presses de la Fondation nationale des sciences politiques, 1986, p. 71, and Raymond Boudon, *L'art de se persuader des idées douteuses, fragiles ou fausses*, Paris: Seuil, 1990, p. 270.

mostly transformed after the 1970s. As in any crisis, the personal status of all individuals was re-evaluated, and certain forms of legitimacy became the criterion of access to political or economic resources. An examination of the social background of these new élites reveals the significance of two groups. One of these, the *ulema*, whose role was not especially important before the war, became extremely influential. Almost all the political parties were lead by religious figures. The other group was that of educated individuals, who emerged from the towns to provide the most dynamic leadership of the resistance. During the war a progressive polarisation came about between the educated Islamists and the fundamentalist *ulema*. With the supremacy of the Taliban a 'clerical revolution' installed a regime unique in the history of the Muslim world.

Finally, what dynamic can be adduced to account for the tendency in the 1990s towards the progressive concentration of power and the elimination of the weakest actors? Commanders and parties unable to accumulate resources were in practice driven out, in favour of complex organisations run by *ulema* or by the educated. The war in this instance instigated a modernisation of the forms of organisation. In addition, the international order favoured concentration by excluding in practice any alteration of the frontiers. Control of the state and in practice of the capital, Kabul, was the major objectives of the actors. Since another feature of the situation was that the internal frontiers could not be stabilised, partition on a regional basis was unable to end contestation. In another context Norbert Elias has described an example of the mechanism of a progressive centralisation of power.[41] Although there were opposing sets of objectives, competition between actors tended to result in one of them achieving a monopoly. This process operated to the benefit of the Taliban up till the American intervention, which simultaneously re-established regional authorities and put an end to rivalry for the capital, which was henceforth placed off limits by the presence of international forces. This unstable situation, with inadequate international aid, facilitated the reconstitution of the façade of a state, which however was for the moment unable to impose its will over the rest of the country, where the civil war continued.

[41] Norbert Elias, *La dynamique de l'Occident*, Paris, Calmann-Lévy, 1975.

With the intention of testing these hypotheses, the first part of the book concentrates on the sociogenesis of the Afghan state and developments from 1960 to 1970. The second part examines political mobilisations in the local and then the national context. The third part looks at the dynamics of the conflict, from the standpoint of the government, and that of the guerrillas. The fourth section looks at developments after the Soviet withdrawal, and especially at the abortive reconstruction of a central political authority, the ethnicisation of the war, and the aims of the fundamentalist *ulema*. The fifth and last section deals with the American invasion and the return of fragmentation.

Part I. THE ORIGINS OF THE AFGHAN REVOLUTION

1. The Sociogenesis of the Afghan State

The political history of Afghanistan may be interpreted as the emergence of a state whose development has re-ordered the relationships between social groups.[1] After the death of Aurangzeb (1707), the vacuum created by the collapse of the Mughal empire and the decline of the Safavid empire allowed Mir Wais, at the head of the Ghilzai tribal confederation, to drive out the Persians in 1709. In 1747 the election of Ahmad Shah (1747–1773) as chief of the Durrani tribal confederation marked the inception of an Afghan dynasty which, after the battle of Panipat against the Indians in 1759, expanded its empire as far as the Indus. Originally elected by the tribes as an agent of military coordination, the *amir* attempted afterwards to keep the proceeds of the conquests for himself. In 1775 Timur moved the capital from Kandahar to Kabul in order to distance himself from the Durrani tribes. However, he was unable to escape the effects of the tribal system, and continued to rule over an empire with fluid boundaries which progressively shrank to the dimensions of present-day Afghanistan under the pressure of British and Russian imperialism. Up to the end of the 19th century incessant revolts resulted in the emergence of what were for practical purposes independent provinces in Kabul, Kandahar and Herat. Attempts to establish a centralised authority inevitably failed due to the weakness of the urban economy and to wars of succession which reduced the country to ruin.[2]

In any explanation of the sociogenesis of the Afghan state from the end of the 19th century, account must be taken of the part played

---

[1] On the building of the Afghan state, reference will be made to the studies made by Hasan Kakar, *Government and Society in Afghanistan: the Reign of amir Abdur Rahman Khan*, Austin, TX: University of Texas Press, 1979, and Vartan Gregorian, *The Emergence of Modern Afghanistan*, Stanford University Press, 1969.

[2] Gregorian, *op. cit.*, p. 69.

by the imperial powers, Britain and Russia, which defined the frontiers of Afghanistan and supported the state at critical moments. Subsequently the development of the institutions of the state took place side by side with the maintenance of patrimonial practices within the governing class. Meanwhile the state, whose source of legitimacy was progressively transformed from Islam to Pushtun nationalism, faced challenges from the *ulema* and the tribes.

The role of imperialism

From the close of the 19th century onwards, the internal balance of forces within Afghan society was diverted into an unnatural course by Britain and Russia, which laid down the frontiers even before a state existed which was truly able to impose its authority on the territory. In fact, those two powers on the whole favoured the establishment of an Afghan state, once the impossibility of direct control was recognised. The frontiers of Afghanistan thus came into being through a process involving both negotiation and war between the British, the Russians and the Afghans. In 1891 the British created the Wakhan corridor, which separated India from Russia and thus gave Afghanistan a border with China. Two years later Britain's Colonel Durand drew the 'Durand Line' which demarcated the frontier between Afghanistan and the Indian empire.[3] Drawn up exclusively in the light of military considerations, the Durand Line divided the Pushtun tribes, and was to be the origin of a lingering dispute between Afghanistan and Pakistan. Finally, between 1904 and 1906 the British demarcated the Afghan-Persian frontier.

In order to forestall disorder on their frontiers, the British were to make a priority of the stability of Afghanistan, ensuring that conflict between the *amir* and the tribes did not result in disadvantage to the *amir*. In 1883 Gladstone granted the Afghan sovereign an annual subvention, financed by a tax levied on the population of India. The annual revenue of the kingdom of Afghanistan was at that time 12 to 13 million rupees. In relation to this the additional British contribu-

---

[3] Dr Azmat Hayat Khan, *The Durand Line: its Strategic Importance*, University of Peshawar and Hanns Seidel Foundation, 2000. Strictly speaking, the Durand Line was not a frontier, but rather the limit of the British zone of influence, which was the justification for Afghan claims on territory populated by ethnic Pushtuns when Pakistan was established.

tion was substantial, amounting to 1.8 million rupees per year from 1893, in addition to a supplementary fund available in case of emergency, thus bringing the total to 28.5 million rupees between 1883 and 1901.[4] During periods of tension, the British provided money and arms whenever the central power in Afghanistan appeared to be in difficulty, especially during the tribal uprisings of 1880, 1882 and 1887. Later, in 1924, during the revolt of the Mangal tribe at Khost, King Amanullah, with British approval, enlisted Soviet and German pilots for punitive air raids. After the overthrow of Amanullah in 1929, the British and the Soviets intervened to come to the assistance of the respective parties. When, after some months, British support enabled a tribal coalition led by the future ruler Nadir to be established, the Russians went so far as to risk a brief military incursion into the north of Afghanistan in support of Amanullah.[5] In the following period, British assistance in the reorganisation of the army was equally significant, with the provision of 10,000 rifles, 5 million cartridges and a sum of £180,000.[6]

Neo-patrimonialism

The construction of the state, once begun at the end of the 19th century, was to continue from that date in spite of some reverses. The concept of neo-patrimonialism[7] applies well to a somewhat ambiguous situation, in which the development of institutions continued but was accompanied by the continued predominance of a restricted group which was able to perpetuate its hold on power.

The institutionalisation of the state. The project of establishing a state on the western model came into existence with Abdul Rahman Khan. He, by refraining from nominating his heirs to positions as

[4] Hasan Kakar, *op. cit.*, p. 90.
[5] Georges Agabekov, *OGPU: the Russian Secret Terror*, New York: Brentano's, 1931; and Anthony Arnold, *Afghanistan: the Soviet Invasion in Perspective*, Stanford, CA: Hoover Institution, 1981, p. 19.
[6] Hasan Kakar, *op. cit.*, p. 321.
[7] The neo-patrimonial state is defined by the appropriation of the partially institutionalised political centre by a group essentially oriented towards the maintenance of its own power. On this issue see Jean-François Médard, 'Etat patrimonialisé', *Politique Africaine*, September 1990.

provincial governors, set a limit to the patrimonialisation of power.[8] The very broad autonomy of the provincial governors was suppressed in favour of a more centralised system, which strengthened the authority of the *amir*. The size of the provinces was reduced, which improved administration and offered a more restricted platform to any potential claimant to the throne. Two examples illustrate the transition towards the institutionalisation of power. First, the royal treasury in 1922 distinguished between the personal expenses of the king and those of the state. The transition towards an institutional system was thus definitively set in train, all the more so since a constitution was adopted in 1923. Secondly, the constitution of 1964 provided for an elected parliament and ruled that members of the royal family could no longer hold ministerial office.

In addition, the recruitment of administrators reinforced the autonomy of the state. In the 19th century the *gholam-i shah* (the king's slaves), in fact orphans or other children under the protection of the *amir*, constituted the backbone of the royal administration. The state thus established for itself a group of loyal supporters, structurally linked to its interests, and divorced from tribal loyalties. The *gholam-i shah*, who often married into influential families, would provide in due course the personnel of the reformist circles of the first decades of the 20th century.[9] Similarly the *pishkhedmat*, who were the sons of notables, kept close to the *amir* as sureties for the loyalty of the group whom they represented, performed various duties at the royal court. This system of recruitment was supplemented by the educational system, of which one function was to educate administrative élites for the state. Thus the military college at Kabul, founded by Habibullah in 1904, mainly recruited the sons of the *khans* of the Durrani tribal confederation, of whose loyalty the regime wished to be assured. The college was to provide a significant proportion of the higher

---

[8] The patrimonial state is characterised by leadership of a traditional kind, where the decision-making power is viewed as the perquisite of the prince and his followers. Before Abdul Rahman Khan, it would be appropriate to speak of 'Sultanism', because of the extent to which power appeared to be the personal property of the *amir*, divisible between his heirs at successions. Cf. Max Weber, *Economie et Société*, Paris: Plon, 1968, p. 231.

[9] See Dr Fazal ur-Rahim Marwat, *The Evolution and Growth of Communism in Afghanistan 1971–1979*, Karachi: Royal Book Company, 1997, p. 106.

administrators in the first two decades of the 20th century.[10] From the 1950s the university progressively took over the task, but the administration then found itself unable to absorb the growing cohorts of graduates. The administration remained relatively unexpanded, as the number of officials was estimated at 40,000 in 1969, in a population of around 10 million people.[11]

To an even greater extent than the civil administration, the army was a priority for investment by the Afghan state. The development of a national army was undertaken in response to the stimulus of the tribal revolts which punctuated the state's drive towards centralisation. Military investment was thus justified by immediate security considerations, since as late as the 1950s the state found difficulty in quelling a rebellion solely by the use of its army and was obliged to raise tribal levies. The clashes of 1924 during the Khost rebellion were an indication that the balance of forces was not always favourable to the central authority, as the debacle of 1929 a short time later also showed. In July 1930 the army, unable on its own to put down a revolt in Kohistan to the north-east of Kabul, was obliged to call on the Pushtuns. In contrast with these internal threats, the protection of Afghanistan against neighbouring powers was always a secondary consideration. The wars against the British in the 19th century, an essential element in Afghanistan's historical memory, were waged by the tribes. The army's only external engagement, which was in any case on a limited scale, was the war of independence against Britain in 1919,[12] and even in this case the assistance of the Wazir and Mahmud eastern Pushtun tribes was necessary. On this criterion the troubles of 1959 marked a turning-point, since for the first time a tribal rebellion was easily crushed by the army. The process of imposed modernisation already attempted under Amanullah was able

---

[10] In the first place Habibullah founded a school for the sons of notables (*maktab-i malikzadeh*), which later became the royal military college (*madrasa-yi harbi-yi sirajiya*).

[11] The figure given by the American governmental agency USAID, cited by Gilbert Etienne, *L'Afghanistan ou les aléas de la coopération*, Paris: PUF, 1972, p. 45.

[12] Unable to occupy Afghanistan, the British nevertheless imposed their control on its external relations. After the war of 1919 Afghanistan was accorded full international recognition and welcomed its first foreign embassies. See Ludwig W. Adamec, *Afghanistan 1900–1923: a Diplomatic History*, Berkeley: University of California Press, 1967.

once more to get under way, and the policies of Daud, from his first term as Prime Minister onwards (1953–63), relied on a military institution whose political significance was growing.

At the beginning of the century the army was a crucial item of expenditure, with 50 per cent of the budget allocated to it.[13] Amanullah (1919–29) was an exception in that at the beginning of the 1920s he cut the military budget, which was to be one of the reasons for his downfall.[14] Subsequently the army became once more a priority. Nadir Shah and his successors devoted more than half the budget to it, and in the 1960s it attracted a third of the current account expenditure. The large size of the army explains in part the levels of expenditure. In the first years of his reign Abdul Rahman Khan set up a paid army of 43,000 men, which had risen to 100,000 by the time of his death in 1901. After a reduction under Amanullah, the army rose again from 40,000 to 70,000 men between 1934 and 1941, and with conscription after 1941 reached 90,000,[15] in a remarkable contrast to the small complement of civil officials.

As in many countries, the army was a central element in the construction of the state. Owing to the numbers who underwent training, and as a model organisation, it had considerable influence within the state apparatus. Its evolution may be traced in the light of two issues, technical modernisation and recruitment.

Rather than real industrialisation, the *amirs* initially sought technological advance in the field of armaments. Openness to western ideas in the 19th century was accepted, but was in principle limited strictly to the technical sphere, and in particular to the manufacture of arms, which could improve the equilibrium of the *amir*'s power with that of the tribes. Dost Muhammad (1826–39 and 1842–63) was the first to call on foreign experts, who modernised his army through the introduction of military uniforms and infantry. Under Abdul Rahman Khan the closure of the frontiers, in spite of its disastrous effects on the economy and culturally, was no barrier to the controlled importation of military technologies. The *amirs*' workshops were restricted essentially to the manufacture of ammunition

---

[13] Under the *amir* Shir Ali in 1877–8 the budget for the army already represented 43 per cent of the total. Hasan Kakar, *op. cit.*, p. 88.

[14] Leon Poullada, *op. cit.*, p. 111.

[15] Vartan Gregorian, *op. cit.*, p. 296.

and guns, and their extent was limited, with a workforce of 1,500 at the beginning of the century, rising to 5,000 in 1919.[16] In the 1940s the state called on British technicians, but the major turning-point came in 1955 with the Soviet-Afghan cooperation accords. These related to the training of officers and the provision of supplies, and effectively made Afghanistan a client of the Soviet Union.

An analysis of military recruitment displays two phenomena: the gradual transition to conscription and the training of an officer corps. In the 19th century several attempts to provide the *amir* with forces independent of the tribal levies failed, since the military significance of the Durrani confederation's horsemen greatly restricted the choices open to the government. Nevertheless Abdul Rahman Khan succeeded in establishing a professional army, paid and hierarchically organised, which was recruited from among the politically most reliable groups. The process of recruitment followed the changing loyalty of the communities: the Hazara, the Qizilbash and the Ghilzai, who were dominant up to 1880, gave way after various uprisings to a majority of Durrani. Nonetheless the *amir* recruited from all the ethnic groups, stationing his troops outside their province of origin, a practice continued under all later governments.

Until the 1940s recruitment was based on the supply of a number of soldiers by the village or the clan, rather than being chosen by the state. In particular Habibullah set up the system of *hasht nafari* (eight men), i.e. the enlistment of one man in eight, chosen by the community. The transition to a conscript army was not achieved without difficulties. Obligatory military service, decreed for the first time by Amanullah in the 1920s, was rejected by the Pushtuns, which gave rise to substantial over-representation in the army of other ethnic groups. In 1941 the international situation allowed the government to persuade the *Loya Jirga* (Great Council)[17] definitively to accept universal military service, which led in turn to the abandonment of

---

[16] *ibid.*, p. 190.

[17] The *Loya Jirga* is a council of tribal chiefs, convened for the first time by Mir Wais at the time of the rebellion against the Safavid Empire. Later the *Loya Jirga* became an assembly of tribal chiefs, religious leaders and notables gathered to endorse a new sovereign or a constitutional change. Cf. Ludwig W. Adamec, *Historical Dictionary of Afghanistan*, Metuchen, NJ: the Scarecrow Press, 1991, p. 150; and Fida Yunas, *Afghanistan, Jirgahs and Loya Jirgahs: the Afghan Tradition (977 AD to 1992 AD)*, Pakistan, 1997.

community recruitment. However, the men of certain eastern and Ghilzai Pushtun tribes were exempted from military service because of their status as 'guardians of the frontier'. In practice this left them free to indulge in smuggling and participate in the destabilisation of the Pushtun tribes on the other side of the Durand Line.

In the first half of the century officers were generally recruited from groups which had links with the authorities: the *pishkhedmat*, the *gholam-i shah*, the sons of notables (*khanzadeh*), and members of the royal clan. Later the government of Daud (1953–63) set up military schools throughout the country. These were free, and became a means of social advancement for many children from small merchant or peasant families.

The maintenance of patrimonial practices. However, the development of institutions of state never resulted in a fully coherent system, nor in the abandonment of patrimonial practices. After the 1950s the Afghan state stressed its institutional character, but power remained largely the personal prerogative of the king and the governing class. The inheritance of power clearly illustrates the low level of institutionalisation. Abdul Rahman Khan laid down rules of inheritance, in order to avoid the wars which had drawn the numerous claimants to the throne into mutual conflict in the 19th century. This situation was complicated by the fact that the *amirs* frequently had several dozen children. However, up to the present there has been no instance of a regular succession to the throne, except that of Abdul Rahman Khan himself in 1901.[18]

---

[18] In 1919 Amanullah in fact imposed himself by force against the opposition of his uncle Nasrullah. Daud, Taraki, Amin, and Najibullah were victims of *coups d'état*. Karmal (1980–6) was ousted by Najibullah on the direct orders of the Soviets, without what could be called a coup, since the succession procedure, as under other communist regimes, was not on a firm legal footing. The situation was just as ambiguous in the case of Zahir who, though the legal heir after the assassination of Nadir, was unable to exercise real power before the 1960s. The coming to power of Daud as Prime Minister in 1953, without there being a coup, symbolised a new balance of forces and allowed a new generation within the dynasty to come to power (to the surprise of many, Daud agreed to go at the request of Zahir in 1963). Even the legality of the presidency of Rabbani (1992–2001) was disputed, and *mullah* Omar (1996–2001), whose government was not internationally recognised, lost power as the result of his defeat by the United States.

Up till the 1970s the Afghan governing class comprised several thousand individuals who, through their wealth or prestige, wielded a decisive social and political influence. Within this class four groups were distinguishable: the tribal aristocracy, the intellectuals (university personnel and religious dignitaries), administrators and merchants.[19] However, the frequency of marriage between governing class families, whose members were linked by extended networks, meant that the division into distinct groups was not absolute, though without the implication of any automatic convergence of attitudes or agreement on decisions. Historically the primary element of the governing class was the royal clan, the Muhammadzai, which had distanced itself progressively from its tribal origins in order to achieve a distinctive status within the state. The role of the Muhammadzai dated from the reign of Abdul Rahman Khan. There was a change in the attitude of the *amir*, particularly after the Ghilzai revolt of 1886–8, after which he systematically raised the prestige of the royal clan, designating it as the *sharik-i daulat* (the partner of the state), thus underlining the privileged position of its members.[20] In the contemporary period the Muhammadzai were over-represented in decision-making positions, especially in the armed forces, because of their supposed loyalty to the dynasty. In the last period of his presidency (1973–8) Daud, having split with the communists, continued to seek the support of the royal clan, of which he was a member, demonstrating the persistence of such loyalties even after the end of the monarchy.

In the course of the 20th century, the development of the state led to the gradual enlargement of the governing class, which became an urban, and even a Kabuli, group. The predominant use of Persian was an indicator of its increasing distance from the tribes, who were Pushtu-speakers, although the Durrani aristocracy always maintained their links with Kandahar, their region of origin. With the

[19] Abdullah Aziz, *Essai sur les catégories dirigeantes de l'Afghanistan, 1945–1963*, Berne-Paris: Peter Land, 1987, p. 55. In addition, Leon Poullada assesses the élites (the royal family, senior officials, tribal chiefs, wealthy merchants, major landowners) at 2–3,000 people: see *The Pashtun Role in the Afghan Political System*, New York: Asia Society, 1970 (Afghanistan Council Occasional Paper no. 1).

[20] In particular they constituted the royal cavalry (*risala-yi-shah-i qandahari*). The *amir* also employed the Muhammadzai in his personal guard. At moments of crisis, however, he turned more readily to the Safi or the Gardezi.

exception of the religious establishment, this class derived its cohesion from a common aspiration towards western-style modernity. A foreign university education was commonplace for students from these families, who frequently went on to find employment in the higher ranks of the administration. The governing class also laid down new norms of behaviour, particularly in dress and language. In addition the onset of industrialisation enabled its members to obtain dominant positions within the economy, thanks to their contacts within the governmental structure. The national bank (Bank-i melli), established in the 1930s, operated in the first instance with private capital and played a part in the creation of most of the industrial ventures of significant size, such as the cotton company Spinzar. Not till the 1960s was there any development of smaller-scale industries, which were never able to obtain sufficient capital.

Beyond the ranks of the national élites, the central authority could also count on the loyalty of particular communities. From the time of Timur, the *amir* employed two strategies, both normal within imperial structures, to ensure the loyalty of his supporters. In the first place, an external community, in this case the Qizilbash, who were Shi'ites of Iranian origin, became the source of recruitment of court administrators and of a military élite.[21] In addition, the *amir* favoured particular Afghan tribes, for example the Safi of Tagab, who was represented in the royal guard, and who provided Abdul Rahman Khan with his most reliable support. In the contemporary period the Nuristanis exemplified the attachment of a particular group to the state. Settled on the Afghan-Pakistan frontier, and converted late to Islam at the close of the 19th century, the Nuristanis, often recruited into the army, secured numerous material privileges. This enabled them to develop their valleys while the relations of the

---

[21] The Qizilbash are the descendants of a Shi'ite community established by Nadir Shah in the Shindawal quarter of Kabul in the 18th century. They have served various Afghan *amirs* in the administration and in the army. In particular, they constituted the majority of the *gholam-i shah*. However, after supporting the British in the war of 1839–42 they were obliged either to leave the city or to practise *taqiyya* (religious concealment). From the reign of Abdul Rahman Khan the Qizilbash gradually lost their influence, though they held on to a significant role in the senior ranks of the administration. Many continued to practise a reduced form of *taqiyya* (concealment), admitting to being Shi'ites only in private.

neighbouring tribes, though Pushtun (the Safi), with the government were poor.

The legitimacy of the state

To ensure its survival the militarily weak state was obliged to avoid disputes, and accordingly paid particular attention to issues of legitimacy. In this project the language of Islam and that of nationalism were often employed simultaneously.

Islam. With varying degrees of success all holders of authority have used Islam as a fountainhead of legitimacy, either primarily or secondarily, with the exception of the communists in 1978–9. However, in its attempts to lean on religious legitimacy, the Afghan state has had a less convincing case than, for example, the Moroccan regime with a long tradition behind it.[22] In Afghanistan the *amir* has claimed Islamic legitimacy since the beginning of the 19th century. It was laid down at that time that sermons in the mosques should be preached in his name, and this obligation was reaffirmed in the constitutions of 1923 and 1931.[23] When certain *mullahs* at the time of the political disturbances in the spring of 1971 no longer preached the Friday sermon (the *khotba*) in the *amir's* name, this constituted a direct challenge to his legitimacy and as such brought retribution from the authorities. But although the Afghan state has always claimed religious legitimacy, its form has often varied greatly. From Abdul Rahman Khan to Amanullah, legitimacy was seen as coming directly from God, and the role of the *ulema* was merely to endorse this. After 1929, however, clerical recognition became in itself the source of legitimacy, and the *ulema* saw themselves as granting legitimacy to the ruler.

Under Abdul Rahman Khan and his successors Habibullah and Amanullah the *ulema* were obliged to recognise the divine origin of

---

[22] See especially Mohammed Tozy, 'Le prince, le clerc et l'Etat. La restructuration du champ religieux au Maroc' in Gilles Kepel, Yann Richard (eds), *op. cit.*, and Rémy Leveau, *Le fellah marocain, défenseur du trône*, Paris: Presses de la Fondation nationale des sciences politiques, 1985, p. 261.

[23] The Afghan constitutions of 1923, 1931, 1964, 1977 and 1987 all recognise Islam as the official religion.

the power of the *amir*. This was a break with the tradition of their predecessors,[24] for whom legitimacy had been that of a *primus inter pares*, the first *amir* having been elected by a tribal assembly at Kandahar. In his memoirs[25] Abdul Rahman Khan presented himself as the bearer of a religious mission which he was obliged to fulfil in the interests of the salvation of the Muslims of Afghanistan. He strongly rejected tribal justification, favouring by contrast the Islamic legitimation of royalty.[26] The practical consequences of this rhetoric were very real. Afghanistan lost to some extent its character as a Pushtun empire, and a degree of equality between its Muslim subjects began to appear. After the suppression of the levy imposed on non-Pushtun subjects (the *sarmardeh*), taxes were no longer in principle variable as between different communities,[27] but were equal for all Muslims. Abdul Rahman Khan also used Islamic terminology in the introduction of new taxes, which made them more comprehensible and conceivably more acceptable.[28] This form of legitimation also allowed royalty to claim a monopoly of the right to declare *jihad*[29] and to condemn as *kafir* (heretical) all those who opposed their power. This measure was also a means of reinforcing his control over the religious establishment. Here may be seen the reflection of the conflicts in which Abdul Rahman Khan found himself in opposition to the *ulema* of Kandahar, who had declared a *jihad* against him on the grounds that he was supported by the British.

To confirm this religious legitimacy, Habibullah (1901–19) was to be solemnly consecrated as *amir* in a ritual devised by Abdul Rahman

---

[24] This was not, however, a total innovation. See Nikki Keddie, *Sayyid Jamal ad-Din al-Afghani*, Berkeley: University of California Press, 1972, p. 55.

[25] *The Life of Abdul Rahman Khan* (1st ed. 1900), Karachi: Oxford University Press, 1980.

[26] He also wrote a handbook on the rights and duties of the good Muslim, *Zia ul Mellat va Din* (The light of the state and of the faith).

[27] The Kandaharis were exempt, the Ghilzai and the Uzbeks paid little, and the Tajiks were the most heavily taxed.

[28] Taxes were justified, on the basis of an interpretation of the Quran, as a religious duty. On Abdul Rahman Khan's economic reforms see McChesnay, 'The economic reforms of Abdul Rahman Khan', *Afghanistan* XXI (3), autumn 1968.

[29] Abdul Rahman Khan was certainly not the first to launch appeals to *jihad*. Dost Muhammad did the same in 1939, and held the title of *amir al-mu'minin* (commander of the faithful).

Khan himself. The accession to the throne of Amanullah (1919–29) followed the same pattern at the outset, and his declaration of a *jihad* in 1919, at the time of the war of independence against the British, increased further the popularity which he enjoyed in the early years of his reign. Although he rapidly distanced himself from the *ulema*, he maintained his religious legitimacy by posing during the 1920s as a defender and potential inheritor of the Caliphate.[30] In a manner symptomatic of current thinking, a constitutional amendment of 1923, endorsed by the *Loya Jirga* (Great Council) in 1924, introduced yet further discriminatory measures against non-Muslims, including the obligation to wear distinctive clothes and the imposition of higher taxes.

However, Amanullah's position was ambiguous because of his simultaneous claim to be espousing a modernising ideology. Thus the 1923 constitution, while confirming the hereditary monarchy, abandoned the principle of the divine legitimacy of royal authority in favour of a constitutional and nationalist model. In addition, the fall of Amanullah in 1929 led to a substantial modification of the relations of the *ulema* with the state, and their link to its legitimation. The imamist concept of legitimacy, which accorded to the king the right to govern in the name of God, was replaced by a more contractual notion of legitimacy, which sprang from the state's acknowledgement of the *shariat*, under the supervision of the *ulema*. Thus the king was no longer the 'servant and protector of the true Islamic faith' as he had been under article 5 of the 1923 constitution.[31] Indeed, after the revolt of 1929 the *ulema*, who had played a key role in both the fall of Amanullah and the installation of the new ruler, gained in independence and presented themselves as possessing the autonomous authority necessary for the ruler's legitimation. After 1929 the incorporation of the *ulema* into the highest ranks of the state further endorsed the political weight of what was already an influential group. Significantly a Jamaat ul-Ulema (society of the *ulema*) was established to certify the conformity of the state's laws to the *shariat*.[32] Its role was significant in the early years,[33] but then dimin-

---

[30] Gail Minault, *The Khilafat Movement*, New York: Columbia University Press, 1983.

[31] Nighat Mehroze Chishti, *Constitutional Development in Afghanistan*, Karachi: Royal Book Company, 1998, p. 67.

[32] A similar step was taken in 1924 after the revolt of the Mangal.

[33] We owe to it the translations of the Quran into Dari and Pushtu.

ished progressively with the arrival in power of Daud in 1953 and the adoption of measures much disputed by the *ulema*, such as the abolition of female veiling in 1959. In 1963 the role of the Jamaat ul-Ulema was devolved to the department of Islamic affairs (Edare-yi sho'un islami) and then to a parliamentary commission, which marked its definitive disappearance. By this time, however, the language of nationalism had already become dominant.

Nationalism. The idea of nationalism made its appearance in the first decades of the century, with the establishment of a constitutionalist movement (Mashruta Khawan).[34] Mahmud Tarzi (1865–1933) was one of the key figures of this movement with his periodical *Saraj al-Akhbar-i Afghaniyah*[35] (The Illumination of the Afghan News), which was published from 1911 to 1918. The father-in-law of the future King Amanullah, Tarzi was an intellectual, open to ideas of modernity, whose influence was to be crucial in the evolution of the intelligentsia at the beginning of the 20th century. The construction of Afghan nationalism lay at the heart of the concerns of these reformers, who were concerned at the absence of national sentiment and the country's lack of development. The difficulty was to bring together nationalism and an acknowledgment of the principles of Islam, in the context of a situation which somewhat resembled the end of the Ottoman empire.

In the view of these reformers, national identity should be common to all the ethnic groups, and founded in the last resort on Islamic values. However, an underlying ambiguity remained: should the direction taken be towards the recognition of the other ethnic groups, or alternatively towards their assimilation to the dominant group on the Kemalist model as seen in Turkey? The reformers opted in the event for the construction of a national identity based on the Pushtun ethnicity, and in particular the Pushtu language.[36] The appeal to Islam may therefore have justified, or even disguised, a project to

[34] See Dr Fazal ur-Rahim Marwat, *op. cit.*, pp. 99 ff.

[35] See V. Gregorian, 'Mahmud Tarzi and Saraj-ol-Akhbar: Ideology of Nationalism and Modernisation in Afghanistan', *Middle East Journal* 21 (3), 1967.

[36] Significantly, the obligatory learning of Pushtu was advocated by Tarzi, in the *Saraj al-Akhbar-i Afghaniyah* of 14 September 1914, quoted by S. A. Mousavi, *The Hazaras of Afghanistan: An Historical, Cultural, Economic and Political Study*, Richmond: Curzon Press, 1998, p. 158.

construct a Pushtun nation-state, and was coupled with a fierce criticism of the conservatism of the *ulema*, such as one could expect from the modernists. In spite of its low circulation, Mahmud Tarzi's periodical significantly assisted Habibullah's earliest efforts at liberalisation.[37] Such modernising ideas were also later to evoke a sympathetic response from Amanullah. In a sense this movement provided the mould for the main reformist tendencies up to the coup of 1978. The communists explicitly acknowledge it, and it is also possible to identify it more indirectly as a precursor of the Islamists in view of their modernisation and interpretation of Quranic texts outside the exegetic tradition of the *ulema*.

Nevertheless, various constraints held back the state's dissemination of a nationalist ideology, and as late as the 1920s the *amirs* did not appeal to nationalism as a legitimation of their authority. In fact it was religious legitimation which allowed them to rally the support—essential for the *amir*—of a faction of non-Pushtuns. Abdul Rahman Khan and Habibullah even encouraged the use of Persian rather than Pushtu as an official language, and the language of education was Persian, even in the Pushtun areas. In no sense did Abdul Rahman Khan owe his power to the Pushtun tribes. The Durrani opposed him at the time of his accession to power, and most of the tribal chiefs had been exiled to India.[38] Above all, nationalism remained a concept alien to Abdul Rahman Khan, who relied on the oppositions inherent in a segmented society rather than on broad Pushtun solidarity, in a manner consistent with a principle of legitimation which remained religious. However, even without consistent ideological justification, the government was dominated by the Pushtuns, who made use of the state as an instrument of 'internal imperialism', especially in the colonisation of the north, and with a tax system which allowed certain privileges to persist. For example, inequalities remained within the army: the Durrani regiments, and especially those linked to the royal clan, were better paid than the others, which gave rise to discontent.[39]

---

[37] In Central Asia the reformist movement of the *Jadids* also paid close attention to this publication. See Leon Poullada, *op. cit.*, p. 42.

[38] Moreover, the *amir* was the last Afghan sovereign to speak Pushtu, Turkish and Persian. His exile to Russia probably promoted a less narrowly Pushtun view of Afghanistan.

[39] Hasan Kakar, *op. cit.*, p. 113.

Nationalism became the state ideology when Nadir Shah[40] was confirmed as ruler in 1930, after the exile of Amanullah and the fall of Habibullah II 'Bacha-yi Saqao' (Son of the water carrier), the Tajik rebel who seized power in January 1929 and held on to it for nine months. The temporary loss of power by the Pushtuns displayed the potential leverage of the non-Pushtuns, leading the former to close ranks. The role of the tribes, and in particular of those of the east, was crucial to the capture of Kabul by Nadir. A new terminology emerged from this readjustment of the balance of power: since the king had been elected by a *Loya Jirga* dominated by the tribes, the basis of his legitimacy could not be identical to that of his predecessors. Nadir was 'chosen by the people, in recognition of his service', as clearly laid down by the 1931 constitution, which only the *Loya Jirga* had the authority to interpret or modify.

Royalty became once more the political focus of the tribes, and at the same time there was a slide away from dynastic legitimacy and towards Pushtun nationalism. The government was unable to control the *ulema*, and progressively turned to nationalism as a form of legitimacy alternative to that derived from Islam. As an instance of this, the legal distinctions between Muslims and non-Muslims were dispensed with, which tended to promote a nationalist rather than a religious definition of citizenship. Therefore, the legitimacy of the state increasingly rested on nationalism, an ideology in which the feeling of belonging to the national community was presented as 'natural', since it was deemed to result from a shared history or even a shared biological basis.[41] In this way legitimation on the basis of tribal genealogy evolved towards legitimation based on 'race'. The construction of a historical memory then became a central concern. From the 1930s Pushtun nationalism, given its impetus by the intelligentsia, made use of history to 'demonstrate' the common origin and destiny of the populations which had their existence on Afghan soil. Thus archaeology was pressed into service to establish the 'Aryan' origin of the peoples living in Afghanistan. The influence of the Kemalist model was plain to see, as was that of nationalist or even racist European theories from the inter-war period.[42] The debate

---

[40] From 1926 the king bore the title 'Shah', rather than '*amir*'.

[41] Ernst Gellner, *Nations and Nationalism*, Oxford: Blackwell, 1983.

[42] The rise of National Socialism in Germany was favourably received by the Afghan nationalists, and especially by Daud, who then attempted to impose the

which took place within the *Loya Jirga* leading up to the adoption of the 1964 constitution displayed clearly the misgivings of the non-Pushtuns over these ideas. The non-Pushtun participants demanded and obtained an amendment of Article 1 to reaffirm that the expression 'Afghan' applied to all citizens and not exclusively to the Pushtuns (in common parlance Afghan was often taken to mean Pushtun).[43]

The linguistic issue took on a growing significance[44] since the state implemented a consistent policy of Pushtunisation which was to continue till the 1970s. Although Persian was understood by a large minority of the population either as a first or second language, the government was to attempt to impose Pushtu as the national language,[45] when hitherto its use had not been obligatory even within the administration. The Pushtu Academy (*Pashto Tulana*) founded by Amanullah expanded, and government publications increased in number. In 1936 Pushtu was raised to the status of a national language, on an equal footing with the Persian of Afghanistan—known as *Dari* to distinguish it, somewhat artificially, from the Persian of Iran. In the same year the government imposed Pushtu as the language of education, before recognising this as unfeasible, leading to the adoption of Pushtu/Persian bilingualism in 1946.[46] In the 1960s administrative measures were put in place with the target of publishing 50 per cent of written material in Pushtu.

This policy encountered the hostility of the non-Pushtu-speakers. The debate in Parliament in 1971 on the requirement that officials should learn Pushtu exposed once more the dichotomy between the Pushtu-speaking deputies and the others. A further problem was that the intelligentsia and the court spoke and wrote Persian, the traditional language of culture. King Zahir himself had only rudimentary Pushtu.

---

use of Pushtu, at the expense of Persian. See Mir Mohammad Sediq Farhang, *Afghanistan dar Panj Qarn-i Akhir* (Afghanistan in the last five centuries), Peshawar: Derarsheh, 1988, p. 632.

[43] Nighat Mehroze Chishti, *op. cit.*, p. 96.

[44] J. Petrusinska, 'Afghanistan 1989 in sociological perspective', *Central Asian Survey*, Incidental Papers Series no. 7.

[45] Pushtu, meanwhile, was spoken by less than 10 % of the population as a second language. See *Encyclopaedia Iranica* 1 (6), Costa Mesa, CA: Mazda, p. 504.

[46] A distinction was drawn between the national language, Pushtu, and the official language, Persian. See Shafie Rahel, *La politique culturelle en Afghanistan*, Paris: Les Presses de l'UNESCO, 1975.

In the army the recruitment of officers underwent a major trans-formation. Daud (1953–63) wished to use the army as an instrument for the Pushtunisation of the state, and to that end he gave priory to the recruitment of Ghilzai and eastern Pushtuns into the military colleges. In the 1970s the young officers were Pushtuns, or less fre-quently Tajiks.[47] The Hazaras and Uzbeks, at the bottom of the ethnic ladder, were in practice excluded from the military profession.

This insistence on Pushtun nationalism at the expense of Islam was a source of tension between communities. The non–Pushtun populations, who were probably in the majority,[48] felt themselves excluded, while for the rural populations, whether Pushtuns or non-Pushtuns, religious legitimacy was the only comprehensible princi-ple. Under the presidency of Daud (1973–8) Pushtunisation entered a more aggressive phase in relation to the other communities. For example, the radio broadcasts in vernacular languages initiated at the end of Zahir's reign were cancelled. In 1978–9 the extreme Pushtun nationalism of the communists, in spite of their theoretical support of minorities, was to play its part in the outbreak of the insurrection.

Challenges to the state

During the process of its formation the state often faced challenges. To crush these, Abdul Rahman Khan relied on a police system, with a network of spies, which deflected all forms of protest short of open rebellion. For instance, journeys of more than a few kilometres out-side Kabul had to be authorised by the police. It was not till the 1964 constitution that Afghans were given the right to free movement in-side and outside the country. Breaking with the historiographical tradition which has represented the *amir* of Kabul as a 'positive' fac-tor for Afghan unity, the historian Jonathan Lee was one of the first to draw attention to the detrimental consequences of the hyper-centralisation of the state, which was reduced to impotence by the

---

[47] Hasan Kakar, *op. cit.*, p. 211, and Barnett Rubin, 'The old regime in Afghanistan: recruitment and training of a state elite', *Central Asian Survey* 10 (3), 1991.

[48] Even if one finds texts where the Pushtuns are said to be in a majority, with the effect of justifying *a posteriori* their domination of the political system. Census re-turns were in fact unreliable, and available data relating to ethnicity has not been fully explored.

ill-health of the ruler, and of the campaigns of pacification with their adverse effects on intercommunal relations.[49] The reliance on policing was an indication of the fragility of the state, which was still threatened by demands for autonomy from unruly communities, and too weak to negotiate, even when this would have strengthened its legitimacy in the longer term. Habibullah, the successor to Abdul Rahman Khan, taking advantage of his more certain exercise of power, was able to abandon some of these police practices, but conflicts once more became regular occurrences.

The challenge to the state came essentially from the tribes (Pushtuns, Uzbeks and Hazaras) and from the *ulema*. However, these oppositional thrusts were not necessarily in the same direction. The *ulema* protected their privileges, especially in education and the judicial system, but they did not dispute the necessity of the state's existence since they hoped to utilise it—for example, to impose the *shariat* in place of tribal customs.[50] On the other hand the tribes denied the state's right to play a part in their affairs, and in the case of the Pushtuns it was understood at best as the representative of the domination exercised by the tribes in Afghan territory. In unsettled times the behaviour of the tribes tended towards pillage of the towns and of state property. Thus, after the sack of Kabul in 1929 the eastern Pushtun tribes were in no particular hurry to re-establish any kind of central government.

The Tribes. When Abdul Rahman Khan (1880–1901) set himself the task of ensuring by military means his domination over Afghan territory, a number of regions still enjoyed *de facto* autonomy. After the military campaigns at the end of the 19th century the Ghilzai tribes, which had been virtually independent till the 1820s, as well as the Turkmens, the Hazaras and the Durrani of Kandahar, no longer represented a serious threat to the central government. In future these

[49] See Jonathan Lee, 'Abd al-Rahman Khan and the "maraz ul-muluk"', *Journal of the Royal Asiatic Society* 3 (1–2), 1991, pp. 208–42. The *amir* is said not to have suffered from gout but probably from cirrhosis of the liver, chronic encephalopathy and porphyria. 100,000 people are said to have been executed by the authorities during his reign. See F. Martin, *Under the Absolute Amir*, London, 1907.

[50] A centralised authority was often favourable to the *ulema*. These played an increasing role within in the imperial bureaucracies of the Ottoman, Safavid and Mughal empires.

tribal confederations would not provide the framework for political mobilisation. Subsequently uprisings mainly concerned the eastern Pushtun tribes, the only ones to have retained any military strength.[51] This semi-autonomy was partly a result of the geographical position of these tribes, which the state wished to be able to bring into play against the British empire, and later against Pakistan.[52]

From the 1950s onwards the state had the military capacity to put the tribes to flight. Although the Safi revolt of 1947–9 still proved difficult to suppress, the troubles of December 1959 showed that the balance of forces had changed. When the Mangal took arms in protest against the building of a road which threatened their income and their independence, they were unable to stand their ground against a mechanised army, and thousands fled into Pakistan from where they only gradually returned. In the same year the state was sufficiently strong to demand the payment of taxes by the Kandahar landowners, who had traditionally refused to comply on the grounds of an exemption granted to them in the 18th century. The police intervened and then the army, and in the end the state won the day, even though the eastern Pushtun tribes continued largely to evade payment of the tax.

However, the state did not always choose to clash head-on with the power of the tribes. The simple act of imposing administrative frontiers which did not accord with the boundaries of the tribal territories was in itself a way of undermining the strength of communal attachments. The result was in some areas the substitution of solidarity based on location for solidarity founded on clan. Another factor was that the villages were in any case less and less homogenous in their tribal affiliations, except in the east. Existing communal antagonisms were also exploited, and sometimes encouraged. For example, the divisions between the Hazaras and the Qizilbash were carefully

---

[51] The most significant of these in recent times have been as follows: in 1933, the Mohmand tribe; in 1937, the Mohmand, Shinwari and Ghilzai tribes in the east; in 1945, incidents in the Kurram valley; in 1947–9 the revolt of the Safi tribe; in 1955 tribal stirrings near Kabul; riots at Kandahar and in the east in 1959; in 1968 the war between the Jaji and Mangal tribes; the agitation among the Shinwari in 1970.

[52] Similar phenomena occur in the case of the Kurds, on the periphery of the Ottoman Empire. See Van Bruinessen, 'Evliya Çelebi and his Seyahatname', in *Evliya Çelebi in Diyarbekir*, Leiden: E. J. Brill, 1988.

cultivated in order to avoid the emergence of a united Shi'ite front. In the same way Amanullah played off the tribes against each other to curb the Mangal revolt of 1924, although this strategy was to fail in 1929.

Frequent transfers of population also facilitated control over the tribes.[53] From the reign of Abdul Rahman Khan, there were movements—both forcible and voluntary—of predominantly Pushtun groups to the north of the country. The aim of this interior colonisation was to ensure the security of the frontiers and exert more effective control over tribes prone to rebellion against the central authority. The government granted lands to the colonists, and afterwards traded on Pushtun solidarity in the face of the dispossessed indigenous populations. The earliest migrations began in 1883, with a programme of colonisation in Badghis, the objective of which was to counter the threat of a further Russian annexation. The failure of this initiative after the loss of Panjdeh in 1885, gave rise to a more ambitious programme, using Pushtun nomads rather than the Jamshidis, who were prone to be tempted by Russian offers of an accommodation. Colonisation was undertaken thereafter with varying degrees of success across the whole of northwest Afghanistan. Transplantation was sometimes punishment for a rebellion, as in 1890 when a penal colony of Suleiman Khel was set up at Baghlan. In addition, the populations involved were not always Pushtuns: at the beginning of the 20th century groups of Uzbeks were forcibly installed in the neighbourhood of Kabul and Jalalabad. The final forced transfers seen to have been those of the Safi after the revolt of 1947–9. However, from the 1920s the exploitation of new lands in the north at Kunduz led to the settlement, though here on a voluntary basis, of several thousand Pushtun families. Interior migrations organised by the state continued till the 1960s, making their contribution to the strength of the central government, which from this point on was in a position to arbitrate between the different communities.

Under Abdul Rahman Khan the significance of the tribes was acknowledged by the existence of a *darbar-i shahi* (council of tribal chiefs), whose deliberations, were strictly consultative. After the events of 1929 a strategy of integrating the tribes into the national institu-

---

[53] Richard Tapper (ed.), *The Conflict of Tribe and State in Afghanistan*, London: Croom Helm, 1983.

tions was declared. The 1931 constitution provided that Parliament should sit from May to October, which necessitated the presence in Kabul of the principal tribal chiefs. The Shah thus hoped to limit the risks of rebellion by gathering together the tribal leaders between the seasons, after the end of the year's agricultural labour, at a time which otherwise lent itself to the mobilisation of the tribes. In addition, in recognition of the role of the tribes, a *Loya Jirga* was supposed to meet at least once every three years, although this was not always to be observed, especially as the council duplicated the work of Parliament. Finally, the institution of a Minister for the frontiers was evidence of the state's vigilance over the turbulent eastern Pushtun tribes.

In one case at least, internal conquest left a trauma whose effects are still felt today. No campaign was as difficult as that which achieved the subjugation of the Hazarajat, the central region of Afghanistan populated by the Hazaras.[54] The origin of the Hazaras remains relatively obscure. Contrary to a popular supposition they are not largely the descendants of the armies of Genghis Khan, as their Mongoloid physical appearance, which contrasts strongly with the Pushtuns and Tajiks, might suggest. They are actually an ancient group, with Turkish and Mongol links.[55] They speak a dialect of Persian, known as Hazaragi, in which Turkish and some Mongol words occur. The total population of Afghanistan is not precisely known, still less its ethnic composition, but most writers agree that the Hazaras constituted some 10% of the population, that is to say more than a million people, in the 1970s. They make up 80 per cent of the Shi'ite population, the remainder of whom are Qizilbash and Tajik.[56]

The date of their conversion to Shi'ism is unknown, but it was probably in the first part of the 16th century, in the early days of the Safavid dynasty (1501–1786).[57] In any case, not all the Hazaras are

[54] In particular the provinces of Bamyan, Ghor, Uruzgan, Wardak, Ghazni and Jozjan. For a history of the Hazaras see Hasan Poladi, *The Hazaras*, Stockton, CA: Mughal Publishing Co., 1989.

[55] See S. A. Mousavi, *op. cit.*, pp. 19 ff. The Hazaras do not always have pronounced physical characteristics, and their social identification is more in terms of cultural markers. There are also regional variations, perhaps the result of intermarriage with Pushtuns and Tajiks.

[56] Persian-speaking non-Hazara Shi'ites are found on the frontier with Iran, mainly in Herat and the province of Nimruz.

[57] Hasan Poladi, *op. cit.*, p. 118.

Shi'ites. Sunni Hazara communities are to be found to the south of Mazar-i Sharif, in Dara-i Hazara (a valley adjacent to Panjshir), Rustaq and Takhar, where Babur reports their presence from the 16th century.[58] However the non-Shi'ite Hazaras tend in general to repudiate their ethnic allegiance in favour of the claim that they are Tajiks, on account of the widespread conflation between Shi'ites and Hazaras, with their consequent stigmatisation by the Sunnis. The claim to be an ethnic Hazara implies in practice an affirmation of Shi'ite faith. In this case ethnic and religious affiliations reinforce one another, while on the other hand there are no links of solidarity between the Sunni and Shi'ite Hazaras.

Though they recognised their attachment to the kingdom of Kabul, to which they paid tribute, the allegiance of the Hazaras to the *amirs* who succeeded up to the end of the 19th century was largely nominal. At times the unification of Hazarajat under the authority of a tribal chief even threatened the authority of Kabul. When Mir Yazdan succeeded in pacifying Hazarajat under his leadership from 1843 to 1863, Dost Muhammad had him imprisoned. At the end of the 19th century the central authority could no longer tolerate the *de facto* independence of Hazarajat and the banditry of some of its tribes. In consequence the *amir* of Kabul waged a series of campaigns, mainly between 1891 and 1893, which resulted in a real integration of Hazarajat into the Afghan state.[59]

This war, similar at its outset to the campaigns carried out in Turkestan or against rebel Pushtun tribes, turned into a bloody repression of which the memory persists even today. Religious mobilisation explains in part the tenacity of the two sides. The declaration of *jihad* by the *amir* of Kabul, and that of the Shi'ite *ulema* in response, was to justify the worst atrocities, and in particular the enslavement of a segment of the Hazara population; Hazaras were sold in the markets of the capital as late as the first years of the 20th century. The *amir* also sent Sunni *mullahs* to convert them.[60] Already displaced

---

[58] Zahiruddin Muhammad Babur, *Babur-Nama* (trans. Annette Beveridge), London, 1922; reissue, Lahore: Sang-e Meel, 1987. Sunni Hazaras also exist in significant numbers in Badghis, in the region of Qala-i Naw, where they were settled by Nadir Shah.

[59] See Hasan Kakar, *The Pacification of the Hazaras of Afghanistan*, New York: Afghanistan Council, the Asia Society, 1973.

[60] Louis Duprée, 'The Political Use of Religion: Afghanistan' in K. H. Silvert (ed.),

from their mountains by the Pushtun expansion of the 18th and 19th centuries, the Hazaras lost a significant part of their cultivable land. Within a number of years a hierarchical tribal system had given way to a disorganised assembly of notables of whom the state made use as local agents. These traumatic events were to give rise to a strong sentiment of identity which was to have its consequences in the present conflict.

Following these events, *amir* Habibullah (1901–19) proclaimed an amnesty. However, few Hazara returned from exile and it was not until the accession to the throne of Amanullah, who repudiated anti-Shi'ite discrimination, that some of those who had fled came back. In the rebellion of 1929 the Hazaras actually supported the king. Significantly, slavery was abolished by decree in 1921, a measure confirmed in the 1923 constitution. However, the Hazaras, though defeated, remained an element unassimilable by Pushtun nationalism, while their adherence to Shi'ism placed them in opposition to the Sunni *ulema*.[61]

Alien to the two modes of legitimation of the Afghan state, and relegated to the bottom of the ethnic hierarchy, the Hazaras suffered from social and economic discrimination. The nomadism of the Pushtun tribes in the central regions of Afghanistan was a particular source of oppression against them. For example, during their seasonal displacements a police agent normally accompanied the Pushtun nomads, and conflicts with the sedentary Hazaras were generally settled in their favour. Trade with the Hazaras and the lending of money at usurious rates of interest also enabled the nomads to seize their land. In the 1970s the nomads went less often to Hazarajat to trade because of the circulation of trading lorries from the neighbouring towns, but the competition for land grew more intense because of increasing demographic pressure.

Descriptive and anecdotal observations all point in the same direction.[62] In the 1960s and 1970s the Hazaras' land was no longer

---

Expectant People: Nationalism and Modernization, New York: American Universities Field Staff Report, 1967.

[61] The Constitutions of 1923, 1931 and 1964 recognised Hanafi Islam as the official rite. The Constitution of 1977 marked a concession to the Shi'ites by omitting this specification.

[62] The cultivation of intensively terraced mountain plots in a good indication of the pressure for land. See also M. Gaweki, 'The Hazara farmers of central Afghan-

sufficient to feed them, which seemed to be the result of two factors. First despite particularly high infant mortality owing to worse sanitary conditions than elsewhere,[63] demographic growth was no longer containable. And secondly, the Pushtuns developed the raising of flocks and herds, restricting the amount of land usable by Hazara peasants. From the 1960s poverty led many of the Hazaras to move to the towns, mainly Kabul and Mazar-i Sharif. In due course this phenomenon of rural exodus accelerated, displacing the centre of gravity of the community towards the towns where the Hazaras became a community generally looked down on, often working as bakers or as unskilled workers.

These circumstances explain why during the past century uprisings in Hazarajat have been frequent, and popular recollection preserves the memory of the most notorious figures associated with the resistance to the state.[64] During Amanullah's reign, Naim Khan rebelled, together with his two sons, because of the encroachments of the Pushtun nomads. He was taken captive at Panjao and imprisoned in Kabul. Another well-known chief, Yusuf Beg, a *khan* from Shahristan, fought for nineteen years against the government before finally being arrested. He was taken to Kabul and executed on the orders of the Prime Minister Hashem Khan (1933–46). Books about Yusuf Beg, published in Teheran by the Hazara community, are still circulated in Afghanistan. However, the most celebrated figure remains Muhammad Ibrahim Khan, a *khan* from Shahristan known as Bacha-yi Gaw Sawar (the boy riding the bull). His nickname comes from a tale told about him in which he is said to have ridden on a bull which ascended to paradise when its right ear was pulled. During the winter of 1945–6 Ibrahim Khan headed a rebellion against a new tax on animal fats. The police post at Shahristan was occupied, and the central authorities lost control of the district for a whole winter. In the spring a delegation of Hazara notables led by the gov-

istan: some historical and contemporary problems', *Ethnologia Polona* 6, Poland 1980.
[63] There were only some ten dispensaries for the whole of Hazarajat, and no doctors outside the NGOs.
[64] David Busby Edwards, 'The Evolution of Shi'i Political Dissent in Afghanistan' in Juan R. I. Cole, N. R. Keddie (eds), *Shi'ism, and Social Protest*, Yale University Press, 1986.

ernor of Kabul came from the capital to offer terms. The government cancelled the tax, but Ibrahim was taken to Kabul and placed under house arrest. He was accused, together with Ismail Balkhi (see below) of planning a coup and imprisoned till the 1960s. He died soon after his release but remained a well-known figure in Hazarajat.

In addition to these revolts led by prominent figures, disturbances were commonplace, often connected to the presence of the nomads. The leaders of these uprisings were local *khans*: apparently there were no popular uprisings. Uruzgan, the home territory of Ibrahim Khan, Yusuf Beg and Naim Khan, seemed most susceptible, on account of the Pushtuns settled in the south of the province, and also because of the minimal presence of the state in this inaccessible region.[65] It would be unsafe to claim that these men were the forerunners of Hazara nationalism, especially where documentary records are so sparse. However, a generation later the first Hazara nationalists, often the sons of the *khans*, who by this time were students in Kabul, held them up as symbols of resistance to the Pushtun state.

The ulema. In contrast to the tribes, who were progressively marginalised by the military power of the state and by social evolution, the men of religion came to represent after the 1950s a real counterweight to the established authority. The *ulema* constituted a social group with its own system of education, both private and governmental, as well as its own transnational networks, and its own material and moral interests, which provided a mobilising impetus. In contrast to the *ulema*, the *mullahs*[66] were not a well-defined or homogenous class. There is no priesthood in Islam. A person who is qualified to lead the prayers is known as an *imam*, and as a *mullah* if he fulfils this function regularly and professionally. However, *mullahs* educated in the *madrasas* displayed solidarity with the *ulema*, especially those whose principal activity was to lead the prayers.

---

[65] The province of Uruzgan long remained under the domination of the *khans*, with a strong tendency to conflicts, both internal and with the Pushtuns.

[66] In Central Asia and Turkey, as distinct from the Arab countries, the expression *mullah* was not restricted to Shi'ites. The *mullahs*, less well integrated into the administration, were sometimes paid by the government, but more often remained in charge of village communities. If there was no school in the village, they would offer an elementary education to the children. See *The Encyclopaedia of Islam*, Leiden: E. J. Brill, 1993, p. 223.

In the 19th century the *ulema* were involved in governmental affairs only in the context of the initial legitimation of a ruler,[67] although they might occasionally play a part in the proclamation of a *jihad*, or in opposition to administrative measures deemed to be at variance with the Quran.[68] Through their often conflictual relationships with the state, the men of religion affirmed their status as a coherent group with an identity and with collective interests. The state sought to integrate the *ulema*, but the influence of the great religious families, together with the effects of fundamentalist ideological tendencies, motivated them to retain their autonomy while mobilising against modernising reforms.

The instrumentalisation of Islam as a source of legitimacy accounts for the effort made by the state from the close of the 19th century to integrate the *mullahs* and the *ulema* into the administration. Abdul Rahman Khan assimilated the *ulema* up to a point into the administrative system by the institution of qualifying examinations, while *mullahs* participated in the indoctrination of soldiers in all the regiments of the army. In 1896 Abdul Rahman Khan attempted to circumscribe the economic autonomy of the *ulema* and the brotherhoods (*tariqat*) by taking partial control of the religious endowments (the *waqf*), especially in the towns.[69] In certain cases the *amir* did not hesitate to punish those reluctant to comply: after the Ghilzai revolt of 1886–8 he cut the emoluments of the *ulema* in the Ghazni region. The role of the state was later reinforced by Amanullah, and then in the 1960s by the Etemadi government, which set up a *waqf* depart-

---

[67] Because of the absence of strict hierarchy among the *ulema*, a claimant to the throne always found a way to ensure his recognition by some group from among them. At the beginning of the 18th century Mir Wais, in order to justify his revolt against the Safavid Shi'ites, procured a *fatwa* from Mecca, which enabled him win the help of the tribal chiefs of Kandahar.

[68] In the 1830s the invasion of a non-Muslim power provided the opportunity for the *ulema*, in declaring a *jihad*, to demonstrate their influence.

[69] See Donald Wilber, 'The Structure of Islam in Afghanistan', *Middle East Journal* 6 (1), 1952, pp. 41–8; Ashraf Ghani, 'Islam and State-Building in Afghanistan', *Modern Asian Studies* 12, 1978, pp. 269–84. Similar phenomena are found in Iran (see N. Keddie, *Scholars, Saints and Sufis*, Berkeley: University of California Press, 1972, p. 7) and in Turkey (see Albert Hourani, 'Ottoman Reform and the politics of Notables' in W. R. Polk, R. Cambers, eds, *Beginnings of Modernization in the Middle East*, University of Chicago Press, 1968, p. 58). The clergy continued to be significant landowners in certain areas, especially, it would seem, in Kandahar.

ment within the Ministry of Justice. In 1970 the state reduced once more the influence of private individuals by placing certain of the pilgrimage sites (*ziarat*) under direct government control.[70]

However, education was the crucial factor in controlling the *ulema*. Before the modern period there was no training centre for them in Afghanistan. Before the Bolshevik Revolution of 1917 they were normally educated in Central Asia and till the 1920s at Deoband in northern India, where Afghans were the second largest group of foreign pupils.[71] At the beginning of the 20th century the Afghan *amir* went as far as to fund construction at Deoband, and offered an annual contribution, which the Deobandi school refused in the interests of preserving its independence. In the 1920s Amanullah attempted to curb the influence of these educational centres, which were notorious for the their dogmatic rigidity. Education at Deoband, and at certain Central Asian *madrasas* was declared no longer to be a qualification for official positions.[72] From the 1940s onwards a national system of religious education was set up by the state, with the aim of facilitating the integration of the *ulema* into the state machinery, and of maintaining control of the content of the teaching provided. The creation of the 'School of Shariat' in 1944 was complemented in 1951 by the establishment of a faculty of theology, linked to that at Al-Azhar University in Cairo. The governmental *madrasas*, opened one by one in the principal towns of the country, trained *ulema* who in due course were attached to the various organs of the state, serving in particular as judges, as academics, or by taking charge of religious education in the secondary schools.

Nevertheless, this governmental enterprise was always limited in its extent, and by the 1970s the majority of the *ulema* were still produced by the private *madrasas*, which had their continued existence guaranteed by the 1931 constitution. The government *madrasas* were in fact to produce the Islamists who were the most antagonistic towards the central authority. This issue is discussed below.

---

[70] See Louis Duprée, 'Saint Cults in Afghanistan', *American Universities Field Staff Report*, South Asia Series XX (1), May 1976. The Charter of the Awqaf Administration of 1969 is given in an appendix.

[71] Barbara Daly Metcalf, *Islamic Revival in British India: Deoband 1860–1900*, Princeton University Press, 1982.

[72] Amanullah was later obliged to rescind this measure.

The education of the Afghan *ulema* was therefore carried out largely outside the governmental structure, which accounts for the influence of the reformers of the Indian subcontinent. From the beginning of the 19th century, the fundamentalist philosophy inspired by the Indian reformer Shah Waliullah (1703–1762) was found in Afghanistan. Although these reformers were stigmatised by the British as 'Wahhabites', there is no historical proof of any direct affiliation to the Arab movement, and a separate origin is more probable. One of the sources of inspiration common to both Shah Waliullah and the Salafists, who rejected the designation 'Wahhabi', lay in the writings of Ibn Taymiyyah,[73] who condemned the excesses of popular religious fervour inspired by Sufism, even though he was himself affiliated to the Qadiri *tariqat*. It can be seen with hindsight that he was especially significant for his theory of *takfir* (apostatisation), although he failed to define with complete clarity in what conditions a Muslim could be regarded as an apostate, and did not call for rebellion against existing Muslim governments. Ibn Taymiyya was nevertheless one of those rare theologians whose rhetoric did not systematically justify the *status quo*. In this he differed from his teacher Ibn Hanbal, who refused to recognise a right of resistance even to a government which ordered actions contrary to divine ordinances. Ibn Taymiyya, on the other hand, recommended disobedience and even revolt. A respected though marginal author, he has since been claimed as an authority both by reformers of the school of Waliullah and by Islamist writers such as Sayyed Qutb and Maududi, who are not themselves *ulema* and find in him a justification for their political theories.

Such reformist ideas were found particularly in the teaching given at the *madrasas* of Deoband and Patna in northern India, which educated part of the Afghan *ulema*. The Deobandis taught strict observance of the Islamic ethical code, and were opposed to the British presence, as well as to any syncretistic approaches towards Hinduism. Distinguishing themselves from the school of Deoband, the Ahl-i Hadith adopted a particularly radical standpoint, and had maintained relations with the Salafis from the mid-18th century.[74] They preached

---

[73] On Ibn Taymiyya see E. Sivan, 'Ibn Taymiyya: Father of the Islamic Revolution', *Encounter*, May 1983.

[74] Marc Gaborieau, Nicole Grandin, 'Le renouveau confrérique (fin XVIIIe–XIXe siècle)' in Alexandre Popovic, Gilles Veinstein (eds), *Les voies d'Allah*, Paris: Fayard, 1996.

the destruction of the tombs of *pirs* to prevent them becoming places of worship, but they were not opposed to Sufism as such; indeed controversy over the links between Sufism and Salafism was often deceptive, since even among the Salafis there existed a minimal Sufi current. Consequently, from the time of Sayyed Ahmad Barelwi (1786–1831) it would be preferable to speak of reformist Sufism, as opposed to the popular practices involved in the worship of saints.[75]

What influence did these movements have over the Afghan *ulema*? Deobandi tendencies have long been present in Afghanistan, where Deobandi texts have been known since the 19th century. For instance, in 1912 the Pushtuns of Karachi, under the influence of the Afghan *amir's* representative, took the side of the Deobandis in a controversy with those who adhered to the orthodox Hanafi school over the status of the Prophet Muhammad.[76] In the course of the discussions concerning the 1931 constitution certain *ulema* disputed Article 6, which includes a reference to saints in the context of the Shah's oath of fidelity, thus adopting a typically reformist position.

After the partition of India certain of the Afghan *ulema*, who would traditionally have gone to Deoband, were instead educated at *madrasas* in the North-West Frontier Province of Pakistan, where the Deobandi influence was strong. In 1959–60, 15 per cent (60 out of 397), of the students at the *madrasa* Dar al-Ulum Haqqaniyah were Afghans, a proportion which grew to 37 per cent in 1970 (204 students out of 550).[77] Movements of the most fundamentalist kind also exercised regional influence. In particular many *ulema* in the frontier provinces of Badakhshan and Kunar were educated in *madrasas* identified with the Ahl-i Hadith and the Deobandis. In Afghanistan the Najm ul-Mudaris *madrasa* near Jalalabad also served as a channel for fundamentalist tendencies close to this movement.[78] Nevertheless, in

---

[75] Frederick de Jong, Bernd Radtke (eds), *Islamic Mysticism Contested: Thirteen Centuries of Controversies and Polemics*, Leiden: E. J. Brill, 1999. Marc Garborieau, 'A Nineteenth Century Indian Wahhabi Tract against the Cult of Muslim Saints: al-Balagh al-Mubin' in Christian W. Troll (ed.) *Muslim Shrines in India*, Delhi: Oxford University Press, 1990. Marc Gaborieau and Nicole Grandin, *op. cit.*, object to the term 'neo-Sufism', which implies a break with tradition.

[76] Sahrah Ansari, *Sufi Saints and State Power: the pirs of Sind, 1843–1947*, Lahore: Vanguard Books, 1992, p. 80.

[77] See Jamal Malik, *Colonization of Islam: Dissolution of Traditional Institutions in Pakistan*, Lahore: Vanguard Books, 1996, p. 207.

[78] Olivier Roy, *op. cit.*, pp. 75 ff.

pre-war times the majority of Afghan *ulema*, who followed the Hanafi rite, were opposed to the 'Wahhabis', lumping together under that term many of the reformists.[79] For example they rejected the doctrine of the Ahl-i Hadith, since the cult of saints remained very popular in Afghanistan.[80]

The dominant faction in the pre-war period professed adherence to a version of Islam close to the Sufi and Deobandi tradition. The Mujaddidi family was a typical rallying point for the traditionalist *ulema*. This family was also behind the initiation of a modernising reform in the teaching of the private *madrasas*. Indeed, in the 1930s Fazl Omar Mujaddidi founded the Nur ul-Mudaris *madrasa*, in the Ghazni province, which was the venue of a genuine reconstruction of private religious education. In reaction to the setting-up of governmental *madrasas* his son Ibrahim in the 1970s introduced 'modern' subjects, including science, sport and English, equipping a new generation of *ulema* who were able to compete with those from the government schools.

The autonomy of the *ulema* in relation to the state was also linked to the role of a number of influential families, notably the Mujaddidi and the Gaylani, who dominated the informal Afghan religious hierarchy and played a leading part in all efforts to mobilise them as a group. From these two families came the most renowned *ulema* and the most influential *pirs* of the two main religious brotherhoods present in Afghanistan—the Naqshbandiyya and the Qadiriyya.[81] The Gaylani and the Mujaddidi were not originally from Afghanistan, but their prestige had allowed them to lead the local *ulema*. Qayyum Jan Mujaddidi, who came from India in the early 19th century, set up a *madrasa* in the Shor Bazaar, from which arose the name by which he and his descendants were known: Hazrat Sahib-i Shor

[79] Here the *ulema* enjoyed the support of the State, which was apprehensive of antagonistic positions. As late as the 1970s an *alem* in Kandahar had Wahhabi preachers imprisoned (interview, Kandahar, 1992).

[80] See Nighat Mehroze Chishti, *op. cit.* On the persistence of non-Islamic traditions, see Marc Gaborieau, 'Typologie des spécialistes religieux chez les Musulmans du sous-continent indien: les limites de l'islamisation', *Archives des sciences sociales des religions* 55 (1), 1983, pp. 22–51.

[81] On the Naqshbandiyya, see Marc Gaborieau, Alexandre Popovic, Thierry Zarcone (eds) *Naqshbandis. Cheminements et situation actuelle d'un ordre mystique musulman*, Istanbul-Paris: Isis, 1990.

Bazaar.[82] There were also branches of the family in Herat, Logar and Ghazni provinces. The second important family, the Gaylani, arrived in Afghanistan in 1905. Other branches of this family were previously in Afghanistan, but the last to arrive achieved dominance. Sayyed Hasan Gaylani[83] had moved to Afghanistan because of differences with the *pir* of the Qadiri brotherhood in Iraq. He was well received by *amir* Habibullah, who granted him a pension, and settled near Jalalabad where he became the principal *pir* of the Qadiri brotherhood in Afghanistan.

These two families, though often opposed to the authorities, belonged to the governing class, and their strategy of forging matrimonial alliances with the royal clan earned them an important position among the élites. The Mujaddidi, who adhered to the Naqshbandi tradition, were awarded a role as the counsellors or arbitrators of the ruler, and in particular took upon themselves the right to confer legitimacy on new sovereigns and to adjudicate on whether their actions conformed to Islamic principles.[84] The Gaylani, who were much less confrontational, also had less influence among the *ulema*. Their ties with the royal clan were close.

For the Shi'ites the centres of education have always been outside Afghanistan, particularly at Qom in Iran and Najaf in Iraq, and the authorities made no attempt to integrate their religious establishment.

---

[82] Qayyum Jan Mujaddidi was descended from Shaikh Ahmad Sirhindi, who was born in Kabul in 1564 and buried at Sirhind in India in 1624. Shaikh Ahmad Sirhindi was recognised as the *Mujadid alf-i thani* (the bringer of millennial renewal), since according to Muslim tradition a reformer periodically arises to bring religion back to its principles. See Ludwig W. Adamec, *Historical Dictionary of Afghanistan*, London: Scarecrow Press, 1991, p. 167. According to family history Qayyum Jan arrived at the end of the 18th century, see David B. Edwards, 'The Political Lives of Afghan Saints: the Case of the Kabul Hazrats' in Grace Martin Smith (ed.), *Manifestations of Sainthood in Islam*, Istanbul: Isis Press, 1993.

[83] A descendant of the founder of the Qadiri brotherhood, *pir* Baba Abdul Qadir Gaylani (1077–1166), was born in Baghdad in 1862. The eldest son of Sayyed Hasan, Sayyed Ali, who later inherited the position of *pir*, died in 1964, and his successor was Sayyed Ahmad Efendi Sahib Gaylani. On the frequent visits by the Gaylani of Iraq to India at the close of the 19th century, which aroused the suspicions of the British, see Gölhan Çetinsaya, 'Ottoman Administration of Iraq, 1890–1900', Ph.D thesis (unpublished), University of Manchester, 1994, p. 55.

[84] This Naqshbandiyya strategy of acquiring influence is evident in the significant number of senior officials who are Naqshbandis, especially from the Barakzai and Sadozai tribes.

A genuine cultural renaissance manifested itself in some *madrasas* from the 1960s onwards. Ismail Balkhi (1922–68), an intellectual known for his abilities as an orator, was one of the leading figures of this movement.[85] Sayyed Beheshti attracted the *taliban* (students) from the entire Hazarajat to Waras. At Kandahar, the cultural movement *Sobh-i Danesh* (dawn of knowledge), inspired by Asef Muhseni, made available a modernist education; in addition to strictly religious topics, the movement's monthly publication dealt with social issues, Marxist dialectic and other subjects.[86] In the majority of cases training in Iran or Iraq was part of this renaissance, which gave rise to a growing politicisation of the students emerging from the *madrasas*. The politicisation of the Shi'ite clergy preceded the Iranian revolution.

The autonomy of thought of the *ulema* and their organisation accounted for the frequency of clashes with the state. From 1919 the *ulema* opposed Amanullah, who wished to speed up the process of modernisation. In 1924 Amanullah, fearing a plot inspired by the British, arrested *pir* Mujaddidi and executed a number of *ulema*. In 1929 the *ulema* played a key role both in the spread of the rebellion and the seizure of power by Nadir. From the 1950s opposition once more intensified between the *ulema* and the authorities, who had resumed the modernisation of society. Some fifty *mullahs*, of whom a number were members of the Mujaddidi family, were imprisoned as the result of their opposition to the unveiling of women in 1959, a measure especially symbolic since Amanullah had already included it in his programme of reform. The parliamentary regime which took office in 1964 afforded the opportunity for a substantial number of men of religion to enter Parliament, around a quarter of the first assembly.[87] The *ulema* and their *taliban* (students), under the influence

---

[85] Sayyed Muhammad Ismail Balkhi, originally from the province of Jozjan, was a remarkable intellectual and preacher who studied at Mashad and Qom. His speeches calling for equality for the Shi'ites, as well as for the democratisation of the country, had an impact in student and cultured circles beyond the Shi'ites themselves. He was arrested in 1946 for an attempted coup, and remained in detention for fourteen years. His influence on the Shi'ite movement as a whole in Afghanistan was critical. On the politicisation of these groups see David Busby Edwards, 'The Evolution of Political Dissent', *op. cit.*

[86] See Olivier Roy, *op. cit.*, p. 202.

[87] Louis Duprée, 'Comparative profiles of recent parliaments in Afghanistan', *American Universities Field Staff Report* XV (4), July 1971.

of Ibrahim Mujaddidi, who succeeded his father in 1956, were at that time organised into an informal group known as the Khodam ul-Forqan (servants of the Quran).

In 1970 a number of *ulema* were again imprisoned, this time after clashes with Marxist students. In the spring of the following year, religious figures from Kabul and its neighbourhood organised the largest demonstration so far seen in the capital, involving tens of thousands of people. The protest was directed against the appearance in a communist journal of an article deemed offensive to religion, and in particular against the use in celebratory coverage of the hundredth anniversary of the birth of Lenin of the term *dorud* (greetings), an expression reserved for the Prophet Muhammad. Ibrahim Mujaddidi and Gholam Muhammad Niazi were the instigators of the movement, which demanded an end to the education of women and a return to veiling (*purdah*),[88] while the protests of the *mullahs*, who roused the tribes in Laghman and Nangrahar, induced the government to negotiate. It will be seen that at this time the political parties enjoyed nothing like the same ability to mobilise.

As has often been the case in the Muslim world, law and education were the two points of friction with the state. The *ulema* were to an extent marginalised in both these fields, above all by the overtly modernist policies of Daud (1953–63). In the judicial domain relations between the *ulema* and the state were initially good. Aiming to counter tribal and customary law, Abdul Rahman Khan widened their role, in particular through the nomination of *qadis* (judges) in all districts. Ashraf Ghani has shown in a study of the case of the province of Kunar how the *qadis*, closely controlled by the state, were able by employing a jurisprudence antithetical to customary law profoundly to modify the way in which conflicts were resolved.[89] Nevertheless, many issues continued to be settled outside the legal system.

---

[88] Leftist movements then mounted a demonstration involving several thousand women. Shots were fired and a number of the demonstrators were burned with acid, in Kabul and other towns. See, Linda Clark Richter, 'The impact on women of regime change in Afghanistan', *Journal of South Asia and Middle Eastern Studies* 3 (2), winter 1983, p. 6.

[89] With the result that women were empowered to become more autonomous agents, while they were excluded from customary law. See Ashraf Ghani, 'Disputes in a court of Shari'a, Kunar Valley, Afghanistan', *International Journal of Middle Eastern Studies* 15, 1983.

The recent subjection of Hazarajat and Nuristan, which had been Islamised only at the close of the 19th century, also tended to enhance the power of the *ulema*, who issued their judgements independently with a right of appeal only to the *amir*. Amanullah still devoted one day each week to the dispensation of justice.

In due course conflicts became inevitable between the state, which introduced a legal code on the European model, and the *ulema* who regarded the *shariat* as the principal legal source and wished to retain the monopoly of justice. Indeed, the effect of all the legal codifications carried out by the state was to diminish the role of the *ulema*. For example, the penal code of 1924 laid down the priority of specialised legal codes in the commercial and military fields, which lay beyond the jurisdiction of the *ulema*. Codification also allowed recourse to legal sources in competition with the *shariat*, such as the *pushtunwali*, the customary Pushtun law. After 1929, however, the secularisation of the law went into reverse, with the civil and criminal law directly inspired by the *shariat* at the expense of imported law.[90] The movement towards secularisation gradually resumed after 1945, but the *shariat* and the right of reference to an Islamic judge continued, so that the coexistence of two alternative principles of justice led to some confusion. Personal law remained generally under the authority of the Islamic judge in the new civil and penal code of 1976, but punishments were defined, which deprived the *qadi* of a margin of interpretation. Finally, judges increasingly tended to be drawn from the faculty of law and political science.

In teaching the state attempted to displace the *ulema* and the *mullahs* in favour of compulsory education controlled by the administration in which the teaching of non-religious subjects had first place. Nevertheless, at least in the 1930s and 1940s, the *ulema* retained a controlling power over education. In consequence the secondary schools for girls were closed till the end of the 1930s, and religious subjects regained their predominance. After the arrival of Daud in 1953, secularisation once more became the dominant tendency, not least because of the increasing presence of western experts in this sphere.

---

[90] Nevertheless the constitution was ambiguous on the point. See Night Mehrose Chishti, *op. cit.*, p. 65. See also M. G. Weinbaum, 'Legal élites in Afghan society', *International Journal of Middle East Studies* 12, 1980, pp. 29–57.

The conjunction of the tribal and religious oppositions. Up to the 1950s the principal danger for the state remained the conjunction of the two opposition forces, tribal and religious. It proved fatal to Amanullah in 1929 having already dangerously threatened his power in 1924. Though there were major contradictions between the religious code, the *shariat,* and the tribal law, the *pushtunwali,* Islam was nevertheless an essential element of Pushtun identity. In addition to their performance of the prayers and the rituals, the *mullahs* interpreted the law during tribal *jirgas,* or gatherings. Occasionally the externality of the *mullahs* to the tribal system enabled them to intervene as intermediaries, similarly to descendants of the Prophet (*sadat*) and holy men (*pirs*). The influence of a particular *mullah* was in practice variable, and was enhanced if significant *waqfs* were under his control. The role of the *mullah,* as an interpreter of the Quran, implied a constant tension with tribal practices, since he sought to impose other values, religious rather than customary, as well as an alternative justice, Quranic as against *pushtunwali.* In contrast to the *pirs,* the *mullahs* did not necessarily seek to minimise conflicts, but looked rather for an 'Islamic' solution.[91] The *mullahs* therefore sought autonomy within the tribal structure.

The conjunction of opposition by the tribes and by the religious establishment in general occurred through the intervention of charismatic *mullahs,* who made possible the temporary suppression of tribal differences and the adoption of a unified stand against an authority denounced as apostate (*kafir*). This was demonstrated by the numerous rebellions led by them.[92] These *mullahs* might even be illiterate, since they derived their legitimacy from their charisma and not, like the *ulema,* from learning. Even in the absence of a charismatic figure, the *ulema* were able to sustain a tribal revolt by declaring a *jihad,* as in 1924 during the Khost rebellion. In that year, for instance, at the time of the revolt of *mullah* Abdullah Ahmadzai, known as *mullah-i* Lang, against King Amanullah, the Mujaddidi

---

[91] This opposition between *mullahs* and *pirs* is found in many tribal societies in the Muslim world. On the situation in Morocco, see Ernest Gellner, *Saints of the Atlas,* London: Weidenfeld and Nicolson, 1969.

[92] Instances in Pakistan and Afghanistan are numerous: the Akhund of Swat, *mullah-i* Lang, the Fakir of Ipi, Shami *pir* or Hadda-yi Sahib; cf. David Busby Edwards, 'Charismatic leadership and political process in Afghanistan', *Central Asian Survey* 5 (3–4), 1986.

supported *mullah* Abdul Ghani, one of their disciples, who directed the uprising of the Ghilzai at Ghazni.

However, any accord between the *ulema* and the tribes would be provisional, to the extent where one could speak of a mutual instrumentality. In fact, the model of tribal action did not undergo permanent change under the influence of the religious leaders, and alliances formed under the leadership of charismatic personalities were always temporary by nature. In reality, tribal revolts were generally occasioned by attempts by the state to place limits on the independence of the tribes, for example through the suppression of the *badraga* (the levy imposed on travellers by the eastern tribes), or the imposition of compulsory military service, or the introduction of identity cards. The religious aspect was generally marginal when set against the preservation of tribal autonomy.

The events of 1929 showed clearly the complementarity between the strategy of the *ulema* and that of the tribes. The revolt against Amanullah was launched by the Shinwari tribes for economic reasons, with no genuine religious dimension. This is why they were able later to respond to the call to revolt launched in 1938 against Zahir Shah by a charismatic *mullah*, Muhammad Saadi al-Keilani, who called for the reinstatement of Amanullah. The same tribes who engineered his downfall in 1929 were to call for his return ten year later. However, in 1929 the *ulema* opposed to Amanullah's project of modernisation capitalised on the revolt against him by declaring a *jihad* against the ruler, who could not stand up to the tribes because his army was not strong enough. So far the situation followed the normal pattern, with the *ulema* and the tribes in alliance, but the capture of Kabul by Habibullah 'Bacha-yi Saqao', a Tajik brigand,[93] created an unprecedented situation. Habibullah, crowned ruler by Akhundzada, the *pir* of Tagab, was supported by the network of fundamentalist *ulema* and by the Naqshbandis of the north;[94] he is supposed to have been the *murid* (disciple) of the *pir* Shams ul-Haq Mujaddidi Kohestani.[95]

---

[93] Habibullah was born in 1890 in Kalakan, the son of a water-carrier (*saqao*), and became a bandit after deserting from the army. See Mir Muhammad Sediq Farhang, *Afghanistan dar panj qarn-i akhir* (Afghanistan in the last five centuries), Peshawar: Derarshesh, 1988., p. 561.

[94] Olivier Roy, *Afghanistan. Islam et modernité politique*, Paris: Seuil, 1985, pp. 86 seq.

[95] Muhammad Naser Kamal, *Afghanistan sarzamin-i aria* (Afghanistan, an Aryan country), Peshawar: Danesh Ketabkhane, 1999, p. 151.

However, the Mujaddidi maintained an ambiguous attitude towards him, because of their links with the Muhammadzai dynasty and the Ghilzai tribes.[96] After some months power was regained by the tribes united under the banner of Nadir Khan, when the Mujaddidi family played a decisive role in rallying the support of the Ghilzai. The key point was the incompatibility of the various strategies. Since the *ulema* at this point were unable alone to sustain the ruler against the tribes, they rallied to the pretender to the throne. By the 1960s and 1970s such opposition movements seemed to be a thing of the past, as the state embarked on a modernisation of the country which led to a different configuration of opposition forces.

---

[96] The *ziarat* of Shirind was a place of pilgrimage for the Ghilzai nomads, which was the reason for their connection with the Mujaddidi.

2. From Mobilisation to Revolution

At a time when the state was no longer threatened by opposition from the tribes and the *ulema*, developmental processes within Afghanistan produced a revolutionary situation. This was because the educated classes, dissatisfied with their role in society, began resorting to collective organisation. From the 1970s onwards the largely dysfunctional political system, unable to mobilise support, paved the way for the communists to carry out a coup, a situation which led eventually to the civil war and the Soviet invasion.

Internal constraints and the model of development. After the initial efforts of Abdul Rahman Khan (1880–1901), the revolt of 1929 against Amanullah obliged his successor Nadir to exercise great prudence. Up to the start of the 1950s the state was principally concerned to acquire the means to maintain its own autonomy, indeed its very existence, since it did not enjoy real military superiority over the tribes. Its modernising effort was at that time relatively limited, and it suffered some notable defeats. Later, no longer apprehensive of military defeat, the authorities were able to embark on social change, placing the emphasis on education, infrastructure and industrialisation.

In Afghanistan the accumulation of capital and the process of modernisation had been the state's business. For this reason the Jewish and Hindu communities, very active up to the beginning of the 20th century, were progressively excluded from international commerce, as the state established monopolies over external trade. The difficulty of mobilising internal resources to embark on the modernisation of the country led the Afghan state to seek international finance, and this produced social and political tensions.

The mobilisation of internal resources

Since the destruction of the systems of irrigation in the south and west of Afghanistan by Genghis Khan and Tamerlane, the country's

61

territory has seldom afforded the necessary resources to maintain central authority. This was why the Pushtun empires of the 18th century were mainly financed from the Punjab.[1] Subsequently, the Afghan state experienced difficulties in raising sufficient revenue to finance its development. To find the money to maintain the army and create infrastructures, Abdul Rahman Khan brought in a number of new taxes, but the revenue raised remained small. In the 1920s Amanullah's ambitious modernisation project, as well as the end of British aid, led him to increase his fiscal pressure substantially and to raise taxation solely in the form of cash—a policy made possible by Afghanistan's relative prosperity between the two world wars. Thus the budget of 1928 shows that 30 per cent of the revenues of the state came from taxation on agricultural produce: a threefold increase over the previous situation. One of the main reasons for the unpopularity of Amanullah lay in his fiscal exactions and their consequences: corruption within the administration, and banditry. In 1927 there was even a physical attack on the Minister of Finance by discontented peasants.

Amanullah's eventual failure demonstrated the impossibility of financing ambitious modernisation projects rapidly without external assistance,[2] and this was even more the case after the events of 1929, when the regime of Nadir Kahn came under additional pressure. The new constitution required the consent of the *Loya Jirga* before the introduction of new property taxes, so—unable to modify the tax regime to any significant extent—the government continued through the 1930s to depend on customs duties for two-thirds of its revenue,[3] a notably high figure which persisted till the 1970s. The urban economy was more highly taxed overall, which put a brake on its development. On the other hand, the great landowners easily evaded property taxes. Finally, the Second World War brought a substantial fall in the state's revenue because of the reduction in the overseas sales of the fleeces of the *karakul* (the wavy-haired sheep) and the flight of capital to the city of Peshawar (now in Pakistan).

---

[1] Hasan Kakar, *op. cit.*, p. 176.
[2] This statement should be qualified, as is shown by the development of Kunduz, undertaken in the 1930s by the Bank-i Melli without external assistance.
[3] Hasan Kakar, *op. cit.*, p. 317.

International funding

After various hesitations, and in spite of the fact that by accepting a degree of dependence the Afghan state broke with the isolationism and wariness institutionalised by Abdul Rahman Khan, the solution offered by external finance was unavoidable from the close of the 1940s. The principal advantage of this approach was that it avoided on the one hand argument over the implications of modernisation and especially its costs, and on the other a clash with the *ulema* and the local notables. International circumstances were auspicious. Rivalry between the United States and the Soviet Union was being fought out through competition in the field of aid, and at least in the short term Afghanistan gained the full benefit. From 1950 relations between the great powers were regulated by an informal agreement between the Soviets and the Americans which defined their zones of influence, respectively to the north and south of the Hindu Kush.[4] The volume of aid for the period 1950–77 was $2 billion, or more than $70 million a year.[5] From the 1960s more than 40% of state revenue was derived directly from foreign aid.[6] Between 1950 and 1969 this came mainly under bilateral agreements, with more than 80 per cent of the aid budget divided between the United States, which provided 31% of the total, and the Soviet Union (54%). In the 1970s an evolution towards multilateralism began to be evident: the United Nations and the World Bank provided 20% of the aid, while the US and Soviet Union shares fell to 21 and 29% respectively. There was in overall terms a fall in American aid from the close of the 1960s, while the Soviet presence was strengthened, especially the number of Soviet specialists. The training of military officers and civilian administrators by the Soviet Union also enabled the KGB and the GRU to pursue an effective policy of recruitment with effects that were to make themselves felt in the 1970s.[7]

---

[4] René Cagnat, Michel Jan, *Le milieu des Empires ou le destin de l'Asie centrale*, Paris: Laffont, 1981, p. 190.

[5] Jacky Mathonnat, 'Une économie impulsée de l'extérieure' in Pierre Centlivres *et al.*, *La colonisation impossible*, Paris: Les Editions du Cerf, 1984, p. 169.

[6] Barnet Rubin, 'Political Elites in Afghanistan: rentier state building, rentier state wrecking', *International Journal of Middle East Studies* 24, 1992, p. 97.

[7] Marie Broxup, 'The Soviets in Afghanistan: the anatomy of a takeover', *Central Asian Survey* 1 (4), 1983.

By accepting international aid the government progressively lost control of its development programme, as was clear from its development plans from 1957 onwards, which consisted of efforts to co-ordinate after aid had been received. The role of foreign experts was decisive in the selection of aid projects, through which the donors sought visibility to demonstrate their technological prowess, but which succeeded only in creating modernised enclaves. Industrial development, which owed much to the Bank-i Melli, was concentrated predominantly in Kabul where a number of light industries appeared, although before the revolution the number of workers involved never exceeded 40,000. Similarly, large-scale projects which needed diverse groups of workers and their families to be assembled at specified locations, such as the Pul-i Khumri cement works, enjoyed only limited success.

Instead of facilitating a controlled transition, Afghanistan's development strategy only reinforced the distinctions between regions and social groups. This may be a feature common to all economic development, but the disruption was particularly evident in the Afghan case since modernisation led to ever greater contrasts between the ways of life and the aspirations of the urban and rural populations. Life in the Westernised parts of Kabul, where most foreign experts worked, was clearly separate from the rest of the country. Two consequences of this strategy were especially detrimental economically: the agricultural crisis and the dependence on foreign aid.

Apart from certain large-scale irrigation projects, like that in Helmand, agriculture was not at the forefront of the donors' priorities, especially those of the Soviets, which was a reflection of their own failures. There was not to be a 'Green Revolution' in Afghanistan.[8] The end of the civil wars had made possible a steady growth in the Afghan population from the beginning of the 20th century. From the 1960s there was pressure on agricultural sector, and the diminishing improvements in productivity were no longer sufficient to match the increase in the population. Thereafter peasant income, which had been stable from 1935 to 1966, fall in real terms.[9] The drought of

---

[8] Concerning Afghan agriculture see Gilbert Etienne, *L'Afghanistan ou les aléas de la coopération*, Paris: PUF, 1972.

[9] For a critique of the adverse effects of aid see Pierre Gentelle, 'L'Afghanistan et l'aide internationale de 1950 à 1978. Espaces modernisables, sociétés rétives', *Revue du Tiers Monde*, October-December 1979.

1970–1 and the resulting famine in 1972 revealed the demographic tensions and the fragility of the agricultural equilibrium. In 1972 some 8,000 people are said to have died of starvation, and some livestock also perished, which drove the peasants heavily into debt.[10] Only the urban centres were linked at this time by paved roads. The lack of secondary roads accounts for the absence of an integrated market—the price of wheat varied from one region to another—and explains how localised famines could occur. On the other hand, the following years showed that in normal times Afghanistan was self-sufficient in food.

More generally Afghanistan experienced the onset of a rural exodus, partly towards Iran and Pakistan. In certain places such as the Andarab valley north of Kabul, 40% of the male population went to work in the towns in the winter.[11] Kabul underwent spectacular development, from 450,000 people in 1965 to 600,000 on the eve of the war. A third of those living in the city had not been born there. Overall the growth of the urban population exceeded that of the rural population, increasing by 3.4% in contrast to 2.5%, although Afghanistan remained an essentially rural country on the eve of the revolution of 1978, when 86% of Afghans still lived in the villages.

In the 1970s foreign aid declined because of the minimal United States interest in Afghanistan in a period of détente. The Soviets, particularly represented through their provision of technical aid, gave less new credit at the same time as the burden of debt was becoming more significant, while the dates for repayment of existing Soviet loans began to fall due. The repayment of loans, which represented 27% of payments in foreign exchange at the start of the 1970s, rose to 40% in 1975.[12] This situation put further pressure on the political system, which was obliged to find additional sources of finance.

The politicisation of the educated class

However, it was in education rather than the economic sphere that modernisation had its greatest effects, laying the groundwork for the

[10] See Hasan Kakar, 'The Fall of the Afghan Monarchy in 1973', *International Journal of Middle East Studies*, 9 May 1978. The production of wheat is said to have fallen by 20 % and the number of sheep by 40 %. World Bank, *op. cit.*, p. 27.

[11] Louis Duprée, 'Settlement and Migration Patterns in Afghanistan: a tentative statement', *Modern Asian Studies*, 9, 1975.

[12] Richard S. Newell, 'The government of Mohammad Musa Shafiq: the last chapter of Afghan liberalism', *Central Asian Survey*, July 1982, p. 57.

emergence of an educated generation from which almost all political activists were drawn. The earliest generation was educated in the
1920s within the system put in place by the principal western powers in the shape of their patronage of high schools.[13] As an outcome
of the liberal episode of 1946–52, the first trade union and political
movements, illegal but tolerated, saw the light of day in Afghanistan.[14] These included the Union of Students, the first student union,
founded in 1946, which was reformist, looked back with nostalgia to
the days of Amanullah, and was anti-imperialist, which meant in
practice anti-American. Another key organisation was the Wikh-i
Zalmayan (Awakening of Youth) formed in 1947.[15] This group, first
established in Kandahar, brought together a large segment of the politicised intelligentsia, including notably Daud, the future president;
Nur Muhammad Taraki, the future founder of the communist party;
Shamsuddin Majruh, a senator; Muhammad Musa Shafiq and Muhammad Hashem Maywandwal, both future Prime Ministers; and
Abdul Majid Zabuli, founder of the Bank-i Melli. This group's inclination was nationalist rather than marxist, even though future communists participated in it. It also had an anti-monarchist component,
and the idea of setting up a republic was openly discussed—royalty
never enjoyed great legitimacy in the eyes of the Afghan governing
classes. However, in spite of its moderate demands, governmental
suppression put an end to this first experiment after a demonstration
in 1952 demanding the recognition of political parties.

From the 1960s the state's educational policy led to a rapid increase
in the numbers of high school pupils and of students.[16] Between

---

[13] These were the French Istiqlal lycée established in 1922, the German Nejat
School in 1924 and the British Ghazi School in 1928.

[14] Clandestine movements in fact began to develop early in the century: a Jamiyat-i
Siri-yi Melli (Association of the National Secret) emerged under Habibullah,
though its activities were quickly minimised after it was uncovered and suppressed following a plot against Habibullah in 1909. In addition, the intelligentsia consolidated around Mahmud Tarzi, who supported Amanullah's reforms,
but Amanullah's fall in 1929 and Nadir's Shah's authoritarianism obliged the
modernising intellectuals to observe a certain discretion, at least until the 1940s.
Thus the Halqa-yi Jawan-i Afghanistan (People of the Afghan Youth), a secret
society of supporters of constitutional reform, was broken up under the conservative regime in place from 1929.

[15] See Dr Fazal ur-Rahim Marwat, *op. cit.*

[16] There were 8,500 students in 1971 and around 15,000 in 1978. Cf. Etienne

1957 and 1967 the number of children receiving school education rose from 126,000 to 540,000.[17] Collective action, especially strikes of students and primary school teachers,[18] began to occur, a symptom of increasing politicisation, which was promoted by a number of factors. Because of the shortage of teachers of Afghan nationality, foreign assistants, who generally viewed the politicisation of their students favourably, played an important role within the university. Two-thirds of the books used by students were in a foreign language (English, French, German or Russian)—a significant indicator of the growing assimilation of foreign culture by the Afghan élites. The relatively liberal policies of the 1960s, and in particular greater press freedom, also increased awareness of political ideas.

These mobilisations were in the last resort the result of the students' difficulty in integrating themselves into society after leaving the university. Without a sufficiently developed private sector, the appearance of numerous educated job seekers on the labour market highlighted the difficulty of providing sufficient employment, with the public sector remaining the principal outlet.[19] Professional success after leaving university depended more on family influence than on ability or on what qualification had been obtained, which condemned the majority of graduates to the lower ranks of the administration, where they were badly paid and underemployed. Indeed high school or university education had created a psychological detachment which, especially for those from the provinces who had been physically cut off from their origins, made return to their families difficult. These former students found themselves in a situation which they perceived as unjust, given their abilities and the needs of

---

Gille, 'L'accession au pouvoir des communistes pro-soviétiques' in Pierre Cent-livres *et al., op. cit.*, p. 181.

[17] World Bank, *op. cit.*, p. 26. In 1974, 30 % of pupils of primary school age were at school, though there was a very marked under-representation of girls: Centlivres *et al., op. cit.*, p. 77. By 1973–4 around 11 % of the population could read. See *Encyclopaedia Iranica*, Costa Mesa CA: Mazda Publishers, 1998, p. 239.

[18] On the student movements of 1966–8 see Louis Duprée, *op. cit.*, p. 619. There were 39 strikes in 1966, 80 in 1967, and 133 in 1968: see Dr Muhammad Anwar, 'The third Afghan constitution (part VII): political parties and newspapers', *Central Asia* 11, Area Study Center, University of Peshawar, winter 1982, p. 5. Around 15,000 people demonstrated following the death of a student killed by the police in the June 1969 demonstrators.

[19] See *Encyclopaedia Iranica, op. cit.*, p. 239.

society. This frustration was in part due to their material circumstances: the salaries were miserable and fell by half in real value between the 1960s and the end of the 1970s.[20] However they were also psychological, as the personal and collective ambitions nurtured during their school or student years collided with the reality of a society which had little tolerance for their ideas. The relative sequestration of the sociable student life, in a country where the population was largely illiterate, reinforced the sense of identity among the group. The army underwent a similar crisis with its young officers. In spite of a degree of ethnic and social inclusiveness in the officers' academies, the key positions in the military were reserved for the Durrani, especially those of the royal clan, who were presumed to be faithful to the dynasty. In addition, those young officers who had spent time in the Soviet Union were kept out of positions of responsibility, since the royal authorities feared, sometimes justifiably, that they might have become communists.

In the 1970s the political parties were not highly structured organisations, but served mainly as discussion forums. The capital was the centre of political activity, although some militants were to be found in towns such as Herat and Jalalabad. At the University of Kabul there were dozens of groups, with only fluid boundaries between them. In the case of the Maoists the various provincial branches were for practical purposes autonomous. These organisations, which at their outset often wavered between adopting the status of student unions or that of political parties, generally concentrated on the publication of a periodical. However, in a largely illiterate country, the public they were able to reach was limited. In the absence of exact studies, the total number of militants and sympathisers of all the parties at this time can be estimated at some thousands. Thus the two branches of the communist movement included at most several thousand members at the beginning of the 1970s, of whom 2,500 belonged to the Khalq and 1,500–2,000 to the Parcham, about the same as the Islamists and the Maoists.[21] The Pushtun nationalist movement and that of the social democrats, who recruited less exclusively from among the students, had even fewer adherents.

---

[20] World Bank, *Afghanistan: the journey to Economic Development*, report no. 1777a-AF, 1978, p. vii.

[21] Louis Duprée, *Red Flag over the Indu-Kush*, Part V, AUFS report no. 28, 1980, p. 3.

A feature which these political movements had in common was that they never achieved any penetration in the countryside. Students—mainly Islamists—who returned to their villages during the summer to spread political propaganda were only isolated instances. The parties were never able to mobilise beyond the educated classes because of their lack of contacts in the rural communities, though distinctions must be made between the different regions, especially according to the prevalent type of social organisation. For example in a highly segmentary tribal context, as with the eastern Pushtuns, political activism was almost non-existent, while in Badakhshan, among the Turkmens and in the south of the Hazarajat, where the politicised sons of local notables exploited their social connections, the situation was much more open.

In the 1970s movements multiplied and the ideological options widened.[22] A religious tendency solidified around *mawlawi* Faizani, an *alem* from Herat, who established the Khodam ul-Forqan at the beginning of the 1950s and later moved closer to Ibrahim Mujaddidi.[23] Elsewhere *ulema* inspired by the Egyptian Muslim Brotherhood held their earliest meetings around 1957, led by Gholam Niazi, dean of the Faculty of Theology and a graduate of Al-Azhar University, later to be executed under Daud.[24] Its distinctness from the student branch, which emerged ten years later more or less independently, was marked from the outset, even though the two movements were in contact. The Islamist students, who were not *ulema*, mainly adhered to the Sazman-i Jawanan-i Mosalman (Organisation of Young Muslims) and acknowledged as their founder Abdul Rahim

---

[22] For a treatment of the various tendencies see Basir Ahmad Daulat Abadi, *Hazab va Jarayanat-i Siyasi-yi Afghanistan* (Parties and political events in Afghanistan), [Pakistan]: Moallef, 1982.

[23] Dr Mohammad Anwar Khan, 'The Emergence of Religious Parties in Afghanistan' in Fazal-ur-Rahim Marwat, S. Waqar Ali Shah (eds), *Afghanistan and the Frontier*, Peshawar: Emjay Publishers, 1991, pp. 1 *seq.*

[24] This movement, whose organisation was loose, is supposed to have been known by the name Tahrik-i Islam (Islamic Movement): cf. Olivier Roy, 'L'Islam', in Pierre Centlivres *et al.*, *op. cit.* p. 108. For the origins of the Islamic movement see also Olivier Roy, 'The origins of the Islamist movement in Afghanistan', *Central Asian Survey* 3 (2) 1984, and Assem Akram, *Histoire de la guerre d'Afghanistan*, Paris: Balland, 1998, pp. 212 *seq.* Other groups were active in the 1960s, notably that of Menhajuddin Gahiz, who ran the magazine *Gahiz* (Morning) until his death in 1972.

Niazi, a student, who died after an illness in 1970. Among the Shi'ites the dominant personality was Ismail Balkhi, who founded the Qiyam-i Islam (Revolt of Islam) in the 1950s. In December 1950 Balkhi was accused of having plotted a coup together with Muhammed Ibrahim 'Bacha-yi Gaw Sawar', and was imprisoned until 1964.[25]

The pro-Soviet communists belonged to the Hezb-i Demokra-tik-i Khalq-i Afghanistan (Afghan People's Democratic party), founded on 1 January 1965 with Nur Muhammad Taraki as secretary-general and Babrak Karmal as deputy secretary-general. In the spring of 1967 the party split into two factions, Khalq (The People) under the leadership of Nur Muhammad Taraki and Parcham (The Flag) under Babrak Karmal.[26] A local splinter group, the Setam-i Melli (National Oppression) made its appearance in the early 1970s.[27]

The Sazman-i Demokrat-i Nawin-i Afghanistan (Modern and Democratic Organisation of Afghanistan), known as Shola-yi Jawid (the Eternal Flame), mustered the Maoists within a very loose organisation. This movement was established on 4 April 1968 and led by Dr Hadi Mahmudi, together with his nephew Abdur Rahman Mahmudi, as well as Akram and Sadiq Yari, all of whom were Hazaras from Jaghori. The party recruited mostly among the Hazaras and the Qizilbash of Kabul, as well as in the Kunar valley in cooperation with Muhammad Hashem Khan, perhaps because of the presence of the Chinese in this province in the context of a cooperative agricultural project.

The social democrats set up the Hezb-i Demokrat-i Mottaraki (Progressive Democratic Party) under the leadership of Hashem Maywandwal. On 24 August 1964, when Maywandwal was Prime Minister, this movement—not officially a political party—proclaimed

---

[25] Dr Fazal-ur-Rahim Marwat, *op. cit.*, p. 246.

[26] On the Afghan communist movement, see Anthony Arnold, *Afghanistan's Two-Party Communism, Parcham and Khalq*, Stanford, CA: Hoover Institution Press, 1983.

[27] The Setam-i Melli itself in due course split into two factions. In 1974 the founder of Setam-i Melli, Taher Badakhshi, became leader of the SAZA (Sazman-i Zamat-keshan) while Bahruddin Bahes took the leadership of the SAFZA (Sazman-i Fedayin-i Zamatkeshan). The origin of the split seems to have lain in the careful strategy of Taher Badakhshi, who remained in contact with the Parchamis and was opposed to the more radical vision of *mawlawi* Bahes, who favoured violent action.

its allegiance to Maywandwal in a radio transmission.[28] In contrast to most of the other movements, it adopted a reformist position and refrained from vehement criticism of the monarchy.

The Pushtun nationalists gravitated towards the Jamiyat-i Afghan Demokrat (Afghan Democratic Party) or the Afghan Mellat (Afghan Nation) set up by the engineer Gholam Muhammad Farhad.[29] The latter party, established on 8 March 1966, took an ultra-nationalist political line, particularly on the question of Pushtunistan and the Pushtun language. At the same time the Hazaras also joined nationalist organisations, frequently those set up by the diaspora in Pakistan and Iran, including notably the Hezb-i Moghul (Moghul Party), which was active among the Hazara community in Iran,[30] and the Tanzim Nesl-i Haw Hazara (Organisation of the Hazara New Generation) in Quetta, Pakistan.[31] It appears in addition that Uzbek militants, without setting up a political party, were also in contact with each other.

[28] Dr Fazal ur-Rahim Marwal, *op. cit.*, p. 246.

[29] Gholam Muhammad Farhad, an engineer trained in Germany, had been elected mayor of Kabul in 1948, before becoming a member of Parliament.

[30] The Berberis, the Hazara population in the region of Mashad who had arrived in Iran from the 18th century onwards and called themselves Khawaris, are said to have numbered about 500,000.

[31] The Hazara population settled in Quetta from the mid-19th century, but Pakistani nationality was not granted to them till 1963. From the mid-1960s the Hazaras of Quetta developed a strong nationalist tendency, in particular through the Tanzim Nesl-i Naw-i Hazara Moghul (Organisation of the New Generation Hazara-Moghul). The Tanzim, established in 1971 and particularly active in the cultural field among the Hazara community in Quetta, had an ideology based on an ethnic and racial nationalism, in which the Hazaras portrayed themselves as the descendants of Genghis Khan. This positive image of conquest and force contrasted with the humiliating and tragic situation of the Afghan Hazaras. Thus a tapestry representing the Mongol horde has pride of place in the office of the director of the Tanzim. Hazara nationalist works dealing with the history of the Hazarajat do not rely on the religious distinction but rather on 'race' as the criterion for belonging to the community. The Hazarajat, according to most of these nationalist authors, extends over a remarkably wide area. All people related to the Hazaras are included, regardless of their avowed identities, such as the Sunni Hazaras of Panjshir and of Qala-i Naw. For example, see Muhammad Gharjestani, *Tarikh-i nowin-i Hazarajat* (Modern History of Hazarajat), Peshawar, 1988. In addition, all territories that have belonged to the Hazaras are included, even if today they are occupied by other populations (this applies especially to areas towards Kandahar and Ghazni). The Tanzim strives to maintain the Hazara identity of the

POLITICAL PARTIES BEFORE 1978

Name	Formation	Membership	Ideology	Leaders
Hezb-i Demokratik-i Khalq-i Afghanistan	1965 (split into Khalq and Parcham, 1967)	Persian speakers for the Parcham. Pushtun speakers for the Khalq	Communist	Nur Muhammad Taraki. Babrak Karmal
Sazman-i Jawanan-i Mosalman	1968	Urban (Kabul)	Islamist	Abdul Rahim Niazi
Shola-yi Jawid	1968	Urban (Kabul, Herat, Mazar-i Sharif) Shi'ites Qizilbash, Hazaras of Jaghori, Kunar	Maoist	Osman Landay, the Yari brothers, the Mahmudi family
Afghan Mellat	1966	Townspeople, Pushtuns	Pushtun Nationalist	Gholam Muhammad Farhad
Hezb-i Demokrat-i Mottaraki	1966	Urban élites	Social Democrat	Hashem Maywandwal

It must be asked whether commitment to political parties mobilised feelings of communal solidarity. Political adherences were based primarily on universal propositions such as Islamism, Maoism and Communism, since their point of reference is either the *umma* or the global proletariat. Only the Pushtun nationalists and the Hazaras used explicitly community-centred language, but in student circles their impact was less than that of the other groups. There was no especially obvious dominant ethnic element among the Islamists or the Communists, seen overall. On the other hand, the political parties, the factions within them and most splinter groups clearly reproduced communal divisions, whether tribal, religious or regional. Following an initial commitment to an ideological principle, militant activity probably tends to promote solidarity on the basis of a broadly regional or communal basis. The Afghan political parties functioned as networks of solidarity (*qowm*): adherence to a

---

immigrant community by organising courses and publishing a periodical in Persian and Urdu, *Zulficar*, but the majority of the Hazaras are today educated in Urdu. The ability to write Persian is rare among the younger generation.

political party was developed into a broad solidarity which brought with it far-reaching implications extending far beyond the avowed political aims of the movement. These might relate to security, for example from the consequences of feuds, and to wide-reaching exchanges, as in marriage. Thus Shi'ite students are over-represented in the Shola-yi Jawid, led by the Hazaras of Jaghori, although the Herat group is not principally composed of Shi'ites. Another example was a splinter group of the Khalq, the Setam-i Melli, which arose from opposition to the Pushtuns who dominated the movement by Tajiks, broadly from the province of Badakhshan. Among the Islamists the *ulema* were most often Persian-speakers, while the lay student members were mostly Pushtu-speakers.

However, these differences in the field of recruitment are inevitably traceable to social factors, urban and tribal affiliations, which were more significant than ethnic affiliation as such. Thus factions within the Hezb-i Demokratik-i Khalq-i Afghanistan at first sight reproduce the antithesis between Pushtu-speakers and Persian-speakers. However, when Persian speakers such as Gholam Dastagir Panjshiri, Shah Wali or the Uzbek Sharay Jozjani left Parcham for the Khalq in 1968, the opposition between provincials and Kabulis re-emerged. The Parcham—which, while avowedly Persian-speaking, was also bourgeois and Kabuli—could not absorb these provincial elements. In this case rural-urban opposition offered a more satisfactory explanation than ethnic affiliation. In addition, Pushtun Islamists in general emerged from mixed Persian- and Pushtu-speaking areas with weak tribal institutions.[32] The case of Sebghatullah Mujaddidi provides further evidence of social contradictions. Mujaddidi, who had been imprisoned in 1959 for an assassination attempt on Khrushchev, was close to the Muslim Brotherhood. Nevertheless, his attempt to become leader of the student branch of the Islamic movement encountered strong opposition, particularly from Gulbuddin Hekmatyar, because of his family connection with the élites.[33] If the interpretation offered here is correct, social trajectories—more than social positions—are a more determining factor than the broad

---

[32] Olivier Roy, 'Le double code afghan. Marxisme et tribalisme', *Revue française de science politique* 35 (5), October 1985.

[33] David B. Edwards, *op. cit.*, p. 184.

ethnic affiliations of Pushtuns, Tajiks and so on. Within the same ideological movement individuals gravitate together according to their social profile. The modalities of political engagement can be seen as related to two particular social trajectories, namely those of students with links to the governing class and of provincial students with no ties with the élites.

Some of the students linked to the governing class are found in leftist groups such as Parcham, where activists linked to the royal clan itself are not exceptional. Daud, who worked with the Parchamis after he was ousted from power in 1963, appealed to them on his return to politics in 1973, since he believed them to be linked to the existing order and up to a certain point loyal to it. Social status provided the explanation why, with only one exception, the communists elected to parliament in 1964 and 1969 were all Parchamis rather than Khalqis.[34] The Parchamis, who for the most part were Kabulis, adopted a more liberal attitude on moral issues than the Khalqis, with female militants in particular playing an active role in the movement.

The leader of the Parcham, Babrak Karmal,[35] was a good representative of his faction. He was born in 1929, the son of Muhammad Hussein, a general who at one point had been governor of Paktya. The family was linked to the royal clan and belonged to the wealthy bourgeoisie of the capital. Karmal's Pushtun origin has been questioned, and it was the case that he spoke only Persian. He was a typical product of the Kabuli bourgeoisie, very distant from the peasant and tribal world. As a student at the Nejat School, he became a German translator after studying political science and law. In the 1960s he attached himself to the Halq-i Jawan-i Afghanistan movement (People of the Young Afghans); afterwards he participated in the foundation of the Hezb-i Demokratik-i Khalq-i Afghanistan and became leader of the Parcham branch after the movement split in 1967.

Provincial members of the educated class, who had only distant prospects of cooptation into the establishment, were attracted by re-

---

[34] Elected in September 1965 to the Wolesi Jirga: Babrak Karmal, Anahita Ratebzad, Nur Ahmad Nur, Fazl ul-Haq Fezan. The defeated candidates were Muhammad Taraki, Afizullah Amin (by a small margin), Sultan Ali Keshmand, Abdul Hakim, Sharay Jozjani. In 1969 only Karmal (in Kabul) and Amin (in Paghman) were elected. The latter was the only Khalqi ever to have achieved election.

[35] See Anthony Arnold, *op. cit.*, pp. 19 *seq.*

volutionary movements such as the Khalq or the Sazman-i Jawanan-i Mosalman. These two movements adopted the same compartmentalised and militaristic style of organisation in a bid to substitute party solidarity for the 'natural' solidarity of the family, and thus make up for the inferiority of their members' social position. Ideology was therefore an experience both radical and all embracing. The Islamist students criticised traditional Islamic instruction, and therefore the *ulema* themselves. In a similar way Khalq accused the Parcham of collaboration with the authorities and the bourgeoisie. The biography of the principal Islamist leader, Gulbuddin Hekmatyar, exemplified this kind of career.

Hekmatyar was born in the autumn of 1948 near Imam Saheb in the province of Kunduz. His father was a small peasant farmer from the Ghilzai Kharuti tribe. After primary education in Imam Saheb he was sent to the military school in Kabul and in due course passed the examination for entry to the Faculty of Engineering. By his own account, Gulbuddin's adoption of Islamism goes back to 1966, when he heard on the radio the news of the hanging of the Egyptian Islamist Sayyed Qutb. Contradicting rumours claiming that Gulbuddin had been a communist in his youth, witnesses in Imam Saheb are unanimous in saying that even then he was sympathetic to the Islamists.[36] Hekmatyar made himself noticed on the campus at Kabul through his energy, natural authority and ability as an orator. He took part in the conference of the Union of Students in 1970 as an active member, then as an elected official in 1972–3. At the same time he became leader of the student branch of the Jawanan-i Mosalman in the early 1970s. As a fugitive in Peshawar from 1974, he became leader of the Hezb-i Islami.

Though just as provincial and equally without resources, the students of the government *madrasas* were in a somewhat different position from the other students. Their politicisation was linked to their status as functionaries and to their contacts with the Egyptian Muslim Brotherhood, as is shown in the contrary case by the absence of Islamists among the *ulema* who came out of the private *madrasas*. They shared the same ambitions as the educated group, but their political positions, though revolutionary, did not imply an insulation from

[36] Various interview at Imam Saheb, October 1991.

society as complete as that of the students. In contrast to the rest of the educated group, they enjoyed a recognised position, and in the countryside even a certain amount of prestige.

The biography of Rabbani[37] is typical of an Islamist *alem*: provincial, influenced by the Egyptian Muslim Brotherhood, and imbued with the Sufi tradition. Rabbani was born in 1940 at Fayzabad in Badakhshan, the son of a small landowner. After primary school he left for Kabul to study at the Abu Hanifa school (Dar al-Ulum-i Shariat), and then till 1963 at the Faculty of Shariat at Kabul. He was a teacher at the Faculty in Kabul from 1963 to 1966, and then went to Al-Azhar, where he took his degree in 1968. Rabbani, himself a member of the Naqshbandi Sufi order, then prepared his doctorate on Jami, the mystical poet of Herat. He also undertook the translation of the book *In the Shadow of the Quran* by the Egyptian Muslim Brother Sayyed Qutb. He became professor of philosophy in the faculty of Shariat, and he edited the periodical *Majalle-yi Shariat* (Shariat Review). As a member of the Islamist faction from its origins, he organised student groups under the direction of Professor Niazi in the 1960s. After going into exile in Pakistan after Daud's coup, he became in 1974 the leader of the Jamiyat-i Islami.

The failure of the parliamentary regime

The dysfunctionality of the constitutional monarchy had a number of causes: parliament's ineffectiveness, its inability to respond to economic crisis, and its failure to incorporate the nascent political parties.

The ineffectiveness of parliament was due in the first instance to the absence of legal political parties, which was a barrier to the construction of coherent political platforms.[38] The elections scheduled for 1974 did not in fact take place, but the king had never intended to authorise the participation in them of the political parties, which prevented the Prime Minister Mohammad Musa Shafiq from estab-

[37] See Ludwig W. Adamec, *op. cit.*, p. 201.

[38] Within Parliament, several factions were nevertheless distinguishable: the conservatives centred on the Mujaddidi family and the leftists around Babrak Karmal. In addition, informal groups centred around figures such as Khalilulah Khalili, an intellectual close to the king, and his movement Wahdat-i Melli (National Unity); Abdul Majid Zabuli, a businessman, and Mir Muhamnmad Sadiq Farhang, an intellectual and a senior official.

lishing his own movement. In addition, the authorities limited the access of the candidates to Parliament. In 1969 some Parcham candidates had pressure put on them by the government or were imprisoned. Members of the intelligentsia, disadvantaged by lack of money and their lack of access to rural locations, were unable to play a part the institutional process. Further, the absence of political parties meant that candidates were obliged to defray personally the costs of their election campaigns, which amounted to considerable sums. Generally those elected were local notables who were able to mobilise a considerable clientele on the strength of their names. As shown by the very low levels of participation, of the order of 10%, parliamentary elections offered the occasion neither for political mobilisation nor for the legitimation of the constitutional monarchy.[39]

The role of Member of Parliament was acted out as a version of that of the *khan*, and the extent to which the concerns of the electors were conveyed to the administration was governed by the conventions of patronage. Corruption scandals, for example in the organisation of the pilgrimage to Mecca, were attributable to the desire of the elected representatives to replenish their funds. Due to the legal constraints no professional political class was to emerge capable of giving expression to social demands and of enforcing party discipline.

Because of the low representation of the educated classes among its members, Parliament and the government were made up of social groups whose interests were divergent, which became to some extent a further obstacle to the system. While the majority of the members of Parliament were rural notables, *ulema* or landowners of low educational attainments, of whom about one-third were illiterate,[40] cabinet members and high officials belonged to the governing class, which was favourable to the rapid westernisation of the country. A particular issue was that Parliament contained a majority of landowners, who in due course were to take steps towards lowering the property tax in order to satisfy both their local clientele and their own interests. This tax had scarcely been readjusted since Amanullah,

[39] For a number of examples of the levels of participation see Louis Duprée, *op. cit.*, p. 590. The constitution of 1964 envisaged an Upper House (Meshrano Jirga) representing the provinces, and a Lower House (Wolesi Jirga), respectively elected for five and four years.

[40] Nighat Mehroze Chishti, *op. cit.*, p. 121.

except very modestly in 1965. As a result it represented the equivalent of only 0.5 per cent of agricultural income at the start of the 1970s, and in some provinces such as Badakhshan, it was in any case imposed only very sporadically. By 1978 the ratio of fiscal receipts to GNP was 7%, a figure which had doubled since 1973 but was still one of the lowest in the world.[41] The state was therefore unable to deploy significant resources. As a result the salaries of government officials were derisory, which created a tendency towards corruption and fraud, over customs duties in particular, and in time resulted in a loss of revenue.

In day-to-day terms the representative system installed by the constitution of 1964 was broadly ineffectual. When a quorum was lacking, legislation could not be adopted by Parliament, which substantially impeded the process of administration. On occasion laws approved by Parliament were not promulgated by the king, including for example legislation relating to political parties and to municipal and provincial councils. Thus Zahir Shah forfeited the support of the business community when he failed to ratify laws to protect the Afghan market, exposed as it was to competition from Pakistan and Iran. In the 1970s the parliamentary regime seemed unable to cope with the mounting economic problems, a failure which indirectly called into question the king's credibility. On the other hand the Assembly did play some part in the expression of popular dissatisfaction. For example, the inability of the corrupt and ineffectual administration to distribute international aid to the provinces most affected by the famine of 1972 was condemned by members of Parliament, who strongly attacked the Prime Minister, Abdul Zahir.[42]

The parties had no mobilisation strategy which reached beyond their own militants, and social crises did not lead to popular mobilisation. In Afghanistan there were no 'de-ruralised peasants'[43] avail-

---

[41] Gilbert Etienne, *op. cit.*, p. 64, and World Bank, *op. cit.*, p. 14. To put the Afghan case into perspective, it is well known that fiscal exactions in Iran have always been lower than in European states: see Saïd Amir Arjomand, *The Turban for the Crown*, Oxford University Press, 1988.

[42] In the same way, Musa Shafiq was challenged over the treaty signed in March 1973 with Iran on the sharing of the waters of the Helmand river (the treaty was later repudiated by the Khalqis following 1978).

[43] Farhad Khosrokhavar, 'Hasan K., paysan dépaysanné, parle de la révolution iranienne', *Peuples mediterrannéens*, 14, 1980.

able for an Iranian-style mobilisation, since the exodus from the countryside had not yet led to the appearance of shanty-towns or deprived suburbs. The demonstration mounted by the Hezb-i Demokratik-i Khalq-i Afghanistan before the coup of April 1978 brought out only 10–15,000 people in Kabul, but was later counted as a success. No popular movement favourable to Zahir Shah was in evidence during the coup of 1973, any more than there would be at the time when Daud fell in 1978. In the latter case the combatants, in spite of the hundreds of victims, did not arouse any following among the population of Kabul; only the president's immediate supporters fought for him, courageously it must be admitted, like Amin's guards who put up a stiff resistance to the Soviet commandos in December 1979.

Hindsight must be avoided in interpreting the events of 1979 in a way that would lead to the supposition that the communist takeover was inevitable. The salient characteristic of this period was the opportunism of various protagonists in a situation which none succeeded in resolving to their own advantage. Daud succeeded in taking power on 17 July 1973, preventing the former Prime Minister Maywandwal from launching a long-planned coup, while the current Prime Minister Musa Shafiq favoured a take-over by the king's son-in-law, Abdul Wali. Daud's tenure of the presidency from 1973 to 1978 failed to stabilise the situation, as was shown by the failed attempts by the Islamists in the summer of 1975, and then in September 1975 and December 1976 by the military, before that of the communists in 1978.[44]

On the other hand, the outcome of the various coups was not entirely a matter of chance, but reflected the ability of various actors to organise small groups of militants and to infiltrate institutions. Given the lack of widespread mobilisation of the population, everything depended in the event on the ability of the actors to control the country's institutions, and in particular the army from within. From the 1950s onwards, the military establishment became the primary objective for any group which wished to take control of the state. Up to this point the normal route to power had been to seek external support, tribal or foreign, and to intrigue within the royal clan. Henceforth, however, conflicts would be settled within the state

---

[44] See Louis Duprée, *Afghanistan, op. cit.*, p. 762.

apparatus by way of coups. Daud's chances of success, or those of the communists, were directly related to the level of their support within the army. The coup of 1973 was carried out on the basis of the support Daud had retained among the officers from his first period in power, in 1953–63, when he had played a key role in the army's modernisation. Daud's lack of vigilance subsequently allowed the Khalqis to infiltrate the police and the army, where they became the most influential group, thus laying the basis for the coup of 1978. In addition, most of the officers had been trained in the Soviet Union, which paved the way for the involvement of the Soviet forces. However, the coup of 1978 demonstrated a lack of cohesion within the officer corps, which did not rally in numbers around the communists. On the other hand the Islamists, lacking leverage within the machinery of the state, had no chance.

Authoritarian mobilisation and repression under Daud

The coup of 17 July 1973 was carried out without difficulty because Daud had the backing of the officers. Zahir Shah, who had few supporters to call on, chose to prolong his sojourn in Rome into a permanent exile. In spite of the proclamation of the republic, Daud's rise to power did not take the form of a fundamental split within the governing class, but seemed rather to be a change of allegiance within the interior of the royal clan. In the event, Daud set up an authoritarian regime which made the government isolated and fragile, in spite of an undeniable improvement in the economic situation. Benefiting from an international situation favourable to the Afghan economy, the government dramatically increased taxes at the rate of 18% per year in 1973–7.[45]

In the political arena Daud moved rapidly to undermine all the representative institutions, and in particular Parliament. The notables forfeited part of their influence with the administration, since the state saw itself henceforth as dealing with individuals and not communities. This is why it was ordered that personal names with a tribal or communal connotation should be altered, in order to counter communal solidarity, at least symbolically. Daud also planned to enhance his support with the creation in 1976 of a unique political

---

[45] World Bank, *op. cit.*, p. 30.

party, the Hezb-i Enqelab-i Melli (Party of the National Revolution). In the constitution of 1977 a key role was assigned to this institution, when all the deputies of the Melli Jirga (National Assembly) automatically became members of it and it was given the role of putting forward the candidature of the president of the republic. After the constitution's ratification of 1977, Afghanistan officially became a one-party state, with the president responsible only to an extraordinary session of the *Loya Jirga*.

However, the party launched by Daud did not put down strong enough roots to serve as a counterweight to the opposition, and especially to the communist opposition. The failure illustrated Daud's inability to create political structures sufficiently attractive to mobilise the officials, the students and the modernist notables within the framework of the Hezb-i Enqelab-i Melli. The communists were similarly to fail to establish a numerically significant party after their seizure of power.

To avoid any challenge Daud systematically suppressed the opposition, both legal and illegal. Following the coup the former Prime Minister and leader of the social democratic Hezb-i Demokrat-i Mottaraki, Hashem Maywandwal, who had been in power in 1965–7, was arrested in September 1973 and executed—perhaps on the orders of Daud, or possibly on the initiative of Parchamis who had infiltrated into the police intending to radicalise and isolate Daud's government. Daud then attempted to get rid of the Islamists with the aid of the communists, who were well represented in the police.[46] In 1974 some Islamist militants were arrested, while others fled and took to the hills near Keshem in the province of Badakhshan, where they were led by Dr Omar.[47] The most visible militants, including Masud and Hekmatyar, went to Pakistan, where they were welcomed by the regime of Zulfiqar Ali Bhutto, who was currently on bad terms with Daud.

At the beginning of 1975 a movement bringing together Islamist students and *ulema* was established in Pakistan.[48] Its structures com-

---

[46] Tahir Amin estimates at 600 the number of Islamists who fell victim to purges under Daud. See 'Afghan Resistance: Past, Present and Future', *Asian Survey* XXIV (4), April 1984.

[47] *Afghanews* 5 (2), 1989.

[48] According to the militants of one group or the other the new structure was called Jamiyat-i Islami or Hezb-i Islami. Which came first is a factor in the estab-

prised a Shura-yi Marqazi (central council) open to all members, which elected a Shura-yi Ejray (executive council) of ten members, including Hekmatyar and Masud. Since the *ulema*—Niazi, Rabbani, Tawana *et al.*—were mostly still in Afghanistan, the students took charge. During the summer of 1974 Rabbani, the designated successor of Gholam Niazi, who was already in prison, arrived in Pakistan and set up in opposition to Hekmatyar, the former leader of the Islamist students in Kabul and responsible at that time for military operations and relations with the Inter Service Intelligence (ISI: the Pakistani secret services): a key post in the circumstances of the time. Elections took place and an *alem*, Qazi Amin, was elected as a compromise candidate with the backing of both Rabbani and Hekmatyar, but gravitated rapidly towards the latter. Rabbani then embarked on a pilgrimage to Mecca, which was a way of keeping his distance.

The Islamist movement began at this point to plot a coup, with the assistance of the Jamaat-i Islami and the Pakistani secret services, who trained the militants and provided money for the purchase of 300 rifles. The coup attempt took place in July 1975. The Islamists pursued a strategy of dispersing small groups of fighters throughout the provinces. They infiltrated themselves particularly in Badakhshan under Dr Omar; in Panjshir under Masud; in Herat where they were led by Nasratyar; in Laghman with *mawlawi* Habib ur-Rahman; in Paktya under the directions of Hekmatyar, who was to remain in Pakistan; and in Nangrahar, where the leader was Adam Khan. In all, there were no more than 2–300 combatants who, without backing in the army, had no chance of overturning the regime.

In Panjshir, for example, Masud divided his group of about forty individuals into three sections, to take control of the whole valley.[49] Masud himself, accompanied by the 'engineer' Ishaq, took charge of

---

lishment of legitimacy. It may be that the appellation 'Jamiyat' was used in a more or less official manner, during the period of the formation of the Islamist movement. On this subject, see also the serie of articles by Tawana, long established as Rabbani's deputy, *Afghanews* 5 (7), 1989.

[49] An account of the events, together with the list of 37 participants, is given by Abdul Hafiz 'Mansur', *Panjshir Dar Doran-i Jihad* (Panjshir during the Period of Jihad) Peshawar, 1991 (1369 AH), pp. 48 *seq.* Reliance is also placed here on various accounts gathered in the north in the autumn of 1991.

the central sector of the valley (the *alaqaderi* of Rukha) during the night of 21/22 July and wounded the *alaqadar* (deputy governor). In the morning the inhabitants woke to find banners on the walls of the government building proclaiming 'Death to Daud' and 'Death to the Russians'. Supposing the culprits were bandits, they alerted the army which sent in helicopters and tanks. Isolated and hunted by both the army and the population, the Islamists fled in disorder, and most succeeding in returning to Pakistan.

Other groups were even less successful. In all, ninety-three individuals were arrested and tried, of whom three were condemned to death. In addition to the revolutionaries' lack of organisation, the principal lesson—as significant as the results of elections would have been—was the total lack of support from the population, who neither knew nor understood the Islamists. This attempted coup also gives some indication of the movement's roots—it was in fact weak and geographically restricted. Nothing took place in the south, in the region of Kandahar, or in the west. Only the northeast and the frontier with Pakistan were affected. The coup had no chance of success, as the Pakistani military men who helped to lay the groundwork for it must have been aware. It might therefore be supposed that the Islamists had been manipulated by the Inter Service Intelligence, whose intention was to deliver a warning to Daud; according to some sources, the ISI may even have tipped Daud off in advance. In spite of the acknowledged lack of preparation of the young militants, who had placed a little too much emphasis on Guevarist *'foco'* theory, the Islamist movement had nevertheless embarked on an adventure which cost it many lives, particularly as the result of the backlash subsequently unleashed in Afghanistan. The fiasco also marked the definitive split in the Islamist movement between the Jamiyat-i Islami, led by Rabbani, and the Hezb-i Islami led by Hekmatyar.

After the operations against the Islamists, Daud decided to exclude the communists from the new cabinet formed in January 1977, but many senior officials of openly Parchami sympathies were nevertheless assigned positions of responsibility, especially in the Ministry of the Interior. Daud's immediate entourage was infiltrated by the communists, including for example Yaqubi, the future head of the secret services under Najibullah. Meanwhile the Khalqis continued their clandestine infiltration of the army, an operation facilitated by

Daud's purges within the military establishment and the rise of a new generation of officers.

The position of the communists was also made difficult by the new foreign policy of Daud, who sought to re-adjust his hitherto pro-Soviet position. His rise to power in 1973 had actually been welcomed by the Soviets because of his links with the Parchamis and the good relations he had maintained with Moscow at the time of his previous period in power in 1953–63. In particular, Daud set in train military cooperation with the Soviets following his visit to Khrushchev and Bulganin in September 1956. From that time on, about 100 Afghans went each year for training in Soviet and Czech military schools, with Tajik translators. In fact the earliest requests for military assistance had been made to the United States, since mistrust of the Soviet Union remained strong in the Afghan governing classes of the 1930s and '40s, but in 1955 the United States—because of poor Afghan-Pakistani relations, refused to finance the modernisation of Afghanistan's military machine. Daud because of its claim to Pakistan-controlled Pushtunistan, turned to the Soviet Union. Cooperation with the Soviets later took on an economic aspect when, following the closure of the Pakistani port of Karachi to Afghan products, Afghanistan arranged to send its exports through Soviet territory.

Daud's return in 1973 gave a new impetus to Afghan-Soviet co-operation. In the 1970s more than 100 civilian experts arrived each year, and from 1973 onwards every battalion of the Afghan army had its Soviet adviser. On the diplomatic front the treaty of neutrality and non-aggression of 24 June 1931, which replaced the treaty of friendship of 28 February 1921, was re-adopted on 10 December 1975 to run till 1980 with an automatic renewal every five years. Lastly, on 30 July 1977 a thirty-year commercial pact was signed.

However, Daud also attempted from this stage onwards to make regional agreements, with the aim of accelerating Afghanistan's development and bringing it out of its seclusion. In 1976 the country took a step towards the recognition of the Durand Line as the international frontier. This was a move towards abandoning its irredentist ambitions, tending towards the resolution of the old quarrel with Pakistan. An agreement would have represented a decisive change in Daud's strategy, from which he hoped to obtain economic benefits and a more propitious regional environment. Daud and Zulfiqar Ali Bhutto exchanged visits in 1976. Changes in the situation in Pakistan—where the elections of 1977 led to Zia ul-Haq's successful coup as well as changes within Afghanistan—would in the end prevent the finalisation of an agreement. During a visit to Iran the same year, Daud obtained a promise of aid for the construction of a railway in western Afghanistan. The following year, 1977, Daud visited Egypt, Pakistan and Saudi Arabia, confirming the re-direction of his foreign policy towards the conservative states of the region, and his decision to keep his distance from the socialist camp. It was in this spirit that he attacked Cuba's adherence to the Soviet line during the preparations for the non-aligned summit of May 1978, and the Cuban delegation which arrived in Kabul a few days before the coup had a conspicuously cold reception. These internal and external developments in Daud's foreign policy were destined to precipitate his break with his communist allies.

Utopia and violence: the communists in power

The retrenchment of the Americans on the international scene, together with Daud's policies after 1975, prompted the Soviets to consider instigating a coup and consequently the reunification of the Khalq and the Parcham. This took place on 3 July 1977 after several months of negotiations under Soviet auspices. The coup, initially set for August 1978, was brought forward due to circumstances. In the event, 17 April 1978 saw the assassination of Mir Akbar Khayber, a leading Parcham ideologue and a confidant of the Soviets. Though there is no definite evidence, it seems likely that Amin, the Khalq's number two, had wished both to rid himself of a rival and to precipitate a political crisis. Mir Akbar Khayber, who controlled the military faction of Parcham's membership, was potentially a rival to Amin by virtue of his age and position. Whatever the truth of the matter, the funeral of Khayber on 19 April turned into an anti-government demonstration, since Daud was generally thought to have been responsible for the assassination, and 10–15,000 demonstrators shouted slogans against the government, the United States and SAVAK, the Iranian secret police. In response, the police on 26 April arrested the leaders of the Hezb-i Demokratik-i Khalq-i Afghanistan, including Taraki and Karmal. On the other hand Amin, who had supporters

within the police, was only placed under house arrest and was therefore able to issue orders to launch the coup according to the plan
already agreed. Thus began the 'Revolution of Saur (April/May)'.

On 27 April at 9 a.m. the garrison of Pul-i Charki—the Fourth
Armoured Brigade, commanded by Captain Aslam Watanjar—advanced on Kabul with fifty tanks, while Colonel Abdul Qader led a
mutiny at the air base at Bagram, north of Kabul. Captain Watanjar
attacked the Ministry of Defence while another group took control
of Kabul airport, and then at mid-day placed himself with nine tanks
outside the presidential palace, where Daud had assembled his cabinet to decide the fate of the communists arrested the previous evening. Daud resisted, at the head of the 1,300 men of the Republican
Guard, and fighting went on through the night. Seven or eight MiG
21 combat aircraft from Bagram bombarded the palace and the general staff headquarters, while a counter-attack by two fighters, which
had come from Shindand on Daud's orders, failed. Daud was finally
killed, still fighting, at around 5 a.m. on Friday 28 April, together
with eighteen members of his family. A thousand people, mostly soldiers, are also said to have lost their lives in the fighting. The tanks of
the Fourth Armoured Brigade then left for Jalalabad, where some
officers had refused to join the coup, and the commander of the garrison there was also killed. At 7 p.m that evening the coup was proclaimed on Radio Kabul, and the newly-formed Shura-yi Enqelabi
(Revolutionary Council) undertook to embark on socialist reforms
while respecting Islam. On 30 April the Revolutionary Council announced its *firman* (decree) no. 1:[50] Afghanistan would henceforth
be the Democratic Republic of Afghanistan under the authority of
Taraki,[51] who became president of the Revolutionary Council and
Prime Minister.

[50] Significantly, the text was read first in Pushtu by Taraki and then in Persian by
Karmal.
[51] Taraki, who was born in 1917 at Moqur in the Province of Ghazni, was a Ghilzai Pushtun, from a modest though not poor family. He studied at the high school
at Ghazni and was then employed in India by the Pushtun Trading Company.
He met Khan Abdul Ghaffar Khan, the leader of the Pakistani Pushtun nationalist
movement (the 'Red Shirts'), who was a fervent admirer of Lenin. Working as
an employee of the Ministry of Economy, he won a reputation as a novelist, poet
and translator. After going to Washington in 1953 as press attaché, he asked for
political asylum in the United States, then spent three years in Pakistan. In 1956

From then onward, the Soviet Union worked towards the swift absorption of Afghanistan into the socialist bloc, and at the end of May 1978 it became a 'member of the socialist community'. On 5 December 1978 the two countries signed a treaty of friendship, cooperation and good neighbourliness, which specifically provided for enhanced military cooperation. In addition, the Afghan police, hitherto trained by West Germany, began to receive experts from East Germany.

The role of the Soviet Union became all the more crucial since relations between Afghanistan and the United States were undergoing a period of serious crisis. On 14 February 1979 the American ambassador Adolph Dubs was kidnapped by militants belonging to the Setam-i Melli, a splinter group of the communist movement, which wished to exchange him for their imprisoned leaders, and especially for Taher Badakhshi, Badruddin Bahes (who was possibly already dead), and Wasef Bakhtari. The police, with their Soviet officers, immediately attacked, against the advice of the Americans, and Ambassador Dubs was killed in the exchange of fire. This provoked an immediate reaction from the United States: the planned level of civilian aid, which had been set at $15 million, was cut by half, and military aid of $250,000 was cancelled. Meanwhile the regime had already initiated a package of reforms aimed at radical social transformation, at a time when the tensions between Khalq and the Parcham were worsening: the situation which would in the end lead to the Soviet invasion.

Once in power, the communists emphasised the centralist and authoritarian aspects of Daud's regime. On 9 June the Revolutionary Council announced its initial thirty-point programme of economic and social reform.[52] *Firman* no. 6 of 12 July 1978 forbade usurious loans and cancelled mortgages on land-holdings of less than 2 hectares if they dated from before 1974, cancelling a proportion of mortgages taken out in subsequent years. Because of the agricultural

---

he was employed as a translator by the American embassy in Kabul, and was probably working for the KGB at this period. He was a founder-member and the first secretary-general of the Hezb-i Demokratik-i Khalq-i Afghanistan in 1965, and then became leader of the Khalq after its break with Parcham two years later. See Anthony Arnold, *op. cit.*, pp. 17 *seq.*

[52] For an English translation of the statutes see Louis Duprée, *Red Flag over the Indu-Kush*, part 3, American Universities Field Staff Report, South Asia Series, 1980.

crisis, peasant farmers had been obliged to take out loans bearing rates of interest typically of the order of 50 per cent. The burden of debt was in consequence bitterly resented in the countryside, but this *firman*, which targeted the relationship of patronage between proprietor and farmer, would in the event be only very partially applied. *Firman* no. 7 of October codified the practice of *mahr* (dowry). The ceiling was fixed at 300 afghanis—a nominal sum—and women under the age of sixteen and men under eighteen were forbidden to marry. This decision was the only one to be justified on the basis of the *shariat*. However these measures, well intentioned as they were, succeeded only in undermining the legal status of women in marriage since traditionally the wife recovered her dowry in the case of a divorce, which gave her real protection against repudiation. Finally, *firman* no. 8 of 2 December 1978 set out the framework of an agrarian reform (*islakat-i arzi*) which was intended to bring into being a class of peasant farmers supportive of the regime. A single family was not supposed to own more than 6 hectares of land of the highest category (the statute defined seven categories of land). Redistribution would be carried out primarily in favour of day labourers working the land, then of landless peasants in villages. The reform also provided for the setting-up of agricultural cooperatives for those who owned less than 5 hectares. In practice it was not possible to implement the reform since it failed to make available to new owners the water and seeds needed to exploit the land. In addition, in those regions (the majority) where the link between peasant farmers and proprietors remained strong, it generally met with resistance. These reforms, as well as the policing practices of the regime, gave rise to popular uprisings, which exacerbated internal conflicts within the regime itself. These are examined in detail in the next chapter.

Tensions between the two factions, the Khalq and the Parcham, were not eased after the acquisition of power. In theory an equilibrium existed between the two factions. Taraki, as secretary-general of the party, president of the Revolutionary Council and Prime Minister, had Karmal as his deputy in each of these positions. However the apparent cooperation between the two factions disguised an advantage for the Khalqis, who were better represented among the military. Also there was a nucleus of militants, such as Qader, a Parchami and Watanjar (a Khalqi who later went over to the Parcham) whose fidelity was primarily to the Soviet Union. These militants gave their obedience directly to Moscow, which would in due course extend its protection to them in the context of the internal party struggles.

From the end of May the Parchamis disappeared from the reports of official activities in the press, which signalled their fall from grace. In early July their principal leaders were appointed as ambassadors, which kept them away from real power.[53] The Parchami ministers were not replaced by others, except for the Minister of the Interior, who was replaced by Watanjar. The great ease with which the Parcham was eliminated showed that the institutional balancing mechanisms within the party had not been enough to counterbalance the influence of the Khalqis inside the army. On 27 November 1978 the majority of the Parchamis were excluded from positions of power, so that the Political Bureau fell under the control of the Khalqis.

The Parcham leaders, now scattered among the embassies, in due course planned a coup with Soviet assistance which was to have taken place in September 1978. However, on 17 August General Abdul Qader the Minister of Defence, Colonel Rafi the Minister for Public Works, Sultan Ali Keshmand the Minister for Planning and Shahpur Ahmadzai the chief of staff of the army were arrested and charged with plotting a coup. Their confessions were published by the *Kabul Times* of 23 September 1978. Ahmadzai and Akbar were executed, but Keshman, Qader and Rafi, who were also condemned to death, had their sentences commuted, probably at the behest of the Soviets. A further coup was attempted in mid-September by a number of soldiers under Watanjar's command, but competition was now mostly between members of the winning side. Indeed the elimination of the Parchamis at once opened the door for overt expression of the internal tensions within the Khalqi faction. In particular the conflict between Taraki and Amin was aggravated.[54] Amin,

---

[53] On 27 June Baryalay, the half-brother of Karmal, and Najibullah were appointed ambassadors to Pakistan and Iran, followed on 5 July by Babrak Karmal himself, who was sent to Czechoslovakia. Nur Muhammad Nur, a former Minister of the Interior, went to the United States, Abdul Wakil to Britain, and Anahita Ratebzad to Belgrade.

[54] Amin was born in 1929 at Paghman. He came from a Ghilzai family of minor officials, and became the principal of the Avesina High School after training as a

the Minister of Defence, became Prime Minister on 27 March 1979 and increasingly strove to replace Taraki as head of the party.

On Monday 10 September 1979 Taraki, returning from the non-aligned summit in Havana, stopped over in Moscow and in complicity with the Soviet leaders decided to have Amin killed at Kabul airport, with the connivance of Watanjar, Gulabzoy and Asadullah Sarwari, chief of the AGSA (the Afghan Secret Services). However, Amin—apprised of the plot by Nawab, Sarwari's deputy at the AGSA—changed the guard at the airport and then arranged for the dismissal of Gulabzoy, Watanjar and Sarwari, who all took refuge in the Soviet embassy. Over the following days Taraki invited Amin several times to the House of the People, the former presidential palace, in order to have him killed, but Amin, aware of a plot, refused to come. On 14 September he finally accepted the invitation and came unarmed to the office where he was awaited by Taraki and the Soviet ambassador Puzanov.[55] Sayyed Daud Tarun, one of Amin's supporters, went in first and was killed by Taraki's men. Amin then fled to the Ministry of Defence, gathered some troops and had Taraki arrested, without a fight. Taraki was strangled a week later in his cell. His death, attributed to illness, was announced in a brief newspaper report. Amin had already had himself proclaimed president, on 16 September, and immediately received a message of congratulation from Brezhnev.

Why did the Soviets fail to keep their Afghan allies under control at a time when many of them were agents for the KGB or the GRU (Soviet military intelligence)? This probably had to do with the revolutionary process, which favoured extremism, as well as to the resilience of the networks of solidarity within the party, which forestalled purges. At first more favourable to the Parchamis, whose coup, planned for September, they had supported, the Soviets then helped Taraki against Amin, whose brutality had alarmed them. The consistent line taken by Moscow had been to promote a gradual transition tending towards the long-term integration of Afghanistan

---

schoolteacher and obtaining an MA at Columbia. He was the only Khalqi ever to be elected, in 1969, after being trounced in 1965. His active and organised contribution was crucial to the success of the Hezb-i demokratik-i Khlaq-i Afghanistan in the organisation of the April 1978 coup.

[55] Fikriyat Tabeev became ambassador in Puzanov's place in November 1979.

into the Soviet bloc. In the event, from the takeover of power by the Hezb-i Demokratik-i Khalq-i Afghanistan, the Soviets sought to calm the revolutionary passions of their protégés, as they were conscious of the risks of social upheaval which reforms could bring. At their request the Afghan government held over certain measures such as the agrarian reform of 1979. The Soviet advisers also suggested, though unsuccessfully, a more cautious line in education. To win popular favour there was even a major celebration on the Prophet Muhammad's birthday.

The worsening of the situation subsequently induced the Soviets to increase their military aid and from time to time to intervene directly, as during the Herat rebellion (see the next chapter). The Afghan communists, especially Taraki, repeatedly sought an increase in military aid. However, in the spring of 1979 the prospect of a massive direct intervention continued to be rejected by all the Soviet officials responsible for Afghan affairs, highly aware as they were of the diplomatic costs and the risk of becoming bogged down.[56] The deterioration of the military situation during the summer of 1979, with the capture of the town of Gardez by the rebels, impelled the Soviets to boost their aid, and in July in particular to station 400 men at Bagram airport north of Kabul. The signing of the Afghan-Soviet treaty of friendship and cooperation on 5 December 1979 enabled the Soviet Union to send in 10,000 men, who would lay the groundwork for the invasion. The assassination of Taraki, who had personal links with Brezhnev, as well as Amin's seizure of power finally put the issue of direct intervention on the agenda, but the aim was no longer so much to help a friendly regime as to restore order in the internal affairs of the party through the elimination of an element which was out of control.

What is now known about the decision-making process serves as a good illustration of the workings of the Soviet system as it entered its decline.[57] The decision to intervene was taken following a meet-

---

[56] In the face of the worsening situation a working committee on Afghanistan was formed, which included Ustinov (Minister of Defence) Andropov (KGB) and Ponomarev (International Department of the Party). On Soviet attitudes to the Afghan communists, see Odd Arne Westad, 'The Soviets and the Afghan Communists', *International History Review* XVI (1), February 1994.

[57] See Jean-Christophe Romer, 'Les mécanismes de prise de décision en URSS. Le cas afghan 1978–1979', *Relations Internationales* 85, spring 1996; also the docu-

ing of a number of the members of the Politburo on 12 December—the day when NATO made public its position on the so-called 'Euromissiles'. Since the KGB, the diplomatic service and the army were opposed to intervention, it appears that the responsibility for the decision rested on the alcoholic and depressive Brezhnev and on ideologues such as Suslov and Ponomarev, who are said to have desired to safeguard the dogma of the so-called 'irreversibility of the construction of socialism'. Rather than from an overall strategy, the decision sprang from a synergy between bureaucratic authority and the mechanical rehearsal of a repertoire of responses which had brought results in the past, for example in Hungary and Czechoslovakia.

On 22 December 1979 Amin left the House of the People to set up his headquarters in the south of Kabul, at Darulaman, where he thought he would be safer. On 23 and 24 December the Soviets, who were in control of Kabul airport, sent in reinforcements, and in the evening of 26 December 300 Soviet commandos took up positions 3 kilometres from Darulaman. On 27 December at 7 p.m the palace was surrounded and the commandos attacked Amin's residence. At the same moment the telecommunications centre of Kabul was destroyed by an explosion, and the Radio and Television building was stormed. At 8.30 p.m. a message from Karmal, still in Central Asia, was broadcast on the radio. Amin and his men resisted courageously and the fighting continued until 1 a.m. Amin, who was alive, was taken to the Soviet headquarters and executed. Engagements with his supporters continued till the evening of 28 December, but from then onwards Soviet control was unchallenged.

ments of the Politburo (in German and Russian) in Pierre Allan *et al.* (eds), *Soujetische Geheimdokumente zum Afghanistankreig (1978–1991)*, Hochschulverlag der ATH, Zürich, 1995.

Part II. MOBILISATIONS

3. The Commanders

'Edicts are the Sultan's; the mountains are ours.'—Dadal Oghlu

In response to the violence of the state, and afterwards to invasion by a foreign power, the population rose up in revolt and embarked on a Holy War, a *jihad*. The mobilisation of the countryside took place in the context of local solidarity networks, organised around 'commanders'. The social backgrounds of these leaders provide an explanation of the different kinds of organisation which were set up.

The revolt

Why was there a breach between the communists and the population? The reception given to the new regime in its first weeks was by no means consistently hostile. Indifference was the principal reaction, but certain urban groups, as well as landless peasants in such areas as Laghman, supported the reforms. Measures taken by the regime, particularly in agrarian reform and the reduction in women's dowries, did not amount to radical change. Land redistribution had begun to be tried out under Daud.[1] The question of limitation of dowries was subject to widespread debate, with some Islamists favouring it in the interest of facilitating marriage for the poorest people. Because of the high value placed on the written word in Afghan society, such projects as the promotion of literacy never attracted fundamental objections from the rural population if they were carried out in a spirit of respect for local customs, and in particular the separation of men and women. In practice, however, teaching adults to read without prior dialogue, together with forced labour, visits by

[1] Daud's reform in 1976 limited land holdings to 30 *jerib* for each individual in order to permit the donation of 600,000 hectares to 676,000 families. In practice there was no genuine redistribution, particularly on account of the manipulation of the land register by large landowners. Hermann-J. Wald, Asis Nadjibi, 'Land Reform in Afghanistan', *Internationales Asienforum* 8 (1–2), 1977, pp. 110–23.

the census authorities and agrarian reform, created considerable tension. The failure of the communists was due mainly to their administrative inadequacy, as well as to a proclivity towards regimentation which did not compensate for the absence of legitimacy. Above all it was due to their resort to violence.

In the first instance the state did not have sufficient administrators to put its reforms into practice.[2] It did not have any representation below the level of the *alaqadari* (the sub-district), and the officials were mostly remote from the villagers. Because of their location on the periphery of villages and their contemporary architecture, government buildings symbolised the externality of the state. The typical official, the *mamur,* dressed in the European style and wore the *karakol* cap rather than a turban, or even went bare-headed (*sarluchi*). The officials were conduits for the importation of urban manners and professed modern values alien to the villages. To cap it all, non-Pushtuns found themselves confronted largely by Pushtun officials who were frequently suspected of privileging members of their own community. Language was a further barrier between the administration and the rural population.

The level of integration was certainly not the same in the case of the great nomadic tribes, who kept their distance from the government, as it was for the peasants of the oases, who were subject to the activity of the administration on an everyday basis. Outside the towns, however, the legitimacy of the state was unrelated to its ability to administer the population, which was undemanding other than in the provision of schoolteachers, who were often requested by the villages. In the case of rural communities, the state was held at arm's length by a profusion of 'micro-strategies', in particular by corruption, which became a means of limiting the effective influence of the administration on daily life. In some instances officials were quite simply paid not to intervene. However, this externality of the state did not present a barrier to its becoming a source of profit, particularly for the Pushtuns. The antagonism between the world of the administration and that of the tribes, in theory virulent, did not prevent nepotism and the exercise of patronage.

[2] Thomas Barfield, 'Weak Links on a Rusty Chain: Structural Weaknesses in Afghanistan's Provincial Government' in R. Canfield, M. N. Shahrani (eds), *Revolutions and Rebellions in Afghanistan*, Berkeley: University of California Press, 1984.

Links between the two worlds were necessary, but the abolition of the *arbab*, who served as intermediaries between the administration and the population, had recently removed this linkage. Attempted under Daud, this measure was rapidly abandoned, as it would also be after the Soviet invasion. Secondly, the efforts of the authorities to mobilise the population were in due course to prove counter-productive. Political life in Kabul and even the coups aroused only limited interest beyond the educated class. Some nomadic communities in the northwest still remained unaware of the overthrow of the king and the installation of the republic some years after they had happened. The regime therefore made efforts to overcome popular indifference. Radio stations throughout the country spread the new regime's propaganda, but the unfamiliar Marxist-Leninist language fell harshly on the people's ears. To the south of Kabul, in Logar, the villagers were obliged to repaint the doors of their houses red as a sign of support for the revolution and, bizarrely, to demonstrate against the Chinese invasion in Vietnam. Officials also compelled the villagers to applaud, which was considered a Russian custom and therefore *kafir*.[3] At the Istiqlal lycée in Kabul, where the doors were also painted red, the Khalqis held compulsory half-hour political meetings every morning before school. Amin later abolished them.

This strategy of authoritarian mobilisation did not make up for the illegitimacy of the communists, and the aggressive atheism of their politics rapidly lost them all credibility with both the rural and urban populations. This rejection showed that religious legitimacy continued to be a determining condition for acceptance of the state. To make up for the abandonment of religious justification, the government played on Pushtun solidarity as well as on the multiple antagonisms present in a fragmented society, but the systematic nomination of Pushtuns to all key positions, and in particular the posts of provincial governors, only served to exacerbate opposition by the non-Pushtun population at a time when the language of nationalism was failing to attract even the Pushtuns themselves.[4] For example, in

---

[3] Interviews in Logar, autumn 1992 and February 1997.

[4] This policy was implemented in spite of official pronouncements and a number of other measures such as the abolition of obligatory Pushtu courses and the occasional use of Uzbek and Baluchi in the official media.

the province of Wardak the government armed the Pushtuns so that they could attack the Hazaras, while in Nuristan it played on the conflict between the Pushtuns and the Nuristanis. In both cases the government's policy failed.

However, it was finally the policy of repression undertaken by the authorities which alienated the governing class, the non-communist intelligentsia and, before long, the entire population. Going beyond anecdotal explanations and immediate causes of the uprising, it was the violence of the state rather than its reforms that lay at the root of the crisis. As often with revolutionary movements, a degree of para-noia on the part of those in control unleashed a cycle of increasingly violent repression. When the doctrinaire vision of the Khalqis, which in any case ran contrary to their own system of patronage,[5] failed to arouse any social response, they were obliged to impose their reforms through a widespread resort to violence. Repression first affected political opponents identifiable as such. Certain generals who had been close to Daud and two former Prime Ministers, Musa Shafiq and Nur Ahmad Etemadi, were immediately executed by the Khal-qis. The Islamists already imprisoned under Daud were executed *en masse* on 4 June 1979 in Pul-i Charkhi prison. Similarly, 18 January 1979 saw the assassination of ninety-six men from the Mujaddidi clan, who were potential opposition leaders, while forty-two women and children were arrested.

In proportion to the growth of opposition, the Khalqis took a hostile attitude to entire classes of the population. Indeed, although the communists were not the inventors of political violence, it had hitherto been targeted against declared enemies of the authorities. The communists broke new ground, launching campaigns of liqui-dation against the *khans* and the *mullahs* where there was no infrac-tion or open hostility. In early November 1979 a list of 12,000 victims of the Khalqi period was published by Yaqubi, the Minister for Security, which gave an idea of the scope of the massacres carried out in the prisons.[6] Following the fall of the regime, mass graves

---

[5] For example, from the spring of 1978 Afizullah Amin armed the members of his tribe (the Kharuti) more on the basis of tribal patronage than on political affiliation.

[6] No precise count exists, but the policy of suppression during the Khalqi period was probably the cause of tens of thousands of deaths. For the Pul-i Charkhi

were discovered, notably at Bamyan and Herat, which provided evidence of the severity of the repression. Since the numerous notables carried off and executed without trial, including *mullahs* and landowners, had been leading members of their community, their disappearance brought in its wake expressions of solidarity.

During the spring of 1978 revolts multiplied.[7] They did not have an openly political dimension and mostly took the form of the capture of the nearest government outpost, the disarming of troops and sometimes the execution of officers, mostly without any attempt by the rebels to broaden their movement. Nevertheless, after some months the countryside was out of control.

The geography of the rebellion illustrated two important phenomena. First, the role of the tribes was not a determining factor. The myth which represents the uprisings as a new phase of the confrontation between them and the state must be set aside. The eastern Pushtun tribes, although since 1929 they had originated the principal rebellions, maintained their calm till the spring of 1979, and in some places even later. Their wait-and-see policy can perhaps be explained by the attitude of the Khalqi officials, who were able to contain them due to the existence of tribal solidarities. In Kandahar the revolt did not occur till very late, just before the arrival of the Soviets. The rebellion of 1978 was radically different from previous ones since its mobilisation took place within all the communities, both rural and urban. The rejection of the regime was universal, a phenomenon yet more evident after the Soviet invasion.

Secondly, the uprisings were not organised: there was no overall plan and there were no networks which would enable a revolt originating in one community to spread to the national level. Nevertheless, in the province of Badakhshan a number of Islamists, and in

---

prison alone Mike Barry suggests a figure of 27,000 executed during this period, *op. cit.*, p. 264.

[7] The first revolt took place in Nuristan in May. See Vincent Schneiter, 'La guerre de libération au Nuristan', *Les temps modernes,* special issue July–Aug. 1980. For a list and a chronology of the uprisings see *amir* Etemad Daneshiyar, *Jang-i Afghanistan wa shuravi amel forupashi jehani komunism* (The war between Afghanistan and the Soviets, a Factor in the Fall of the Communist World), Peshawar: Markaz-i taqiqiyat-i enqelab-i islami Afghanistan (Centre for the Study of the Islamic Revolution in Afghanistan), 1992, p. 83.

particular Basir Khan, provided the impetus, while to the south of Kabul, from Logar to Ghazni, the networks of *mullahs* linked to the Khodam ul-Forqan coordinated the uprisings, though at the provincial level at most. Three examples will show the diversity of the different situations: the rebellion in Herat, that of the Shi'ites in Hazarajat and Kabul, and the student movements.

The Herat rebellion. The uprising in Herat in March 1979 was unique in the Khalqi period. Although other provincial towns experienced uprisings, especially the mutinies of the garrisons in Mazar-i Sharif and Kabul, nowhere did power fall entirely into the hands of the insurgents. The government here suffered a severe psychological blow and became aware that it faced opposition even within the towns. In addition the suppression of the uprising led to the intervention of Soviet air power directly from the Soviet Union, in an anticipation of the invasion which was to take place in December. The Herat rebellion showed the complexity of the mechanisms of mobilisation and in the end demonstrated their broad spontaneity.[8]

Agrarian reform was not a determining factor in the Herat rebellion. This had in essence been completed before the uprising began, with little opposition due to the absence of ties of solidarity between the large-scale landowners, who were often townsmen, and the farmers.[9] On the other hand, the persecution of the religious élites and the notables by the communist authorities seems to have been a decisive factor. The *pirs* and the *ulema*, who represented the religious tradition in its most 'retrograde' aspects, were the prime targets of the Khalqis. Many were killed or imprisoned, while others went into exile in Iran or Pakistan.

---

[8] Essentially, these events have been reconstructed on the basis of interviews undertaken during stays in 1988, 1989 and 1993.

[9] R. Grönhaug, 'Scale as a Variable in the Analysis: Reflections Based on Field Materials from Herat' in F. Barth (ed.), *Scale and Social Organisation*, New York: Wenner-Gren, 1973; and Olivier Roy, *Afghanistan, Islam and modernité politique, op. cit.*, p. 143. According to the government press, 50,000 hectares were distributed to 25,000 families up to the summer of 1979 (*Kabul New Time,* 6 August 1979); in that year fifty-one cooperatives were formed, of which thirty-four remained in 1984 (*Kabul New Time,* 10 March 1984). The later disappearance of most of the cooperatives is explained by the action of the *mujahidin* and the lack of government support.

Shortly before the uprising in the city, revolts took place in a number of villages in the province, including Salimi, Ghoryan and Zindajan. However, these were not organised and differed in their immediate causes: a census in Salimi and forced labour on a road in Gharyan. On the morning of 15 March the peasants of the surrounding area gathered around the mosques together with the townsmen and, encouraged by the *mullahs*, converged on Herat, attacking all the symbols of the state and of communism indiscriminately. The revolt of the 17th division, which began immediately after that in the town, brought the army on to the side of the rebels. This reinforcement enabled them, in the course of the day, to gain control of all the government buildings. The success of the revolt in Herat was probably due to the confluence of two separate phenomena. First, the city formed part of an urban agglomeration which ran from Zindajan in the west to the Pushtun Zargun in the east. There was no clear geographical or ethnic separation between the town and the neighbouring villages. The rebellion therefore had at its disposal a wider arena than in most instances, with the government unable to prevent villagers from the surrounding regions entering the city. At Ghazni, by contrast, the clear separation between the Pushtun countryside and the Tajik bazaar hampered effective coordination and therefore the capture of the town. The second factor related to the participation of the troops. The rebels, who did not have arms, would probably have been scattered by a military contingent that had remained loyal to the government.

The city remained in the hands of the rebels for a week, and according to witnesses these were days of total anarchy. The bazaar was repeatedly looted, contradictory rumours circulated, and no organisation appeared able to control events. A number of Soviet advisers were killed although, contrary to what is sometimes said, their bodies were neither mutilated nor dragged through the streets.[10] Although, according to one eyewitness, this explosion of violence was a 'revolution without a leader', a number of individuals nevertheless stand out. Among the soldiers of the 17th division Sardar Khan, a Maoist artilleryman, and Gholam Rasul Khan, an officer, played a significant role in such coordination as existed. The future leaders of the prov-

---

[10] It is likely that between 150 and 200 Soviet advisers were killed during the revolt. Other foreigners in the city were spared.

ince, Captain Ismail Khan and Allauddin Khan, had a lower profile. On the civilian side an impression prevails that there was great confusion. Gul Muhammad, a *khan* from Gozargah, a Barakzai Pushtun, came to the city with a number of rifles and headed one of the earliest armed groups, while two former convicts, Kamar-i Dozd and Shir Agha Shongar, set up their own band.[11] A committee was also set up during the week of the town's liberation, and in spite of sometimes contradictory reports it appears that Shir Agha Shongar and Kamar-i Dozd were its dominant personalities. Outside the city all the *uluswali* (districts) were captured, except for the command posts at Obeh and Pushtun Zargun. The surrounding provinces also rose in revolt. The uprising of the Badghis followed that of Herat several days later, and because news of the events had come rapidly to Qala-i Naw, the provincial capital, was directly connected to it. In the south, in Farah, most of the *uluswali* were captured several days before the events in Herat, but there seems to have been no link between these two uprisings.

After the onset of the rebellion, the Kabul government accused the Iranians of having encouraged it because of a speech made by Shariat Madari and an attack on the Afghan consulate in Mashad. Around half the inhabitants of Herat are Shi'ites, and the government suspected them of being influenced by the Iranian revolution. The return of Afghan labourers from Iran also prompted a propaganda move by Kabul, which claimed that 4,000 Iranians disguised as Afghans had entered the country. Having denounced the foreign role in the uprisings, the government embarked on a particularly brutal programme of repression. The commander of the base at Kandahar, Major-General Sayyed Mukharam, organised a force of some thirty tanks and around 300 men to re-take the town. The soldiers arrived at Herat on 20 March, waving Qurans and green flags, and the rebels, convinced that the revolt must have spread to the whole of Afghanistan, allowed the contingent to enter the town, while the suburbs were bombed by aircraft which came both from the Soviet Union and from the neighbouring air base at Shindand. It is still difficult today to know how many people were killed in 1978–9, but

[11] Kamar-i Dozd was a thief, as is indicated by his nickname 'Dozd' Shir Agha, on the other hand, was from a rich family, but had squandered his inheritance and spent several periods in prison. He was known for his extravagant tastes and predilection for prostitutes, male and female.

the discovery in 1992 of a mass grave containing 2,000 bodies north-east of the town enables a guess to be made. A figure of 25,000 victims was the estimate of government officials.[12]

This spectacular rebellion has been the subject of various analyses. Giorgio Vercellin suggests an ethnic interpretation, stressing the secular opposition between the Pushtuns and the other communities.[13] He refers to the observations of a 19th-century Hungarian Jewish traveller, Arménius Vambéry, according to whom there were sharp antagonisms at that time between the newly-arrived 'Afghans', i.e. the Pushtuns, and the local populations.[14] However, the same evidence also acknowledges the assimilation of Pushtuns previously resident in the country, and it may be supposed that this process had continued, since none of the eyewitnesses questioned spontaneously suggested that there had been an ethnic clash. In addition, the personalities of some of the leading figures, such as Gul Muhammad, a Pushtun Barakzai, appears in itself to rule out such motivations, while the first uprising took place in Salimi, a Pushtun village. Finally, nothing in the state of inter-ethnic relations in the province would allow the supposition that the Pushtuns of Herat, often well assimilated into the urban environment, might have been the object of resentment from the Persian-speaking majority. However, though research does not permit the hypothesis of a rebellion directed against the local Pushtuns, there remains the fact that the Khalqi period was characterised by a takeover of the state by the Ghilzai and by eastern Pushtun tribes. In this sense the rebellion of Herat, a Persian-speaking town, did have anti-Pushtun implications. In a similar interpretation, Richard Newell argues that the rebellion was Shi'ite and anti-Pushtun,[15] but this runs up against the same obstacles, with the additional difficulty of explaining the uprisings outside the city, where the Shi'ites are very much in the minority.

---

[12] Interview with a Parchami expatriate in Germany, 1989. Olivier Roy gives a wide margin, estimating there were between 5,000 and 25,000 victims: *Afghanistan, Islam et modernité politique, op. cit.*, p. 146.

[13] Giorgio Vercellin, *Afghanistan 1973–1978. Dalla repubblica presidenziale alla repubblica democratica*, Venice: Università degli studi di Venezia, 1979, pp. 61–4.

[14] Cf. Arménius Vambéry, *Voyages d'un faux derviche en Asie centrale*, Paris: You Feng, 1987, pp. 240–1.

[15] Richard Newell, 'The Government of Muhammad Mussa Shafiq: the last chapter of Afghan Liberalism', *Central Asian Survey*, 1982, p. 92.

Was the Herat rebellion at least partly the result, as Olivier Roy believes, of the work of the Islamists?[16] Although there were contacts between the militants of the Jamiyat-i Islami and the officers of the 17th division, it is incorrect to suggest an infiltration of the army by the Islamists. The Jamiyat-i Islami office in Mashad, whose activities were favoured by the Iranian revolution, had begun to make contacts among the more senior officers of the 17th division in Herat, including Ismail Khan, Allauddin Khan and Abdul Ahad, some weeks before the rebellion. After the rebellion's spontaneous outbreak the officers joined the rebels, with whom—and this is the crucial point—there had been no prior dialogue, for the good reason that there had been no pre-existing organisation on the civilian side. Furthermore, some of the leaders from the army side were Maoists, such as Sardar Khan, which ruled out a mutiny organised by a group of officers belonging to the Jamiyat-i Islami. The *ulema* also did not seem to have been connected in any particular way with this group, since the majority of them afterwards joined the Harakat-i Enqelab. The disparity in the personalities of the leaders—*khans*, fugitives from justice and officers—allows the hypothesis of a rising organised by a political movement to be excluded. The evolution of the rebellion was rather an indication of the weakness of political and other organisations in Herat.[17] In this perspective the reticence of the *ulema*, who took only a minimal part in the rebellion's active phase, seems to have been especially revealing. In the end those who took part—peasants, *ulema* and students—are convinced of the spontaneity of the movement. The eyewitnesses of the episode, who were also participants, stress the indiscriminate nature of the mob, the disorder, the air of acute crisis sometimes degenerating into arbitrary violence. The one cry which echoed through the city was '*Allahu Akbar*' (God is the greatest), while many of the inhabitants huddled in their houses in fear of being denounced as pro-government or Maoists, or falling victim to the hunt for those who were *sarluchi*—with uncovered heads, indicating lack of piety.

[16] Olivier Roy, *Afghanistan, Islam et modernité politique, op. cit.*, p. 145.
[17] S. C. Stack notes the relative absence in the pre-war period of trade unions or associations in local life: 'Herat, a Political and Social Study', unpubl. Ph.D. thesis, University of California, Los Angeles, 1975.

The Shi'ite uprising. In Hazarajat a number of notables took an optimistic view of the communist coup: it at least delivered them from Daud, whose aggressively nationalistic policy had led to the widespread installation of Pushtun officials.[18] However, troubles were rapidly unleashed by the announcement of the reforms brought in by the regime, locally represented by young officials who were both inexperienced and arrogant. These reforms were never to be applied in reality, but the uprising was prompted by the provocative attitude of the young Khalqis and by the victimisation of the *khans* and the Shi'ite clergy in both Hazarajat and Kabul. Notables of the former regime were particularly targeted, as was shown by the imprisonment of many former parliamentarians. In response government buildings and especially schools, which were seen as centres of communist indoctrination, were destroyed by the rebels. In Hazarajat the rebellion took on a character of unequivocal opposition to the state and to the Pushtuns. It began prematurely in October 1978 immediately after that in Nuristan. Following the winter which severs all communication in Hazarajat, local uprisings directed against the administrative centres began in March and April. By June the entire region was free of government control, which from then on was restricted to the fringes of Hazarajat, in the bazaars of Jaghori and of Bamyan which is only partly Hazara. This success resulted particularly from the minimal administration present in Hazarajat, as well as from the mountainous terrain and the lack of means of communication. The rebellion was in general both spontaneous and unanimous: the entire population would participate in attacks on governmental administrative posts. In some places *khans* led the rebels, in the tradition of Bacha-yi Gaw Sawar, but a hitherto unobserved phenomenon was the role played by the *ulema*, often the heads of private *madrasas*, who thereafter formed the backbone of the new political class of Hazarajat.

In the spring of 1979 the first signs of rebellion also appeared among the Shi'ite community of Kabul. In this period of crisis the indiscriminate repression practised by the government reinforced

---

[18] To qualify this statement somewhat, it may be seen that certain *khans* still look back with some affection to the era of Daud, which marked the onset of the modernisation of Hazarajat, in contrast with the characteristic of Zahir Shah's administration.

the solidarity between the two Shi'ite communities of the capital, the Hazara and the Qizilbash. The Shi'ite religious élites were decimated by the Khalqis in 1978–9, especially in the towns. Religious authorities such as the *ayatollahs* Waez and Akay Alem were incarcerated in the regime's prisons, as were young intellectuals such as Binesh, Muhseni's deputy. In reprisal for this persecution, the Hazaras, who controlled this market, prevented the supply of wood to the capital. At the end of May 1979 Amin met the leaders of the Hazara community, but evidently no agreement was reached since riots took place in Shendawal, the Shi'ite quarter of Kabul. An attempt by four Hazaras to capture a police post caused the death of a Soviet officer and unleashed extremely brutal measures of repression. The army used light armour, and several dozen died. Three hundred Hazaras, picked up at random, were taken to the Pul-i Charki prison and executed the same day. Helicopters dropped leaflets alleging Iranian involvement. It is true that on 21 June Iranian radio broadcast a message from *ayatollah haji* Sayyed Hasan Tabatabay, urging the Afghans to 'continue their resistance'. The roster of the 12,000 victims who died under Taraqi, published by Amin on 10 October 1979, shows that 7,000 Hazaras were shot at Pul-i Sharki in a few months. The fiercest suppression of the Shi'ites was the result of fear of Iranian influence, widely overestimated, and of traditional contempt for the Hazaras.

The student movements. In the towns, and particularly in Kabul, the presence of secondary school and university students, sometimes Maoist or Islamist militants, gave a particular character to the protests.[19] In the capital the student demonstrations were incited by leaflets (*shabname*) and appeals to *jihad* proclaimed at night from the roofs of the houses. In particular the Maoists planned an action on 21 April, the Day of the Flag: the anniversary of the replacement of the old red, black and green flag by the red flag of the revolution. Leaflets were circulated on 19 and 20 April, and on 21 April the first demonstration took place.

[19] The focus here, for analytical reasons, is on the students. However, the general atmosphere of the city was one of resistance even before the arrival of the Soviet forces. Kabul would later be mobilised in its entirety against the Soviet occupiers between 21 and 24 February.

By 26 April the strike at the university was near-total. On 28 April the police took severe action against a student march, leaving many dead and wounded. The girls of the Surya and Rabe Balkhi Schools then took the initiative of beginning strikes at school and encouraged the boys of the Ghazi School to follow suit. On 29 April a demonstration set off towards the university buildings. Six students died under Parchami fire and some thirty were wounded. A girl from the Rabe Balkhi School, shot dead by the Parchamis, became the symbol of the student revolt. In another development the garrison at Bala Hisar, south of the town, rose up on 5 August 1979 at the instigation of Maoist groups which had infiltrated it. The government then used its MiGs to bombard the fortress and rapidly retook the base. In the following months police controls would increasingly forbid open opposition.

These three cases demonstrate that despite a lack of organisation there was unanimity among the population during this first phase. The educated class and the town-dwellers in particular sided largely with the opposition. A further factor was that the authorities failed in their attempts to exploit communal antagonisms. This unanimity was due in particular to the religious significance which had been attached to the rebellion.

Jihad

At the outset the uprisings were fuelled by the multiple demands of the population, and their moral rejection of political authority; later their various justifications coalesced under the banner of *jihad*, which served to legitimise the rebellion. *Jihad* is a religious concept which veiled the political perception of the struggle, since it is an exchange between man and God, and not between two adversaries. In 1978–9 the people did not mobilise against the communist government in the name of an ideology: militants were rare among the rural population, and their rhetoric—including that of the Islamists—was incomprehensible to a population whose literacy was as undeveloped as its politicisation. The political parties had not made themselves known, or indeed were not established at all, until after the uprising, which they exploited but did not initiate.

The religious interpretation was imposed on events thanks to a conjunction of factors. Historical memory enabled Islam to appear as the legitimation of popular rebellions against the invading *kafir*, as had been the case with the British in the 19th century, and against the state, as in 1929. With the Soviet invasion resistance was also seen as patriotic, and the parallels between Babrak Karmal and Shah Shoja[20] became common currency in the pamphlets calling for *jihad* against the occupier. In addition, Islam remained an essential component of individual identity. Religious practice was general in the pre-war period, while atheism was practically unthinkable, at least in the countryside, though the Uzbeks and the Hazaras were often less observant than the Pushtuns. For the Pushtuns Islam was tightly linked to tribal values, even when these did not have a religious origin, for example in the case of the concept of 'honour' (*namus*). Finally, the establishment of an Islamic republic in Iran, which had not resonated only with the Shi'ites, presented a contemporary model of religious revolution. In this initial phase there was no contradiction between these multiple references.

This religious interpretation of the rebellion was promoted by the *ulema* and the *mullahs*, a group strongly united in their struggle against the communist authorities, who had proclaimed a *jihad* against the regime. Represented everywhere in the country, they constituted an informal but efficient network for the transmission of information, as the rebellion of 1929 had already shown. In instances where the uprising was coordinated, for example in Logar or in Ghazni, the *ulema* played the leading role. In most insurrections the sermons of the *mullahs* were crucial: the people often assembled at the mosque before marching on the government command post. In the mosques, the habitual scene for discussion among the villagers, the *mullah* would use his influence to put forward a religious exegesis of resistance to authority, and his intervention often served to convince the hesitant by removing their doubts as to the illegitimacy of the authorities. Later the *mujahidin* gathered in military centres, but in villages far from the combat zones the mosque played a central role up to the 1990s in bringing combatants together. Lastly the religious leaders often enabled communal antagonisms to be overcome, but this unanimity was only temporary, and the former splits, often reinterpreted in political language, later came to the fore again.

---

[20] From the name of the *amir* put on the throne by the British in 1839, who became a symbol of collaboration with foreign imperialism.

With the proclamation of *jihad* by the *ulema* the rebellion took on a universal nature, aiming thereafter at the overthrow of the illegitimate authorities. The justification in terms of Islam gave a direction to individual efforts: *jihad* is experienced as both a personal obligation and a religious duty.[21] The concepts of *mujahid* and of *shahid* lie at the heart of the conceptions of individuals in relation to the nature of their commitment.[22] The declaration of *jihad* in particular justifies emigration (*hijrat*) and the special treatment of *mujahidin*, whose status is defined by the religious texts as a balance of duties and privileges. The rules relating to purification, especially in the funeral ceremony, are modified. In contrast to the normal practice, the corpse is not washed, since the body of one who dies as a *shahid* is pure, and paradise has already been promised to him. In another illustration, according to a poster outside a mosque in Badakhshan, *mujahidin* in combat are permitted to enter a mosque wearing shoes, in accordance with an ancient legal principle dating from the era of the Muslim conquests.

Following a long-standing tradition great fighters who have died in battle become the object of popular veneration comparable to that given to the *pirs*: 'In pre-war Afghanistan, martyrs were not distinguished from other holy men whose tombs were the object of visitation.'[23] Thus at certain mosques in Herat prayers are still said for the martyrs of 19th-century wars against the British. Frequently a 'Front' would retain the name of its first commander and in this way place itself under his patronage. The exploits of the great *mujahidin* who have died in combat are recounted, and placards about them are displayed throughout the country. The prestige attached to the destiny of a *shahid* reconciles those left alive to their loss. This may explain the willingness of the *mujahidin* to sacrifice themselves, and the high morale of the population up to the Soviet withdrawal—i.e. the exact moment when the concept of *jihad* became less relevant.

---

[21] *Jihad* (etymologically 'effort') is the act of participating in the defence of the Muslim community or in its expansion. See *The Encyclopaedia of Islam*, Leiden: E. J. Brill, 1960, p. 551.

[22] In the tribalised Pushtun regions the ideal of the warrior, who obeys the Pushtun tribal code, replicates that of the *mujahid*, which nevertheless offers stronger legitimation.

[23] 'Dans l'Afghanistan d'avant guerre, les martyres ne se distinguaient pas des autres saints hommes dont on visitait les tombeaux,' Pierre Centlivres, Micheline Centlivres-Demont, *op. cit.*, p. 58.

'Qowm' and commanders

Conflicts, provided they are short, do not necessarily bring with them any profound change in social organisation, and may even fulfil certain functions. Confrontations which occur at regular occasions in the year, outside the periods reserved for agricultural labour, and which rarely occasion more than a few fatalities, are sometimes seen as demographic controls. This functionalist approach, though distinctly underestimating both real disturbances of the social balance and the regulatory role of the state, does offer an explanation of the repetitive aspect of such confrontations.[24] However, from 1978 onwards violence had unprecedented effects. The state withdrew from the countryside, and the consequences of minimal administration and of military constraints meant that the *mujahidin* became progressively less identified with the general population. A new social role appeared: the commander.[25] This was an individual, attached to a party, who fulfilled at the local level the functions of military and political leadership. In the 1980s there were several thousand commanders in Afghanistan, whose influence varied substantially, ranging from Masud, the organiser of an army of more than 10,000 men, down to a village notable at the head of a handful of *mujahidin*. However, the commanders were aware of belonging to groups which fought or collaborated to achieve the same goals.

What was the relationship between belonging to a *qowm* and the process of mobilisation? Before the war elections displayed the mobilisation and coalition of ethnic groups for the election of deputies

[24] On this, see Louis Duprée, 'Tribal Warfare in Afghanistan and Pakistan: a reflection of the segmentary lineage system' in A. Ahmed, D. Hart (eds), *Islam in Tribal Societies*, London: Routledge and Kegan Paul, 1984. Nevertheless, historical studies demonstrate the frequency of serious disruption in Afghan history. In Afghan Turkestan the population accepted the arrival of the Kabul government in the 19th century, since the continual conflicts between *khans* were giving rise to serious disorder and were perceived as unacceptable. In addition, a functionalist account brings up all the criticisms usually aroused by an approach of this type, and in particular the fact that war is only one possible means of demographic control (in competition with such means as birth control and emigration), so that why it occurs historically in this particular society remains to be explained.

[25] It is also interesting that this word, *Commandant,* was itself new, and of foreign origin. *Amir* is sometimes used of important commanders, but has not gained its place in the common language to designate of this new social role. An analysis of the local and regional organisations is given in Barnett R. Rubin, *The Fragmentation of Afghanistan*, New Haven and London, Yale University Press, chapter 10.

(*wakil*) on the basis of local issues: for example, the Hazaras of Qala-i Naw got their *khan* elected ahead of the Pushtun candidate, an Uzbek might be elected by non-Pushtuns against a Pushtun candidate, and so on. In other cases concrete interests or a common way of life, independent of ethnicity, provided a basis for electoral mobilisation.[26] On the contrary, social classes were not groups with solidarity, nor could they be mobilised: there was no peasantry, and still less a working class conscious of itself as such.[27] During the war it was possible to distinguish two situations: one where mobilisation was within the framework of an existing *qowm*, and another where the commander had mobilised several *qowms* or parts of *qowms*.

If mobilisation took place within the framework of an existing *qowm*, the network of solidarity collectively sustained a party and a commander. At what level is a *qowm* capable of itself becoming the framework of mobilisation? Over-broad sources of solidarity, such as macro-ethnic affiliation (i.e. Pushtun, Tajik and so on), do not constitute a framework for mobilisation, and nor do tribal confederations such as the Durrani or the Ghilzai. In the latter case Ghilzai identity had become a 'historical relic', as Anderson remarks.[28] In fact the Ghilzai confederation was broken up by the appearance of the Durrani confederation, and the political context no longer accommodated it. During the war this identity was not an active basis for mobilisation, even though the Ghilzai were over-represented in the Harakat-i Enqelab. The absence of extended *qowms* capable of political mobilisation is accounted for in part by the action of the state, which had destroyed the tribal structures.

A network of solidarity on a smaller scale, not necessarily of a territorial nature, generally served as the primary framework for mobilisation. Among the eastern Pushtuns tribes or the Ghilzai, the mobilised *qowm* was generally the clan, several thousand individuals at most. In the mountains the field of action of the commanders was often

---

[26] See particularly Micheline Centlivres-Demont, 'Types d'occupation et relations inter-ethniques dans le nord-est de l'Afghanistan', *Studia iranica* (Paris), 5 (2), pp. 269–77.

[27] The analyses offered by Richard Tapper seem here to assume rather than to demonstrate a transition to a class-based structure, 'Ethnicity and Class: Dimensions of Inter-Group Conflicts in North-Central Afghanistan' in R. Canfield, M. Shahrani (eds), *op. cit.*, pp. 230–47.

[28] 'Tribe and community among the Ghilzai Pashtuns', *Anthropos*, 70, 1975, p. 596.

dictated by geography: from one valley to another, or at different altitudes in the same valley, the solidarity networks differed. Similarly a fraternity of artisans practising the same trade could serve as the basis for the establishment of a group.

To take a particular example, the fraternity of the delinquents of Kandahar, the *payluch* (the shoeless ones), functioned as the framework of mobilisation under the leadership of Abdul Latif, an innkeeper before the war but now leader of the *payluch* and as such responsible for relations with the local authorities. Little is known of this brotherhood, which is similar to that of the *koka* in Kabul, the *luti* (from *lut*, 'hooligan') in Iran, or the *shabab* in Tripoli (Lebanon).[29] The brotherhood brought together the young men of the bazaar, often the sons of butchers, innkeepers and such like—all professions lacking prestige. Their distinguishing signs of membership were a large knife, a yellow robe and distinctive slippers. The *payluch* were obliged to observe a code of honour and solidarity between members, and therefore constituted a *qowm*. They organised dogfights near a *ziarat* close to the town and smoked quantities of hashish.[30] Given the responsibility for the security of certain streets, probably as some kind of racket, they sometimes also acted as contract killers. Though on the margin of legality, the *payluch* formed part of the social life of the bazaar in Kandahar and today former members are not stigmatised. The son of the chief of the *payluch*, Gul Agha, who had been educated up to the top class at the secondary school in Kandahar, had been a government official before the war. At the moment of the Soviet invasion the *payluch* were massively mobilised behind their leader to take part in the fighting against the occupiers. They seemed afterwards to have disappeared as an organised group, since many were killed in the early years of the war.

---

[29] Interview with a former *payluch* (Kandahar, 1992). The organisation of young men from popular urban origins into *futtuwa* was an invention of the caliph Nasr, of which the *payluch* are perhaps a survival. Cf. E. Ashtor, *A Social and Economic History of the Near Middle East in the Middle Ages*, Berkeley: University of California Press, 1976, p. 234.

[30] There is a link stronger than that of mere geography between these three activities: the visit to the *ziarat*, the use of hashish and the dogfights. Pressing the point somewhat, it could be said that the urban style of Kandahar is here perfectly expressed—to which should be added music, which was ubiquitous in the town before the arrival of the Taliban.

Although political mobilisation brought solidarity networks into play, it was not a mechanical transposition of various *qowms*.[31] Mobilisation might sometimes not be ascribable to a *qowm*, since a commander may benefit from the support of a number of networks or partial networks. In some instances the *qowm* may support more than one commander, the better to protect itself from political events. Political mobilisation in existing networks is autonomous, but whether mobilisation takes place within an existing *qowm* or whether it brings into existence a new structure, its mode of operation continues to be that of a network of solidarity.

The social profile of the commanders

The social origin of the commanders mainly corresponded to four ideal types: the holy man (the *pir* or the *sayyed*), the *alem*, the *khan* or the educated man. These were not primarily political or military figures, but could become so through a capacity to mobilise men and resources. These different types of status were related to resources of different kinds: respectively religious charisma,[32] religious knowledge, wealth, and the modern education sanctioned by the state. In addition, the *khan*, the *pir* and the *alem* were all important figures in their local communities; the influence of the educated class was less definite. However, the prestige attached in the villages to learning was undeniable, and social contacts made at school or at university opened up access to political networks. For those lacking initial resources social mobility was limited: ordinary fighters could assert themselves at the local level through their courage or their organisational abilities, but very few went on to run larger groups.

These four 'ideal types' did not exist in the real world, where for the most part the situation was more complex. A single individual could bring to bear a diversity of resources, such as his status as an

---

[31] For example, A. Shalinski studied a group of *muhajirin* of Fergana and noted that they belonged simultaneously to the Hezb-i Islami and to the Jamiyat-i Islami: 'Ethnic reaction to the current regime in Afghanistan', *Central Asian Survey* 3 (4), 1985.

[32] It should be recalled, following Max Weber, that charisma is a social and not a psychological phenomenon. It is the recognition by a group of disciples of the exceptional quality of an individual, in this case a religious quality. *Economie et societé*, vol. I, Paris: Presses Pocket, p. 320.

alem, his territorial inheritance which might earn him a role as a *khan,* and his membership of a family of *pirs.* So the principal commander in Kunduz, Aref Khan, an educated man who was the son of the former mayor of Kunduz and a major landowner, had at his disposal a number of different resources. Men of the educated class who became commanders often belonged to notable families, and it is therefore difficult to distinguish between what they owned to those connections and to their scholarly achievements. Where an educated man did not belong to the dominant branch of an influential family, such as Amin Wardak or Fazlullah, his educational status might allow him to be preferred to other candidates for the position of commander. In other cases *pirs* were often also significant landowners and acted as *khans,* to whom they might up to a point be assimilated. *Pirs* and *sadat* might also be *ulema,* at least in the regions such as Herat and Ghazni that were dominated by orthodox Sufism. In Hazarajat *khans* often gave their daughters in marriage to *sadat.*[33] On the other hand, *ulema* and *khans* were normally distinct categories in pre-war Afghanistan, especially among tribal populations.[34]

The emergence of the new élites allows these types of resources to be re-evaluated in the context of social upheaval. As a result of the *jihad,* religious personalities—*ulema, pirs* and *sadat*—found their legitimacy enhanced. In addition, local social structures governed the probability that an individual of a particular social background might become a commander. In fact, the political map showed regional patterns in the social origins of the commanders, to an extent which rules out a random distribution: for example the *ulema* were dominant in the province of Ghazni and in Hazarajat, and the *khans* maintained their hold among the Baluchis of Helmand. In some sense the value of religious prestige or scholarly achievement, and their capacity to be transformed into a political resource, varied from region to region. Afghanistan was not socially homogeneous, and this was especially true after the disappearance of the state.

[33] R. Canfield has described the relations between *pirs* and *mullahs* in the Bamyan region, 'Ethnic Regional and Sectarian Alignments in Rural Afghanistan', in Ali Banuazizi, Myron Weiner (eds), *Religion, the State and Ethnic Politics,* Syracuse University Press, 1986.

[34] However, Jamal Malik, *op. cit.,* p. 244, on the basis of a study of the social origins of students in the *madrasas* of the NWFP (some of whom were Afghans), points to a not insignificant number of sons of *khans* in the recent period (11.3%).

What tendencies emerged? First the sweeping scale of the changes must be stressed. The national élites were virtually eliminated. The presence of the *ulema* was the most novel factor, together with the rise of the educated classes. Regional differences were a factor: in different areas pride of place was taken either by the educated or the *ulema*. The changes also had a generational aspect: most of the commanders were born in the 1950s, since the material conditions and the high mortality rate favoured younger fighters, who were physically capable of guerrilla warfare. Among the *khans* the new generation took the form of a transfer of power to heirs who had received an education. These points will become clearer through individual analysis of each of the four categories defined above.

The ulema. In a number of places *ulema* or *mullahs* became commanders, and this direct and long-term exercise of power was something new in Afghan history. Two factors tend to explain this development: their legitimacy in the eyes of the rural populations and their capacity for organisation. The retreat of the *ulema* to the countryside in the two or three decades before the war restricted their influence to rural areas. The example of the Mujaddidi family, which transferred its principal *madrasa* from Kabul to Ghazni, typified a long-term sociological change: the tendency for the *ulema* to become displaced from urban centres, especially if they had not come from the government *madrasas*. Sometimes financially dependent on their congregations, the *ulema* were only rarely major landowners in the pre-war period, and at least in the rural context they remained strongly rooted in their community, the majority of them exercising their functions in the region of their birth.[35] This close link explains why men of religion have often acted as spokesmen for the population, e.g. in Badakhshan where they occupied the position of an alternative authority.[36] In addition, when the state withdrew from the countryside after 1978, the *ulema*, in their capacity as religious scholars, had at their disposal a legitimate and recognised field of knowledge which

---

[35] Some tribal communities, however, made a point of choosing their *mullah* from outside their own group.

[36] M. N. Shahrani, 'Causes and Context of Differential Reactions in Badakhshan to the Saur Revolution' in M. N. Sharhani, R. Canfield (eds), *op. cit.*, p. 152.

allowed them to establish legal relationships between individuals. The war therefore had the effect of giving the *ulema* a monopoly in the field of justice, which reinforced their influence.

The second factor was related to the existence of structures and networks. The *ulema* and those *mullahs* who had followed a course of religious teaching formed part of an institution held together by the strongest personal ties. An *alem* would remain faithful to the master who had given him his *ijaza* (licence to teach), and to his fellow pupils. If he was the director (*mudares*) of a *madrasa* he could also rely on his students (*taliban*) and their families. Further, outside the traditional *madrasas*, where the teaching was rigid and repetitive, the government *madrasas* and a number of private *madrasas* educated *ulema* who were of a modern tendency and more aware of political issues, who would become effective administrators.

The *ulema*-commanders, who existed throughout Afghanistan, were dominant in Ghazni, in the north of Helmand, in Badghis, to the south of the town of Mazar-i Sharif, and in Hazarajat.[37] What were the social structures which facilitated their success? First of all, the weakness of the *khans* favoured the emergence of the *ulema* on the political scene, as is seen in Ghazni. In this province there were numerous *khans* of the Andar tribe, but they had little influence as individuals. The weakening of the ties of patronage therefore had its effect, and the *mullahs* had not faced strong competition. In the deprived regions of Helmand, which were very different from the central regions where irrigation projects had brought about a profound social transformation, the local *khans* were unable to mobilise a significant clientele. On the other hand, deep-seated segmentation was a brake on the appearance of the *ulema* as political leaders, so that the *khans* were dominant among the eastern Pushtun tribes, despite the exception represented by *mawlawi* Haqqani of the Jadran tribe. In addition, the rural nature of the communities concerned made the establishment of the *ulema* easier since there were no alternative urban élites. In the second place, the presence of a prestigious *madrasa*, such as the Nur ul-Mudares at Ghazni, was a factor common to most of the regions dominated by *ulema*-commanders, such as Waras and Nili in the Hazarajat. These *madrasas* were the centres of networks of

---

[37] In Logar, the *ulema* were in competition with the educated class.

ulema who were able to coordinate their activities over what were sometimes far-flung regions.

The pirs and the sadat. In Afghanistan, as in the rest of the Muslim world, particular individuals or objects may enjoy the reputation of possessing a beneficial spiritual quality, *barakat*, which reflects on to those who come to view them. The *pirs* and the *sadat* are the two categories of individuals who enjoy this spiritual quality. These possessors of religious charisma have substantial social effects, since their disciples (*murid*) are potentially available for mobilisation in a political cause.[38]

The *sadat*, descendants of Muhammad through his daughter Fatima and his son-in-law Ali, enjoy no particular privileges in Islam. They are not automatically recognised as the bearers of *barakat*, but nevertheless command a certain prestige[39] and may enjoy a privileged economic position, though there also exist poor *sadat*. Villagers may ask *sadat* to live among them in exchange for gifts, in order to benefit from their *barakat*.[40] Sometimes specialising in pious rituals, they serve as intermediaries and as arbiters, for example in the case of a conflict within a tribe. Their status varies: in the east they have little prestige, while in Hazarajat they are influential.

The *pirs* are spiritual masters, normally within the context of a Sufi brotherhood.[41] Their relationship with their disciples may be ritualised through participation once or twice a week, often during the night of Thursday or Friday, in a *zikr*—a mystical exercise consisting of a recitation of the names of God under the *pir*'s leadership. Professional solidarity may also be expressed through the cult of a deceased *pir*, who may be adopted as the patron of a group of artisans practising the same trade. Popular religion is also expressed, though

---

[38] Louis Duprée, 'Saint Cults in Afghanistan', *American Universities Field Staff Report, South Asia Series* XX (i), May 1976.

[39] The *khwaja*, descendants of the first Caliph Abu Bakr, have a lesser degree of religious legitimacy but often play a comparable social role.

[40] Micheline Centlivres-Demont, 'Types d'occupation et relations inter-ethniques dans le Nord-Est de l'Afghanistan', *Studia Iranica* 5 (2) 1976, pp. 269–77.

[41] The Qadiriyya and the Naqshbandiyya are the most prevalent Sufi orders, although the Chestiyya and Suhravardiyya are also encountered. There are also *pirs* who do not belong to a brotherhood, and *malang*, vagrant preachers who have no organised clientele.

less consistently, through visits to the *pir* and through pilgrimages to relics or to the tomb (*ziarat*) of a *pir*, which is often under the guardianship of the descendants of his family.[42] These practices are widespread. The *ziarat* of Mazar-i Sharif, where a local Afghan tradition maintains that Ali, the Prophet's son-in-law, is buried, attracts tens of thousands of pilgrims every year.

In other places the *pir* presides over a *khanaqah* (a place where Sufis gather) which functions both as a mosque and as a *madrasa*, although this function had declined in the pre-war period. A *murid* would normally be assured of a welcome from his master, who would when appropriate exploit the relationship to his own benefit. The attachment of a *murid* to his *pir* would take the form of a gift in cash or in kind made once or twice a year on the occasion of a visit by the *murid* or of a tour by the *pir.* This source of finance covers the upkeep of the *khanaqah* but the surplus of the gifts of the disciples over the expenses of the *pir* might be considerable, since the *murids* often come from several provinces. The pattern of *pir-murid* relations is structurally that of patron and client, although the goods involved are of a different kind. The hypothesis may be advanced of an extension into the sacred domain of more general social models.[43]

In the context of Sufism there are two ways of approaching the exchanges between the *pir* and the *murid*.[44] Orthodox mystical practices form an integral part of the teaching of the *ulema*. On the contrary, practices connected with the cult of saints are viewed by the *ulema* as magical rituals. Richard Tapper suggests on the basis of a case-study that individuals who take part in Sufism of the 'saintly' variety are often of inferior social status and experience feelings of inadequacy in relation to the values of their group.[45] Whatever the truth of this, the distinction between the two types of Sufism is not a matter of difference between one brotherhood and another, but between different *pirs* and the communities from which they recruit their *murids.* Among the tribal populations the Qadiri *pirs*, but also some *naqshbandis*, are generally attached to a saintly cult.

[42] The guardians (*mutawali*) usually sell amulets (*tawiz*) to visitors.

[43] On Christian saints, see Peter Brown, *Le culte des saints, son essor et sa fonction dans la chrétienté latine*, Paris: Editions du Cerf, 1984.

[44] See Olivier Roy, 'Sufism in the Afghan Resistance', *Central Asian Survey* 2 (4), December 1983.

[45] Richard Tapper, *op. cit.*

In the pre-war period the flow of both manuscripts and oral transmissions seems to have dried up, although the scarcity of historical sources must cast some doubt on the reality of the supposed 'decline' of Sufism, a theme which recurs in literature on the subject. It remains true that the brotherhoods did little recruiting within the young educated class or in the towns, other than in regions such as Herat. Bo Utas relates this decline to the hereditary status of the *pirs*, so that their disciples were not motivated to aspire to excellence in order to become their successors.[46] This probably accounts for a certain ossification in the style of teaching. However, the principle of succession within families is long-standing, so that the decline, a more recent phenomenon, must be explained by other factors, in particular the competition offered by modern schools from the 1950s onwards.

To what extent were such charismatic figures able to make use of their legitimacy to achieve the status of commanders? In the pre-war period certain *pirs* or *sadat* were personalities of local influence, who were sometimes even elected as members of Parliament. The economic and political effects of religious charisma did not therefore appear only with the onset of the war. Because of the long tradition of struggle of the Naqshbandis against the Russian colonisers in the Balkans, Central Asia and the Caucasus, it might have been thought that this brotherhood would become a motivating factor in the *jihad*.[47] In fact the brotherhoods have not been at the heart of the resistance, and have not been the framework for the parties, as has been seen in Turkish and Iraqi Kurdistan at various periods.[48] With some exceptions, mainly in Herat and Maymana, the *pirs* did not become commanders and there was no collective loyalty among *murids* to any particular group.

Locally the *sadat* occupied significant positions, for example in the northeast, but did not make up greatly extended networks. The only exception concerns Hazarajat, where the *sadat* were dominant almost

[46] Bo Utas, 'Notes on Afghan Sufi Orders and Khanaqahs', *Afghanistan Journal* 7, 1980, p. 2. For the theory concerning the decline, see also David B. Edwards, *op. cit.*, p. 187.

[47] It should be noted that the brotherhoods have not played a determining role in the current war in Chechnya.

[48] See Martin van Bruinessen, *Agha, Shaikh and State*, London: Zed Books, 1992, mainly chapters 5 and 6.

up to 1982, though in alliance with the *ulema*.[49] To be a *sayyed* helped notables who were also major landowners to preserve their local clienteles. In the last resort the war did not produce charismatic figures, 'mad *mullahs*' such as appeared in the 19th and 20th centuries in the tribal revolts against the British on the Afghanistan-Pakistan frontier.[50]

How might the relative eclipse of the brotherhoods be explained? The *pirs* were the victims of the Khalqi repression in the 1978–9 and in consequence many left for Iran or Pakistan. Further more the brotherhoods, with their recruitment among the urban and educated groups in decline, did not have men at their disposal who were able to become guerrilla leaders, and suffered from the effects of competition from other élites, the educated class and the *ulema*, who had taken control of various parties and tended towards action of a more organised kind. Nevertheless it will emerge in the course of the analysis of the biographies of the leaders of the political parties that membership of a brotherhood was still a considerable advantage. Thus the influence of the Mujaddidi family depended partly on its position

---

[49] In Hazarajat the influence of the *sadat* was related to that of the *khans*, but with the eclipse of the *khans* the networks were broken up, since the *sadat* were not spread throughout Hazarajat. Though numerous in Yakoalang and at Behsud, they were virtually absent from the south of Hazarajat. This factor partly explains the initial alliance between the *sadat* and the *ulema* who were more evenly distributed. In addition, most *pirs* are *sadat*, which explains the significant clientele they enjoyed and also their competitive relationship with the Shi'ite clergy. Traditionally the role of the *sadat* was to provide links between social groups, especially at times of crisis. Their activity during the war may be seen as an attempt to perpetuate this role, though on a scale and in ways which were different. The failure of the *sadat* was due to the impetus of the Iranian revolution, which favoured the rise of clergy trained in Iran who were generally hostile to popular forms of religion. The conflict between the *ulema* and the *sadat* was therefore also a competition for the monopoly of religious legitimacy. Nevertheless, the *sadat* were not eliminated in contrast with the *khans*, and their prestige among the lowest classes of the population allowed them to resist from their strong points, for example Waras, Behsud and Naur. A major landowner such as Sayyed Hasan Jaglan was able to mobilise hundreds of men at Naur. A *sayyed* such as Beheshti, on the other hand, was able to use his status as a *mudares* to speak on equal terms with the *ulema* and to mobilise his *taliban*.

[50] See Akbar S. Ahmed, *Millennium and Charisma among Pathans: a critical essay in social anthropology*, London: Routledge and Kegan Paul, 1976.

within the Naqshbandi brotherhood. The same observation holds for the relationship of the Gaylani with the Qadiri brotherhood.

The khans. A *khan* is a local notable who exercises an influence related to his status as a landowner or as a tribal leader. He maintains a clientele whose size is measured by those who are obliged to him, from among the relationships in which he is dominant. He feeds others and obtains services for them: he cannot operate without an open table, gifts to the local *mullah* and so on. He therefore invests his capital and his time in a network of relationships while personifying the values of his group, in particular that of generosity. He also plays a role as intermediary between the community and the outside world, whether government officials or a passing stranger, and he thereby obtains numerous advantages, particularly through his dealings with the administration. Nevertheless, his behaviour is directed towards the acquisition of prestige, rather than material benefits. Thus in his relationship with a *mulgerey* (companion) the *khan* feeds or helps his client, but this clearly differs from the payment of wages. In effect the *khan* makes use of his companion, who remains a free man, as an emblem of his status as a person of influence.[51]

The power of the *khan* consists primarily in his capacity to exert influence. He has no means to impose his will other than persuasion, debate and gifts. His power has no legal basis, although in certain regions such as Hazarajat and Badakhshan his domination over the peasants can be very forceful. This is not a matter of traditional power, since there is no handing down of immutable and more or less sacrosanct rules, but rather of a system of influence which is relatively open to newcomers. Between *khans* there is a degree of competition for dominance, and 'personal qualities' are obligatory to attract continued fidelity.[52] The son of a *khan* does not automatically inherit the position of his father, although the power of acquired status tends to favour family continuity.

Two types of *khan* are distinguished by the more or less hereditary nature of their situation. In the eastern Pushtun tribes or among the

---

[51] See Whitney Azoy, *Buzkashi: so that his name shall rise*, Philadelphia, PA: University of Pennsylvania Press, 1982.

[52] Fredrik Barth, *Political Leadership among Swat Pathans*, London: Athlone Press, 1959.

Ghilzai the competition between *khans* results in a degree of instability among individual positions, while in other cases, there is what might almost be described as an aristocratic form of authority. The great families of Kandahar in particular, but also those of Hazarajat,[53] of Badakhshan and among the Baluch, enjoy a legitimacy which is founded not only on their economic resources but also on their genealogy, which is in itself a source of legitimacy.

After the 1960s economic transformations acted to the detriment of the clientele relationship between the *khans* and the peasants. Relations lost their mystique, becoming more overtly economic. Social relations altered, and the very idea of a clientele began to erode. In Ghazni, for example, the introduction of tractors broke the cycle of reciprocity, and the position of *khan* tended to disappear.[54] In Hazarajat the *khans* lost their erstwhile social supremacy. Their decline did not date only from the war, but had already been in evidence much earlier, probably from the end of the 19th century when the Hazara tribes had been conquered by Abdul Rahman Khan. However, social changes from the 1950s onwards further accelerated a decline which was to the benefit of the merchants and craftsmen. Everywhere sedentarisation, economic liberalisation and the alleviation of insecurity tended in the direction of increasing the influence of the state and the weakening of the *khans'* power.

How did the *khans* react to the new conditions imposed by the war? Those whose clientele was at the village level did not have the same level of resources to dispose of or employ the same strategies as those who wielded their influence on a provincial or national scale. The disappearance of the great notables was a major consequence of the war. In Hazarajat they were overthrown in the very regions where their power had been most absolute, such as the Uruzgan province and Jaghori, while many smaller *khans* had survived in regions such as Behsud. These were notables who had sometimes possessed several dozen villages. In the Kandahar region the great Durrani fami-

---

[53] According to the particular place in Hazarajat, there exists a quasi-aristocratic system with much importance ascribed to genealogies (in the province of Uruzgan), or a system of competition between notables, similar to that of the eastern Pushtun tribes (this applies in Behsud).

[54] Jon Anderson, 'There are no Khans any more: economic development and social change in tribal Afghanistan', *op. cit.*

lies went into exile, sometimes to Quetta, and no commanders of any significance were drawn from their ranks.

The power of the *khans* suffered as a consequence of the fall from grace of the state partly because of their role as its representatives. However, this effect should not be exaggerated: the *khans* lost power mainly because of the link between military force and hostile policies. Assimilated to the old 'feudal' order, they were exposed to the hostility of the Islamists and, in a less obvious way, of the *ulema*, not to speak of the government, for whom they represented an easily identifiable target. In some cases pressure from the Islamists, which went as far as assassination, prompted their withdrawal from the political scene, especially in Laghman. In Hazarajat the *ulema* sometimes bitterly opposed the landowners, whom they accused of injustice against the peasants. At Yakaolang, where most of the landowners were *sadat*, open conflict was to last for several years until the *ulema*, supported by the peasants of the neighbouring mountains, eliminated the great landowners of the valley. The *khans*, preoccupied with their personal rivalries, showed themselves unable to band together to make common cause against either the *ulema* or the Islamists. More significantly, they did not even succeed in holding on to their local power by calling into play their relationships with their erstwhile clients, which speaks volumes about the violence of the social changes.

In addition, the richest and the most influential disposed of the economic and cultural resources to be able to establish themselves easily in Pakistan or in the West. Those *khans* who had connections with the governing class therefore went into exile and played only an indirect, though sometimes significant, political role, such as those from Kandahar who established themselves in the Pakistani city of Quetta. On the other hand, at the village level the *khans* were able to set themselves up as commanders, since here they did not encounter the competition of the educated class or the *ulema*, whose numbers were insufficient to administer the population in all the villages.

Regional variations were explicable in terms of the intensity of fighting and the power of the tribal system. In regions little touched by the war, the *khans* retained their dominance, since the war was a less significant agent of change. Furthermore, the lessening of economic activity had the effect of preserving established positions, at

least for the land owners. The Baluchis in the south of Helmand and
the Aymaq provided instances of this persistence in the social structures. In addition, in some tribalised areas such institutions as the
jirga became once more the real locus of power, since the commanders were often the heads of clans. This phenomenon of retribalisa-
tion was to be seen in all the Pakistan frontier regions, where the
solidarity of communal affiliation and the tribal code did not permit
autonomous political activity.

The educated class. Though restricted in numbers, the return of the
educated group to the countryside was important since it provided
leaders for the resistance and particularly for Islamist parties.[55] As the
fighting became more generalised, many educated young men left
the towns or returned from abroad, making their way back to their
villages of origin where their families were known. Masud, a native
of Panjshir, had lived mainly in Kabul, and from 1974 in exile in
Pakistan, before settling in his native valley in 1979. In the same way
Zabihullah returned to Marmul, at a time when he was teaching in
Mazar-i-Sharif. Dr Fazlullah and Amin Wardak, who were students in
Kabul, returned respectively to Baraki Barak in Logar and to Jeghatu
in Wardak.

The lack of leadership was in fact the crucial problem for the
Afghan guerrillas. Organisation, especially in the military field, necessitates a minimal level of technical competence, and in particular the
ability to read and write. Members of the educated class therefore
became commanders, especially since their status also gave them the
ability to negotiate directly with the groups in Peshawar.

However, the elevation of a member of the educated class to the
role of commander generally also required either affiliation to a party
or the support of a family. For example, in the first phase of the war,
militants returned to Afghanistan with a few followers and imposed
themselves locally as commanders, without consultation with the

[55] In the case of Badakhshan the principal commanders, with the exception of
some *khans*, had emerged from the educational system, which was well developed in this region. On the other hand it would be hard to argue, even in
Badakhshan, that all the leaders were educated men, as Shahrani does (*op. cit.*,
p. 164), in view of the contrary examples of Sayyed Wakil and of Kheyradmand—who were respectively a *khan* and an *alem*.

local population, as Masud had done in Panjshir. In certain places in Hazarajat such as Lal o Sarjangal, or Deh Kundi (Khedir), power was overtly seized by force, without prior political effort. Several dozen young Hazaras, who had gone to study or work in Iran, came back armed and took control of their regions of origin.

Nevertheless, the adjustment of the young townsmen to life as guerrillas was far from easy. Many stayed in Peshawar, unable to find a niche in Afghanistan. The rejection of westernisation, which was identified with the state, placed the educated class in an awkward position. Anecdotally, but significantly, table manners—the return to the traditional style of eating with the hand from a common dish—caused the younger men some distress. Some were never able to adapt to these new living conditions and preferred to undertake political work in Peshawar or in the West.

The presence of educated commanders was particularly frequent in the northern regions of Afghanistan, such as Herat in the northeast. In the south, where tribal organisation dominated, the educated class had difficulty in imposing itself in competition with the *khans*. In Hazarajat or in Ghazni the educated group was pushed aside by the *ulema*.

Models of organisation

'The commanders? They have taken the place of the old *khans*, but they are more powerful!' (Ahmad Shah Masud in an interview, autumn 1991)

Analysis of the social origins of the commanders allows the way they exercised power to be scrutinised, with two preliminary remarks. First, the correspondence between a commander's social background and a particular way of exercising power is only on the level of probability. For example, an educated man might exercise power in the manner of a *khan*, in a very traditional way. Secondly, one should emphasise the independence of the commanders from the parties, which explains why party affiliation is not brought in at this stage of the analysis. In fact there was little control over the activity of the commanders by the parties based in Pakistan or Iran. In the absence of national coordination, the strategy of the commanders remained largely autonomous, especially in the early years of the war. Local political alliances were made on the initiative of the commanders, and within a single party there might be contradictory strategies. Also precise lines were not laid down by the parties in relation to the organisation of *muja-hidin* groups. Discipline, such training as might be offered, and the way of life differed little from one party to another, but depended rather on the social background of the commander and the community within which he operated. On the basis of actual cases, two models of how power was exercised might be constructed: the 'patrimonial', which was the more normal at the start of the war, and the 'institutional' in the case of the complex organisations which progressively took control of widespread areas.

The patrimonial model. In the patrimonial model there was no clear separation between the public and private domains. The commander made no distinction between his personal revenues and those of the party, or between his personal actions and those in which he represented a political movement. His status was dependent on his personal reputation or his family rather than an institution. His field of action was defined by the extent of the networks of solidarity which supported him, and in particular of his extended family, occupying all posts of importance. In addition, the system of succession to power was symptomatic of the low level of institutionalisation and of the weight of family connections. Since the status of 'commander' was part of the inheritance of the individual, it could be handed on, in most cases to brothers, or sometimes to a son. The party to which the commander belonged would restrict itself to the ratification of the choice of the new commander.

In a patrimonial system the commander exercised personal power, without delegation or administrative structure. No attempt would be made to establish an administration, or to set up schools or courts. On the contrary, the people were obliged to pay a *mullah* to give primary instruction to children, and to turn to an *alem* on judicial questions. Nor did the commander embark on the establishment of a real military organisation since, even when he headed an armed force, he behaved above all as a private person. No hierarchical structure was instituted: rather, the commander maintained relations with his clientele through favours and gifts. If he was sufficiently wealthy, he lodged his *mujahidin* in his own house and fed them, which reinforced his personal authority.

The commander partly took upon himself the traditional functions of the *khan* in the relationships of the community with the 'exterior'. He would exploit his position to enrich himself and to become an owner of land. His position as an intermediary effectively enabled him to appropriate a proportion of humanitarian aid, as well as of any assistance provided by political or religious factions, and of local resources, whether by means of taxation or of seizure. He might also marry into influential families desirous of making an alliance with the local authority. The guesthouse, where travellers of standing would normally be entertained, was a perquisite of the commander, and he kept open table in order to maintain his reputation for generosity. The distinction between a *khan* and a commander lay in the absence of relations with the state in the case to the latter, although he might be surrounded by the wider network of partisan solidarity. While the power of the *khans* was entirely informal, the commander could impose his will by force and was not obliged to rely on appeal to the consensus or on the use of indirect pressure.

The institutional model. As distinct from the patrimonial model, the institutional model constituted a bid to set up an alternative state, with regulations and a civil and military administration. Many educated commanders established organisations resembling this model, including notably Masud in Panjshir, Ismail Khan in Herat, Zabihullah in Mazar-i-Sharif, and Najmuddin in Badakhshan. However, numerous traces of patrimonialism survived: for example bodyguards tended to come from the home village of the commander, while personal profiteering by leaders continued to be a frequent occurrence.

While in a patrimonial system the commander controlled networks of solidarity, in an institutional system he exercised authority over a population occupying a defined territory, imposing consistent standards concerning the treatment of individuals. Solidarity networks ceased to be the only paradigm for the recruitment of officials and *mujahidin*. There was a meaningful distinction between public and private goods, and a system of taxation could be established. Officials ran a rudimentary administrative system, expressing the aims of their organisation in ideological language. Succession to power, though not necessarily following precise rules, takes place outside the commander's family. Military organisation was professional, and the *mujahidin*

were sometimes paid, recognising hierarchical authority and occasionally wearing uniforms. Objectives were conceived on a broader
scale, with strategies developed over longer periods. On the basis of
this general model, three 'ideal types' can be constructed: a clerical
model, set up by the *ulema*; a state model, set up by the educated
class; and a partisan variety, established by the Islamists.

The clerical model sprang directly from the involvement of *ulema*,
which did not imply that all *ulema* organised a system of this type:
some remained with the patrimonial system of organisation. Administration was conducted according to the principles of Islamic law.
Official positions were given in principle to *ulema* or to their *taliban*,
who were normally pupils of the same *madrasa*. Two examples of this
model may be cited. In the province of Helmand in the 1980s, the
commander *raïs* Abdul Wahid set up a typically clerical system at
Baghran, in the province of Helmand. All the officials were *taliban*
from his *madrasa*. The *mujahidin*, who were closely controlled and
professional, wore uniform and observed strict discipline, while authorisation from the commander was required for population movements. In the province of Ghazni the administration of the provincial
shura (council) was entirely in the hands of the *ulema*. However, no
strict hierarchy existed among the *ulema*, as at Baghran: in contrast a
more consensual system prevailed, although Qari Baba continued to
be the dominant personality up to 1994. These characteristics were
in essence those which would later be found among the Taliban,
who appeared to implement the same system on a national scale.

In the state model a bureaucratic organisation took upon itself the
functions of government, such as education, taxation and justice. No
attempt was made to impose a precise ideological model, beyond the
consensual principle of the Islamic state. This type of organisation
was therefore linked not directly to an ideology but rather to a social
class. The recruitment of officials was carried out among the educated
class, including soldiers and state functionaries,[56] but not necessarily
among the Islamic militants as the example of Herat showed. In this
province in 1980 Ismail Khan set up his own regional organisation,
the Emarat, open to commanders belonging to all parties. He was

---

[56] The commanders often recruited their officials in the universities where they
themselves had been students: engineers in the case of Masud, teachers for
Zabihullah, and soldiers in the case of Ismail Khan.

not himself an Islamist and his relations with the local Islamist network, which was run by the Afzali family[57] and Nurullah Emat, were difficult. Ismail Khan was a former officer, and he attempted to reproduce within his organisation the functions of the state. From the beginning of the war he was unique in recruiting his senior aides with no regard for communal or political affiliation. Of the four leading figures in the Emarat, three were from outside the town proper, namely Ismail Khan and Allauddin Khan, who were both from Shindand,[58] and Muhammad Aref from Shamali. These three 'outsiders' had in common the fact that they were all former soldiers. They were far from being the only military men in the Emarat, and it was certainly this link with the military which gave the organisation its coherence at the top.

The partisan model was a variant of the state model, in which the underlying structure was more the party than the state. The structures were of a different type than those which have been described, since the movement had revolutionary principles. There was some similarity with Maoist guerrilla movements, although the ideological structure was different. The population was led by militants with ideological commitment, in addition to, or sometimes instead of, technical abilities. The objective was to politicise the population.

Masud's organisation was the most developed example of this kind of structure in Afghanistan.[59] He had been a militant Islamist since adolescence, and his involvement in the movement drove him into exile in Pakistan in 1974, whence he returned in 1975 to take part in

---

[57] Hafizullah Afzali was a student in the university at Kabul in the 1970s, and took part in the coup in Panjshir in 1975, where he was killed. See Abdul Hafiz 'Mansur', *op. cit.*, p. 52, and the anonymous *Biography of Commandant in Chief Safiullah Afzali and the Resolution of Afghan Mujaheddin and Refugees*, Liestal: Bibliotheca Afghanica, n.d. His brother led a Front in Ghorian, in the province of Herat, and never acquiesced in the leadership of Ismail Khan, in particular because of his lack of legitimacy in the eyes of the Islamists.

[58] Whether the *uluswali* of Shindand was regarded as belonging or not to the province varied from one period to another.

[59] There are many written accounts of Masud and films about him, but few are of any quality. The demands of the media, which tend to focus attention on Masud's personality, obstruct understanding of his political organisation. Jean-José Puig gives a relevant analysis of his career in 'Le commandant Massoud' in Gérard Chaliand (ed.) *Stratégies de la guérilla*, Paris: Payot, 1994. See also Abdul Hafiz 'Mansur', *op. cit.*

the Islamists' abortive coup.[60] After a period in Nuristan he took up residence in Panjshir, where the rebellion broke out in July 1979, and eliminated rival groups, in particular the Maoists. For this professional revolutionary ideological issues were central, in spite of the priorities of combat. In 1980, through the agency of his brother, he embarked on the establishment of political teaching for the peasants in Panjshir: in the event the classes failed, and the plan was abandoned. Officials used very political language,[61] and their horizons were not limited to Afghanistan: their movement fell within an international revolutionary context. Another factor was that Masud's expansionism provoked a long series of clashes with other commanders, which brought about, for example, his military occupation of the neighbouring valley of Andarab. Masud was also the only commander to organise on a substantial scale training courses for Afghan guerrilla leaders as well as for foreign Islamists, who included Kashmiris, Turks and others. Internationalism was a characteristic trait of Masud's model, at least up to the fall of Kabul in 1992.

In the face of attempts by lay members of the educated class to build political organisations, the rural population kept its distance. In reality there was a fundamental ambiguity in the relationship between the population and the educated class: where the latter wished to establish an impersonal political relationship, the rural population interpreted this new type of authority differently to avoid recognising the regulation being imposed on them, and to continue relying on personal relationships, shading sometimes into clientelism, which

---

[60] Masud was born in 1956, the third of six sons, into a wealthy family in the Panjshir valley; his father was an officer. He spent his childhood in Kabul, and attended classes at the French Istiqlal lycée (although he rarely spoke French, he retained his competence in the language). He studied at the Polytechnic high school, and joined the Islamist movement. After the failed coup in the spring of 1974, in which he did not take part, he fled to Pakistan. He was trained by Pakistani officers and led the group which carried out the coup of 1975 in Panjshir. In 1976 Masud, who was close to Rabbani, found himself accused by Hekmatyar of having betrayed the movement, on the basis of statements obtained under torture from a friend of Masud, Jan Mohammad, who was later assassinated by Hekmatyar. Though arrested, Masud escaped death and returned to Panjshir in the spring of 1979. See Anthony Davies, 'A brotherly vendetta', *Asiaweek*, 6 December 1996.

[61] Quoting for example Mackinder, one of the founders of geopolitics. Interviews with officials of the Shura-yi Nazar, autumn 1991 and spring 1992.

they found easier to manipulate. The issue was not the acquisition of power but its justification, and how it worked in practice. Therefore, when Masud travelled in the country, and as the number of personal petitions increased, there was a short-circuit of the regular procedures in favour of an appeal to a charismatic personality who makes 'just' decisions in the light of a moral code. In the short term the commander's power appeared to be enhanced, but in fact his political programme was jeopardised. The recognition of charisma functioned in this instance as a transaction, in effect a compromise, between the institutional motivations of the educated class and the apolitical goals of the peasants.

In theory, the 'cult of personality' would be a response to this ambiguity, combining the recognition of a leader with the process of organisation undertaken by the educated class. The educated class were the driving force behind the transition to a cult of personality, since they were able to use it as a means of imposing ideological or administrative constraints in the name of the charismatic personality. This phenomenon was observed, up to a point, in the regions controlled by Masud: it was in these regions that tensions were strong since the model was the most ideological.

Finance

Economics lay behind the choice of a war of attrition, with offensives over a limited time involving only a few men. The commanders did not administer the economy, which could otherwise have been a source of income, since they had neither the organisation nor the legitimacy to do so. Even movements between the *mujahidin* and the government's regions were only occasionally controlled, generally with the aim of obstructing some move by Kabul. The government did undertake massive purchases of wheat from time to time with the aim of blocking the *mujahidin*'s supply chain, using the nomads as intermediaries; this caused a rise in prices. However, the economic dimension was not absent from strategy, examples being the creation of bazaars and the diversion of trade routes as a result of the clashes and rivalries between commanders, particularly in Badakhshan and Hazarajat. There was also interaction between military logistics and economics, since the commanders strove to control the means of communication. The resources of the commanders could be seen as deriving essentially from three sources: taxation, external assistance[62] and the traffic in drugs.

Taxation. The issue of taxation was important in two ways. First, taxation was an important source of local finance, which enabled the commanders to be independent of both the parties and external aid. It was therefore a good indicator of the state of relations between commanders and the population. The levies raised by the *mujahidin* were in theory Islamic taxes.[63] *Zakat* is raised on cash and on goods, such as flocks, and mineral extraction, to the level of 2.5% of the value held in a year. *Ushur,* raised on harvests at the rate of 10%, was of considerable importance, since the commanders controlled few bazaars, at least at the start of the war. The proceeds of these two taxes are normally given to the poor, to needy travellers and to the *mujahidin,* which served as a justification for their appropriation by the commanders. Still, there was an evident dilution of the Quranic principle that the recipient of this obligatory gift should be freely chosen.[64] As an exception to the rule laid down above, there were also non-Islamic taxes, in particular tolls on the roads. The commander here enjoyed a resource which was all the more advantageous in that it did not risk disaffecting the local population. Taxation on shops, which does not seem to have an Islamic basis, was in general low. Finally, a widespread form of participation was to feed the *mujahidin* in the nearest *markaz.* This was the first form of popular contribution to the resistance. For all these taxes self-assessment of contributions was the rule rather than the exception, owing to the lack of specialised officials, and also to the refusal of the peasants to allow the commander to interfere in their affairs. Since many regions were politically fragmented, the payment of tax was the symbol of affiliation to a particular commander, from which sprang the strategy of seeking protection by paying taxes to several commanders.

[62] In the absence of reliable information, no attempt will be made to analyse in detail the distribution of military aid.

[63] Joseph Schacht, *An Introduction to Islamic Law,* Oxford University Press, 1982.

[64] The *zakat* should be distinguished from the *sadaqat,* which is a voluntary act of charity.

In the early years of the war contributions from the population were widespread and spontaneous. The turning-point came as the *mujahidin* became increasingly professional in 1985–6, with the growth in foreign aid, especially from the United States. Popular contributions were sidelined, at least in the case of the major commanders, who relied on external humanitarian and military aid. In many regions the population found themselves deprived of a bargaining counter and unable to exert pressure on the commanders.

Humanitarian aid. It may appear controversial to put humanitarian aid among the resources available to the commanders. However, although the avowed objective of the NGOs was to give aid to the population,[65] the commanders profited from it directly—and indirectly through its influence on their prestige or legitimacy. The distinction between humanitarian aid and aid not regarded as such is in any case open to criticism. Assistance given by Islamist networks did not admit a distinction of this type. The building of a hospital or the gift of arms served the same objective, namely to ensure the victory of the *jihad*. However, the two routes were distinct, both from the point of view of the donors and in the conditions under which aid was given. Thus the distinction should be maintained.

In the early years of the war humanitarian aid had two characteristics. First it was crisis aid—essentially gifts of cash, together with a medical presence and the setting-up of dispensaries. The aid came mainly from private organisations run by well-wishers, rather than from institutional organisations as became the case still later. By their nature the medical organisations were more professional, but with almost that sole exception aid operations at that time had a distinctly amateur and sporadic character: the amount of aid provided was economically negligible, its importance resting above all on the reports of the situation it brought to the attention of western public opinion.[66] A significant evolution took place from 1986 onwards

---

[65] Some 256 NGOs have been involved in aid to the Afghans, of which about fifty operated in Afghanistan. Helga Baitenmann, 'NGOs and the Afghan war: the politicisation of humanitarian aid', *Third world Quarterly* 12 (1), January 1990, pp. 62–85; and Pierre Centlivres and Micheline Centlivres-Demont, 'Etat, islam et tribus face aux organisations internationales'. Le cas de l'Afghanistan, 1978–1998', *Annales* 54 (4), July–August 1999.

[66] For example the testimony given in the United States by Juliette Fournot, the head of the MSF (Médecins Sans Frontières) programme in Afghanistan, to the

with the arrival of American money.[67] Professional sources of finance provided an impetus towards the professionalisation of the staff. The NGOs, which were highly dependent on institutions (e.g. agencies of the United Nations and of the European Community and USAID), were no longer autonomous in their strategy and became the agents of their backers. The borderline between NGOs and international organisations therefore became less well defined.

Humanitarian aid was a significant factor for a commander, as the number of commanders or their representatives who hovered in the anterooms of the NGO offices in Peshawar made evident. Besides, the humanitarian aid agencies were often the sole source of information on the conflict, and they naturally spoke about the regions they knew. In consequence most journalists followed in the tracks of the humanitarian workers because of their logistical facilities, and the existence of a source of information and a viable 'story'. The political map therefore became distorted to the benefit of those commanders who enjoyed humanitarian aid. The reverse of the coin was that the prestige of a commander might suffer if he could not guarantee the security of the humanitarian aid workers.

In addition, a commander did not usually have the means to undertake administrative action, in particular because of the lack of doctors, teachers and engineers. Humanitarian aid enabled a response to be made to the more urgent demands of the population, particularly in medical care. For example, a dispensary brought a commander little income, but he would be credited for his astuteness in having persuaded an NGO to work in his territory. Aid was also a resource for the commander in that he was able to find positions for his clientele and above all his family within the NGO project. In addition, since the commander ensured the security of the NGO, he would arrange, normally at inflated rates, for it to pay a number of *mujahidin*. The security argument also allowed the com-

---

Congressional Task Force on Afghanistan, *Hearing on Medical Operations in Afghanistan*, 4 March 1985.

[67] US $400 million for the period 1980–4 (combining humanitarian and military aid) and $250 million for the year 1985 alone: John H. Lorentz, 'Afghan aid: the role of private voluntary organisations', *Journal of South and Middle Eastern Studies* XI (1–2), autumn–winter 1987, p. 103. $250 million were attributed to international agencies between 1985 and 1989: Helga Baitenmann, *op. cit.*, p. 75.

mander to exercise a strong influence over the situation in which the project operated, which was the guarantee that he could keep it under his control. In numerous cases personal profit to the commanders was an acknowledged fact, particularly where land was reclaimed. Sometimes such projects related to zones in which the commander had a personal interest, but in other cases profit came from a tithe on the aid provided. This was not necessarily seen as illegitimate by the population, all of whom depended on the size of the amounts held back.

In large organisations, which were emerging from the patrimonial model, the NGOs played an important role in the functioning of the administrative apparatus, as with Masud and Ismail Khan, though at a lower level in the case of the latter. Masud, who had set up a relatively complex administration, was entirely dependent on the aid of the NGOs in all civil matters, such as health, reconstruction and, to a great extent, education.

In addition to the western countries, Islamic networks such as the Muslim Brotherhood or the Salafists (the Ahl-i-Hadith) were active from their bases in Peshawar. The Muslim World League, whose director in Peshawar in the 1980s was Abdul Hasan, deployed the largest budget for the maintenance of the *mujahidin*, amounting to several million dollars annually. Saudi Arabia, the most important donor, did not appear to control the use of its funds closely, and local employees were generally identified with the Muslim Brotherhood. Additionally, the Saudi Red Crescent was funded directly by the Saudi government, but here too the personnel often belonged to the Muslim Brotherhood tendency. Among the other groups, the Maktab-i Khidmat-i Mujahidin (Mujahidin assistance office) was centred at the beginning of the war around Abdullah Azzam and his assistant Osama Bin Laden. In particular this group published the magazines *Jihad* and *Bunian-i Makhus*. Its finance came principally from the Gulf and from British Muslims. The distribution of aid to the *mujahidin* was not centrally planned, and this fragmentation was a reason for the multiplicity of sources of finance and the groups present in Peshawar. An additional issue was that sources of finance such as Syria, Iraq, Saudi Arabia and Libya were often antagonistic to each other politically. A further factor was the cooperation between the

Muslim Brothers and the Saudi financiers, in spite of their ideological separation. The situation of Abdullah Azzam is an indication of this distribution of responsibilities.[68]

Drug trafficking. The third source of finance was the opium trade.[69] After 1979 circumstances came together to cause a real explosion of production in Afghanistan. The revolution in Iran had the effect of bringing to a halt all production in a country which was a traditional consumer, with around 2 million users, and also an entrepot on the smuggling route to Europe and the United States. In addition, Ira-

[68] Abdullah Azzam is a figure who throws much light on the mobilised networks. Born in Palestine in 1941, he was of Jordanian nationality. After reading Muslim law at Damascus University from 1967 to 1973, he took a doctorate in that subject at Al-Azhar and taught Islamic Studies at the University of Jordan from 1973 to 1980. In 1981 he became a professor at King Abdul Aziz University in Jeddah, but lived in Peshawar where he took part in the *jihad*. He died in November 1989 as the result of a car bomb in circumstances that remain obscure.

[69] Though illegal in Afghanistan, the consumption of hashish was tolerated, and it was not unusual to see smokers in parks or buses, as well as in *saqikhana* (places where opium and hashish were smoked). Opium was rarely used, and only among the poorest classes. Part of the production was exported, mainly to Iran, via Herat to Mashad and Chakansur, sometimes after being refined in Kabul. Smuggling to Europe and to the United States was routed through Kabul airport. The profit derived from opium was significant, more so than from hashish, which explains why the zones of consumption and production did not necessarily coincide. For example, the Jalalabad and Balkh regions were producers, but without significant consumption, since the opium was destined for export or for the Turkmens. Opium was frequently grown for sale because of the price it commanded, while hashish was consumed locally. The cultivation of the poppy, which is planted in the autumn, forms part of a cycle of cultivation including wheat and vegetables. In January 1972 the police confiscated pure heroin and refined hashish prepared for export, which marked the discovery of an illegal trade no longer carried out on a local level but forming part of the international market. The 1970s also saw an increase in consumption. While hashish was frequently used, opium continued to be confined to the most deprived populations. It is likely that the opening of Afghanistan to tourism was an important factor, both in the increase of production for export, and in consumption, through imitation. In early 1972 the Afghan government set up two committees for the suppression of the opium traffic, which indicated the onset of an awareness of the problem, and perhaps reflected an apprehension of appearing to be subject to American pressure like Turkey. The reduced production of opium in Vietnam after 1973 would also have had the effect of increasing production in Afghanistan and Pakistan.

nian smugglers fled to Pakistan to avoid the authorities and continue their activities. By coincidence, the harvest was bad that year in Asia, which increased international prices. At the same time (in February 1979) Pakistan decided, because of Zia ul-Haq's policy of Islamisation, to ban the production and use of opium. Hitherto a low level of production had been permitted, and use was tolerated in official government venues. Because the crop in 1979 was exceptional, and the price increased because of the ban, the Pakistani producers, mostly in the North-West Frontier Province, converted their opium into heroin. Thus all the circumstances came together to make Afghanistan a major producing region: the increased international prices, the existence of refining laboratories and international smugglers in Pakistan, and the absence of control over the Afghan countryside.

Three regions produced 90 per cent of the Afghan opium exported: Badakhshan, Helmand and Nangrahar. The north of Helmand[70] was one of the world's leading areas of production Opium might be described as the dominant crop, since it occupies the largest land area and yields the most revenue. Two factors favoured the producers. First the Baluchi smugglers, of Iranian and Afghan nationality, switched from smuggling electrical goods to trafficking opium. Secondly, the principal commanders of north Helmand, beginning with the most important among them, *mullah* Nasim, gave their blessings to the crop by providing transportation and security. Although *mullah* Nasim did not himself cultivate opium poppies, he levied a tax on exported opium which guaranteed him useful revenue.

The situation was very different in Badakhshan. The principal producing areas were Fayzabad, Keshem, Jurm and Baharak. How-

---

[70] The province of Helmand may be divided into three areas clearly distinguishable from each other, ethnically, economically and politically. Baluchi country begins in the south, from Mirabad, in the *alaqaderi* of Deh Shu. Durrani Pushtun tribes, the Alizai, the Ishaqzai and the Alikozai, occupy the northern districts of the province: Musa Qala, Nausad, Baghran and Sangin. The central part of the province—Marja, Lashkargah and Girishk—is ethnically very mixed because of the irrigation projects. There are also Pushtuns, sometimes from Farah or Wardak, as well as Hazaras and Uzbeks. In each of these three regions the economy is different, with a predominance of dry crops in the north. The peasants of north Helmand began to produce opium in pre-war times for export to neighbouring Iran via the Baluchis. Production was carried out on a local basis and alternated with other crops such as wheat.

ever, it appears that in Khash 60 per cent of the land was given over to the production of opium, which made it the largest crop. Similarly, in Peshkan the land was not irrigated and therefore did not lend itself to other forms of cultivation, so that the peasants grew only poppies. Traditionally the population used opium, especially the Ismailis, and poppies were grown on small individual landholdings. Badakhshan was a province always on the edge of famine. Its situation greatly deteriorated in the 1970s, because of population growth. In this context the cultivation of poppies was of the highest importance for peasants who were thus able both to obtain money and to ensure their own personal access to the drug. Although the commanders did not earn large returns from the growth of poppies, it was politically difficult for them to forbid it because of the overall level of poverty.

Production in Nangrahar, primarily destined for export, began long before the war. Opium, which in pre-war times had been a secondary crop, now became the principal source of revenue for many families, especially in Nangrahar's poorest districts. In prosperous regions the proportion of land given over to the cultivation of poppies was some 10 per cent, and this figure increased for poorer lands. In contrast to Badakhshan the local commanders were directly involved in cultivation, as landowners, and in its transportation to Pakistan. The presence of the same tribes in both Pakistan and Afghanistan facilitated the movement of the drug and its delivery to the North–West Frontier Province's laboratories.

4. The *Jihadi* Parties

In parallel with the drive towards mobilisation inside Afghanistan, political organisations made their appearance in Pakistan and Iran. They adopted a stance opposed to the regime in Kabul, whose legitimacy they wholly rejected, and established duplicate authorities, in a situation characteristic of civil war. In the analysis of the political situation we first examine the formation of these parties, followed by the exclusivity of their representation of the *mujahidin*. Finally a typology is presented, relating to the various types of ideology, organisation and recruitment.[1]

The formation of the parties

In 1978–9 the situation was so fluid that dozens of organisations attempted to turn popular mobilisation to their advantage. This was a chaotic period characterised by ephemeral alliances, when attempts to achieve unity were as rapidly followed by schisms. Parties canvassed known personalities to preside over their coalitions, although in the event all that was on offer was the opportunity to create new organisations. In opposition to the initial movement towards unity, which was justified in terms of the military and moral exigences of the *jihad*, ideological divergences and competition for resources served as a contrary impetus towards fragmentation. The pattern of schisms which led to the emergence of the Sunni and Shi'ite parties is examined below in detail.

In 1978 Hezb-i Islami and Jamiyat-i Islami, which were already in existence in Peshawar, came together as the Harakat-i Enqelab-i Islami (Movement for the Islamic Revolution), under the leadership of *mawlawi* Muhammad Nabi, a former member of Parliament and an associate of the Mujaddidi family. Nabi laid claim to the political inheritance of the pre-war Khodam ul-Forqan, since the assassina-

---

[1] See Barnett R, Rubin, *op.cit.*, pp. 196 ff.

tion of Ibrahim Mujaddidi and his son Ismail had left the Mujaddidi family without a leader.[2] In fact the most politicised *harakati* commanders recognised the continuity between the two movements. However, the strains between Hezb-i Islami and Jamiyat-i Islami continued, and each soon took its own way, with Harakat-i Enqelab remaining under the leadership of *mawlawi* Muhammad Nabi.

Mawlawi Muhammad Nabi subsequently surrendered the leadership to Sayyed Gaylani, a *pir* of the Qadiri brotherhood and a member of the pre-war governing class, in a new movement, the Mahaz-i Melli (National Movement). However, *mawlawi* Mohammed Nabi rapidly recovered control of the Harakat-i Enqelab, leaving Gaylani at the head of Mahaz-i Melli. In addition the Jebhe-yi Nejat-i Melli (National Salvation Front) was established as a new coalition under the presidency of *mawlawi* Sebghatullah Mujaddidi, who had been in Peshawar since October 1978.[3] However, most of the parties—including Hezb-i Islami, Mahaz-i Melli and Harakat-i Enqelab—refused to participate in this Front. The Jamiyat-i Islami became for a time Mujaddidi's sole partner, but later it regained its independence, leaving Mujaddidi as the leader of Jebhe-yi Nejat-i Melli.

At the same time Hezb-i Islami split at the end of 1979. *Mawlawi* Khales emerged as the leader of a party that retained the same name—it will be referred to as Hezb-i Islami (Khales). His separation from Hekmatyar may be explained in terms of personalities: *mawlawi* Khales probably felt that the difference in their ages and his own position as an *alem* gave him precedence over the young Islamist. Khales' style, with little concern for organisational niceties, also put him at odds with the Hezb-i Islami line.

In January 1980, when the Islamic conference took place in Lahore, the six parties—Hezb-i Islami, Hezb-i Islami (Khales), Harakat-i Enqelab, Jamiyat-i Islami, Jebhe-yi Nejat-i Melli, Mahaz-i Melli—embarked, at the urging of Jamiyat-i Islami, on a process of unification which resulted on 19 March 1980 in the formation of an alliance, the Ettehad-i Islami Baray Azadi-yi Afghanistan (Islamic Union

---

[2] Another consideration was that the only remaining heir, Muhammad Amin Mujaddidi, was too young: he spent the war years in Islamabad.

[3] Sebghatullah Mujaddidi, the founder of the Jebhe-yi Nejat-i Melli, was unable to lay claim to the inheritance of his cousin Ibrahim. In the event, Sebghatullah was not fated to become the *pir* of the Mujaddidi family, and in any case before the war he took a controversial position close to that of the Muslim Brotherhood.

for the Liberty of Afghanistan). The secretary-general Sayyaf, an Islamist *alem* recently freed by the communist regime, then went into an alliance with Hekmatyar against the other movements, but afterwards broke with Hekmatyar while retaining control of the Ettehad. At this point the seven Sunni parties came into existence.

Nevertheless in 1980 the number of more or less autonomous groups was still substantial, and the monopoly enjoyed by the seven parties was imposed only piecemeal. Besides the Maoist groups (see Chapter 6), there were regional parties, mainly in the province of Kunar.[4] Kunar was the first region to rebel in 1978, and due to its position on the Pakistani frontier it rapidly escaped government control. Owing to the violence of the fighting, only 20 to 30 per cent of the population remained there out of 330,000 inhabitants before the war. Independent fronts made their appearance: thus Muhammad Anwar Amin, a Nuristani *khan*, became leader of the Jihad-i Islam-i Nuristani (Islamic Jihad of Nuristan), a party which found itself in competition with 'Da Islami Jahad Da Para Da Kunar Da Qowmuno Ettehad' (Alliance of the *aqwam* of Kunar for the Jihad), formed in 1980. In the early months, the parties in Peshawar provided arms and sent men to fight alongside the Nuristanis, except for Hezb-i Islami, which tried to take military control of the region. Muhammad Anwar became the principal Nuristani leader, though due to lack of support his movement was progressively marginalised.

In the case of the Shi'ites the politicisation of the confessional parties, which had already begun before the war, became the rule after 1978.[5] Religious sentiment, mobilised through the appeal to *jihad*, precluded membership of the Sunni parties[6] and favoured the leadership of the *ulema*, who were seen as the coherent force within the community. The Shi'ite political scene was characterised by opposition between the predominantly Hazara parties, including Shura, Nasr and Sepah, and the parties with predominantly non-Hazara

---

[4] David J. Katz, 'Responses to Central Authority in Nuristan: the case of Väygal Valley Kalasha' in M. N. Shahrani, R. Canfield (eds), *op. cit.*, pp. 94–119.

[5] See Rolf Bindemann. *Ethnizität und Gesellschaft. Religion und Politik bei den schi'itischen Hazara in Afghanistan, Iran und Pakistan*, Berlin: Das Arabische Buch, 1987, Occasional Papers no. 7.

[6] There were several instances of Shi'ites joining Hezb-i Islami. The Mustazaffin, a small group whose membership was largely Shi'ite, also accepted Sunnis.

leadership, such as Harakat-i Islami and the Mustazaffin, which were present either outside Hazarajat or in its border areas.

During the war a number of parties either coexisted or confronted each other in Hazarajat. However, in the earlier period the Shura-yi Enqelabi-yi Ettefaq-i Islami-yi Afghanistan (Revolutionary Council of the Islamic Union of Afghanistan) held sway as a consultative organisation. The Shura's earliest manifestation was a gathering of several hundred independent delegates and representatives of parties, whose aim was to establish an autonomous authority in Hazarajat.[7] The assembly was held at Waras, in the province of Bamyan, in August and September 1979, and appointed Sayyed Beheshti as its leader. This Shura was an initiative unique in Afghanistan in terms of the number of delegates who came together to agree on effective cooperation over such an extensive territory. Even before the Soviet invasion, the convening of the Shura signalled Hazarajat's political renaissance. Meanwhile the central authorities, careful to avoid gathering together the Hazaras into a single administrative entity, had divided them up into several provinces. The assembly at Waras demonstrated the power of Hazarajat's identity, at a time when among the Sunnis the *shuras* of the *mujahidin* were systematically replicating the existing administrative divisions. The only similar case among the Sunnis was the Nuristani party mentioned above.

One of the principal parties which took part in the Shura was the Sazman-i Nasr (Party of Victory). Nasr was founded by a group of *ulema* trained in Iran who had been active in the pre-war years both in Hazarajat and among the Hazara community in Kabul, Ghazni and Mazar-i Sharif. Some of them had travelled in Syria, Lebanon and Palestine, and had fought against Israel in the 1970s. However, the movement devoted itself primarily to political propaganda: the operation of libraries and publication of leaflets (*shabname*). Nasr was officially established in the summer of 1979 in Mashad by three *ulema*, Mir Hussein Saddeqi, Azizullah Shafaq and Abdul Ali Mazari.

The founders of the third significant party in Hazarajat, the Sepah-yi Pasdaran-i Islam (Army of the Guardians of Islam), were intellectuals who were active in Iran at the moment of the revolution. In the

---

[7] At Yakaolang, after the capture of a military post, a committee was formed to participate in the constitutive assembly of the Shura-yi Ettefaq: in a good example of the unanimous spirit of those times this included members of Nasr, *khans* of the Harakat-i Islami and the principal of the local school, who had no party affiliation.

liberal atmosphere of the early days of the Iranian revolution, under the government of Bazargan, various Shi'ite parties[8] came together to set up the Jebhe-yi Azadibakhsh-i Afghanistan (Front for the Liberation of Afghanistan) whose name was derived from an organisation linked to the Iranian Pasdaran. Two or three months later these parties separated, after setbacks which resulted from ideological differences and from the antagonism between *ulema* and lay members. The young intellectuals who had taken a key role in this Front did not immediately set up another party, but linked up with the Iranian Pasdaran to fight in Afghanistan. At the time the leader of this group was Ibrahim Qazimi, an engineer in his thirties from Behsud, educated at the university in Kabul. The decision to give official recognition to the Pasdaran as an Afghan movement was taken by the Iranians in 1983, following a two-month trip to Hazarajat by the Iranian Jaffar Zade, who visited Ghazni and Behsud. The party then adopted the title of Sepah-yi Pasdaran-i Islam (Army of the Guardians of Islam), choosing as its leader a former member of the Shura, Akbari, an *alem* trained in the Iraqi city of Najaf. Ibrahim Qazimi, who had ceded his influence to the religious establishment, migrated to Canada in early 1984 and disappeared from the political scene. The creation of the Sepah by Iran was the result of a desire to take back control of the Shi'ite movement: Nasr was regarded as too independent, in particular as the result of its history before the Iranian revolution. Sepah also represented the victory of *ulema* who were close to the Iranian clergy over young intellectuals who were too independent for Teheran's taste.

Outside Hazarajat the Khalqi government's assassination of *shaikh* Waez, who was the representative of the Ayatollah Khoei in Afghanistan, left *shaikh* Mohseni as his heir and one of the leaders of the non-Hazara Shi'ite community, although he had mainly been known in Kandahar. After a narrow escape from police who had come to arrest him in the spring of 1978, Mohseni removed himself to the Iranian city of Qom where he established the Harakat-i Islami.

The Sazman-i Mujahidin-i Mustazaffin (Organisation of the Poor Mujahidin) was a small party of intellectuals based at Shashpul in the province of Bamyan, and was the only organisation in Afghanistan to

[8] Nasr, Niru, Rad, Nehzat, Mujahidin-i Khalq (Mustazaffin), Jombesh-i Mustazaffin.

accept both Shi'ites and Sunnis, both in practice and in terms of doctrine. The movement seems to have originated in the 1960s in the time of Zahir Shah, with the Pasdaran-i Enqelab-i Islami (Guardians of the Islamic Revolution), which in 1977–8 became the party of the Mujahidin-i Khalq-i Afghanistan (Mujahidin of the Afghan People). In 1979 the party adopted its present name. The other Shi'ite parties were sparsely represented on the ground, sometimes mustering only a few dozen men. Their origin often lay in the ties of patronage between Hazara *ulema* and Iranian *ayatollahs*: this was the case with the Nehzat-i Islami-yi Afghanistan (Islamic Movement of Afghanistan), the Hezb-i Dawat-i Islami (Party of Islamic Preaching), and the Hezbollah.[9] The Nehzat-i Ruhaniyat wa Jawan-i Afghanistan (Reja) (Movement of the Afghan Clergy and Youth), the Niru-yi Islami-i Afghanistan (Islamic Force of Afghanistan) and Rad (Thunder) had leaderships drawn more from the laity and attracted less support from Iran.

Monopoly of representation. Over time the exiled parties gradually established their exclusive right to speak for the *mujahidin*, especially through their ability to define the parameters of legitimate ideology, as well as through their control of resources—subject to the control exercised by the countries in which they operated—and through the membership of the commanders.

The parameters of legitimate ideology. The concept of *jihad*, which in the eyes of the great majority of the population was the sole legitimate principle, entirely governed the doctrine of the political parties. The plainest indication of the centrality of religion was the position occupied by the *ulema.* In the event, the absence of a professional political class in the pre-war era and the significance invested in reli-

---

[9] Hezbollah was not in reality a structured party but rather an ensemble of groups financed and armed by Iran. The two important Hezbollah groups were at Herat and at Kandahar. In Kandahar Hezbollah, led by *haji* Mukhtar Sarwari, played an active part in the struggle against the Soviets. Sarwari opposed *shaikh* Mohseni, who was accused of accepting American aid. The two groups in Kandahar and Herat maintained relations, but there do not seem to have been mechanisms for liaison, even though *shaikh* Ali Wusuqi was described in Kandahar as the leader of the Afghan Hezbollah.

gious legitimation enabled the *ulema* to dominate the political field: they led all the parties, with the exception of only one of any signifi- cance, Hezb-i Islami. The lay parties, which did not satisfy this re- quirement, were swiftly eliminated (see Chapter 6). In contrast with the pre-war period, when the range of ideological systems—com- munist, Islamist and nationalist—was unrestricted, the parties in exile were distinctly more homogeneous. By this token the Islamists lost their monopoly over legitimation on the basis of Islam, even though their ideology remained distinctive and opposed to that of the tradi- tional *ulema* and the members of the former governing class.

The control of resources. The ability to control the political arena and to maintain a monopoly of representation required the control of external aid, and in the absence of resources of their own the parties subsisted by appropriating a portion of the aid intended for the *muja- hidin* and the refugees. Relations with host countries were crucial for the parties. No movement could survive without the assistance of Iran or Pakistan, and Harakat-i Islami, for example, had alternately enjoyed support from both.

For the Sunnis the principal host country for refugees and exiled combatants was Pakistan, whose cooperation was also essential in the transfer to the *mujahidin* of the arms and financial support provided by Saudi Arabia and the United States. Since Pakistan largely con- trolled the distribution of aid, its attitude was crucial for the survival of the groups which came into existence in 1978–9. In December 1979 the Soviet invasion of Afghanistan was a threat to Pakistan, but it was also useful to the regime of Zia ul-Haq whose military dicta- torship had been ostracised by the international community, espe- cially after the hanging of the former Prime Minister Zulfiqar Ali Bhutto. After some hesitation Pakistan accepted full American assis- tance, in the shape of $3.2 billion of direct military aid and total aid of $7.2 billion during the 1980s.[10] In addition, Pakistan was given an IMF credit of $1.6 billion, the largest hitherto granted to a develop- ing country. In exchange for western support, Pakistan became the

[10] P. Dikshit, '1993: Afghanistan Policy', *Strategic Analysis*, Nov., vol. XVI no. 8, p. 1073. For a historical approach to Pakistani foreign policy, see S. M. Burke, L. Ziring, *Pakistan's Foreign Policy: an historical Analysis*, Oxford University Press, 1990.

conduit for western aid to the Afghan resistance and a sanctuary for the anti-Soviet guerrilla movements. The several billion dollars of aid available for the resistance was therefore in practice distributed by Pakistan.[11]

On the other hand, far from acting simply an instrument of the West, Pakistan made use of its position as an intermediary to control the parties and develop its own policy. In institutional terms Pakistani supervision was exercised in three ways: political and military affairs were supervised by the ISI (Inter-Services Intelligence Directorate), international contacts and negotiations were carried on by the Ministry of Foreign Affairs, and aid to the refugees was administered by the Commissioner for Afghan Refugees. The role of Pakistan was crucial from the first in the formation of the exiled Afghan political parties which appeared in 1978–9. The Pakistani government therefore decided to halt the formation of new groups and to stabilise the number of parties, in the case of the Sunnis, at seven. Similarly, for the entire duration of the war a Pakistani general took part in the meetings of the exiled parties, while strategy on the ground was broadly laid down by the Pakistan military. The Pakistan administration also played a decisive part in the allocation of aid to 3.2 million Afghans within its borders, of which a significant part seems never to have reached the refugees. Finally, Pakistan acted in the field of diplomacy as the representative of *mujahidin* parties who were never invited to participate directly in negotiations.[12]

Pakistan's Afghan policy, from the Soviet invasion up to the events of 11 September, displayed great stability and did not depend on the party in power. For this reason support for Hezb-i Islami continued after the death of Zia ul-Haq and only ceased because of the movement's failure on the ground. Similarly, the alternation between Nawaz Sharif and Benazir Bhutto had no consequences for Afghan policy, with Benazir continuing to support the Taliban. The reason for this continuity lay in the influence of the military establishment and also in a broadly consensual view of Pakistan's national interest.

---

[11] The single American donation amounted to around $2 billion and the Arab countries provided a similar sum. See Charles G. Cogan, 'Partners in Time: the CIA and Afghanistan since 1979', *World Policy Journal*, 10 (2), 1993, pp. 73–82; William Maley, *The Afghanistan Wars*, London: Palgrave, 2002, pp. 76 ff.

[12] D. Cordoves and S. S. Harrison, *Out of Afghanistan: the inside story of Soviet withdrawal*, Oxford University Press, 1995.

The strategic plan, often expounded by the Pakistani military, was to endow Pakistan with 'strategic depth' in relation to India, through the installation of a pro-Pakistan government in Kabul, and furthermore to create a Muslim region capable of standing up against India economically, demographically and perhaps even militarily. The balance of power with India and the issue of Kashmir therefore entirely determined Pakistan's Afghan policy. In particular, a pro-Pakistan government in Afghanistan should be able to block the return of an alliance of Afghanistan and India against Pakistan.[13]

In line with such arguments, the Pakistan authorities backed those Afghan religious movements which appeared to share an *a priori* ideological solidarity with Pakistan, which itself had embarked on a process of Islamisation. In the 1980s Gulbuddin Hekmatyar had proposed a confederation between Pakistan and Afghanistan, aiming to please his Pakistani protectors. On the other hand, Pakistan had played a key role in the elimination or marginalisation of the Maoist or nationalist movements within the Afghan resistance, because they represented a potential threat to Pakistani domination.

However, the situation in practice was more complex than might be supposed from what has so far been said. Pakistan's Afghan policy had actually been set in train by officers who held an 'orientalist' view of Afghanistan. The model which influenced the ISI officers who were in charge of contacts with the Afghan commanders was implicitly that of the Pakistani tribal region, where central authority manipulated tribal divisions on the British 'divide-and-rule' model. This is probably why the ISI assisted the development of the Khales faction of the Hezb-i Islami which opposed Hekmatyar's Hezb-i Islami in the early 1980s, even at a moment when it supported the latter. In general the Pakistani intelligence services systematically divided the Afghan parties by setting the commanders against each other. This strategy did not only affect the military: up until 11 September at least, Afghanistan was seen by the Pakistani political class as an extension of Pakistan's frontier zone, and therefore the Ministry of the Interior rather than that of Foreign Affairs took the leading role, even in diplomatic contacts with the Afghan movements.

---

[13] See Ahmad Iqbal, 'A mirage misnamed strategic depth', *Al-Ahram Weekly*, Cairo, no. 392, 27 August–2 September 1998. Also Major Abdul Rahman Bilal, *Islamic Military Resurgence*, Karachi: Ferozsons, 1991.

In the implementation of its strategy Pakistan made use of a network of Afghan clients, of which Hezb-i Islami, followed by the Taliban, were the most important. As has been observed, the relationship between the Islamists and the ISI went back to the 1970s, especially in the organisation of the coup of 1975. Hekmatyar, the future leader of Hezb-i Islami, liaised at that time with the Pakistan intelligence services and had made himself the privileged ally of Islamabad. Subsequently Pakistan distributed a large proportion of the aid to Hezb-i Islami: probably around 40%. Hezb-i Islami also took advantage of its good relations with the Pakistan administration to establish itself in the refugee camps and to assassinate its political adversaries, particularly the leftists, nationalists and royalists.[14]

With the Shi'ites Iran played a role symmetrical to that of Pakistan, although it did not exercise such close control over the establishment of parties since some were based in Afghanistan and therefore less dependent on external aid. Iranian policy went through a number of stages. Its complexity and lack of consistency at certain moments arose from there being multiple centres of decision-making which were sometimes violently opposed to each other. Iran's policy of fragmentation through the creation of parties was probably not so much a Machiavellian encouragement of discord, even though in theory Iranian control would thus have been enhanced, but rather the result of internal struggles within Iranian politico-religious circles.

In Afghanistan, Iran sought above all to preserve its relationship with the Shi'ites, while at the same time not providing them with any significant military assistance in order not to damage its own relations with the Soviet Union.[15] The Persian-speaking Sunnis kept their distance from Iran, which offered them no significant help. The reality was that the regime in Iran prioritised its struggle against Iraq, while offering largely verbal support to the *mujahidin*, although it did provide some logistical facilities on its territory. Consequently its relations with the parties which were actually fighting the Soviets were difficult, even when these were Shi'ites, as with the Harakat-i

---

[14] In the 1980s Hezb-i Islami appeared also to maintain private prisons in Pakistan where it was able to detain its opponents.

[15] Well before the Islamic revolution, the Afghan Shi'ites felt themselves to be close to Iran. Portraits of the Shah were to be seen in some Shi'ite houses, and Hazara migrants travelled for preference to Iran rather than to Pakistan.

Islami. On the other hand the Iranians did assist Shi'ite movements which took their inspiration from the Iranian revolutionary model, such as Nasr and Sepah.

The affiliation of the commanders. The parties' monopoly over the representation of the *mujahidin* was yet further extended in Afghanistan through the recruitment of the commanders, hence the fundamentally asymmetrical relationship between these two types of actors.[16] The parties depended on the bellicosity and organisational capacity of their commanders to attract further foreign donors and enhance their influence, although media manipulation might in the short term affect how they were perceived and therefore influence the flow of aid. On the other hand, what the commanders were able to raise from the population was used locally, with nothing returning to the centre of the organisation.

When a commander joined a party, it was because he thereby derived immediate and concrete benefits. In practice commanders were only able to maintain their influence if they succeeded in obtaining arms and money. Here the parallel drawn by Mike Barry between the activities of the *khans* and those of leaders of parties is illuminating.[17] The primary activity of the parties was the distribution of arms, while most movements also ran military training courses: for example, teaching the use of anti-aircraft weapons. The parties also gave support to the commanders or to their *mujahidin* when they spent periods in Pakistan or Iran.

At their origin the relationships between the commanders and the parties did not depend principally on ideological identification, but on access to resources provided from abroad. However, this statement must be qualified, especially for those commanders who had a political affiliation which pre-dated the war. Non-material issues generally played a considerable part in the relationship between a commander and a party. Party affiliation provided protection, and also legitimacy in relation to other groups. In the event a commander not attached to a party could be suspect—was he, for instance, a

---

[16] The leaders of the main Hazara Shi'ite parties were not in exile, but remained in Hazarajat. Only Mohseni, who was not a Hazara and recruited principally in the towns, lived in Pakistan. There did not exist therefore the same kind of relationship between the parties and the commanders as for the Sunnis.

[17] Mike Barry, *op. cit.*, p. 15.

Maoist?—and other local groups might take this as a pretext to bring him down, especially since they did not fear reprisals. Similarly, affiliation to a party almost inevitably brought with it benefits of solidarity, especially while travelling.

The relationship between a party and a commander also depended on the commander's importance. Many petty commanders lingered for months in Peshawar, waiting for a party to provide them with arms and thus enable them to go home.[18] However, from the moment when a commander became important enough to be able to pay for a representative in Pakistan, his autonomy was enhanced, since he would henceforth be able to make his own contacts with the Pakistan intelligence services and with western embassies. For instance, Abdul Haq, Masud and Amin Wardak had the benefit of direct aid from France or from Britain. Such direct links weakened the parties, who saw the exclusivity of their role as intermediaries threatened.

While membership of a party was the general rule, this did not prevent a commander from having a large measure of autonomy in his choice of which particular organisation to join. This would be, in the majority of cases, a choice for the commander and not the *mujahidin* or the population. Affiliation was undertaken at the initiative of the commander, as the leader of an already existing group which would make contact with a party in order to obtain weapons.[19] In addition, competition between the parties meant that they were obliged constantly to strive to maintain their existing clientele, which hampered the establishment of party discipline. In the event this competition augmented the freedom of action of the commanders who followed the patrimonial model, and changed their allegiance without difficulty from one party to another, although the commanders of the institutional type maintained more stable affiliations. During changes of party the *mujahidin* remained faithful to their commander rather than to the party. Various reasons might lie behind

---

[18] Conflict could erupt between the leadership and the commanders if their demands ceased to be met: in some cases violent incidents took place in Peshawar itself.

[19] However, the commander's room for manoeuvre was not unlimited, and an unpopular party affiliation could diminish his power. In addition early affiliation, often crucial, tended to be made when the *mujahidin*, and therefore the commanders, were not well differentiated from the population.

the commanders' changes of party, though the prospect of obtaining more arms, and therefore of consolidating their power, was often enough. Another common situation was the existence of a conflict between commanders of the same party. For instance, in Badakhshan Jamiyat-i Islami was largely dominant at the beginning of the war, except in Keshem which was under the control of Hezb-i Islami. However, internal conflicts within Jamiyat-i Islami in the Argu region prompted the expulsion of the commander Jamaluddin and his replacement by *mawlawi* Kheyradmand of the Hezb-i Islami.

As the war continued, the parties never succeeded in leaving behind this disunity between the leaderships and the commanders. With only rare exceptions, occurring mainly when the leadership was situated in Afghanistan, the parties would continue to be coalitions of commanders.

A typology of the parties

The classification of the Afghan parties generally adopted has proved inadequate. The customary distinctions drawn between 'moderate Islamists', 'radical Islamists', 'moderate fundamentalists', 'traditionalists' and so forth are confused and hard to justify, since they depend on non-empirical criteria which arise from the subjective involvement of an observer, often a westerner, with the movements. In addition the relevant areas for analysis—ideology, organisation and recruitment—have not been distinguished.

Three models of party may be hypothesised, derived from the types of commander: the Islamist, the clerical and the patrimonial. This typology is based on a statistical correspondence between social position, ideology and method of political action. The ideology of the educated class tended to be Islamist, while that of the pre-war élite was conservative, and the *ulema* of the private *madrasas* were often fundamentalists. Similarly, a bureaucratic style of organisation was linked to the involvement of the educated group or of the *ulema*, while the pre-war élites adopted a more informal structure, based on patronage. Finally, the recruitment of commanders was socially close to that of the leadership: *ulema*-commanders were found in clerical parties, educated commanders in Islamist parties and *khan*-commanders in patrimonial parties.

The characteristics of an Islamist party were therefore an Islamist ideology and leadership, of lay or religious origin; with a bureaucratic organisational style and recruitment from the educated class. A clerical party was characterised by a fundamentalist ideology, combined with a clerical bureaucracy, and a leadership consisting of *ulema*-commanders. Finally a patrimonial party brought together a conservative or reactionary ideology, a leadership drawn from the pre-war élites, a patrimonial organisation, and recruitment from the *khans*. These categories applied fairly well to the majority of the parties in terms of their leadership, organisation and ideology, but recruitment was by its nature more complex since, as is shown later, they involved local considerations.

This typology also enables the identification of mismatches and irregularities, since the links between the various phenomena—ideology, leadership, organisation and the recruitment of commanders—were not in practice absolutely consistent. In practice there might be a contradiction between recruitment and leadership, or between recruitment and avowed ideology. In all such cases local issues and incidental motivations should be examined for the understanding of particular situations. The personal histories of the leaders often provided some explanation. In addition, a party might evolve moving closer to an alternative ideal type. Ideological frontiers between Islamists and fundamentalists had a tendency to become blurred, which was not unique to Afghanistan. However, recruitment would generally follow a set pattern.

To return to the selected categories, Hezb-i Islami, Jamiyat-i Islami and, among the Shi'ites, the Mustazaffin corresponded closely to the category of Islamist parties, although the situation of Jamiyat-i Islami was more complex owing to the mixture of *ulema*-Islamists and lay Islamists in its leadership. Jebhe-yi Nejat-i Melli and Mahaz-i Melli were instances of the patrimonial model. Hezb-i Islami (Khales) was similar to this model in its organisation and recruitment, but its leader, an *alem* who did not belong to the pre-war ruling class, expressed himself in fundamentalist terms. Harakat-i Enqelab was the sole example of a Sunni clerical party, to which may be added the majority of the Shi'ite parties, especially Nasr and Sepah. Harakat-i Islami, headed by an *alem* but with a membership of notables and an Islamist ideology, was hard to fit into a category, as was also the Ettehad, with an Islamist leader, a fundamentalist doctrine and a frankly opportunist recruitment policy. The proposed classification will be more satisfactorily demonstrated by way of a detailed examination of four issues: leadership, organisation, ideology and recruitment, always distinguishing between Sunnis and Shi'ites.

THE SUNNI PARTIES

Name of party	Leadership	Orgnisation	Ideology	Recruitment
Hezb-i Islami	Islamist (Gulbuddin Hekmatyar)	Bureaucratic	Islamist	Educated class
Jamiyat-i Islami	Islamist, clerical (*mawlani* Rabbani)	Bureaucratic	Islamist	Educated class
Harakat-i Enqelab	Clerical (*mawlani* Nabi)	Clerical	Fundamentalist	*ulema*
Jebhe-yi Nejat	Patrimonial (*pir* Mujaddidi)	Patrimonial	Conservative	*khan*
Mahaz-i Melli	Patrimonial (*pir* Gaylani)	Patrimonial	Conservative	*khan*
Hezb-i Islami	Patrimonial	Patrimonial	Fundamentalist	*khan*
Ettehad	Clerical (*mawlani* Sayyaf)	Patrimonial	Fundamentalist	Opportunist

THE PRINCIPAL SHI'ITE PARTIES

Name of party	Leadership	Organisation	Ideology	Recruitment
Shura	Clerical (*sayyed* Beheshti)	Clerical	Conservative	Hazara, *sadat*
Nasr	Clerical (*shaikh* Mazari)	Clerical	Islamist	Hazara, *ulema*
Sepah	Clerical (*skaikh* Akbari)	Clerical	Islamist	Hazara, *ulema*
Harakat-i Islami	Clerical (*shaikh* Mohseni)	Clerical	Conservative	Shi'ite *khan*
Mustazaffin	Islamist (engineer Hashemi)	Bureaucratic	Islamist	Educated class

The leaderships. With one exception only—Gulbuddin Hekmatyar—the leaders were *ulema*, but this category was not homogeneous. Some, such as Burhanuddin Rabbani, *pir* Sayyed Ahmad Gaylani,[20] Abdul

---

[20] Born in 1932, Gaylani was educated at the Abu Hanifa College in Kabul, then at the Faculty of Theology at the University of Kabul where he took his degree in 1960. The Gaylani family soon linked itself to the royal clan through marriage.

Rasul Sayyaf,[21] and Sebghatullah Mujaddidi,[22] had emerged from the government *madrasas*, while others, such as *mawlawi* Yunus Khales[23] and Muhammad Nabi Muhammadi, came out of the private *madrasas*.

In 1952 Sayyed Ahmad married Adela, the granddaughter of *amir* Habibullah, at a moment when the wife of King Amanullah was also of Gaylani descent. Before the war the *pir* was mainly occupied in secular pursuits: among other activities he was the Peugeot concessionaire, and his activities as a brotherhood leader were modest. He placed the preservation of his network of clients above his pursuit of spiritual practices.

[21] Sayyaf was born in 1946 at Paghman, near Kabul. He was a pupil at the Abu Hanifa theological school where he graduated in 1963, then at the Islamic College at Kabul University where in 1967 he took his degree with distinction, then becoming a teacher at the Faculty of Shariat where he taught *hadith*. In 1969 he went to Al-Azhar University, and graduated with distinction. He returned to Afghanistan in 1972, where he taught and helped to publish *Shariat*. His involvement with the Islamist movement was already notorious, which resulted in his arrest in 1974 as he boarded a plane to the United States to undertake legal studies. He was freed by Babrak Karmal in 1980 and went to Pakistan, where he achieved election as president of the Ettehad-i Islami (Islamic Alliance).

[22] Born in Kabul in 1925, Sebghatullah Mujaddidi was the son of Muhammad Masum Mian Jan Mujaddidi. He was educated at the Habibia School, and afterward spent six years at the Faculty of Law and Jurisprudence at Al-Azhar University, where he graduated in 1953. Until 1959 he taught at various schools, as well as teaching Quranic studies and the *shariat* at the Teachers' College in Kabul. He had links with the Egyptian Muslim Brotherhood, and enjoyed good relations with Rabbani, with whom he had in common membership of the Naqshbandi *tariqat*. In 1959 he was accused of participation in a conspiracy against Khrushchev during the latter's visit to Afghanistan. He was imprisoned until 1964, then lived in the United States from 1968 to 1970. He founded the Jamiyat-i Islami-yi Ulema-yi Mohammadi in 1972. Once more exiled from 1974 onwards, he headed the Islamic Centre in Copenhagen, returning to Peshawar in 1978, where he set up the Jebhe.

[23] Born into a poor family around 1919 at Nuqur Khel, Khales was a Pushtun of the Khagiani tribe, and studied in private *madrasas* before going to complete his training at the Haqqaniyyah *madrasa* in Pakistan. In the 1960s he worked for Kabul Radio, where he presented religious programmes. He seems to have enjoyed a certain popularity, owing to the direct and often humorous style of his contributions, and he also collaborated on a monthly magazine, *Gahis*. Around 1960 Khales published a translation of the book by Sayyed Qutb, *Islam wa Adalat Ijtima'i* (Islam and Social Justice). His involvement with the radio station and the magazine ended with the rise to power in 1973 of Daud, who swiftly showed his antagonism to the Islamists: under Daud one of his sons was killed. Khales's membership of the Islamist movement appears to date from this time. In 1975 he went into exile in Pakistan, taking up residence in Islamabad. From 1975 to 1978 he worked within the Hezb-i Islami.

The life histories of the Islamists, who were often exiled during the 1970s because of their opposition to the authorities, were plainly different from the members of the governing class such as Muhammad Nabi, a former member of parliament, or Gaylani, a former member of the *Loya Jirga*. The Islamist leaders, who had been relatively unknown before the war, had a network of militants at their disposal, while the other leaders were well known and had support among the ruling class and, in particular in the case of Gaylani, within the Sufi brotherhoods. Some leaders held several positions, others did not. In contrast to Hekmatyar, who belonged only to one category—that of Islamist—Gaylani belonged to three: he was a member of the ruling class, a *pir* and an *alem*. Rabbani was an Islamist and an *alem*. Ethnically Rabbani was a Tajik, Gaylani and Mujaddidi were *sadat*, and the others were Pushtuns.

Among the Shi'ites none of the important leaders belonged to the ruling class, and education was not a point of difference, since all were *ulema*. Their community affiliation was a more influential factor. Three types of leader mobilised different networks: the *alem-sayyed* such as Beheshti; the Hazara *alem* such as Mazari,[24] and Akbari; and the non-Hazara *alem* such as Mohseni. The engineer Hashemi, the leader of the Mustazaffin, was the only lay Islamist among the Shi'ites, occupying a position comparable to that of Hekmatyar among the Sunnis, but leading only a group of very small size.

Models of organisation. The party structures in general duplicated the administrative pattern, with titles such as *amir-i welayati* (provincial governor) and so on. Titles were derived from Islamic terminology, such as *amir*, and in general distinguished between military officials (*amir-i nezami*) and political ones (*amir-i siasi*). Beyond these common characteristics, the parties might be organised on patrimonial, bureaucratic or clerical lines.

The bureaucratic style of organisation necessitated a body of rules concerning activities, such as meetings and the assignment of tasks, on an administrative model. Recruitment of students and former government employees accounted for the propensity to bureaucratic

---

[24] Born in 1946, Mazari came from Nanway, a village near Charkent in the province of Mazar-i Sharif. After studying in Qom and Najaf he returned to Afghanistan in 1978.

organisation. The Hezb-i Islami was the closest to this model, while Jamiyat-i Islami, which also recruited among the educated class, did not have the means to maintain an extensive bureaucracy. Hezb-i Islami's organisation was a blend of centralisation and military discipline on the model of the Pakistani Jamaat-i Islami.[25] Its obsession with rules contrasted with flexibility observed elsewhere. Hezb-i Islami set up an alternative society as well as an alternative state, and demanded that its members should end their communal affiliations. The party was intended to take precedence over family or tribal loyalties, a policy which came up against various kinds of resistance.

The organisation's outstanding characteristic was centralisation. Hekmatyar was in a position to make crucial decisions more or less on his own, though this seems to have been modified after successive setbacks and the marginalisation of the movement. While in most parties the commanders were allowed wide autonomy on the ground, the leadership of Hezb-i Islami retained as far as possible strict control over local initiatives. In the 1980s the major commanders had in principle been supposed to stay in daily touch by radio. Internal purges enhanced respect for the discipline of the party, which had the use of prisons in Pakistan where several hundred members of other parties, as well as communists, were detained, tortured and executed.

Among the Shi'ites the Mustazaffin was the best example of a bureaucratic organisation. In total this group amounted to only several hundred men, whose time was divided between military and civilian activities. A sharp distinction was drawn between the officials, who were all members of the educated class, and the ordinary members. The officials were drawn from the original pre-war nucleus, and though the engineer Hashemi was the spokesman and leader of the group, the leadership was collective. The overall level of organisation was the best found anywhere in Afghanistan.

The clerical parties adopted a type of organisation in which the personnel were religious figures. Among the Sunnis this model was found in the Harakat-i Enqelab, where the leadership consisted in

---

[25] See Marc Gaborieau, 'Le néo-fondamentalisme au Pakistan. Maududi et la Jama'at-i-islami' in Olivier Carré (ed.), *Radicalismes islamiques*, vol. 2, Paris: L'Harmattan, 1986, pp. 33–76; also Kalim Bahadur, *The Jama'at-i-islami of Pakistan*, Lahore: Progressive Books, 1978.

principle of *ulema* and their *taliban,* and was the dominant one among the Shi'ite parties in Hazarajat, especially during the Shura of the early years, which replicated the pattern of administration of the state, though with the posts of responsibility occupied entirely by *ulema.*[26] The system set up by the *ulema* of the Nasr and the Sepah was little different from that of the Shura, but was less complex.

Mahaz, Jebhe and Hezb-i Islami (Khales) functioned according to a patrimonial model where no distinction was made between the resources of the leader and those of the organisation. For example, the trucks belonging to Hezb-i Islami (Khales) were the property of the leader, who was thus in a position to embark on commercial ventures in his private capacity. In these parties the commanders employed complex strategies to increase their resources and their clientele. The commanders often directly provided their own finance, and therefore enjoyed wide autonomy. Within Hezb-i Islami (Khales) a number of competing networks could be distinguished.[27] The Pakistani intelligence services controlled the activities of all of them, supporting the various commanders according to their priorities of the moment. In Mahaz the group which surrounded *pir* Sayyed Ahmad Gaylani consisted largely of members of the former governing class, as well as the *pir's* family members. This was the only party to have been family-based to this extent, with the possible addition of that of

---

[26] Hazarajat, and particularly Yakaolang, was incidentally the only place where the population was systematically disarmed. Hazarajat was divided into nine *wilayat* (provinces). Small settlements had a *shahrwal* (mayor). The administration of the Shura, which took over the government buildings, was top-heavy and inefficient to a degree. The representatives of the thirty-four liberated *uluswali* were represented by two or three delegates making up a permanent *shura* which met once or twice a week. There were committees for war, economy, culture and law. Taxes were high, reaching 10% of incomes, much more than among the Sunnis. Militarily the Shura ran four fronts, in Bamyan, Behsud, Naur and Jaghori, coordinated by Sayyed Hassan *jaglan.* There was conscription, requiring one year of military service at the age of twenty-two, with the possibility of sending a paid replacement.

[27] On the one hand, *haji* Din Muhammad and his brothers *haji* Qadir, Abdul Haq and Daud controlled an important part of the party's resources. On the other hand *mawlawi* Khales maintained good relations with Engineer Kabir, his brother, and Engineer Mahmud, which counterbalanced the influence of the other network. *Mawlawi* Haqqani and Amin Wardak were virtually independent powers, each closely linked to the Pakistani intelligence services.

Mujaddidi; in both these cases nepotism reached a level which obstructed their efficiency.[28]

Ideology. 'Scripture is its own interpretation.' (Martin Luther)[29]
   Three ideological positions define the range of the Sunni political
field. These are Islamist, fundamentalist and reactionary-conservative,
each of which relies in different ways on religion for its validation.
The Islamists, in Hezb-i Islami and Jamiyat-i Islami, had a distinct
predilection for ideological issues. This concern—systematically to
validate the actions of the party on the basis of abstract principles—
was a point of distinction from the practice of other movements.
Hezb-i Islami therefore attached great importance to the training of
its members and to the spread of its ideology.[30] Its programmes and
those of Jamiyat-i Islami were important texts since they enumerated
in detail the parties' principles on religion and education, among other
issues. The Islamic revolution, with its founding myth of the original
community of the Prophet, played a key role in political doctrine
and in the self-conceptualisation of these parties. The principal accent

---

[28] Sayyed Hasan Gaylani, Fatima Gaylani, Naser Zia, and Suleiman Gaylani were
among the most active of the Gaylani family within the Mahaz apparatus. Among
the former members of the senior administration were General Salam, General
Katawasi, Asef Muhammad Ikram and Dr Gholam Faruq Azzam. The leadership
of Jebhe was drawn from élite figures from the former regime: for example Muhammad Gulab Nangrahari, Shahid Zemaray the secretary of Mujaddidi, and
family members such as Abdul Shakur Turyalay Osman. The son of S. Mujaddidi, Zabihullah, was the treasurer of the party, while his brother played a part in
the early years before taking up residence in California. The details of these networks may be followed in Ludwig W. Adamec's *A Biographical Dictionary of Afghanistan*, Graz: Akademische Druck- und Verlaganstalt, 1987.

[29] *Oeuvres*, vol. I p. xxiv, Paris: Gallimard, 1999.

[30] For analysis of the programmes, see David B. Edwards, 'Summoning Muslims:
Print, Ideology and Religious Ideology in Afghanistan', *Journal of Asia Studies* 52,
no. 3 (August 1993), pp. 609–28. Hezb-i Islami propagated its ideology essentially
through the party's publications in Peshawar. The daily *Shahadat* and the monthly
magazine *Mujahidin Monthly* were among the party's most widely distributed
periodicals. In addition, meetings were regularly organised in the refugee camps
to allow the party leaders, and especially Hekmatyar, to put their points of view, a
thing the other movements did less often and on a less organised basis. Hezb-i
Islami attempted to take control of the refugees, for example through setting up
schools for orphan children in the camps. Great attention was typically paid to
education in the desire not to leave it to the *mullahs* and to teach non-religious
subjects.

was placed not on re-Islamisation in day-to-day terms but rather on a radical and violent transformation of political society, and putting social relations on a new footing. The Islamist project did not give a special place to the *ulema*, but legitimised institutions on the basis of universal suffrage—masculine and feminine—while nonetheless rejecting western democracy and especially the concept of multiple political parties.

Rationality, science and modernity were also essential elements of the ideology of the Afghan Islamist parties. Hezb-i Islami's model of modernisation, essentially urban and industrial, favoured investment in heavy industry and the nationalisation of major companies—as too did that of Hezb-i Demokratik-i Khalq-i Afghanistan—while explicitly excepting small companies. On the other hand, the peasantry did not loom large in the party's thinking. Hezb-i Islami was the inheritor of the Muslim Brotherhood's ideology, in practice closely allied to *dirigiste* planning, whereby development could be programmed in foreordained steps. The Islamists were influenced by the Third World left in more than one aspect of their programme, all the more since anti-imperialism was a concomitant of the Islamic revolution. Verbal antagonism towards the United States, whatever the complexities of the actual relationship, was a constant in the language of Hezb-i Islami and, to a lesser degree, of Jamiyat-i Islami. Hezb-i Islami took a systematically hostile attitude towards westerners, and incidents—some fatal—were frequent.

However, there were differences between the two movements. The history of the Islamist movement was re-written because of Hekmatyar, who was the object of a real personality cult organised by the party functionaries, while Rabbani set himself up as an arbiter between the various commanders of the Jamiyat-i Islamic. In addition the programme of Jamiyat-i Islami was an appeal to all Afghans, and laid less stress than Hezb-i Islami on the party leader. Although both movements referred to Islamist authors such as Maududi and Sayyed Qutb as the source of their doctrine, Jamiyat-i Islami was inspired by the dominant tendency of the Egyptian Muslim Brotherhood, while Hezb-i Islami identified itself rather with the Pakistani Jamaat-i Islami, which was very hierarchical.[31] Even though Jamiyat-i Islami

---

[31] Maududi was, however, more conservative. For example, he was radically opposed to all agrarian reform: see Seyyed Vali Reza Nasr, *Maududi and the Making*

aimed at the liberation of Soviet Central Asia,[32] it put first the patriotic aspect of the struggle against the occupier. Hezb-i Islami rejected all nationalist ideology and proposed a confederation with Pakistan. However, this suggestion was made with the aim of enhancing relations with Islamabad, and thus in reality primarily tactical.

Hezb-i Islami and Jamiyat-i Islami also took opposing positions on the issue of *takfir*: could a Muslim be declared an apostate by virtue of his recognition of a non-Islamic state, when he continued to perform his religious duties, prayer, fasting and so on? Sayyed Qutb,[33] an important ideologue for the Egyptian Muslim Brotherhood, reintroduced this idea, which was found in the writings of Ibn Taymiyya (1263–1328). Hezb-i Islami practised individual *takfir*, that is to say it took upon itself the right to declare a practising Muslim an apostate, which could imply the death penalty, but stopped short of declaring the whole of Afghan society to be irreligious, as certain groups following Sayyed Qutb had done in the case of Egypt. With this exception Hezb-i Islami, in denying that law had any autonomous existence, operated according to political imperatives, untrammelled by moral or juridical perspectives. Political assassination, justified by *takfir*, was a vital part of the political culture of Hezb-i Islami. This was a divergence from the juridical viewpoint of most of the parties, who turned in cases of difficulty to an interpretation in the spirit of jurisprudence, although the *ulema* were not always the

---

of Islamic Revivalism, Oxford University Press, 1996, p. 74. The closeness of Hezb-i Islami to Maududi may have consisted at a more profound level in its interpretation of texts outside the religious institutions; though Maududi, in contrast to Hekmatyar, had a classical religious education and came from a line of *pirs* of the Chishti Sufi brotherhood.

[32] As witness Ismail Khan, who declared that he wished to die a martyr at Bukhara (interview: Herat, autumn 1988). Jamiyat-i Islami's maps showed Soviet Central Asia as an occupied portion of the *umma*.

[33] On the thought of Sayyed Qutb, who was largely the Islamists' inspiration, see Olivier Carré, *Mystique et politique. Une lecture révolutionnaire du Coran par Sayyid Qutb, frère musulman radical*, Paris: Presses de la fondation nationale des sciences politiques, 1984. On *takfir*, see p. 15 ff. For Qutb, *takfir* was a generalisable concept, implying a break with society rather than individual excommunication. On this point Sayyed Qutb's view was atypical within the Egyptian Muslim Brotherhood and only a few groups of extremists, such as Tahrir, Takfir and Jihad, made *takfir* the basis of their strategy, in the process carrying Qutb's view to an extreme. In particular, this was the justification for the assassination of President Sadat of Egypt.

judges of last resort. For Hezb-i Islami nothing could be just in itself, and truth had no value outside the party, which retained a *de facto* monopoly over the interpretation of the Quran. Jamiyat-i Islami, on the contrary, employed a more limited concept of *takfir*, possibly explained by the presence of numbers of *ulema* within the party.

While the Islamist movements were linked to the phenomenon of mass education, it has been observed that the fundamentalist tendencies, often established by *pirs* or *ulema*, originated with the 19th-century reformists of the Indian sub-continent. In contrast to the Islamists, the fundamentalists preached a 'return' to good Islamic customs, in relation for example to the status of women, to religious practice and to artistic activities. However, this dichotomy should not be stretched too far, since there was also an authentic fundamentalist political project, although it implied the rejection of the modern forms of the state and even of politics as an independent sphere. Within the fundamentalist movement various tendencies were represented in the Afghan parties, whether inspired by Salafism or more in continuity with the pre-war tradition.

The war facilitated a breakthrough on the part of fundamentalist movements whose influence had previously been limited. The ideology of the Ettehad and of certain Hezb-i Islami (Khales) commanders was inspired by such fundamentalist movements. In particular, these parties rejected parliamentary democracy and elections, to which they preferred an 'Islamic' system, in which the *Ahl-i hal wa akd* (pious Muslims, persons respected within the community) played a determining role in the legislative system. The frequent denunciations by Khales and Sayyaf of the Shi'ites, to whom the former even denied the right to vote, reflected in the case of Khales the traditional tensions between the Shi'ite and Sunni Pushtun tribes of the frontier, but it also arose from the scale of Saudi financial support. However, it seemed that neither the commanders of the Ettehad nor Sayyaf himself became Salafists, since they continued to observe the Hanafi Sunni rites. Finally, at the beginning of the war, Harakat-i Enqelab was closer to Mahaz or to Jebhe. Nevertheless, a growing strictness on moral issues indicated a rapprochement to the tendencies mentioned above.

The reactionary or conservative parties, Mahaz and Jebhe, were nostalgic for the old order and the domination of the pre-war élites. Mahaz had no detailed programme, but its ideology may be deduced from the publications of the WUFA (Writers' Union of Free Afghanistan). Mahaz was a royalist party, which arose from the personal links of Gaylani with the royal family and the pre-war establishment. Mahaz demanded a constitutional system inspired by the regime of the West, with separation of powers and a parliament. It favoured the market economy and opposed the social measures proposed by the Islamist parties. Jebhe took a similar line, although it appealed more directly to Islam as the mode of social organisation and did not insist on support for the king as an absolute principle.

Among the Shi'ites the distinction between Islamism and fundamentalism was less relevant. The ideological structure was polarised by attitudes to Khomeini, and placed conservatives in opposition to revolutionaries. In the revolutionary parties such as Nasr and Sepah the *ulema* insisted unanimously on the predominance of the religious leaders in the political field. Their ideology was nevertheless put into practise in various ways by different leaders in different places. Nasr was inclined generally to be populist and puritan, but some officials took a less sectarian and less strictly clerical line. The demand for social justice was also expressed by many of its leaders, and attempts were made to distribute land to the peasants. In addition Hazara nationalism, though seldom appealed to as such, was an element of the ideology of Nasr, Sepah and Nehzat.

By contrast, the Harakat-i Islami of Mohseni, a disciple of *ayatollah* Khoei, did not seek to set up the Iranian revolution as a model. A factor was the opposition between Khomeini and Khoei, who had always rejected the involvement of the *ulema* in politics, and in addition had failed to return to Iran after the revolution. Although *shaikh* Mohseni preached that the social order should conform to Islamist values, he did not proclaim a clerical model of society and remained socially a conservative. The Mustazaffin were once more the exception. The principal sources of the party's ideology were Iranian intellectuals, especially Ali Shariati, as well as, more tangentially, Muhammad Iqbal, a Pakistani Sunni, and Ismail Balkhi. The view taken of Khomeini was somewhat critical, since the party was opposed to the domination of the *ulema* in politics. Utopianism was the most unusual feature of this system of ideas, which sought to recreate a perfect community modelled on that of the Prophet.[34]

---

[34] The parallel with the Iranian Mujahidin-i Khalq was striking, and the two parties in fact had contacts. This ideology was organised around two central ideas:

Distribution on the ground. Since the beginning of the war most Afghans identified with a party and many held membership cards. It was not unusual to encounter an individual with two or three cards from different parties. Multiple adherences in general included a main membership, genuinely entered into, along with others acquired for convenience, often to facilitate travel. In the towns membership was more often to a single party. In practice an individual's choice of a party depended on the opportunity to develop political awareness in the context of environments other than the immediate solidarity group of the extended family, i.e. in school, at the university or in professional life. Among townsmen who had been through the educational system, the various members of a single family might have experienced different social contexts, and therefore may have had access to a variety of choices, while in rural areas it was customary to follow family or clan affiliations. However, whether membership was on an individual or a collective basis, it was only with a commander as intermediary that the Afghan population joined a party. Only the distribution of the party memberships of the commanders was significant.

The political map of Afghanistan was complex, and one cannot necessarily discover the individual reasons for the affiliation of each commander. Of more significance are the imperatives which explain them in more general terms. Two types of affiliation can be distinguished, one based on the imperative of proximity and the other on the imperative of differentiation. The first type results from the search for a leader who is close to a commander in the context of a *qowm*, and the second type from the need for differentiation at a local level, which obliged the commanders to distinguish themselves from each other by their choice of party.[35]

---

first, a unity between Shi'ites and Sunnis, who ought to overcome their differences, and, second, social justice, to be achieved by way of the collective ownership of the means of production, or of a part of them. The influence of Marxism, or at least of socialist ideas, was palpable. The very name Mustazaffin (the poor) was significant. In addition, their positions on the status of women were very liberal in the Afghan context. Uniquely, as far as is known, the Mustazaffin gave women military training.

[35] In addition some affiliations were purely practical. The Ettehad, in particular, was set up on the basis of generous contributions from the Gulf, hence the initial reluctance of observers to regard it as a real party. Opportunist reasons for membership were in this case the rule rather than the exception.

The imperative of proximity. Affiliations were explicable in part on the basis of social proximity: commanders adhered to the party whose leadership was socially compatible in terms of geography, ethnicity or social status. In the end the degree to which a party was able to extend itself on the ground would depend largely on the capacity of the leader to bring various networks under his control. In fact, the real criterion for the choice made by a commander was not in any direct sense the party's ideological stance, but rather the personal characteristics of the leader, in communal, geographical, social and religious terms. The leader of the party was crucial, since the desire for social proximity, on the model of the *qowm*, was operative in the choice of membership. Party leaders brought into play their various qualities to attract various networks: *ulema*, Islamists, notables, members of the ruling class, *murids*. There follows an examination of communal proximities, shared membership of networks, whether political or linked to the Sufi brotherhoods, and finally shared membership of a social category.

In all the parties there was an ethnicity which was dominant at the level of leadership and, though in general less obviously, among the commanders. For example two-thirds of the leadership of Hezb-i Islami was made up of non-Durrani Pushtuns, clearly differentiating it from Jamiyat-i Islami, which was three-quarters Tajik.[36] *Mawlawi* Rabbani was the only party chief who was a Persian-speaker, a Tajik and a Sunni. Mujaddidi and Gaylani were Persian-speakers but also *sadat*. This exclusivity over the representation of the non-Pushtuns certainly played a part in the expansion of the Jamiyat-i Islami. Similarly the leadership of Hezb-i Islami (Khales) was eastern Pushtun, while that of Harakat-i Enqelab was in essence Ghilzai Pushtun, while that of Mahaz was Durrani Pushtun. Among the Shi'ites the leadership and the commanders of the Harakat-i Islami were mainly non-Hazara Shi'ites: Qizilbash and *sadat*.[37] By contrast, Nasr and Sepah were led entirely by Hazaras.

[36] Barnett Rubin, *op. cit.*, p. 87.

[37] The most important areas for Harakat-i Islami were: Kandahar (commander Ali Anwar), Ghazni (Dr Shah Jan, originally from Kakrak), the neighbourhood of Kabul (commander Anwari), Charkent (commander Din Muhammad), Bamyan (commanders Sayyed Adi and Mobarez), and the Unay pass (commander Rezavi). In Herat, Harakat-i Islami benefited in 1989 from the membership of commander Azimi, hitherto the responsible military official in Rad. There was there-

Affiliations therefore could be established as the result of a common macro-ethnic attachment, but also through local proximity. Thus the areas of effectiveness of a party were often those where the leader, in one way or another, had roots. Rabbani, originally from Badakhshan, Khales from Nangrahar, and Sayyaf from Paghman were influential in the provinces where they were born. The geographical extent of Harakat-i Enqelab, also resulted in a strong and durable presence among the Ghilzai and in the province of Ghazni. Muhammad Nabi was himself born into a Ghilzai tribe, the Astonekzai. In addition Ibrahim Mujaddidi had set up the Nur al-Modares school in Ghazni, and, since the recruitment of *taliban* was mainly local, his pupils were principally Ghilzai. The building of this *madrasa* reinforced what was already a long-standing link between the Mujaddidi and the Ghilzai tribes. Historically there had therefore been a Mujaddidi presence among the Ghilzai, which Muhammad Nabi inherited as leader of the Harakat-i Enqelab.

In this Hezb-i Islami was an exception; it was one of those rare cases where the leader of a party had no local or tribal roots. The regions of Hezb-i Islami's strongest influence, for example the neighbourhood of Kabul, were the result of a party structure in which town-dwellers predominated. In fact the Pushtuns of Imam Saheb, Hekmatyar's birthplace, were affiliated not to Hezb-i Islami but to Gaylani's Mahaz. Hekmatyar's membership of the Kharuti tribe, part of the Ghilzai confederation, led to no sizeable recruitment, since Hekmatyar suffered from two disadvantages: first, he was born in the province of Kunduz, far from the territorial base of his tribe, and secondly his family was not especially influential. He was therefore not seen as a representative of the Kharuti tribe, a fact demonstrated by Hezb-i Islami's recruitment among the Suleiman Khel, who were the Kharuti's traditional enemies. The Mustazaffin were also a particular case. The members of this group tended to be townsmen, often from Kabul or the north of Afghanistan, so that basing itself at Shashpul, near Bamyan, did not constitute a return to the leader's

---

fore both an urban distribution and a presence at the periphery of Hazarajat. This geographical position was partly what conditioned the strategy of the party, which was always in a minority in majority Sunni areas. In addition, though the commanders were mainly Qizilbash or *sadat*, the *mujahidin* were partly Hazaras, especially in Ghazni and around Kabul.

qowm of origin as in the case of Masud or Zabihullah, but was only the result of strategic considerations.

The leaders of the parties also mobilised commanders who had belonged to a particular political or Sufi brotherhood network. Because of the personalities of their leaders, Mahaz and Harakat-i Enqelab were the two main groups able to mobilise the Sufi brotherhood networks. Harakat-i Enqelab's links with Sufism were close because the Mujaddidi stood for the orthodox Naqshbandi tradition, and the two networks of *pirs* and *ulema* were difficult to distinguish, as in Herat.

Sayyed Ahmad Gaylani does not have links with all the Qadiris of Afghanistan, and most of those who recognised him as a *pir* did not follow the ritual of orthodox Sufism. His *murids* belonged mainly to Mahaz, especially in Ghazni and Jalalabad.[38] The presence of Gaylani's *murids* was substantial in Ghazni, for example among the *kuchis* (nomads), who joined Mahaz as a group. The largely Qadiri affiliation of the Ghilzai nomads had already been observed in the 1930s by Captain J. A. Robinson.[39] Among the various eastern Pushtun tribes the Ahmadzai mainly joined Mahaz at the outset of the war, in particular under commander Shamali who was active in the region of Jalalabad. The decision of the eastern tribes to throw in their lot with Gaylani was related to the presence of *murids*, as well as to the recruitment of families of *sadat*, such as that of Majruh.[40]

A commander who was a former Islamist militant rejoined his former party. This accounted for the presence of a Hezb-i Islami commander near Keshem in the heart of Badakhshan, a region which belonged mainly to the Jamiyat. This commander, Abdul Wadud, was the brother of Dr Omar, an Islamist executed by Daud who had been close to Hekmatyar. There were also some *ulema* who were former pupils of Rabbani, such as *mawlawi* Shirin in Wardak.

---

[38] The *pir* of Esfandeh, *pir* Ali Mahmad Khalifa, a Tajik, and *pir mullah* Sayyed 'Palawan' had links with Gaylani, who often visited them in pre-war times. In addition, the *amir-i welayati* of Mahaz, Sayyed Nazar Jan, was a Qadiri *pir* also linked to Gaylani.

[39] Captain J. A. Robinson, *Notes on Nomad Tribes of Eastern Afghanistan* (1st edition 1934), Lahore, 1980.

[40] When the Gaylani family arrived in 1905, Habibullah gave him a property at Chaharbagh, where *pir* Sayyed Hasan Gaylani was later buried. His tomb became a *ziarat* and many of the Gaylanis' *murids* are found today in this area.

Finally commanders joined various parties as the result of the similarity of their social origins—whether they were educated, *ulema*, or *khans*—to those of the leadership of the party. The educated class mainly joined the Jamiyat-i Islami and the Hezb-i Islami, which was therefore principally found within those groups. The individual affiliations of students, who were often from the technical faculties as with most Islamist movements, as well as those of former government employees, were of greater importance here than with most of the parties. The case of the province of Helmand showed that Hezb-i Islami's recruitment took place within groups affected by modernisation—schoolteachers, government employees and such like—while its recruitment in the rural and tribalised areas was negligible. Because of the lack of religious legitimacy of its leader, a 'negative' characteristic of Hezb-i Islami's recruitment was the small number of *ulema* who adhered to it and their restricted influence. The Islamist *ulema* in general gravitated towards Jamiyat-i Islami at the time of the schism in 1975, with none of the Islamists who had been at the Abu Hanifa government *madrasa* joining Hezb-i Islami. Those rare *ulema* within the Hezb-i Islami were mostly judges excluded from senior posts. It was not by chance that the two principal splits within Hezb-i Islami were carried out by *ulema*.[41]

Jamiyat-Islami's membership had the same element of educated laymen, but Rabbani's personality also attracted Islamist *ulema* trained at the government *madrasas*. These two groups were found among both the leadership and the commanders. As for the commanders, the party recruited more among the educated class than the *ulema*, the great majority of whom joined the Harakat-i Enqelab—even those who were Persian-speaking, as in Herat, since Rabbani's prestige could not be compared to that of the Mujaddidi family. The *ulema*-commanders of the Jamiyat were generally the products of government *madrasas*, such as that of Abu Hanifa in the case of *mawlawi* Alam at Mazar-i Sharif, or of the faculty of theology at Kabul in the case of Muhammad Ismail Tariq of Laghman.

---

[41] The second of these, which followed that of *mawlawi* Khales, was that carried out by Hekmatyar's deputy Qazi Amin, an Islamist *alem* from a government *madrasa*. From 1980 Qazi Amin, who did not relish his subservience to Hekmatyar, attempted to create a network of support for himself within the party. In 1982 he officially split from Hezb-i Islami, probably with financial aid from Sayyaf, who had an interest in weakening a competitor.

Those *ulema* who were not from the government *madrasas* mainly joined Harakat-i Enqelab because of the personality of its leader Muhammad Nabi, who had been close to Ibrahim Mujaddidi before the war. *Mawlawi* Khales's fundamentalist approach had also attracted *ulema* from the private *madrasas,* both in the west, from Kandahar to Farah, and in the east as in the case of Jalaluddin Haqqani and Shir *mullah* Khel. Among the Shi'ites, Hazara *ulema* made up the officials of Nasr[42] and Sepah.

The *khans* mostly joined Harakat-i Enqelab, Jebhe, Hezb-i Islami (Khales) and Mahaz. Harakat-i Enqelab was the party which attracted the most *khans* at the start of the war, since Muhammad Nabi represented a degree of continuity with the parliamentary regime, in contrast to the Islamist movements.

Within Jebhe, Sebghatullah Mujaddidi was an *alem* who because of his early exile had lost touch with the Islamist movements. In the absence of militant supporters, he relied on his membership of the Mujaddidi family rather than on his Islamist commitment in order to set up his party. Jebhe's recruitment came largely from two sources. The élite schools connected to the government of Zahir Shah, which in Daud's time, were often in opposition, provided the senior staff of the party. Merchants and artisans, often with links to the Sufi brotherhoods, made up the majority of the Jebhe's commanders and *mujahidin.*

Mahaz was the party of those linked to the old order—that of Zahir rather than of Daud. These were people who had suffered from modernisation: the *bazaaris* (shopkeepers and artisans), the governing class and the major notables. Inevitably, therefore, there was a generational difference between the officials of Mahaz and those of the other parties. The *bazaaris,* often Persian-speaking, also made up a significant portion of the membership of Mahaz because of their nostalgia for the days of royalty and the economic structures of that time, which were more favourable to the artisans.

[42] The presence of Nasr was particularly strong in the heart of Hazarajat, especially in Yakaolang, Lal o Sarjangal, Deh Kundi (Khedir). The Nasr officials were all *ulema*: *ustaz* Abdul Husein Sadeqi, of Turkmen, a disciple of *shaikh* Akay Alem (the representative of Khomeini in Afghanistan, who was assassinated under Taraqi); the *ayatollah* Abdul Ali Mazari of Charkent, who spent most of the war in Iran, where he was in close contact with the Iranian clergy; Nadeqi (of Deh Kundi); Azizullah Shafaq of Behsud; *ayatollah* Eftekhari (of Dara-yi Suf); *shaikh* Qurban Urfani; and *hojatoleslam* Zaedi (of Yaokalang).

In the tribalised regions of the east, the Pushtun *khans*, who were often the leaders of sub-groups of their tribe, followed *mawlawi* Khales. His ethnic origin, his reputation due to his pre-war radio broadcasts, and his status as an *alem* enabled him to recruit in a tribal area. His role was therefore not dissimilar to that of the charismatic *mullahs* who crop up in the history of the Afghan frontier.

The Shi'ite Harakat-i Islami commanders were generally not *ulema*, which clearly differentiated them from the pro-Khomeini revolutionary parties. Harakat-i Islami recruited notables: merchants, landowners such as Din Muhammad at Charkent, and some from the educated class such as Dr Shah Jan at Ghazni.

The imperative of differentiation. Membership of a party also followed a system of differentiation: two adjacent but competing groups would affiliate to different and even opposing parties. Local rivalries were translated into political conflicts, and perpetuated as such. There were many examples: the affiliation of the Andar tribe to Harakat-i Islami increased the tendency for the Suleiman Khel tribe to join another party—Hezb-i Islami—because of pre-existing tensions. With two such groups in the same party there would be the risk for the minority group of the power of the majority group being reinforced because it would be better represented in the leadership of the party. In addition, the coexistence of two groups within the same party would prove unmanageable in the case of an armed clash. Through its re-introduction of the autonomy of individual actors, this imperative based on local configurations militated against what could have become the automatic operation of affiliation founded on proximity.

Sometimes the process of affiliation by differentiation reproduced the pattern produced by proximity; however two groups might be similar in macro-ethnic terms—both Pushtun, for example—and still join different parties. This provides an explanation for the presence, at first sight surprising, of some parties in areas which were alien to them. The adherence of *mullah* Naqibullah to Jamiyat-i Islami seems a case in point. Naqibullah was an Alikozai Pushtun, of the Durrani confederation, from the Arghandab valley north of Kandahar. None of his social characteristics—a Pushtun small landowner who had not been politically active before the war—appeared to predispose him to join Jamiyat-i Islami. However, in this region Mahaz

membership was largely Barakzai, Harakat-i Enqelab was dominated by Ghilzai from the neighbouring provinces of Ghazni and
Logar, and Hezb-i Islami was locally Ghilzai. Therefore it was probably more logical for *mullah* Naqibullah to join Jamiyat-i Islami,
which was locally 'neutral' in tribal terms and which also possessed
substantial resources. In addition, the fact of being ethnically marginal within Jamiyat-i Islami may offer advantages, since the party
was impelled to give priority to a Pushtun commander who could
endow it with legitimacy nationally. The same explanation holds
good for the adherence of *raïs* Abdul Wahid of Baghran, in the province of Helmand, to Jamiyat-i Islami in 1988, after a long conflict
with Nasim Akhundzada, his neighbour, when both at first belonged to the same party, Harakat-i Enqelab. In this case strategic considerations may have predominated: Ismail Khan, himself a member
of Jamiyat-i Islami, had made an agreement with *raïs* Abdul Wahid
concerning control over the road between Herat and Quetta.

In a situation of marked fragmentation, the likelihood was that all
the parties would achieve representation, for reasons other than the
imperative of proximity, since the groups present were at least as numerous as the parties. Only the choice of the dominant group, if
there was one, followed the imperative of proximity or representation, while the remainder could be regarded as random choices. The
sole exception to this rule was that two strongly opposed groups would
often belong to the most openly antagonistic parties—e.g. Hezb-i
Islami and Jamiyat-i Islami. Such motiveless partisan affiliations were
found especially in Kandahar, at least up to 1988–9, after which the
pattern tended to become simpler. Many groups adopted contradictory and sometimes very fluid affiliations; adherence here was entirely subservient to an imperative of pure differentiation. There was
also a good example of fragmentation around the town of Kunduz,
where the political map was especially complicated. Within the town
there were populations from all over Afghanistan who had come to
cultivate the land in this northern region. The distribution of the
parties seemed largely random, except for Aref Khan, a Pushtun and a
son of the former mayor of the town, whose pre-war Islamist sympathies had led him to Jamiyat-i Islami.

Hezb-i Islami's recruitment among the Pushtuns was a recurrent
theme in these choices of affiliation, which as a result came to re-
semble an imperative of proximity. Thus the Pushtuns were often

members of Hezb-i Islami when they were locally in the minority, as in the province of Baghlan or at Mazar-i Sharif. Similarly the Ghilzai of Kandahar, who were mainly of the Hottak tribe, were largely Hezb-i Islami in a Durrani environment. However in majority Ghilzai regions, the Ghilzai did not join Hezb-i Islami, but preferred Harakat-i Enqelab. Groups in minority situations joined Hezb-i Islami since this enabled them aggressively to defend their specificity, which was not as much encouraged by the other parties. This provided a good illustration of the effects of the leader's situation: Hekmatyar, himself a minority Pushtun, recruited among populations who saw themselves in a similar light.[43]

Affiliations on the basis of differentiation had the general implication that the parties were more broadly instrumentalised, but they also affected relationships between groups, in general by exacerbating tensions, since party conflicts on a national scale were reproduced at the local level. Affiliations based on context were more numerous among populations organised on a segmentary basis, such as in the eastern provinces and Kandahar, and in multi-ethnic zones, where the need for differentiation was most obvious.

The parties and the refugees

From 1979 refugees arrived in Pakistan at the rate of tens of thousands a month.[44] They were estimated in October 1979 at some 200,000, and would reach a million at the end of 1980 and 2 million in 1981. The largest number of registered refugees was seen in 1990, with 3.2 million, to which around half a million should be added who were not registered.[45] After this, return to Afghanistan became an increasing phenomenon. Figures provided by the UN High Commission for

---

[43] To take a further example, Hezb-i Islami was very largely Pushtun in the province of Baghlan. The Pushtuns were relatively recently settled in the region, between 1930 and 1950, and their relations with the Tajiks and the Ismailis were sometimes tense as a result of competition for land. The coming to power of the Parchamis did not improve the situation of the Pushtuns, since Babrak Karmal made a preferential alliance with the Ismailis, whose support was necessary for the control of the crossroads of Pul-i Khumri. The majority adherence of the Pushtuns of Baghlan to Hezb-i Islami was therefore likely.

[44] On the number of refugees in Iran and Pakistan and their situation, see *Encyclopaedia Iranica* VII (4), New York: Bibliotheca Press, 1995, pp. 383 ff.

[45] *Ibid.*, p. 383.

Refugees have been criticised, since several hundreds of thousands were not counted, either through delay or to escape supervision.

In Pakistan, to simplify the situation, two waves of refugees may be distinguished. Until approximately 1984 the refugees, who were up to 80 per cent Pushtuns, came from the south and the southwest. In some cases their exodus was a protest—a *hijra*—but more often the population simply fled the fighting. Generally they arrived in an organised group, a clan or a village, under the leadership of a *khan* or *mullah*. There was no automatic linkage between the number of departures and the intensity of the fighting, as it is showed by the province of Kandahar, although the exodus from Kunar could be directly linked to the fighting. After 1984 there were more from the north, but they were always a minority among new arrivals. Their arrival was related to the fighting; sometimes to conflicts between groups of *mujahidin*, as well as to bombing and to the deliberate destruction of the harvest. Their exodus, often involving only individuals or families, was undertaken clandestinely, since the main roads had been closed by the government.

The majority of the refugees in Pakistan, around 2.3 million, lived in the North-West Frontier Province. In Karachi there were also 200,000 refugees who were not in general gathered into camps. In 1982 the Pakistani administration had also set up a camp in the Punjab, which by 1987 had a population of 172,000.[46] Because of the scale of the aid, the material conditions of life were not bad. The rate of infant mortality was lower than in neighbouring Pakistani villages. Solidarity groups—clan, village or tribe—were reproduced within the camps. The difference in the way of life was above all due to the lack of land, which had consequences in daily activity and social status. In addition, the size of the groups of people was larger, in Pakistan averaging several tens of thousands.

The refugee population was a considerable prize for the Afghan political parties.[47] For this reason, out of aid totalling $1 billion intended for the refugee camps in Pakistan throughout the entire conflict, it may be estimated that only half reached its destination, the remainder being divided between the Pakistani administration and

[46] Brigitte Picard, 'Les Damnés du Penjab', *Les Nouvelles d'Afghanistan*, special issue 'Les réfugiés afghans', December 1987.
[47] Among the refugees in Iran the role of political organisations was more limited since there were no camps and only the Shi'ite organisations were active.

the Afghan parties, which were active in the camps where they competed with the traditional notables as intermediaries with the administration. Even more than in Afghanistan, the possession of a party card became universal—for the Pakistan administration this document also served as an identity card. The Islamist parties, principally Hezb-i Islami and Jamiyat-i Islami, were the most active in organising the population, with schools, security committees and so on.

The refugees' dependence on aid enabled the parties to present themselves as intermediaries and therefore to acquire real power;[48] they were able to control the refugees and negotiate with the Pakistani state. A second factor, of some importance, was the absence of arms in the camps, which meant a lower risk of vendettas and the consequent fragmentation of parties. Finally, the militants did not need to justify their local strength in numbers. The displacement of populations gave rise to new relationships and facilitated interventions by outsiders.

One may nevertheless question how real were the affiliations to Islamist parties. In some camps such as those in Baluchistan[49] the low level of influence of these parties was attributable to the persistence of strong tribal structures among the refugees. Frequent pro-royalist demonstrations and the hostile reception given to Hekmatyar during his visits were evidence of this. In 1987 the Afghan Information Center, directed by Sayed Bahodine Majrouh,[50] carried out a survey of political opinion among the refugees in the camps. The most

---

[48] See the analyses of Pierre Centlivres and Micheline Centlivres-Demont, 'Hommes d'influence et hommes de partis. L'organisation politique dans les villages de réfugiés afghans au Pakistan' in Erwin Grötzbach (ed.), *Neue Beiträge zur Afghanistanforschung*, Liestal: Bibliotheca Afghanica, 1988, and Micheline Centlivres-Demont, 'Les réfugiés afghans au Pakistan: gestion, enjeux, perspectives' in Rocardo Bocco, Mohammad-Reza Djalili (eds), *Moyen-Orient. Migration, démocratisation, médiations*, Genève: Institut Universitaire des Hautes Etudes Internationales, 1994.

[49] On the refugees in Baluchistan, see A. S. Ahmed, 'The impact of the Afghan refugees on ethnicity and politics in Baluchistan', *Central Asian Survey* 9 (3), 1990, pp. 43–56.

[50] B. Majrouh, the son of Sayyed Shamsuddin Majruh (a former Minister and senator), who was close to Mahaz, ran the Afghan Information Center until his assassination in February 1988. He also left a significant body of poetry, part of which has been translated into French: see particularly *Le suicide et le chant. Poésie populaire des femmes pachtounes*, Paris: Les Cahiers des Brisants, 1988 (translation and adaptation by André Velter).

striking finding was the popularity of the former king Zahir Shah and the desire for a negotiated peace.[51] The selection of the sample was perhaps questionable, but it was also clear that there was no large-scale ideological affiliation to the Islamist parties.

[51] 62% wanted a negotiated solution and 73% wanted unity between the parties. The survey was conducted among a sample of 1,787 'educated' Afghans, a restriction which raised questions of methodology.

Part III. THE DYNAMICS OF CONFRONTATION

5. The Kabul Regime

'*Amadand o sukhtand o raftand* (They came, they burned, they left).' (Hafez)

In the history of the Kabul regime three separate periods can be distinguished. From 1980 to 1986 the Soviets applied a policy whose long-term aim was to turn Afghanistan into a new Central Asian Republic. Between 1986 and 1989, the failure of their project drove them to prepare the ground for withdrawal, while at the same time attempting to leave their Afghan ally stronger through a policy of 'National Reconciliation'. From 1989 to 1992 the regime survived with Russian assistance, but it became progressively weaker. This chapter examines the internal balance of forces within the administration, as well as the Soviet-Afghan strategy and the preparations for retreat, together with the survival of the regime until 1992.

The Party under Karmal

Under Babrak Karmal there was neither institutional stability nor well-defined legal order. His 'ten-point document' published in 1980, served as a provisional constitution till 1987, when the Constitution was finally adopted by a *Loya Jirga*. Legitimation by way of a popular vote was never a priority, even at the symbolic level. In theory the authority of the state rested with the twenty-seven members of the Revolutionary Council who elected the Praesidium, but these institutions were in reality subordinate to the Party. This was structured in the classic manner: the Central Committee, with seventy-three members, elected the eight members of the Politburo and the eight members of the Central Committee's secretariat. Some of the members of the Politburo—including Najibullah, Nur Ahmad Nur, Saleh Muhammad Zeary and Babrak Karmal—also sat on the secretariat of the Central Committee, which further reinforced the concentra-

173

tion of power. There were also the primary organisations of the Party
and its mass organisations, which, outside Kabul, were largely theoretical. In any case the Party never achieved functional harmony because of constant factional clashes. The government lacked unity,
since the most powerful ministries were divided between the Khalqis, who held the ministries of the interior and defence, and the Parchamis, who held the Prime Minister's office and controlled the State
Information Service, the KHAD (Khedamat-i Ittala'at-i Daulati).

A further problem was that the leadership was unable to impose
its will without Soviet support. Indeed, the direct implication of
Babrak Karmal in the invasion had undermined his legitimacy even
within Party circles. He was never able to extend his authority over
the whole of the Hezb-i Demokratik-i Khalq-i Afghanistan; still less
was he able to achieve wider credibility. Babrak Karmal never tried
to establish a cult of personality as did Taraqi or Amin, probably on
the instructions of the Soviets whose desire was to avoid the per-
sonalisation of power. In fact, he governed with the help of a small
family group, together with a number of figures supported by Moscow. In addition to Karmal himself this nucleus included Anahita
Ratebzad, who was his mistress; Mahmud Baryalay, his half-brother,
who was married to one of Anahita's daughters; Nur Ahmad Nur,
also married to a daughter of Anahita; Shah Muhammad Dost, whose
daughter was married to one of Karmal's brothers; and Generals
Yasin Sadiqi and Abdul Wakil, who were Karmal's cousins. Besides,
some appointments were made directly by the Soviets, including
Watanjar, Gulabzoy, Mazduryar, Tanai, Mohmand, Kawal, Panjshiri,
Nazar Mohammed and Gul Dad.

Attempts to widen Karmal's support within the Party were often
prompted by the Soviets, but ended in failure. Some Parchamis opposed him, notably Wakil, Mazdak, Kawiani, Suleiman Laeq, Mangal
and Khazemjo; while the few Khalqis recruited by him were Soviet
trusties formerly close to Taraqi. At the insistence of this group
Asadullah Sarwari, a former head of the secret services, and in that
capacity responsible for the anti-Parchami purge, even came briefly
to hold the post of Prime Minister under Karmal, before being
named ambassador to Mongolia in July 1980: in effect a sentence of
exile. The Parchamis did not have the resources for a purge which
would have decapitated the army and weakened the Party, with the
result that only those close to Amin were removed, leaving Karmal

to govern with a very limited Party base. In the event the Soviet invasion and the return of the Parchamis, who had been brusquely displaced by Taraqi, constituted a major shock to the Khalqis, whose sense of nationalism was unsettled by the presence of foreign troops. Karmal was therefore obliged to govern with a Party whose membership, 75 per cent Khalqi, rejected him. The Khalqis always retained their majority within it, and the bid by the Parchamis to gerrymander the national Party conference in March 1982 by annulling the results of elections in the provinces favourable to the Khalqis ended in failure.

In spite of their original intentions, the Soviets never succeeded in reunifying the Party, since political allegiances worked on the model of the *qowms*. Purges, far from eliminating opposition, only succeeded in deepening splits and exacerbating vendettas.[1] The tensions between the Khalq and the Parcham were never resolved and only the Soviet presence, and pressure from the *mujahidin*, prevented them on the whole from turning into armed conflicts.

The three strategic dimensions

With the limited resources at their disposal the Soviets adopted three complementary strategies: Sovietisation, pacification and open warfare. First the authorities attempted to sovietise the Afghan towns on the model of the Central Asian republics. Secondly, pacification was initiated, employing various tactics such as the setting-up of government militias, recruitment of notables, a nationalities policy and the institution of a government-backed clergy. The objective in this case was not to sovietise: the government aimed only to maintain the neutrality of the population in order to establish buffer zones against the regions held by the guerrillas. The intention, therefore, in contrast with the Khalqi ideal, was gradually to pacify particular regions or segments of the population, while at the same time reestablishing the legitimacy of the state. In the end open warfare broke out in the regions outside government control, where the principal objective of the Soviet-Afghan army had been to expel the population and thus weaken the guerrillas.

---

[1] See Olivier Roy, 'Le double code afghan. Marxisme et tribalisme', *Revue française de science politique*, 35 (5), October 1985.

Sovietisation. The inauguration of the first bridge over the Amu Darya between Termez, then in the Soviet Union, and the Afghan town of Ayratan symbolised the incorporation of Afghanistan within the Soviet sphere. The process of integration depended on direct control by Moscow, and at the same time the promotion of Afghan relations with the Central Asian republics. In the event the reaction of the Central Asian communists to the invasion of Afghanistan was positive, since Afghanistan's inclusion in the socialist camp tended to reinforce their influence in relation to Moscow. In particular the Uzbek leader Rashidov made a point of welcoming Afghan students.[2] In the early years of the occupation, however, the influence of the Central Asian republics remained low. Only after the Soviet retreat were their relations with Afghanistan closer, especially with the latter's northern provinces.

Integration had an institutional dimension. In addition to the occupying troops, some 3,000 Soviet advisers, of whom half were soldiers, oversaw the totality of Afghanistan's institutions, each of which was directly linked to the corresponding Soviet organ. Russian was the customary working language in these bilateral contacts. The Soviets took charge of the general direction of the Kabul regime, and even of day-to-day administration. The most influential Russian figures did not hold official positions. The ambassador[3] had little real influence, but the senior KGB official played a key role. Most Afghans who were in contact with the occupiers stress the 'superiority complex' of the Soviets in their dealings with the Afghans.

For the people Sovietisation meant ideological training in the schools and the indoctrination of workers and officials within the unions, militias, women's organisations etc. Publications in Russian became more numerous, and television propaganda was insistent. Thousands of children were sent to study in Central Asia with the aim of preparing a new Sovietised generation to take the country over by the year 2000. The transformation of urban society continued its progress in various fields, in particular in relation to women, who shed their veils and adopted western dress in Kabul and more

---

[2] Marie Broxup, 'The Soviets in Afghanistan: the anatomy of a takeover', *Central Asian Survey*, 1 (4), 1983.
[3] The post was occupied in the early 1980s by Fikret Ahmedzhanovich Tabiev, an Uzbek-speaking Tatar from Bukhara.

timidly in Mazar-i Sharif. Integration also had its economic dimension: Afghanistan's gas reserves were exploited by the Soviet Union, which did not buy its gas at the international market price, while production fell to half its pre-1978 level. On the other hand the Soviets never attempted any collectivisation of the Afghan economy, especially of trade.

The counter-insurgency. Sovietisation required mastery of the military situation. The Soviets therefore tried to crush the resistance by indirect strategies, a technique which had served them well in the 1920s against the Basmachis.[4] In the Afghan case the KGB was the principal instigator, and the Afghan secret service, the KHAD,[5] was the key instrument of the counter-insurgency policy.

During the war the secret services became a complex organisation, probably the best financed and most efficient institution in Afghanistan. Since accounts of it are fragmentary, the synthesis here suggested does not claim to be more than tentative, being based on a number of interviews with former KHAD officials. From the moment he took power Karmal was to make the KHAD the principal instrument of his policy, while ensuring that its recruitment was primarily Parchami, with the particular aim of countering the Khalqi dominance in the armed forces. The KGB official who oversaw the KHAD therefore took a detailed interest in appointments to the Afghan army, where final decisions were taken in consultation with Soviet officers. Relations between the KHAD and the Afghan army

---

[4] Even before the invasion, the Afghan communists had turned to the Central Asian model. On 8 October 1978 the Khalqi regime set up the first 'Committees for the Defence of the Revolution' in the towns, on the pattern of those set up in Central Asia in the 1920s to counter the Basmachis. See also Marie Broxup, 'The Basmachis', *Central Asian Survey* 2 (1), 1983, and Joseph Castagné, *Les Basmatchis*, Paris: Leroux, 1925.

[5] The employment of spies was a tradition of the Afghan authorities since Abdul Rahman Khan, but a modern intelligence service was only set up in the 1930s. After 1978 the new services were called AGSA (Da Afghanistan da Gatay da Satanay Edara; Afghanistan Security Service), then under Amin KAM (Da Kargarano Istikhbarati Muasasa; Worker's Security Institution). Karmal then set up the KHAD (Khedamat-i Ettelaat-i Daulat; State Information Services) which was to become under Najibullah the WAD (Wezarat-i Amniat-i Daulati; Ministry for State Security), before disappearing along with the regime in 1992. A Riasat-i Amniat-i Melli (National Security Services) was later to operate during the presidency of Rabbani.

were therefore consistently bad. The KHAD was directly linked with the KGB: several hundred Soviet advisers, of Russian, Uzbek and Tajik origin, ran the service, down as far as the regional level. In this sense integration was more real than in the Afghan army, where officers were often in conflict with their Soviet colleagues.

Between 1980 and 1986 the KHAD was run by Najibullah, who had been personally selected by the Soviets, and in particular by Yuri Andropov. At the head of the organisation the director was assisted by between two and four deputies, responsible for some twelve departments, whose number varied from time to time.[6] Najibullah appointed to the KHAD's key positions people with whom he had personal ties. On the evidence of known cases, his family and professional networks, including the Faculty of Medicine, seem to have been crucial.[7] The KHAD employed between 30,000 and 40,000 official agents, who were excused military service, and possibly around the same number of clandestine or unofficial agents. The organisation had its own military unit, including a national guard. The regional organisations were modelled on the central organisation, with a staff of 1,000 in regions where the KHAD functioned fully, for example in Kandahar, Jalalabad, Herat, Kunduz and Mazar-i Sharif. An idea of the importance given to the KHAD can also be gleaned from its finances. At the outset its budget was not fixed, credits being made available according to need. In 1991 it is said to have been granted $300 million.[8]

The primary objective of the counter-insurgency was the re-establishment of authority and of the basic legitimacy of the state in the countryside. To this end the regime set aside its most controversial policies; thus agrarian reform was discontinued by Karmal in March 1981, only to be resumed in February 1982, although it now took account of the 'traditions and religious sentiments of the

---

[6] For a list of the various offices and Najibullah's deputies in the KHAD, see Mohammad Nasir Kemal, *op. cit.*, pp. 442–3.

[7] For example, Najibullah's deputy, General Baqi, a Pushtun engineer from Paktya, was one of Najibullah's distant relatives. Tareq, a Tajik from Parwan, who was the official in charge of the KHAD's internal security, was Najibullah's childhood friend, while his successor, Dr Shir, a Pushtun from Nangrahar, knew Najibullah at the Faculty of Medicine and became his confidant. It was Dr Shir who transferred Najibullah's money to India when the regime fell.

[8] This figure was given by a person close to Najibullah (interview, Kabul, 1997).

people', a position which concealed nothing less than the discontinuation of the redistribution of land. In addition, this policy had four concomitant aspects: the establishment of an official clergy, the policy of nationalities, the recruitment of notables and the establishment of militias.

In relation to religious policy the era of the Soviets represented a break from the Khalqi period.[9] Atheist propaganda campaigns, a frequent occurrence under Taraqi, came to an end, and the regime presented itself as the protector of Islam. Religious freedom was guaranteed in the provisional Constitution of 1980, particularly for the Shi'ites. In the same way, in cases where the legal situation was fluid, judges were allowed to turn to the *shariat* as a source of law. The regime began once more to organise the *hajj*, and multiplied its contacts with Islamic institutions in the Soviet Union and elsewhere. Mosque construction and the restoration of *ziarats* were also utilised for propaganda purposes. Also on occasions the regime resumed the use of Islamic terminology. Those who died fighting for the government were referred to as *shahids*, and the struggle against the guerrillas became a *jihad*. The opposition was stigmatised, in a Quranic expression, as *munafiqun*, or hypocrites. They were also accused of destroying mosques and assassinating *mullahs*, which was sometimes true, since the *mujahidin* often targeted religious figures who had pledged their loyalty to the regime. In addition the *mullahs* were supposed to aid the regime in the dissemination of the revolution, which was presented as a continuation of the reforming policies of Amanullah. The KHAD's Bureau 7 was given the task of secretly disseminating instructions for the *mullahs'* sermons, and of maintaining surveillance over the urban mosques. The Kabul government also made use of *pirs* as agents, for example in the province of Logar, in the *uluswali* of Baraki Barak.

The indoctrination of an Afghan clergy on the Soviet model was an important objective of the counter-insurgency. Karmal gave a new impetus to the transformation of the *ulema* into state officials, a process which had already been under way for a century. The Jamiyat ul-Ulema (Society of Ulema), dormant under Taraqi, was reactivated. In 1982 the authorities set up an Edare-i Shu'un-i Islami (Department of Islamic Affairs) answering directly to the Prime Minister.

[9] See Asta Alesen, *Islam and Politics in Afghanistan*, London: Curzon Press, 1995.

The Shura-yi Ali-i Ulema wa Ruhanyun (Council of the Ulema and the Religious) attached to this department had a consultative role, with *ulema* designated by the Prime Minister; from 1983 the department was attached directly to the Paderwatan (see below) and in March 1985 it became the Wezarat-i Islami wa Awqaf (Ministry of Islamic Affairs and Waqfs) headed by *mawlawi* Abdul Wali Hujat.[10] In spite of his efforts, the government did not succeed in attracting well-known *ulema*: the majority of the religious officials were illiterate *mullahs*, educated in the private *madrasas*.

The second plank of the pacification programme, the policy of nationalities, also failed. In the Soviet Union the communist theory of nationalities laid down by Stalin was unquestioned before Gorbachev, and for the Afghan communists it was the unchallenged intellectual framework. A nationality was defined, according to this 'realist' approach, by a language, a territory, a culture—which might include a religion—and by common economic interests. In reality the practice of the Afghan communists put into play a definition of nationalities which served the political objectives of the authorities. The government distinguished six major ethnic communities: Baluchis, Pushtuns, Tajiks, Uzbeks, Turkmens and Hazaras, together with two minor ones, the Pashaïs and the Nuristanis. Following the Soviet model the communist authorities permitted these groups a large measure of cultural autonomy[11] in exchange for a strict ideological control which relegated cultures to the level of folklore. The objective was to reinforce ethnic segmentation in order to enhance state control. In the context of Central Asia this policy, applied over the long term, led to

[10] A Tajik from the province of Takhar, Abdul Wali Hujat was a former official of the Ministry of Justice who was imprisoned for four years under Zahir for his unorthodox views. He was close to leftist movements such as Setam-i Melli, and became the public prosecutor of Herat under Taraqi, then president of the Department of Islamic Affairs in 1983, finally becoming a Minister in 1985. For an analysis and an excellent biography, see Chantal Lobato, *Un islam conservateur au service du communisme: Kaboul 1980–1985*, Paris: EHSS, 1986, p. 75 and 'Kaboul 1980–1986: un Islam officiel pour légitimer le pouvoir communiste', *Central Asian Survey*, vol. 7 no. 2/3, pp. 83–8, 1988.

[11] The foundations of this policy were in fact laid from the inception of the regime, with decree no. 4, which allowed the use of Turkmen, Baluchi, Uzbek and Nuristani as 'national languages'. The authorities established radio broadcasting in these languages. Two newspapers, *Gorës* and *Yulduz* (in Uzbek and Turkmen respectively), were published in Kabul.

the creation of real nationalisms—Uzbek, Turkmen and more tenuously Tajik—which had not existed some decades earlier.[12]

On the institutional level the Ministry for Tribes and Nationalities replaced the Ministry for Frontiers, which had traditionally been responsible for the management of the eastern Pushtun tribes. In the context of the policy of nationalities the government published periodicals such as *Melliatah-yi Baradar* (Brother Peoples) in the principal languages of Afghanistan. In April 1987 individual systems of transliteration were developed for Baluchi, Pashaï and Nuristani, which at least in theory boosted local particularism at the expense of the *jihad*. The policy of nationalities was also a means of exerting pressure on neighbouring states where the inhabitants belonged to the same ethnic communities. The Baluchis, who were also represented in Iran and Pakistan, were awarded a national day by the communist government, which at the time gave refuge to Baluchis of the Pakistani opposition.[13] On 19 October 1980 Karmal announced on Radio Moscow his support for 'the struggle of the peoples of Baluchistan and Pushtunistan'. There was constant contact between the Pathan nationalist movements and the Kabul government. In 1988 Khan Abdul Ghaffur Khan, the historic leader of the Pathan nationalists, was buried in Jalalabad in accordance with his wishes.

This model was to a great extent inappropriate to Afghan circumstances and therefore impracticable. In reality, as long as the Soviets were there, belief in the *jihad* stood out in opposition to all ethnic and national demands. In addition, the ethnic communities did not enjoy homogeneous territories owing to the displacement of the Pushtun tribes, the territorial dispersal of the Tajiks, and so on, while in general there was an arbitrary quality to the criteria defining a nationality. For example, the Nuristani dialect adopted as a standard was not understood in all the valleys of Nuristan. Finally, the means employed had only a restricted effect: publications had an impact only on an urban and literate public, i.e. a small minority, although radio broadcasts had a larger potential audience.

Only one community, that of the Hazaras, approximated at all closely to the government model. In this territory, which was in any

---

[12] Olivier Roy, *La nouvelle Asie centrale ou la fabrique des nations*, Paris: Seuil, 1998.
[13] Witnesses were able to visit these camps in 1978 (personal information from Stéphane Thiollier).

case strategically unimportant, the Soviets refrained from military operations in favour of an indirect approach. The war was thus the cause of an alteration in the relationship between the Hazaras and the state, especially under Karmal. The regime's recruitment policy and the massive migration of Hazaras to Kabul during the war led in due course to a marked increase in their numbers within the administration. However, attempts to open a dialogue between the government and the Hazaras made no progress, since Hazarajat was the scene of a civil war between pro-Khomeini revolutionary groups and conservatives. The main issue was the refusal of the Kabul government to recognise a defined Hazara territory, probably because of Khalqi objections, since it would have opened the door to a form of federalism. During this phase of the war the policy of nationalities finally collapsed, since the macro-ethnic groups—Pushtuns, Baluchis, Uzbeks and Tajiks—were unable to provide the framework for a political mobilisation. To take effect allegiances needed to be pledged at local level.

After the disaster of the Khalqi period, the Soviets aimed at mastering the situation by enlisting the notables, hoping thus to pacify the countryside and isolate the *mujahidin*. The government's aim was to play its part once again in the traditional pattern of relations between the state and the local notables, while blocking the rise of new élites, especially the Islamists. On 15 June 1981 the Jebhe-yi Melli-yi Paderwatan (National Front for the Fatherland) was set up, with the purported aim of providing an apolitical structure for the notables, in the context of which they could support the government. The Paderwatan brought together peasant organisations, religious and other groups which were intended to 'represent' the Afghan people, and strove to continue the modernising and nationalist tradition established by Amanullah.

In the government's scheme the Paderwatan was intended primarily for the Durrani Pushtuns, in general with a leader from one of the great families of Kandahar. In spite of this the establishment of the apparatus of the Paderwatan was more successful in the predominantly Uzbek northwest provinces. In these regions the *mujahidin* found keeping up their resistance harder than elsewhere because of their distance from the sanctuary of Pakistan, their proximity to the Soviet Union and the difficult terrain, much of it desert. The Uzbeks were also more receptive to the Soviet approach, perhaps because of the neighbouring presence of Uzbekistan which presented a model of modernisation at a time when Uzbeks were in a minority in Afghanistan and had traditionally been excluded from power.

Although there were some successes, the achievements of the Paderwatan were disappointing, especially in the view of the amount of effort invested. By placing their reliance on the traditional notables who were in decline, the Kabul authorities were able to enhance their power only marginally. In addition, notables who swore allegiance were obliged to flee to the towns, thus losing their rural clientele. But in spite of these shortcomings the Paderwatan continued to provide the political framework for recruitment between 1982 and 1987.

Beyond the recruitment of the notables, the Paderwatan's objective was to facilitate the formation of militias, the distribution of which was dictated by geographical considerations. These arose from the need to establish buffer zones between the towns, which the government sought to Sovietise, and the countryside, where the *mujahidin* were too well established for the army to achieve anything beyond combing operations which always needed to be repeated.[14] Gradually militias began to be deployed along the roads, as between Kabul and Mazar-i Sharif, and between Kandahar and Spin Boldak, as well as on the outskirts of the towns where they provided an essential reinforcement for the security perimeters set up between 1983 and 1987 to limit the incursions of the *mujahidin*. It was in these zones that the efforts of the government began to take effect, and the level of military pressure frequently obliged villagers to choose between exile and compromise with the authorities. As a *quid pro quo* for pledges of allegiance the government provided material help, for example with electricity supplies and tractors for the harvest, without demanding ideological commitment in return. The government's classification of the militias was complex. To simplify, a distinction was drawn between units formed by the government and pre-existing groups which had rallied to the government's side.

The militias formed by the government enlisted their members on an individual basis, sometimes because of ideological consider-

---

[14] This section follows the lines of an article written by the author in collaboration with Chantal Lobato, 'The militia in Afghanistan', *Central Asian Survey* 8 (4), 1989, pp. 95–108.

ations, but more often because for financial reasons. Generally they were deployed in areas where some measure of industrialisation had occurred, and where the population was not too strongly in the grip of traditional communal solidarities. For example in Lashkargah, in the province of Helmand, Khano's militia recruited men of all ethnic communities as individuals, though nepotism and family connections, here as elsewhere, played their part.[15] In this militia the ideological content was strong, with a violent rejection of the *mullahs* and of traditional society. The officers continued to employ outrightly atheistic language even after the fall of Kabul to the *mujahidin*. In the province of Jozjan, Rashid Dostam's[16] militia, one of the largest in the country, also proceeded on the basis of individual recruitment. Rashid Dostam, a former gas employee, was typical of a class of Afghans at odds with the traditional rural values. Sometimes landless peasants who had benefited from the agrarian reforms organised themselves to defend their gains, for instance in Kandahar in the Arghandab valley.

The principal purpose of the urban militias was to preserve urban security and to occupy territory in the wake of Soviet-Afghan offensives, in order to 'assist the peasants' and enlighten them about 'the nature of the Revolution'. For example, after the Soviet offensive of July 1984 in Panjshir, 4–600 members of the Sepah-yi Enqelab (Army of the Revolution) were sent for two months into the valley, in an operation extensively covered by Kabul television. The operation was repeated over a further two weeks in 1985, with equally little result. That same year the dispatch of 200 members of this militia to Kandahar was also a failure, particularly because of the resignations it prompted among the militiamen, who were made to stand guard over government buildings and whose sojourn was compulsorily prolonged. On the other hand, the government's urban militias functioned relatively smoothly in the towns of the north-west such as Maymana and Shibergan, which had never been threatened by the *mujahidin*.

---

[15] Interview with Khano, autumn 1992.

[16] Dostam was born into a poor family at Khwaja Doki, near Shiberghan. His father was a farmer. Dostam was employed in the gasworks at Shibergan, where he was recruited by the Parchamis. He became a militiaman and did six months military training in Kazakhstan in 1980. Cf. Ludwig W. Adamec, *op. cit.*, p. 66.

However, in the formation of such militias gaining the allegiance of pre-existing groups was a much more effective procedure than individual recruitment. Such groups, if sufficiently large and aggressive, formed rural militias (*Ghund-i Qawmi* or *Kandak*); others were confined to maintaining the security villages under the patronage of the Paderwatan. Militia groups came from various ideological backgrounds: leftists, religious minorities and former *mujahidin*.

The majority of the leftist groups had signed up to the government of Babrak Karmal. In the Taraqi-Amin period government repression constrained the Setamis to retire to the countryside where the militants, most of whom were townsmen, had few roots.[17] In particular their 'progressive' positions were not enough to earn them the support of the peasants when they were attacked by the *mujahidin*, which placed them in an untenable situation. After the Soviet intervention, which brought about the Parcham's return to power, the Setamis progressively rallied to Babrak Karmal, who was a personal friend of Taher Badakhshi, the historic leader of the Setami movement. SAFZA rejoined the government in 1981, although it did not officially take the plunge till 1986 in the framework of the policy of national reconciliation. The Setamis were the source of important militias in the north-east, where they were well represented before the war. Masud's defeat at Shahr-i Bozorg in Badakhshan in 1990 was largely due to the intervention of these militias, though they were helped by Hezb-i Islami.

The Ismaili community, founded upon religious rather than ethnic solidarity, was also courted by the government. The Ismailis lived in two strategic locations: one at Pul-i Khumri, a key position on the road linking Kabul with Mazar-i Sharif, and the other close to the Pakistani frontier in the province of Badakhshan. Although the community based in Badakhshan had too little demographic weight to play an independent role, that in Pul-i Khumri found itself at the heart of the conflict. After a phase in opposition during the Khalqi period, the Ismailis cooperated with the government, since they were repelled by the Islamic position; the Sunnis did not regard them as Muslims. The government was therefore able to recruit them whole-

---

[17] From the moment of the Parchamis' displacement by the Khalqis, the Setamis were subject to severe repression. Taher Badakhshi and *mawlawi* Bahes, who had been imprisoned since the summer of 1978, were executed.

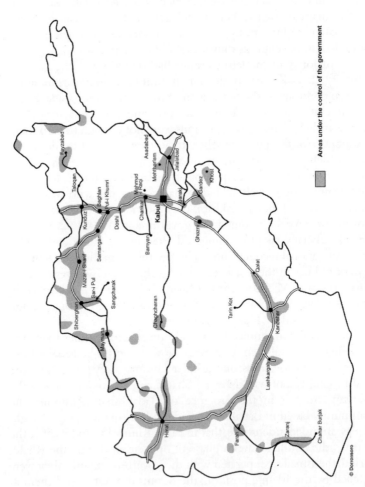

The Kabul regime, 1989.

Areas under the control of the government

sale from 1980 onwards, in exchange for material benefits and autonomy for their community.

Finally, the vigorous rivalry between commanders led to recurrent clashes between *mujahidin*. The government was therefore able
to play the role of a third party in these conflicts, tipping the scales in
favour of one side or the other. In general the recruitment of *mujahidin* was carried out through the Paderwatan, which appointed an
'elder' (*rishsafid*, a 'white beard') to make contact with the target
group. If the negotiations were successful the group officially surrendered its arms, only to take them up again at once, but this time in
the service of the government. Occasionally these encounters turned
out badly: in 1983, seventy government officials were massacred
during an allegiance ceremony near Jalalabad.

The recruited group in no way altered its behaviour, neither sub-
mitting to military discipline nor renouncing their religious practices. Recruitment was therefore not synonymous with the return of
the state. The ambiguous position of those *mujahidin* who rallied to
the government side was a recurrent factor, for example in the region of Herat. Among the most spectacular pledges of allegiance was
that made by Ismat Muslim, an Achekzai Pushtun, whose forces were
deployed along the road between Kandahar and the Pakistan border.
In 1984, following clashes with rival groups, he crossed over to the
government side together with several hundred men of his tribe, a
move he seems likely to have made after payment of $200,000. Ismat
Muslim, the son of a general and educated in the Soviet Union, was
a personal friend of Babrak Karmal and had little sympathy with the
puritan position of the *mujahidin*. All in all, the success of the policy
of recruitment also depended on the ability of the army to put pressure on the *mujahidin*.

Military operations. By restricting the size of its occupying forces,
Moscow attempted to escape entanglement of the kind which had led
Americans to commit more than half a million men in Vietnam.[18]
On the other hand the Soviet contingent, which never numbered
much more than 100,000 men, was unable to compensate for the
weakness of the Afghan army, especially since the Soviet troops, who

---

[18] For an overall view of military operations, see Mark Urban, *War in Afghanistan*,
London: Macmillan Press, 1990.

had little taste for combat as well as being ill-equipped and underfed, were restricted to 'useful' Afghanistan: the cities and the main axes of communication. It seems that no reliable information is available on the make-up of the Soviet forces, not even relating to the number of troops who passed through Afghanistan, though the figure officially quoted is half a million. The first arrivals were volunteers, who believed they were defending Afghanistan against the activities of the CIA, but the truth gradually dawned concerning the hostility of the population and the serious aggression by their own comrades faced by the young conscripts, including beatings and rape. From this point onwards, in the absence of further volunteers, those conscripted were seldom told their true destination.

The prime objective of the Soviet high command was to increase the strength of the Afghan army, in view of the difficulty of keeping control over an area larger than France, with terrain very advantageous to the guerrillas. In 1978 the Afghan army numbered 110,000 men but, eroded by desertion, it fell to 25,000 men by 1980. The number under arms, which was to reach 150,000 in 1988, at the moment of the Soviet withdrawal, remained insufficient in spite of programmes of forced conscription, the lowering of the age of conscription, and the extension of military service to three years, with two years of mobilisation for reservists under thirty-nine. These measures from time to time occasioned protests: in November 1982 the eastern Pushtun tribes demonstrated against conscription, which violated their traditional exemption. The Soviets also wanted to reform the structure of the Afghan army, and to revise its strategy to fit in more closely with their own military system. In 1980 Afghanistan was divided into seven regions, each with a Soviet commander and Afghan officers as regional commanders under his authority. However, the Afghan army continued to be badly organised and was divided into the regular army, the gendarmerie (*Sarandoy*) and the frontier guard. And up to the end armaments were in short supply.

Relations between the Soviet and Afghan armies were not particularly good, and the Soviets always took the Afghans to task in particular for their untrustworthiness. For this reason Masud was always aware of operations in the Panjshir well before they took place, even if he was sometimes surprised by their magnitude. In 1985 a number of Afghan generals were even arrested for passing information to the *mujahidin*. Faced with the multiplication of leaks, the Soviets quickly adopted the practice of informing the Afghan officers only at the last minute before joint operations. The Afghans on the other hand complained about the inertia of the Soviet troops, who declined to become involved when Afghan troops were attacked. The major battles, and therefore the largest losses, involved the Afghan forces, which fought in the front line and defended isolated outposts.

The objectives of the Soviet command were basically to preserve the security of the towns and the lines of communication, and to curtail infiltration by the guerrillas from their sanctuary in Pakistan; frontier control was necessary to deny or obstruct the reinforcement of the guerrillas in men and supplies. However, the level of Soviet involvement and tactics changed over time, as was seen by the varying level of their losses.

There were three distinct periods. Between 1980 and 1983 the Soviets adopted a defensive position, avoiding direct involvement and relying largely on the Afghan forces. The priority accorded to static defence of strategic areas—towns, bases, roads—accounts for the low level of casualties: 1,500 in 1980 and 2000 in 1981. In 1982 Andropov sought to limit the losses and attempted to reach a diplomatic solution. In this period there were few attacks, and government operations were aimed mainly at dislodging the guerrillas from the regions surrounding the towns, where they were infiltrating at night and attacking guard posts. From January to March 1982 the Soviets attempted to improve the defences of the major towns, including Kandahar, Herat and Mazar-i Sharif. They surrounded and destroyed infiltrated quarters, a tactic which resulted in substantial civilian casualties, but in spite of these operations security left much to be desired. At Mazar-i Sharif commander Zabihullah even succeeded in seizing the civil airport in a commando operation, and at Kandahar there were battles in the town every night.

The absence of real results in due course obliged the Soviets to become directly involved, so that in 1984 and 1985 operations were at their height, with a strategy directed at winning the military victory by wearing down the resistance. In 1985 there were six offensives involving more than 5,000 Soviet troops, particularly in Panjshir and in the east, and in the Paktiya region 30,000 men took part in one operation. Soviet losses reached a peak, with 2,300 deaths in 1984 and 1,868 in 1985. During these two years the government also strove to protect the towns with guard posts every 100 or 200 metres, the space between these positions being blocked by anti-personnel mines. To gain entry to the towns three or four security cordons had to be crossed. In Mazar-i Sharif, where the operation was especially successful, the *mujahidin* were unable after 1984 to get into the town, and military pressure obliged them to fall back towards the south. Elsewhere major cleansing operations were regularly launched in areas held by the *mujahidin* to drive the population out of regions the government was unable to control. Finally, after 1986 the Soviets were getting ready to pull out and launched fewer offensives. Losses fell significantly at this time, with 1,300 killed in 1986, 1,215 in 1987 and 759 in 1988.[19]

Inadequate logistics and lack of training for guerrilla warfare were two factors which accounted for the poor performance of the Soviet military. The war uncovered the decline of the Soviet system and indeed marginally accelerated it. The lack of experience of the Soviet troops in mountain warfare, the lack of initiative of the officers, and insufficient knowledge of the terrain were all factors which led to tactical errors, and in particular to excessive use of tanks. The Soviets were insufficiently mobile, surrounding and indiscriminately bombing terrain in reaction to guerrilla offensives, but failing thereafter to occupy it because of the lack of efficient infantry. The war was waged too inflexibly, with aerial bombings between set hours and no night attacks, at least in the early years. Although the ambushes mounted by the *mujahidin* were often clumsy, the Soviets' ability to respond remained low. In the end the logistical problems reached a point where attacks had to be drawn to a close after a week, just at the moment when the *mujahidin* were running short of ammunition. Most of the Soviet prisoners were captured while searching for food.

Although logistics remained hopelessly inadequate up to the end, the patent unsuitability of the Soviets' military structure led to changes in tactics. The army was reorganised into smaller units, and commandos were used to seal off frontiers and mount nocturnal raids. The most significant change related to the increasing role of air power in the conduct of the war. For the Afghan and Soviet forces

---

[19] Even if these figures are not accurate in absolute terms, the year-on-year variation appears to be authentic (see below).

aviation became the decisive factor in the anti-guerrilla struggle, since it was more effective than traditional large-scale operations and allowed casualties to be kept down. In this way bombing raids with MiG 24 assault aircraft became more frequent, with support from MiG 8 observation planes. From 1985 onwards the Soviet forces adopted the technique of covering the flanks of their attacks with helicopter-borne units, especially during mountain warfare. However, because the *mujahidin* became better armed, air support was less effective from 1986 and 1987, which entailed difficulties for large-scale operations and in the supply, and therefore the survival, of isolated outposts.

At the moment when the Soviets withdrew they had succeeded in establishing satisfactory security in the towns in the north and to some extent in Herat, although Kandahar remained largely beyond their control. As for the security of frontiers and lines of communication, their other priority objective, the failure of the Soviets was obvious. Regular attacks launched to wipe out *mujahidin* groups near the roads or in the frontier zone with Pakistan were unsuccessful, largely owing to the nature of the terrain and to the scale of Pakistani support. The multiplication of commando operations and the millions of mines laid on the Afghanistan-Pakistan frontier were similarly ineffective, since the geography of the region meant that no real closure of the frontier could ever be achieved.[20]

Preparations for the retreat

The decision to withdraw from Afghanistan was taken in the spring of 1986. From his accession to power a year earlier Gorbachev had decided to resolve the Afghan crisis, which was impeding his policy of reconciliation with the West. The social mobilisation effected by *glasnost* and *perestroika* was in practice insufficient to counter the shortfall in production in the Soviet Union, which was becoming increasingly dependent on the West in technology. The Afghan war became a test of Soviet 'good will' and of the renunciation of its expansionist policy. The withdrawal was all the more necessary due to

---

[20] Mines were much used: according to the US government, between 10 and 16 million were laid. The Soviets are reported to have installed 2,131 minefields, of which only 1,518 had been cleared at the time of their departure. *Pakistan Times*, 16 August 1988, and AFP 25 June 1988.

the mounting diplomatic and internal costs of the occupation; the war had left the Soviet Union diplomatically isolated. The invasion of 27 December had been carried out in defiance of international law, and the only justification offered by the Soviet government relied on a verbal appeal made by the Afghan leader Afizullah Amin before his execution by Soviet special forces. Outside the immediate circle of Soviet client states this was accepted by no-one, and on 20 November 1980 the General Assembly of the United Nations called for the withdrawal of foreign forces from Afghanistan, and the resolution was thereafter renewed year by year. At the moment of each vote the UN became the scene of a diplomatic confrontation between the Soviet Union and its allies on one side, and a growing majority of UN member states on the other.[21] The repeated censure of the Soviet presence in Afghanistan represented a major setback for Soviet diplomacy in relation to the Third World and particularly Muslim states.

The war was also a source of tensions within the Soviet Union. Though hard to calculate, the cost of the war was probably $4–8 billion a year in the 1980s.[22] The official Soviet casualty figures— 13,369 dead, 311 missing and 35,578 wounded—are an understatement: other estimates tell of 40–50,000 deaths. Unofficial estimates made by the Soviet people at large were considerably higher, while the lack of any credible rationale for the war made it all the more unacceptable.[23] Drug use, which had not previously been significant, also became widespread. From 1983 popular opposition to the war began to be voiced.[24] The relative freedom of expression under Gorbachev later permitted a number of demonstrations to take place, which made clear the popular view of the posting of conscripts. For

---

[21] The first resolution condemning the Soviet invasion met with the approval of 104 countries against 18, with 18 abstentions. The figures for that of 15 November 1984 were 119 for, 20 against and 17 abstentions; that of 13 November 1985: 122 for, 19 against, 12 abstentions. On 10 November 1987, 123 votes were cast against the Soviet Union, an indication of its mounting isolation.

[22] See Anthony Arnold, *The Fateful Pebble: Afghanistan's Role in the Fall of the Soviet Empire*, California, Presidio, 1993, p. 185 ff.

[23] Official figures given in May 1988 by General Lizichev. For an assessment of these figures, which seemed considerably to underestimate the losses, see the article by Valeri Konovalov, 'Legacy of the Afghan War, some statistics', *Radio Liberty*, 1 (4), 1989, and Anthony Arnold, *op. cit.*, p. 190.

[24] Anthony Arnold, *op. cit.*, p. 194.

example, on 20 May 1985 there was a demonstration in Erevan of 200 relatives of conscripts who were about to set off for Afghanistan.

A fact understood by few observers is that Najibullah's accession to power in 1986 signalled a major change in Soviet policy. To safeguard the survival of his regime after the withdrawal, he was to play a double game: within the party he consolidated his authority and set in train structural changes, while in his external relations he attempted to bring the *mujahidin* into a process of political negotiation, and simultaneously undermined their position by going through the motions of a liberalisation designed to attract the population into his camp.

The restructuring of the Party. The advent of Najibullah had been orchestrated by the Soviets against the wishes of a large majority of all factions of the Hezb-i Demokratik-i Khalq-i Afghanistan. In the Soviet view his personal qualities and social background were appropriate to their plans.[25] Andropov had in any event sounded him out as a future successor to Karmal as early as 1982. He was young— aged thirty-nine in 1986—as well as being energetic and something of an orator, in contrast to Karmal. He was also well placed as the former head of the KHAD to develop a counter-insurrectionary policy and to block any coup attempt. In addition his background conferred on him greater legitimacy than that enjoyed by Karmal, both inside and outside the Party. Najibullah was a Pushtun speaker, born in Paktiya, and married to a Muhammadzai (the royal clan), which increased his acceptability to the Pushtuns. Even after the fall

---

[25] Najibullah, the son of Akhta Muhammad, was an Ahmadzai Pushtun from Paktya, born in Kabul in 1947. His father was at one time consul and commercial attaché in Peshawar, where Najibullah learned Urdu and English. After attending the Habibia School, he studied medicine and joined Karmal's group. He took part in student demonstrations and was even briefly imprisoned on two occasions. He married Fatima, a niece of Dr Anas (formerly Zahir Shah's Minister of Culture) and a member of the royal clan. It is likely that he became a KGB agent at the close of the 1960s, and he joined the Central Committee at the time of reunification in 1977. In 1978 he was put in charge of the Kabul Committee, and then—a victim of the purge on the Parchamis—he was named as ambassador to Teheran, and afterwards to Yugoslavia. He later became head of the KHAD, and after appointment as a member of the Politburo in 1981 became its secretary-general at the end of 1985, handing over the running of the KHAD to his deputy Yaqubi.

of the regime he retained the support of certain eastern Pushtun tribes including his own tribe the Ahmadzai.

Najibullah's ascent was obvious by the end of 1985. On 11 January 1986 the KHAD was elevated to the status of a ministry, as a sign of the growing importance accorded to an apparatus of which Najibullah was in practice to keep control. After a month-long 'private' stay in the Soviet Union, Babrak Karmal resigned his post as secretary-general of the party on 4 May 1986, to be succeeded by Najibullah. On 30 September 1987 Najibullah was appointed to the presidency of the Revolutionary Council. On 28–29 November 1987 the *Loya Jirga* approved the new constitution and the appointment of Najibullah as head of state. He would in due course combine the position of head of state with that of president of the Council of Ministers and of the Higher Defence Council. This accumulation of power was a symbol not so much of the concentration of power in his hands as of his isolation. Nevertheless he took care to place his supporters in key posts. Gholam Faruq Yaqubi, his deputy at the KHAD, went on to the Central Committee, and Suleiman Laeq, who had worked a great deal with KHAD in his position as Minister for Tribes and Nationalities, became an alternate member of the Central Committee. Najibullah was also able to rely on the support of Parchamis opposed to Karmal—Kawiani and Wakil—as well as several Khalqis. In addition he mobilised his network of provincial officials and notables from the old regime who had been appointed under the policy of National Reconciliation. For instance, in 1990 Khaleq Yar, Daud's former Minister of Finance and governor of Herat, was appointed Prime Minister in succession to Sultan Ali Keshmand.

The purge of Karmal's supporters was spectacular. Anahita Ratebzad was stripped of her position as president of the Women's Democratic Organisation on 6 August 1986, and on 21 November Panjshiri, Danesh and Qader left the Politburo. To strengthen his grip on the Central Committee Najibullah increased its membership. Some of Karmal's supporters reacted violently to their eclipse. When Najibullah was appointed, pro-Karmal demonstrations took place, especially in Kabul and Kandahar. On 8 May 1987, a few days after Karmal's departure to exile in Moscow, his supporters organised a demonstration outside the Ministry of the Interior. There were also three bomb explosions at Mikrorayon, also perhaps their responsibility.

The announcement of the Soviet departure inaugurated a period of unanimity within the Party, which mobilised to ensure its own survival, especially during the *mujahidin* attack at Jalalabad in the spring of 1989. However, tensions continued to run high and, taking advantage of the progressive withdrawal of the Soviets, the Khalqis several times tried to recover control, making use of their positions in the Defence and Interior Ministries. Two or three attempts were made during the course of 1988. 5 March 1988 saw the start of the trial of 128 conspirators, among whom were officers and Party members. On 14 May 1988 twenty-three of the twenty-nine provincial governors were replaced in order to forestall a coup. In consequence Najibullah sacked the Khalqis most involved. On 19 October 1988 Saleh Muhammad Zeary, leader of the Khalq, left the Politburo. In November Gulabzoy, who was suspected of organising a coup, was replaced as Minister of the Interior by Watanjar. In compensation Najibullah attempted to gratify the Khalq by appointing Tanai, the Khalqi party chairman, as Minister of Defence in August 1988. In the same spirit four Khalqis out of nineteen new members were appointed to the Central Committee in October 1989.

Najibullah, who had become party chief and president entirely at the wish of the Soviets, never consolidated enough support within the party: his supporters were always fewer in number than those of Karmal, while the Khalqis never accepted him, even though he was a Pushtun. This initial weakness obliged him to rely to a great degree on the KHAD, which he continued to manage through his deputy Yaqubi, while in the interests of maintaining his authority he also played on the antagonism between the Parchamis and the Khalqis. These machinations led to a lessening of the Khalq-Parcham split, as hostile groups sprang up.

The policy of National Reconciliation. The expression 'national reconciliation' (translated into Persian as *ashti-yi melli*) was employed by Gorbachev in his Vladivostok speech of July 1986 in relation to crisis situations in the Third World in general and in particular in Afghanistan. From the end of 1985 Karmal had made use of the expression '*naosazi*' to denote a variety of *perestroïka*. The appointment of Najibullah gave a new impetus to reform and implied renunciation of the military solution. From now on the accent would be placed on an indirect strategy.

In the event the major military operations conducted by the Soviet-Afghan command had, more than anything else, given a political boost to the guerrillas. As was often the case, the apparent disparity between the forces led the government to neglect the more purely political aspects of the struggle, a point proved by the example of Masud. Had offensives not been regularly launched against Panjshir, whose strategic importance was sometimes overestimated, Masud could never have achieved the level of recognition he enjoyed. Similarly, attempts to break the position of Ismail Khan in Herat by military means reinforced his legitimacy, solidifying around him the unity of the *mujahidin*, who were mostly divided. Military pressure, which tended to prompt mobilisation, in fact worked against the Kabul government to the extent that the complete annihilation of a group of combatants was always extremely difficult.

At first the significance of the policy of National Reconciliation was misunderstood by observers and by the commanders, who saw in it only a propaganda exercise. Their incredulity, which was real, marred the effect of the declaration of the policy, with which the government had counted on dropping a political bombshell. Nevertheless, the following developments were spectacular: the government set about nothing less than the deconstruction of the communist regime. The issue concerned not so much the 'sincerity' of these changes as their political effects, which would in the end be substantial since they expressed new power relationships. The effects of the policy of National Reconciliation would only truly be felt after the withdrawal.

After several last thrusts in 1986, mainly to ensure the security of the towns, the Kabul government proclaimed the policy of National Reconciliation in January 1987. Following the plenary meeting of the party and the declaration of a unilateral cease-fire from 15 January, the government asked the leaders of the armed opposition to negotiate. In addition a general amnesty was promulgated on 24 January for Afghans engaged in anti-government activities. Finally, on 8 March 1988 Najibullah commissioned the Paderwatan to establish contacts with opposition groups, which were acknowledged as future partners.

The lifting of restrictions on commerce[26] and the new attitude—in public, at least—of respect for religion brought great satisfaction

[26] In addition, a decree of June 1987 raised to 20 hectares per person the initial

to the merchants and officials, who were alarmed by the dissension among the *mujahidin* which seemed to increase in proportion to their closeness to victory. The language of the authorities, as employed for example by provincial governors at ceremonies of allegiance, centred around two themes: first, the affirmation of the Islamic character of the government, which respected and protected the faith; and second, an appeal to patriotic sentiment against Pakistani interference, which some Afghans actually accepted but with reluctance.

The policy of National Reconciliation also had an ethnic dimension. Najibullah, who was able to take advantage of his Pushtun legitimacy, attempted to oust the Tajiks from the Party leadership. However, at the same time his link with the Hazaras was maintained. In 1986 a Hazara Nationality Council (Shura-yi Melli) was established under the supervision of the KHAD's 12th Bureau. In addition a Hazara *jirga*, the Jirga-yi Sarasari-yi Milliat-i Hazara (Central council for the Hazara nationality), was held in Kabul in September 1987[27] while Sultan Ali Keshmand (himself a Hazara) was Prime Minister. Sultan Ali Keshmand spoke in terms with markedly nationalist overtones on the occasion of the inauguration of the Markaz-i Insijam Omur-i Milliat-i Hazara (Centre for the Coordination of the Affairs of the Hazara Nationality) in the summer of 1989.[28] He also set up a Hazara regiment, the 520th infantry, in December 1986. In addition, the new constitution of 1987 recognised the equality of the tribes and nationalities.

In the event, on 30 November 1987, a *Loya Jirga* approved the new constitution, with a general outline that remained close to that of 1964. A *Loya Jirga* made up of tribal chiefs, intellectuals, notables *et al.* was to designate the president of the republic for a term of seven years. The president had a right of veto over parliamentary decisions, which could only be overruled by a two thirds majority. Parliament was elected for six years, while the senate was half appointed by the President and half elected. Finally, there were significant symbolic concessions: Islam once again became the religion of the state, and Afghanistan adopted a flag in which the colour green predominated.

---

ceiling of 6 hectares, which was tantamount to recognition of the failure of agrarian reform.
[27] *Kabul New Times*, 24 September 1987.
[28] S. A. Mousavi, *op. cit.*, p. 177.

From the Proximity talks to the Geneva accords

Diplomacy was not of major importance in bringing about the Soviet withdrawal. In the first instance, the negotiations were a means
for Moscow to put a diplomatic face on its military defeat, since it
had failed to produce a political formula to end the civil war. The
talks were therefore only marginally useful, but they did allow the
UN secretary-general to strengthen his position. In the event the
settlement of the international aspects of the Afghan conflict marked
the end of the Cold War and the emergence of new international
relationships. The role of the UN at this time changed radically, it
appears, and the Afghan issue was one of the first where the organisation, no longer paralysed by the East-West confrontation, made a
bid to embark on autonomous action.[29]

From the earliest months after the Soviet invasion, recriminations
and proposals for negotiations proliferated. Demands for uncondi-
tional withdrawal were issued in January 1980 by a special session of
the UN, then several weeks later by the Organisation of the Islamic
Conference (OIC). At the end of February 1980 Pakistan proposed
a troika, to include the Foreign Ministers of Pakistan and Iran and
the secretary-general of the OIC, to serve as an intermediary between the *mujahidin* and the Kabul government, which however refused to entertain even indirect contacts with the parties in Peshawar.
The Iranians refused to negotiate in the absence of the *mujahidin*, a
factor which, when added to their bad relations with the United
States, largely excluded them from subsequent negotiations.

In its turn Kabul took the initiative and on 14 May 1980 put forward a preliminary proposal to open bilateral talks between Afghanistan and its neighbours Iran and Pakistan relating to a mutual non-
intervention pact, to be guaranteed by the United States. In Kabul's
eyes the Soviet presence was non-negotiable, since it related to Afghanistan's sovereignty, and negotiations should not be seen as a way to
internationalise the crisis.

Faced with this impasse, the UN adopted a policy of indirect rapprochement. In February 1981 the secretary-general Kurt Waldheim
appointed Xavier Perez de Cuellar as his personal representative for

---

[29] For the text of the agreements, see Diego Cordovez, Selig H. Harrison, *Out of
Afghanistan: the inside story of the Soviet withdrawal*, New York: Oxford University
Press, 1995.

Afghanistan. Perez de Cuellar shuttled between Islamabad and Kabul, but their positions appeared irreconcilable: the Kabul regime's demand was for direct negotiations with the Pakistan government, while Pakistan insisted on self-determination for the Afghan people. After Perez de Cuellar's election as UN secretary-general, Diego Cordovez became the new special representative and succeeded in initiating indirect negotiation in Geneva, beginning in June 1982. With the mediation of UN negotiators these brought together Pakistan and the Kabul government of Afghanistan, in the presence of Soviet and American observers. The talks were organised around four issues: a bilateral accord between Kabul and Islamabad on reciprocal non-intervention, international guarantees, a bilateral agreement on the return of refugees and a plan for the withdrawal of Soviet troops. By mutual agreement between Pakistan and the Soviets, the *mujahidin* were not represented. This first series of negotiations ended in failure, since the Pakistanis refused to recognise the Kabul government, which in its turn did not wish to discuss a withdrawal.

Andropov's rise to power between 1982 and 1984 was marked by a relative freedom for diplomatic activity, but without concrete results, due to his rapid departure. At the negotiations of April 1983 in Geneva, Kabul asked for the closure of the camps in Pakistan and the end of support for the resistance; while Islamabad wanted a firm commitment over the duration of the withdrawal, which the Soviets rejected. Nevertheless Diego Cordovez showed optimism and believed that agreement was close, although the Soviet position later hardened with the demand that the security of Kabul should be fully guaranteed before any withdrawal. It appeared in fact that Andropov's influence had begun to wane because of his ill-health. The Soviets returned to their initial position: there could be no discussion of Soviet troops in the course of Afghan-Pakistani negotiations, and the only role for the Americans would be as guarantors of non-intervention. 1984 was a year without results, although the fourth round of the negotiations in August was the first to be held on the basis of 'proximity'—talks were no longer 'indirect'. Henceforth meetings were held at a venue which accommodated both Pakistani and Afghan delegations.

In the spring of 1985 the advent of Gorbachev re-launched the process of negotiation, and in 1986 agreement was reached on three points: the refugees, non-intervention and guarantees. Only the schedule for the withdrawal of Soviet troops remained as an important point of disagreement. The Pakistanis wanted a rapid withdrawal, over three or four months, while the Soviets and, even more, the Kabul regime wanted a longer period. Still, the positions were moving closer. At the round of talks in March 1987 Pakistan asked for withdrawal over seven months as against eighteen months called for by the Kabul regime—by the end of 1987 the demands had become eight months and sixteen months respectively. The issue of a transitional government was also put on the table, since the end of the negotiations seemed to be approaching.

Gorbachev, in his Vladivostok speech of 28 July 1987, proposed the formation of transitional government including the *mujahidin*. By this time Diego Cordovez had already tried to negotiate the formation of a provisional government including the king, Zahir Shah, but he ran into opposition from the Islamist parties, Pakistan and the United States, which inclined towards a military solution. In a BBC interview on 11 May 1987, Zahir Shah said he was ready to take up his responsibilities if the majority asked him to. On 10 June Najibullah said he was also willing to negotiate with the king, but on 16 June Zahir Shah gave his final refusal as a consequence of the negative reactions from the *mujahidin*.

The Soviets finally unblocked the negotiations by renouncing the objective of a political solution as a condition of withdrawal, but maintained their demand for 'negative symmetry', by which they meant a ban on arming the adversaries within the country. On 8 February 1988 Gorbachev made a speech removing the last obstacle with the proposal of a withdrawal within ten months, while setting a deadline of 15 March for an agreement to be reached. In February 1988 Zia ul-Haq, taken by surprise, hastily set up an interim *mujahidin* government. On 2 March 1988 the final round of negotiations began in Geneva. Negative symmetry was finally abandoned after American hesitations, and each side continued to arm its allies.

On 14 April 1988 the accords between Pakistan and Afghanistan were signed in Geneva, with an American-Soviet guarantee.[30] They provided for a Soviet withdrawal in early 1989, but were less than explicit about the political future of the country. On 12 May the

[30] Diego Cordovez, Selig S. Harrison, *op. cit.*, pp. 389 ff.

withdrawal began at Jalalabad and Kandahar, then on 26 July at Shindand. The first withdrawal from Kabul took place in August, by which time, according to Gromov the commander in chief of the armed forces, no more than half the Soviet forces remained, concentrated into the six provinces of Kabul, Baghlan, Samangan, Kapisa, Farah and Herat. The Soviets abided by their commitments and completed their withdrawal on 15 February 1989. On the whole the *mujahidin* did not attack the Soviet forces as they pulled back, choosing rather to occupy the positions they left behind.

In the end responsibility for the application of the Geneva Accords was assigned to Diego Cordovez, who was replaced at the end of his mandate as the secretary-general's representative by a Cypriot, Benon Sevan. However, many believed that the fall of Kabul was now only a matter of months away, while the principal problem had become the reconstruction of the country, entrusted to a UN special agency UNOCA (United Nations Office for the Coordination of Humanitarian and Economic Assistance to Afghanistan). On 12 May Sadruddin Aga Khan, the former UN High Commissioner for Refugees and an influential member of the Ismaili community, was appointed UN coordinator for economic and humanitarian programmes in Afghanistan, at the head of UNOCA.

The post-withdrawal survival of the regime

Up to the coup of 1992 the situation appeared deadlocked: the regime did not fall, and the *mujahidin* proclaimed themselves unable either to push through a military victory or to formulate a credible political alternative. In the event the ongoing Soviet withdrawal had had a number of consequences. The spirit of *jihad* began to flag, while the Kabul regime was no longer so visibly controlled by Moscow. In consequence the language of National Reconciliation came to seem more credible. In addition the regime's military redeployment, departing from a significant number of outposts and small towns, was not without advantages: a more concentrated security system was stronger. The regime also had the benefit of Soviet military aid, while the West had scaled down its assistance to the *mujahidin*. In the end the failure of the attack on Jalalabad in the spring of 1989 brought about a change of view: a *mujahidin* victory began to seem improbable in the short run.

Consequently, the policy of National Reconciliation came fully into play. Wherever where the government refrained from launching attacks, *de facto* cease-fires and more or less peaceful coexistence began to take hold. After the reverses of 1988–9 military deployment began to take a more permanent form, while the morale of the *mujahidin* was damaged by their internal dissent. In the post-Soviet period, the government did not so much attempt to rally the *mujahidin* as to strike agreements with them in the aim of keeping clashes down to an acceptable level. UNOCA tended in the same direction with the specification of cease-fire zones.

One example will serve to illustrate the success of this process. In Kandahar, the major Pushtun city of the south, some particularly aggressive guerrilla groups brought the fighting into the heart of the town. Here violence against the Soviet occupiers had always been spontaneous and immediate. In 1980 four Soviet soldiers, on duty in the heart of the city, were beaten to death by the population in an unplanned attack. The soldiers did not exaggerate when they used to say that a posting to Kandahar was a punishment. The government's attempts to dislodge the guerrillas from the outskirts of the city never succeeded, to the extent that several observers predicted its imminent fall after the Soviet withdrawal. However, under the leadership of the governor, Nur ul-Haq Ulumi, a Parchami from an important local family, the policy of National Reconciliation began to bear fruit, meanwhile aggravating the divisions among the *mujahidin*. In exchange for financial and other incentives—e.g. permission for the *muijahidin* to come into the town without their weapons to visit their families—the parties scaled down their attacks, a particular result of which was that any coordination between *muijahidin* groups for a general attack on the town became impossible. Pakistani initiatives to unite the *mujahidin* were to fail, although some parties, including Hekmatyar's and Khales's Hezb-i Islami, refused to compromise with the government, in order to maintain their access to Pakistani funding.[31]

In a bid to gain wider support, the government organised a not altogether honest reorganisation of political life. Najibullah wanted

---

[31] This split also corresponded to tribal considerations: the Ghilzai, who were dominant in the Khales and Hekmatyar factions of the Hezb-i Islami, rejected the agreement, which was accepted by the Alizai and Barakzai Durrani who belonged to the Jamiyat-i Islami and the Mahaz.

to set up a new party in order to enhance his credibility as a participant in a putative coalition government with the *mujahidin*. On 25 Feburary 1990 he called on the party, the Hezb-i Demokratik-i Khalq-i Afghanistan, to step down from its controlling position. A new movemement, the Hezb-i Watan (Party of the Nation) was officially created on 27 June 1990. As a forewarning of this development, the government press had maintained a discreet silence concerning the Hezb-i Demokratik-i Khalq-i Afghanistan, from the time of the Soviet withdrawal up to the victory at Jalalabad. In fact the Hezb-i Watan inaugurated no profound change since Najibullah was able neither to broaden his political base nor to appoint new officials. The executive committee of the Hezb-i Watan was made up of thirteen members, of whom eleven had belonged to the Central Committee of the Hezb-i Demokratik-i Khalq-i Afghanistan in 1980; 80% were Parchamis, with a balance between pro-Karmal and pro-Najibullah factions.

In addition multi-party pluralism was largely an illusion, although the Hezb-i Watan ceased to play a leading role, it remained the guarantor of the policy of National Reconciliation. In the event Najibullah authorised political parties under the decree of 11 September 1990, but it was Department 7 of the WAD (successor to the KHAD) which clandestinely organised such 'opposition forces' as the Hezb-i Deqhanan (Peasants' Party) and the Hezb-i Islami (the Party of Islam: a Hazara nationalist splinter group based in Jaghori), as well as the 'independent' newspapers such as *Akhbar-i Hafta* (The Weekly News). In the Senate twenty-five out of sixty-two seats were assigned to the opposition.[32]

In spite of these developments the dangers which would prove fatal for the regime were contained already in embryo in the policy followed by the government from 1987. Although the deployment of the military was generally unchallenged, declarations of loyalty remained sparse, with most of the commanders preferring to remain autonomous, outside *ad hoc* agreements with the government. The policy of National Reconciliation was extremely fragile, as the regime managed its internal divisions badly and progressively lost control of the periphery.

With the period of the withdrawal over, tensions within the government worsened. In March 1990 the Khalqis attempted one final

---

[32] Asta Olesen, *op. cit.*, p. 267.

coup, with the help of Hezb-i Islami. The earliest contacts between the Khalqi tendency and Hezb-i Islami probably took place in early 1990, when Hekmatyar met Khan Abdul Wali Khan, the leader of the Pathan nationalist movement, the Awami National Party. For the Khalqis, who opposed Najibullah and his strategy of National Reconciliation, the coup represented the possibility of acquiring power while at the same time achieving Islamic legitimacy through the alliance with Hezb-i Islami, which had already opened its ranks, for reasons of communal solidarity, to a number of Khalqi deserters.

On 6 March Tanai, the Minister of Defence, launched the coup from the air base at Bagram, to the north of Kabul. The government, forewarned of the attempt, kept control of the situation, thanks especially to the KHAD troops who guarded the capital. Najibullah, who took refuge in the bunker at the Presidency, contacted the provincial governors, who remained loyal to him, one by one. On the following day, 7 March, Tanai acknowledged his failure and joined the Hezb-i Islami in Pakistan. On 8 March Bagram air base was recovered from the rebels. On 11 March an anti-Khalqi purge began with the dismissal of five members of the Politburo and seven members of the Defence Council. According to the regime, 623 arrests were made, but the ousting of the Khalqis did not of itself enable Najibullah to reassert his power. He was no longer able to exploit the Khalqis as a counterbalance to Karmal's supporters, who would play a decisive role in his fall in the spring of 1992.

In addition, despite the scale of Soviet aid, which amounted to $14.2 billion in the year of the withdrawal,[33] the financial and political burden of the policy of National Reconciliation progressively undermined the infrastructure of the Afghan state. To pay the militias the government adopted an inflationary policy which resulted in a spectacular increase in the money supply, from 112.5 to 222.7 billions of Afghanis between 1988 and 1990.[34] However, even more than the financial burden, the loss of control over the provinces threatened the regime.

---

[33] See Anthony Arnold, *op. cit.*, p. 185. Thirty MiG 27s were delivered in October 1988, as well as SCUD missiles, used against the outskirts of the capital. The Politburo archives show that up to the end the Soviet Union believed it could keep Najibullah's regime in place (Allan, *op. cit.*).

[34] See Barnett R. Rubin, *The Fragmentation of Afghanistan*, New Haven and London: Yale University Press, 2002, p. 163.

The authorities increasingly relied on the militias and established with them a relationship of clientelism comparable to that which existed between the parties and the commanders. The army banked on the militias to ensure the security of the towns, but also increasingly to carry out major offensives. The militiamen of Abdul Rashid Dostam, originally from the north-west, fought throughout Afghanistan, which put them in a position of competition with the regular army. These men were systematically involved in the toughest fighting, since they were volunteers, sometimes paid by results, and were not liable to desert to the *mujahidin*, from whom they expected no mercy. This militia, officially the 53rd division, comprised 20–40,000 men and answered directly to the president, bypassing the Ministry of Defence.

The militias' effectiveness presupposed local roots, which at first the government encouraged, but it would in due course have negative consequences. In some provinces the chronic problems of the regular army left the militiamen as the predominant local military force. Their bargaining power grew substantially in relation to the state, which was obliged to pay out in order to maintain the loyalty of groups which were nothing less than private armies. This was true for the former *mujahidin* who had preserved their autonomy, but also for militias set up by the government itself, such as that of Rashid Dostam, who were quite capable either of refusing to fight, or of pursuing local policies sometimes running counter to those of the central government. Disobedience was rife, and in many places the authority of the government did not run; it could no longer keep order in certain suburbs of Herat, where the militia held travellers to ransom and settled their differences with the Kalashnikov. In the autumn of 1991 clashes between the militias and the regular army were an indication of the decline of the situation in the province of Herat. The same happened in the north where Dostam's authority took precedence over Kabul officials. The government thus lost the credit it had gained through its policy of moderation and its discontinuation of military operations. Random violence became prevalent, and that of the militias was as arbitrary as that of some of the *mujahidin*.

The central government had few means at its disposal to exert pressure: the secret services—the KHAD and then WAD—were themselves powerless to control the militias which had a real *esprit de corps*, often based on communal solidarity. In the Uzbek provinces of the northwest the most powerful militia leaders had taken control of the Party apparatus and the army. In the face of the militias' growing independence, the central state became unable to control its own security apparatus.

The weakness of the centre relative to the periphery called into question the functionality and even the existence of the state. Traditionally power in Afghanistan was exercised from the centre. The appointment of officials who were generally strangers in provinces where they served for limited periods safeguarded the control of the central state, and precluded to a certain extent the establishment of excessively powerful local authorities. However, for practical reasons the state had fostered the autonomy of the militias, bringing into being a balance of power increasingly unfavourable to the centre. The achievements of pacification were in the end too costly for an exhausted state, which could not survive the disappearance of its Soviet protector. The policy of the government thus led to a gradual loss of control of the periphery, which facilitated the coup of 1992.

6. The Guerrillas

An account of events from the point of view of the *mujahidin* presents more of a problem than their examination from the standpoint of the government. The guerrillas existed in a wide variety of local circumstances, and the Shi'ite and Sunni groups developed in different ways, while the priorities of the commanders on the ground diverged from those of the leaderships in exile. A common thread nevertheless emerges: the tendency towards professionalisation among the *mujahidin*, which emerged in parallel with the prevalence of institutional styles of leadership over the patrimonial model. The changing political dispositions on the ground, in addition to interparty relationships and developments subsequent to the Soviet withdrawal, will be analysed below.

The professionalisation of the fighters

At the outset the Afghan guerrillas lacked mobility, while in many places the tribal model of warfare persisted. The *mujahidin* were strongly identified with particular territories, which accounts for the problems they encountered in operating outside their home regions. The guerrillas did not put a high value on secrecy or mobility, since the government was well aware of their positions on the ground, but placed their faith in the difficulty of access to their mountains and high valleys, as well as in the government's inertia. Ambushes involving more than a few dozen men were rarely mounted, and these were often carried out in the same places, with little attempt at surprise. With the exception of a few commanders such as Masud, attacks against government positions generally aimed not at capturing them—at least not before 1988—but at keeping up pressure on the government while providing an opportunity for individual fighters to display their valour. Overall, the support of the population, in addition to the topography, compensated for any inadequacies, which in any case the Soviet-Afghan forces did not fully exploit.

However, over the years the circumstances of the resistance changed, as they became better armed and trained. In the early months of the rebellion the *mujahidin* fought with old English Lee-Enfield rifles, then came the arrival from Pakistan of Kalashnikovs, which remained their standard weapon throughout the war. At the outset the guerrillas were entirely without heavy arms, but they gradually acquired suitable anti-tank and anti-aircraft weapons. Plastic mines were effective, since the Soviets had nothing with which to detect them, but the antiquated RPG7 anti-tank weapons were responsible for most of the Soviet-Afghan losses. From early 1986 onwards the *mujahidin* obtained around 200 Blowpipe anti-aircraft weapons, and then about 1,000 Stingers between 1986 and 1990. The efficiency of these weapons has been exaggerated, however, and they certainly did not alter the course of the war; Mark Urban has estimated Soviet-Afghan losses due to these missiles at ninety helicopters and planes, of which 15–20 were combat aircraft—i.e. less than 20% of the total losses of some 500 units up to the Soviet withdrawal.[1] Communications were also a weak point for the *mujahidin*: during the 1982 offensive against Panjshir, Masud used handwritten messages to communicate with his troops. Hence the relatively sophisticated radios supplied by western agencies greatly assisted coordination between groups.

The acquisition of better weapons was directly linked to the provision of aid by western and Arab countries. Between 1980 and early 1992, when military aid officially ceased, the United States gave $2–3 billion to the *mujahidin*, to which can be added a similar sum from the Arab countries. However, President Reagan had been highly cautious during his first term, in spite of his anti-communist rhetoric. For 1983 the CIA asked for a budget of $30 million for the *mujahidin* (compared to $24 million for the Contras in Honduras). Charles Wilson, a Democratic senator, obtained an additional $40 million and some Swiss anti-tank guns. In 1985 a distinct turning-point was reached, with a budget of $200 million, which was to reach $280 million by 1989. The other western countries, especially France and Britain, did not publicise the level of their military aid to the *mujahidin*, but

---

[1] Mark Urban, *op. cit.*, p. 296. It is possible that these estimates are too high.

fighters were trained in Europe and Pakistan, while equipment such as radios, missiles and anti-tank weapons was distributed to the parties. Around 80,000 *mujahidin* were reported to have been trained in Pakistan, mainly by Pakistani officers, as well as—more unusually— by Americans.[2]

However, the improvements in armaments only achieved their effect through the introduction of more elaborate organisation, which brought with it an increasing level of integration and coordination. This phenomenon took place with greater or lesser rapidity in different regions. From the earliest years Masud laid the foundations of a permanent army, while in some distant valleys the *mujahidin* continued as they had started, as the inhabitants of a village under arms. These developments were in part related to the patterns of rivalry between the commanders.

Relationships between commanders were generally characterised by competition arising out of personal rivalries, logistical issues, control over strategic positions, and humanitarian aid among other considerations. In addition, mobilisations had often been conducted on the basis of *qowms*, so that commanders sometimes inherited long-standing communal hostilities. For instance, Pushtuns who had recently settled in the north were sometimes subjected to attacks by local populations wanting to recover their land. Other cases had a more social explanation, as in Laghman where the conflict between Hezb-i Islami and Jamiyat-i Islami could be interpreted as a confrontation between great landowners and tenant farmers.

The reality was that no regulatory mechanism existed which could enforce an agreed standard of behaviour and underwrite transactions. The parties, who were themselves in a competitive situation, were hardly in a position to impose discipline on the commanders. Rivalry frequently spilled over into armed clashes. The *jirgas* of some tribal regions, and for a while the *ulema* of Kandahar, were able to

---

[2] For an assessment of the levels of aid, see James Rupert, 'Afghanistan's slide towards civil war', *World Policy Journal*, vol. XI, no. 4, fall 1989; Kirsten Lundberg, *Politics of a Covert Action: the US, the Mujahedin and the Stinger missile*, Harvard Intelligence and Policy Project, Kennedy School of Government, 1999; Alan Kuperman, 'The Stinger Missile and U.S. intervention in Afghanistan', *Political Science Quarterly*, vol. 114, no. 2 summer 1999, pp. 219–63. On the Arab aid see Muhammad Yousaf and Mark Adkin, *The Bear Trap: Afghanistan's Untold Story*, London: Leo Cooper, 1992, p. 77.

play a regulatory role, but such instances frequently came after the outbreak of conflicts, with the aim of reconciliation. A considerable number of commanders were pressured into switching their allegiance, driven into exile or assassinated. Mistrust was the most striking characteristic in the day-to-day attitudes of the commanders. Cooperation between groups was restricted to *ad hoc* operations, and the primary objective of each commander was to secure his own autonomy. *Shura* councils were rarely effective, and only more closely-knit systems, where the commanders were more narrowly constrained by some form of organisation, were able to implement cooperation. Such were Masud's Shura-yi Nazar (Council of Oversight) and in the west the Emarat of Ismail Khan.

Conflicts between commanders were far from rare even before 1992, and sometimes occurred even among those of the same party, especially one whose dominance in a particular region concealed the customary local differences. In 1988, in the west, clashes between the two commanders of the Harakat-i Enqelab in Helmand, *mullah* Nasim and *raïs* Abdul Wahid, left hundreds dead and intermittently interrupted the traffic of convoys between Pakistan and the Herat region. Similarly, in Badakhshan battles between Najmuddin and Basir Khan divided the province politically and to some extent economically over a period of years.

Tashqurghan, on the road between Kabul and Mazar-i Sharif, provides a good example of such situations. In the 1980s clashes between commanders in this small town were endemic. The bazaar was split between different commanders, and no *mujahid* was able to enter the territory of a different party. In an overt manifestation of this hostility, the commanders built fortified towers with firing points and walls two metres thick, sufficient to withstand rocket-launchers. Movement in the bazaar at night was dangerous because of the possibility of ambush, while political assassinations were ordinary occurrences. Violent confrontations emerged even within parties. In contrast to other regions, there were no social or historical factors here which offered a sufficient explanation of these antagonisms.[3] The social origin of the principal commanders was not a divisive factor, since in essence the rural notables, the *bays*, of Tashqurghan

---

[3] For a portrayal of the bazaar in the pre-war period see Pierre Centlivres, *Un bazar d'Asie centrale*, Wiesbaden: Ludwig Riechert Verlag, 1972.

had retained their power. There was no confrontation with the new élites, although the rise of educated individuals provided some explanation for the tensions. The *ulema* had risen in influence, here as elsewhere, but they were still excluded from the political process. Nor did the existence of several communities explain the clashes. The town was predominantly Tajik, with significant minorities of Uzbeks and Pushtuns, but the commanders were not noticeably identified with any ethnic group. The case of Tashqurghan shows that clashes between commanders cannot always be explained by communal tensions arising from social structures; here rivalry between commanders was the decisive factor. Politics was being conducted for its own sake, and the struggle for power was—at least sometimes—its own justification.

Institutional systems were by nature more likely to prevail in the competitive struggle between commanders because of their superior organisation and greater ability to attract and make use of foreign aid. Masud and Ismail Khan progressively expanded their spheres of influence, eliminating or absorbing the smaller groups. The emergence of organisations on a provincial scale was the predominant tendency in the 1980s. This process of amalgamation brought about a transformation of structures founded on networks into territorial structures. At the outset of the war, commanders had generally based their power on individuals linked by solidarity related to a *qowm*. Later, however, the influential commanders were those who controlled a territory. The appearance of territories in due course implied the demarcation of frontiers; real political divisions on the ground were beginning to emerge.

The territorialisation of politics and the concentration of power were the result of the predominance of institutional systems—either clerical or state systems according to their location. In the north members of the educated class set up the most effective organisations, but the *ulema* held sway over Hazarajat and the tribal areas of the south, and the educated class made no inroads into the tribal regions. For example Amin Wardak, himself an educated man, was not able to extend his territory since his base was in Wardak, a Pushtun tribal zone, where he faced strong opposition as he attempted to expand beyond his initial network. Up to 1994, therefore, the Pushtun south remained much more fragmented politically than the north, so that the *ulema* achieved real predominance only in the province of Ghazni and in Hazarajat.

These developments had their impact on the relationship between the *mujahidin* and the population, in which a watershed was reached in the mid-1980s. External aid permitted the *mujahidin* increasing independence from the population, especially from the point of view of finance. The *mujahidin* tended more to gather in their own *marakiz* (bases) which gave concrete expression to the distinction between military and civil territory. In the early days the *mujahidin* generally spent several months at these bases, returning afterwards to cultivate their lands or going to work abroad. However, the destruction of the irrigation systems and the fact that battles had often been fought on the best lands—near villages or on the plains— left many individuals unemployed and available to become full-time fighters. Being a *mujahid* therefore became a career. The *mujahidin* henceforward stood apart from the population, from whom they were no longer indistinguishable as they had been when the war began.

The evolution of the political map

The fighting, the allocation of aid and rivalries between commanders were all factors which affected the geographical distribution of the parties. Our analysis of political changes on the ground includes the elimination of the lay parties, who were the heirs of the pre-war nationalist and leftist movements,[4] and an examination of the Sunni and Shi'ite parties.

The elimination of the lay parties. The leftist parties in general had no social base in the countryside. They had recruited in the urban environment and been unable to adapt themselves to the new political

---

[4] The nationalist movement Afghan Mellat had no presence on the ground. After 1979 its development took place mainly outside Afghan territory. For example, Dr Mohammad Amin Wakman was resident in the United States at the moment of his election to the presidency of the party at a meeting in Peshawar on 8–9 March 1990. Afghan Mellat's claim to a greater Pushtunistan caused it to lose all aid from Pakistan, and doomed its attempts to establish bases in Afghanistan, though it later moderated its irredentist claims and tried to widen its ethnic base. Its main enemy was Hezb-i Islami, which it blamed for the assassination of several of its members in Peshawar, in particular Dr Shewigal on 27 March 1990 and Taj Muhammad Khan in September 1991.

realities. Khalqi policies were discredited, together with 'progressive' ideas such as agrarian reform, the spread of literacy and the liberation of women, all of which had been favoured by a faction drawn from the urban and educated population. Although leftist militants, often the sons of notables, were represented in certain areas, clashes with other parties and a lack of support from Pakistan led to their rapid marginalisation. In addition the government had been able to repress or bring over to its side the largely urban movements, as was shown by the arrest of several hundred leftists in Kabul in early October 1981.

The pre-war Maoist movement, Shola-yi Jawid, had disappeared in the political turmoil of the 1970s, when its principal activists were killed or fled.[5] New organisations appeared in 1979, of which the leading example was the SAMA, Sazman-i Azadibakhsh-i Mardom-i Afghanistan (Organisation for the Liberation of the Afghan People). Other groups of former Maoists, under different titles, kept up a limited level of activity in the interior of the country. Their activities fell into two categories: on the one hand there were autonomous Maoist commanders, and on the other they made attempts to infiltrate other parties.

At the beginning of the war the leader of SAMA, Majid Kalakani,[6] led a 'Front' in the Shamali plain, close to Kabul. Kalakani had been a Maoist militant from the 1960s and was one of the founding members of SAMA. On 27 February 1980 he was arrested after fighting the regime for several months from a base in his village. He was imprisoned and in June 1980 executed. Under heavy pressure from

---

[5] For instance Dr Abdul Rahim Mahmudi, the brother of the founder of Shola-yi Jawid, was able to escape with his brother Adi when some of his relatives were murdered.

[6] Majid Kalakan was born in 1939 and came from the village of Kalakan in Kohdaman, in the Shamali plain. This was also the birthplace of Habibullah Kalakani, '*bacha-yi saqao*', raising the question whether there was a tradition there of opposition to the authorities. His father and grandfather are reported to have been hanged in 1945 during Hashem's regency. The family was exiled to Kandahar until 1953, when Kalakani returned to Kabul. He afterwards went into hiding between 1958 and 1963. During the liberalisation of the 1960s, he joined the Maoist movement Shola-yi Jawid. In 1968 he once more went into hiding and a price was put on his head. A biography of Kalakani—in part the source of this information—was published in French in Brussels in December 1982 in the periodical *Shah Nama*.

other movements, his men disbanded and his movement disappeared.[7] Up to the fall of Kabul in 1992 the Maoists were just as active in the west of the country. In Farah the Jebhe-yi Moallimin (Teachers' Front) brought together several hundred fighters, at Bala Bolak and near the Iranian frontier, whose affiliation, although they did not openly advocate Maoism, was known to all in the region. The unstable political circumstances in Farah afforded them the opportunity to exercise influence on the local level, through alliances forged with local commanders. In Nimruz a 'Front' based at Zaranj was led for several years by two Maoist leaders: Parwiz, a Shi'ite, and Gul Mahmad, a Pushtun sympathetic to SAMA. The persistence of Maoist 'Fronts' in the west was explained by the relative weakness of the other parties, particularly Hezb-i Islami. A significant role had been retained in Nimruz by the notables, which shielded the Maoists both directly, since they were often linked to the notables by family ties, and indirectly, since the Islamists were less influential in this area. Iranian support, which was overt in Nimruz in Parwiz's case, tended in the same direction. It is likely that the Iranian government wanted a clientele independent of Pakistan in its frontier region. The establishment of Hezbollah groups in Herat had a similar purpose.

Attempts to infiltrate are by nature clandestine and tend to be uncovered only if they go wrong. In addition, a distinction between the individual presence of former Maoists and genuine infiltration was not always easy to draw. Such attempts brought two issues into focus. First, they targeted Harakat-i Enqelab, at least in those cases where some record of events exists, for example in Herat and Balkh at the start of the war. The reason for this may have been the party's loose organisation, as well as the family ties between the Maoists on the one hand and the *khans* and *mawlawis* on the other. Secondly, in the absence of popular support, the Maoists were obliged to act in secret and their initiatives mostly failed, at least where their existence aroused the antagonism of the other parties.

Elsewhere the Maoists kept a foothold in Peshawar, despite the regular assassinations of which they had been the victims since the

---

[7] SAMA was afterwards led by his brother Abdul Qayum Rahbar, who was unable to make his base in Afghanistan. He was assassinated in Peshawar on 27 January 1990.

start of the war, the responsibility for which was generally borne by Hezb-i Islami.[8] There was also a secretive but well established Maoist community in Quetta.

The Sunni parties. During the 1980s Jamiyat-i Islami became the dominant party in the north, while Hezb-i Islami (Khales) and the Ettehad also expanded their influence. The losers—Mahaz-i Melli, Harakat-i Enqelab, and Jebhe-yi Islami—began to lose their influence, a tendency which accelerated after the fall of Kabul.

All observers agree on the importance of Harakat-i Enqelab during the first years of the war as the only party which could claim at that time to exist on a national scale. This initial success was related to the support of a majority of the *ulema* and of the *khans*. However, from 1982–3 onward Harakat-i Enqelab declined markedly in the north, to the benefit of Jamiyat-i Islami, particularly in the provinces of Balkh, Herat and Takhar, while in the west its decline benefited Hezb-i Islami (Khales). The inroads of competing parties also threatened Harakat's position in Logar, though less seriously. Areas which stayed solidly under Harakat-i Enqelab's control were the north of Helmand, up to the point of *raïs* Abdul Wahid's defection to Jamiyat-i Islami in 1989, and above all Ghazni where the young and warlike *ulema* monopolised power in spite of the split initiated by *mawlawi* Mansur in 1981.[9]

---

[8] The kidnap and murder of Dr Samad Durrani provides an example of the difficulties of the Maoists in establishing themselves politically in Pakistan. Durrani, from the province of Paktya, was born in 1947 and studied medicine at the University of Jalalabad. He fled to Pakistan at the end of 1979 and set up the Jebhe-yi Mobarezin (Combatants' Front), a movement based on Maoist principles, as well as playing an active role in the Afghan Doctors' Association. In August 1981 he took part in the 'trial' of the Soviet invasion organised by the Peoples' Tribunal in Stockholm. In late 1980 he also set up a school for 'bare-foot doctors'. On 25 May 1982 some members of Hezb-i Islami kidnapped Durrani and executed him shortly afterwards, with the acquiescence if not the complicity of the Pakistan police. A women's organisation, RAWA (Revolutionary Afghan Women's Association), also maintains a militant stance.

[9] This secession, the earliest and the most significant, was carried out by *mawlawi* Mansur, a former pupil at the Nur al-Modares *madrasa* in Ghazni, who had retained his links with the Mujaddidi family as a *murid* and a former student of the *pir*. It is not accidental that *mawlawi* Mansur gave the name of Khodam ul-Forqan to his splinter group of Harakat-i Enqelab, echoing the title of the pre-war movement. He relied largely on Harakati commanders from Ghazni who had come

Weaknesses in Harakat-i Enqelab's leadership account for its decline, but this was probably not decisive: after all, *mawlawi* Khales was no better organised. The nature of Harakat-i Enqelab's recruitment process was itself at issue: many of the commanders were *khans* or *mawlawis* advanced in years who were unable to bring useful cadres to the movement. The commanders' conservatism was a barrier to innovations in both the military and civilian areas. Harakat-i Enqelab's recruits guaranteed it a high level of social legitimacy, but not necessarily any particular aptitude for warfare. A final factor was that Pakistan gave no priority to the support of Harakat-i Enqelab. In 1983 many commanders went over to Jamiyat-i Islami because Harakat-i Enqelab was not arming them sufficiently.

Jamiyat-i Islami gradually achieved predominance in the north, from Badakhshan to Herat. Its success was related to the conjunction of a number of factors: the presence of educated individuals among its members, strong links between its commanders and the rural population, and a high level of external aid. In addition the decentralised structure of the party, resulting largely from the failure of the leadership in Peshawar to impose its will, had at least the advantage of favouring the emergence of powerful local organisations without too much opposition from Rabbani. Jamiyat-i Islami also gained a foothold in the south, especially under *mullah* Naqibullah in Kandahar, though it did not achieve a predominant position anywhere in the Pushtun region. In the mid-1980s Jamiyat-i Islami became the leading party in Afghanistan, in spite of low membership in the east of the country.

The success of Ettehad was essentially due to the financial resources of its Arab patrons. It recruited on an *ad hoc* basis among commanders who wished to change their party, a consequence of which was the random nature of its geographical distribution. Meanwhile Hezb-i Islami (Khales) recruited mainly new commanders in the west of the country, thus spreading beyond its regional base but not leaving behind its sociological roots, since it continued to be largely Pushtun and tribal.

---

from the Nur al-Modares, and who almost all rallied to him. It may be deduced that Muhammad Nabi must have had difficulty imposing his will on the former pupils of the *pir* Mujaddidi, since he was not an alumnus of the Ghazni *madrasa* and had received a more traditional education.

The erosion of Mahaz-i Melli and Jebhe-yi Islami continued. The first retained a regional presence in Kandahar, while the second was totally marginalised. Lacking Pakistani support and any credible organisation, these two parties rapidly abandoned all hope of influencing military developments.

Finally, the decline of Hezb-i Islami was striking. The issue was why, after its initial success, this movement progressively lost its influence, in spite of its numerous cadres and its disproportionate share of Pakistani aid. Its failure is probably connected to rejection by a population unwilling to tolerate the authoritarianism of its officials. In the end Hezb-i Islami made the same mistakes as the Khalq in its behaviour towards the rural people. Furthermore it became marginalised as a consequence of its strategy of confrontation with other parties. Its clashes with Harakat-i Enqelab and Jamiyat-i Islami unleashed what were virtually regional wars, especially in the north, the west and the province of Laghman. The most serious clashes were with Jamiyat-i Islami, especially on Masud's supply routes. At the worst moment of the Soviet offensive of September 1981, Hezb-i Islami attacked Masud through Koh-i Safi, putting him in the perilous position of having to withstand an attack on two fronts. In a further instance on 9 July 1989 Sayyed Jamal, a Hezb-i Islami commander, ambushed some of Masud's men, after which twenty-five *mujahidin* were taken prisoner and executed. A major row ensued and Hekmatyar, who had to explain his commander's actions, spoke of a local settling of accounts. After a long search Sayyed Jamal and three other Hezb-i Islami *mujahidin* were arrested and on 23 December 1989 they were publicly executed. This aggressive strategy did not save Hezb-i Islami, hitherto well established, from being progressively reduced by Masud to isolated Pushtun remnants.

The Shi'ite parties. From the Shi'ite standpoint the war was fought in two distinct theatres. First, inside Hazarajat the conflict was mostly an internal affair, while outside it the war was waged in coordination with the Sunnis and presented no distinctive features. After the war within Hazarajat, there followed changes in the relationship between Sunnis and Shi'ites.

Because of Hazarajat's isolation and the absence of Soviet-Afghan troops, the situation there was an interesting one, which revealed the political dynamics in a distinct region which had no substantial interaction with the state. Tensions suppressed elsewhere because of the exigencies of the *jihad* were fully displayed. Some tendencies such as the growing importance of the *ulema*, the decline of the *khans* and the emergence of ethnic politics were harbingers of developments that took place at the national level in the 1990s.

Soviet military operations in Hazarajat were kept on a very limited scale. Certainly Bamyan rose in revolt in July 1979, but the city was retaken in 1980 by the government, which held it till 1988. Armed columns which occupied Behsud and Panjao during the summer of 1980 stayed only a few days. No operation of any size took place subsequently, other than occasional bombardments of Waras and Behsud. The reason for the Soviets' lack of interest in the interior of Afghanistan lay in their priorities: control over the economically exploitable sector of the country and the major communication routes. This, as has been seen, was no barrier to an awareness by Karmal's government and then that of Najibullah of the opportunities for political leverage presented by Hazara nationalism. In this region the primary dynamic consisted of internal conflicts: first the elimination of lay forces, then conflicts between revolutionaries and conservatives.

At the beginning of the war, almost the whole of Hazarajat was controlled by Shura-yi Ettefaq, led by Sayyed Ali Beheshti, and in the first two years the *khans* and the Maoists were eliminated, as well as the nationalists, who were prey to the hostility of the *ulema* who ran the party.

Within the Tanzim Nesl-i Naw-i Hazara-Moghol[10] movement there emerged a Hazara nationalist party, the Ettehadia, whose original feature was that it consisted of both Pakistani and Afghan Hazaras.

---

[10] This nationalist organisation, mentioned in Chapter 2, had been exploited in the past by the Pakistani government. In 1973 Daud's return to power and his irredentist Pushtun propaganda led the government of Zulfikar Ali Bhutto, using the Hazara radio station based in Quetta, to give its support to the Tanzim in the interests of its promotion of a greater Hazarajat in the centre of Afghanistan. Links with the Afghan community were mediated through the Hazaras, who traded with Quetta. When the war came the Hazara population of Quetta grew, bringing an increase in nationalist activities. For example, Ghajestani, a former journalist and author of a number of books on the history of Hazarajat, lived in Quetta where he ran a *Shura-yi Farangi* (cultural association) before being assassinated in Afghanistan after the fall of Kabul.

Relations between the Tanzim and the Ettehadia were very close, with the former giving logistical support to the latter and providing its intellectual framework. In May 1979 *haji* Rasul, *shaikh* Mohaqeq Turkmeni, Fasei and Akbari (from Jaghori) set up the Ettehadia-yi Mojahidin-i Afghanistan (Union of Mujahidin of Afghanistan).[11] The aim was to provide support for those Hazaras fighting in the interests of a Hazara nationalist renaissance. The movement had its main bases in Jaghori, where the commander was *haji* Barakat. This was the Hazara district nearest to Quetta, the place from which a substantial part of Quetta's Hazara community originated. From there too came the majority of its militants. The first arms convoy set off for Quetta towards the close of 1979, led by *haji* Rasul. At that point Ettehadia was not yet receiving military aid from the Pakistan government, but the Harakat-i Enqelab and Jebhe-yi Islami provided some arms. In the autumn a press conference in Quetta attracted the attention of the Pakistan government and from then on Ettehadia was substantially assisted by the ISI. From Pakistan's point of view, the advantage presented by the Hazara nationalists was that they acted as a counterbalance to the Iranian revolution. Ettehadia at that time played the role of an arms supplier for the other Shi'ite parties—Shura, Nasr and Harakat-i Islami. However, the movement was unable to expand further, due to internal crises and rivalry with the other parties. Following multiple splits[12] Ettehadia ceased effectively to exist, while it also met resistance inside Afghanistan. In 1981 it was militarily vanquished by the other parties after several days of fighting, and thereafter its role ceased. Contrary to allegations which have been made, this party was not simply a channel for

---

[11] Saddeqi, a future leader of Sepah who was also in Quetta, refused to become involved and went directly to Iran, where he already had contacts. Fasei was appointed president, *haji* Rasul vice-president, and Aedri secretary-general. Aedri, later president of the Ettehadia, was a Pakistani citizen. Mohammad Akram Gisabi, a Hazara from Kabul, joined the movement in 1980 and later became vice-president.

[12] During 1980 the first signs of dissent appeared within Ettehadia: Fasei, the president, joined Nehzat and a split ensued, led by *haji* Rasul, who was opposed to Abdul Husein Maqsudi, the new president. *haji* Rasul, who had links with Nasr and the pro-Iranian parties, became leader of a new Ettehadia. For his part Akbari, who had set off with an Ettehadia convoy, joined the Shura, for which he became a spokesman, which further embittered relations between these two parties.

the ISI to supply arms to Hazarajat. It failed first of all as the result of the overwhelming capacity of the Iranian revolution to attract support, as well as its inability in any real way to break into the religious networks. In reality, though some disciples of *ayatollah* Khoei from Najaf were sympathetic to Ettehadia, it was unequivocally lay and even leftist.

The only bid by the *khans* to achieve political expression was by way of the Shura-yi Arbabah (Council of the *Arbab*),[13] whose leading figures, Gharibdad from Behsud and *haji* Nader of Turkmen, were assassinated by Nasr in 1983 and 1984 respectively. In any case this *shura* was never more than an informal group, rather than a structured party. In fact a significant number of *khans* joined Harakat-i Islami, though it was run by a Shi'ite Qizilbash, because of its conservative ideology and its opposition to the pro-Iranian revolutionary parties. However, the lack of any previous Harakat-i Islami presence and the intrinsic weakness of the *khans* precluded its success. In 1985 the Nasr party's assassination of Tawala, the commander of Harakat-i Islami, who was a son of the principal *khan* of Yakaolang, initiated the definitive decline of Harakat-i Islami as a political force within Hazarajat.

Two factors account for the collapse of the *khans*. First, there was the absence of any political connection with Pakistan or Iran which might have given them arms and lent political support. Support from Iran was out of the question, so there only remained Pakistan, which however chose to support first Ettehadia and then Harakat-i Islami. Second, political organisation was lacking, a factor attributable to the traditional rivalry between the *khans*, as well as to their age, which meant that they had little appetite for involvement in political and military activism. The generation which had the ability to organise itself on the political level had already become politically committed before the war, often in the cause of the left. This seems likely to be the most convincing reason for the *khans'* eclipse. They were thus doubly the losers on the political scene, since they were not only swept from power themselves, but their offspring, who were often Maoists or nationalists, were also politically eliminated. The *khans* were the most modernising and educated group among the population of Hazarajat, and their abrupt displacement was to have serious consequences for the population as a whole.

[13] In Hazarajat the expression *arbab* is equivalent to *khan*.

There were many Maoists among the Hazaras from Hazarajat's border regions. In these more developed areas some of the notables' sons attended the university, where most joined Maoist groups. They were active in the province of Ghazni in particular, and especially in Jaghori: the Mahmudi brothers were one example. At the beginning of the war there was apparently a Maoist 'Front' of which five members were hanged in Kabul in 1980. No longer able openly to acknowledge their Maoist allegiance in face of the hostility of the other parties and a section of the population, the Hazara Maoists of the SAMA turned to entryism, targeting in particular nationalist movements such as Ettehadia. Later they mostly withdrew to Quetta.

After the elimination of the lay parties, tensions sharpened between the Shura and the revolutionary pro-Iranian parties, especially Nasr, which soon allied itself with Sepah. In early 1982 there was a Nasr offensive against the Shura, with the complicity of some of the latter's commanders. Husein Saddeqi, the Shura representative in Iran, who had returned to Nili in 1981, went over to Sepah. He led the principal attack on Waras, Sayyed Beheshti's village, which was the Shura headquarters, but could not advance further than Panjao because of a counter-offensive mounted by Sayyed Hasan *jaglan*, the Shura's military chief. At the close of 1982, after this first offensive, the new political position on the ground showed an overall loss for the Shura, which no longer had real control beyond the regions of Waras, Panjao and Naur. The revolutionary parties, Nasr and Sepah, were dug in at Deh Kundi, Lal o Sarjangal and Yakaolang, as well as Dara-i Suf and Turkmen. Shura thus lost control of the centre of Hazarajat, which contained the most mountainous and inaccessible regions.

After sporadic fighting, the second major offensive by the revolutionary parties took place in 1984. On 6 May 1984 Sayyed Beheshti was dislodged from Waras and obliged to retreat to Naur, Sayyed Hasan *jaglan*'s fief. Backing from Harakat-i Islami enabled him to retake Waras in September. The positions on the ground stabilised and thereafter no further large-scale attack was launched, though sporadic fighting continued until 1989. This second offensive in particular revealed the polarisation between the moderates, Harakat-i Islami and Shura, against the revolutionaries of Nasr and of the Pasdaran. The fierce but highly localised struggles in which the parties were later involved are difficult to detail. There was clearly a tendency towards fragmentation: clashes took place between all the parties, for example between Nasr and Sepah at Deh Kundi, and sometimes even within them.

Political autonomy in Hazarajat led to a resurgence of clashes with the Pushtuns. The politically-motivated exclusion of the nomads from Hazarajat became generalised, with the exception of a few areas such as Naur, a traditional crossing point.[14] The collapse of the central government removed the protection enjoyed by the Pushtun nomads, who were also robbed and involved in clashes which closed off their traditional migration routes.

In addition to the clashes with the nomads there was also conflict throughout the war between Hazaras and Pushtuns along Hazarajat's frontiers, especially at Jaghori but also at Anguri in Ghazni province, near Kajran in Ghor, and at Meydan Shahr in the province of Wardak. On the other hand, in the northern Ghazni and in Wardak other than in Meydan Shahr the clashes were limited in scale. In the case of Wardak the reason may have been that the long-standing Pushtun presence in the valley of Wardak, dating from their conquest in the seventeenth century, tended to promote better interethnic relations. There was no living memory of the loss of the land. Also the two communities were geographically well separated by a plateau above the valley. In Ghazni the Hazaras were in part townsmen, accounting for around one-third of the population, and had fought the Soviets and the government troops side by side with the Sunnis throughout the war. The personality of the local commanders also played a role: Shah Jan of the Shi'ite Harakat-i Islami and Qari Baba for the Sunni Harakat-i Enqelab favoured coexistence. The most savage conflicts took place at Jaghori and at Anguri, where the Hazaras apparently went on the offensive to recapture lands confiscated under Abdul Rahman Khan. In the south and in Uruzgan the flight of Pushtun families was reported, especially in the spring and autumn of 1990. Meanwhile Hazaras travelling to Pakistan were often seized for ransom by the Pushtuns.

---

[14] The situation was less tense in previous years: see Alain Guillo, Jean-José Puig, Olivier Roy, 'La guerre en Afghanistan: modifications des déplacements traditionnels et émergence de nouveaux types de circulation', *Ethnologica Elvetica* (Berne) 7, 1983.

Relations between Sunnis and non-Hazara Shi'ites were on the whole better than those between Pushtuns and Hazaras. The non-Hazara Shi'ites, especially in the towns, had developed sophisticated relations with the Sunnis which tended rather towards cooperation than confrontation. When conflicts took place, the political affiliations of the commanders were crucial because although the commanders generally took decisions according to local circumstances, the directives of the parties often had direct consequences for local inter-party relations. Of the Sunnis Hezb-i Islami (Khales) and Ettehad were the most anti-Shi'ite, although the Sunnis generally had good relations with Mohseni's Harakat-i Islami, which was mainly established in urban areas or on the fringes of towns. By way of illustration, the local Harakat-i Islami in Herat (formerly Rad) maintained good relations with Jamiyat-i Islami, but Ismail Khan several times attacked the Hezbollah militias, whom he accused of having links with his enemies.

Inter-party cooperation
The parties in Peshawar repeatedly attempted to coordinate their activities, usually in response to pressure from American or Pakistani donors, but up to the fall of Kabul this cooperation was in name only: it had no effect on the structure of the parties, which remained independent of each other, and had hardly any impact on the situation on the ground.

In April 1981 an assembly of *ulema* summoned the party chiefs. After some days of discussion an alliance was established bringing together Jamiyat-i Islami, the two branches of Hezb-i Islami, Ettehad, Jebhe and the fragments of Harakat-i Enqelab, especially that of *mawlawi* Mansur. However this alliance, entitled Ettehad-i Mujahidin-i Afghanistan, proved ephemeral. After the failure of this initiative two separate coalitions were established on the basis of ideological affinities and personal relations between leaders. On 2 June 1981 an alliance sympathetic to royalist ideas came into existence which included Harakat-i Enqelab, Jebhe and Mahaz.[15] Following the appeal by

---

[15] Mahaz's military weakness led it to adopt the *jirga* (the tribal assembly) as its mode of political-diplomatic action. These ploys never succeeded, in particular as the result of the position of the Pakistanis and the Islamists, who were opposed to the return of the king. The first came in the spring of 1980 at the initiative of

Zahir Shah in *Le Monde* on 22 June 1983 this coalition appealed for the creation of a united resistance front coordinated by the king.

Meanwhile the remaining parties also made attempts to institutionalise their cooperation. On 2 May 1982 at Rawalpindi the announcement was made of a 'complete unification' of the movements. On 25 May 1983 Sayyaf was elected president in a second round against *mawlawi* Khales. Rabbani was entrusted with military affairs and Hekmatyar became vice-president. The president was henceforth to be elected for a period of two years—there had initially been a rotating presidency—but the profound hostility between the groups involved precluded any joint strategy from developing. On 7 March 1984 the alliance was hit by a crisis when Sayyaf, in the absence of Rabbani and Khales, arranged for his cronies to be elected to positions of responsibility in charge of financial and military affairs.

In the end the two alliances disintegrated, and on 1 April 1985 the parties proclaimed the formation of the 'Alliance of Seven' for which Hekmatyar became the spokesman.[16] The earliest initiatives towards the formation of a para-governmental structure date from this period. On 22 July 1986 the Alliance announced the establishment of offices in New York and in Jeddah (to liaise with the Organisation of the Islamic Conference). On 17 January 1987 this alliance set up a High Council of Mujahidin bringing together the seven Sunni parties. They participated for the first time together at the Islamic Conference in Kuwait, and on 29 January 1987 Sayyaf addressed the conference but failed to obtain the status of observer which the *mujahidin* had been seeking—unsuccessfully—since 1980. Afghanistan's seat remained vacant, as it had been since 1980.

Omar Barakzai, and therefore fell outside the sphere of influence of the Gaylani family, who opposed it. The second, in the autumn of 1981, was planned by a committee of former ministers and parliamentarians. This *jirga*, which was planned to take place in Quetta, ended in disarray after being moved to Peshin because of the opposition of the Pakistani government. The third *jirga*, which never got beyond the planning stage, was the result of an appeal by the king on 22 June 1983. Later there were repeated attempts to convene a *jirga*, but these met with limited success due to alterations in the balance of forces within the country which closed the door to this kind of procedure.

[16] The precise name of this alliance appears to have been Shura-yi Ettehad Islami Haftgane (Council of the Islamic Union of the Seven).

As for the Shi'ite parties, all attempts to unite had taken place under Iran's auspices, and were translated into an impetus towards unity in the face of the Sunnis which existed at the level of diplomacy rather than on the ground. In 1982 the first attempt at alliance brought together various small parties within the Jebhe-yi Mottahid-i Enqelab-i Islami, which in 1984 became the Etilaf-i Chaharganah (Union of Four Parties). In 1985 an alliance based at the Iranian city of Qom under the patronage of Ayatollah Montazeri brought together Nasr, Sepah, Niru and Harakat-i Islami. Two years later the principal constituents of another alliance, Shura-yi Etilaf-i Islami, were Nasr, Sepah and some small groups of Khomeini supporters, excluding Shura-yi Ettefaq and the Mustazaffin. Relations between the parties continued to be hostile on the ground, so that this alliance operated only in the diplomatic sphere, and specifically in negotiations with the Sunnis over the setting-up of a parliament in exile.

The announcement of the Soviet withdrawal meant that the issue of cooperation needed to be faced once more, this time as a matter of urgency. On 11 May 1988 a provisional constitution was adopted and on 19 June the Sunni parties announced the formation of an interim government. This assisted the first efforts of the *mujahidin* to establish a diplomatic presence. Rabbani was delegated by the alliance to make a tour of Africa. In addition he was received by President Reagan on 9 November 1988, and by the UN secretary-general. From 3 to 5 December he was at Taef, where he negotiated with a Soviet delegation led by Vorontsov, the new Soviet ambassador in Kabul.

However, this interim government did not represent the resistance movement as it existed in reality. Each party was allocated two ministers, which did not reflect their presence on the ground and entailed an over-representation of the Pushtuns. In a government of fifteen members there were eleven Pushtuns, two Tajiks, one *sayyed* and one Hazara. The Pushtuns were mostly Durranis from Kandahar, including one with no party affiliation. The two Tajiks were members of Jamiyat-i Islami. The process of choosing representatives exacerbated the ethnic opposition between the parties.[17] An additional issue was that the Shi'ite parties were not represented.

---

[17] The Kabul government simultaneously announced the formation of a new cabinet, led by Hasan Sharq, of which the ethnic make-up was much more balanced.

The Soviet withdrawal accelerated the setting-up of a provisional government, which was already present in embryo in the interim government. The presumed imminence of victory led the Pakistani leadership to promote the establishment of a body to represent the *mujahidin*. The convocation of a *shura* announced by Mujaddidi in January 1989 was the prelude to the provisional government's formation. The members of the *shura* were mainly Pushtuns, since each party automatically sent sixty delegates. Presence on the ground was not taken into account, and the over-representation of eastern Pushtuns was blatant. Disagreement immediately broke out among the parties on the role of the Shi'ites and the part to be played by the king.

All Shi'ite attempts to obtain a place within this government failed. The crucial disagreement was over the number of seats to be allocated to the Shi'ites within a common *shura*. Notwithstanding, Mujaddidi—delegated by the Sunni parties—reached a preliminary agreement in Teheran on 5 February with Muhammad Karim Khalili, the spokesman for eight Shi'ite parties, which were allocated eighty seats in a *shura* of 539 members. However, this agreement was not endorsed by the Sunni parties, who offered the Shi'ites sixty seats out of 440, in contrast with the 100 seats for which the Shi'ites were asking. Opposition to the Shi'ites from Hezb-i Islami, Hezb-i Islami (Khales) and Ettehad precluded agreement, and these parties were supported by Pakistan and Saudi Arabia, with the aim of keeping Iran's influence to the minimum.

Despite the absence of the Shi'ites, the *shura*, composed of 400 members, including some twenty intellectuals living in Europe, opened its deliberations in the Pakistani city of Rawalpindi. On 23 February Mujaddidi became president, with 174 votes, prevailing over the other leaders. Sayyaf was appointed Prime Minister. On 9 March the provisional government was recognised by Saudi Arabia, followed by Sudan, Malaysia and Bahrain. A number of countries, including Britain and France, sent ambassadors. On 6 April 1989 Peter Thompson was appointed the US representative to the provisional government with the rank of ambassador, and on 16 April the provisional government was accorded Afghanistan's seat at the Islamic Conference.

The provisional government, financed by Arab and western benefactors, set up its headquarters in Peshawar. Corruption and inefficiency were its two most striking characteristics. The appointment of provincial governors was followed neither by the establishment of an administrative structure within the country, nor even by enhanced coordination between the parties. Overall, the government showed little cohesion. For example, the dispatch in January 1991 of a contingent of 2,000 *mujahidin* to assist the coalition against Saddam Hussein was carried out against the wishes of some of the parties, notably Hezb-i Islami. Developments on the ground were in any case destined to make an irrelevance of this government, set up as it was in anticipation of the rapid collapse of the Kabul regime.

The mujahidin after the withdrawal

The period from 1989 to 1992 was one of transition. The *jihad* of the early years was over, but the survival of the Kabul regime continued to obstruct the establishment of the emerging new political configuration. The rise of the *mujahidin* was especially swift during the Soviet withdrawal. The morale of the fighters, who were aware of having won a historic victory, was very high. In addition arms flooded in from Pakistan. During the summer of 1988 a large number of military positions and towns fell into the hands of the *mujahidin*, including in June Meydan Shahr (later retaken by the government), Muhammad Agha and Qalat-i Ghilzai; in August Kunduz, Dara-i Suf and Bamyan; and in early September Imam Saheb and Spin Boldak. Asadabad fell on 11 October, and 21 October saw the capture of Mahmud Raqi, the provincial capital of Kapisa. By the time the Soviet withdrawal was complete the Kabul regime held only some sixty urban centres, and six provinces out of twenty-five had fallen entirely into the hands of the *mujahidin*.

However, these victories were partly illusory, since they were the result more of the redeployment of the government's defences than of any improvement in the coordination or logistics of the *mujahidin*. In fact, in the context of the post-withdrawal situation, Pakistani strategy was aimed at the capture of the towns in order to precipitate the collapse of the regime. However, the guerrillas did not possess the human or military resources to bring to completion a campaign which necessitated the military coordination of thousands of men. A further factor was the suspension of US aid to the resistance from December 1988 to July 1989: a crucial moment, just as the Soviets were stepping up their arms shipments to the Kabul regime.

After the withdrawal of the Soviet forces from Jalalabad in May 1988, this city became the main objective of the Pakistani military, which believed that its fall would result in the fall of Kabul, enabling Hekmatyar to seize power. In this sense the fall of Jalalabad represented a risk for the other parties, and Masud is said to have allowed the passage of a number of large convoys in March and April 1989 to save the government forces from being starved of supplies.[18] The Kabul regime, aware that its future was at stake, sent 15,000 men to Jalalabad, which had already been reinforced by troops from other positions the government had abandoned. On 6 March 1989 Hezb-i Islami (Khales) and Mahaz-i Melli *mujahidin* began their offensive with the acquisition of Samarkhel, to the east of the city, which they captured by bribing the officer in command. The *mujahidin* then attempted to take the city's airport but suffered heavy losses; in particular, Scud missile strikes threw the attack into chaos, while at the same time government reinforcements advanced along the Kabul-Jalalabad road. Meanwhile, on 10 March the guerrillas attacked from the north and then in the following days also from the south. However, government air support prevented the guerrilla fighters from massing and the *mujahidin* were driven back. Fighting went on into April but by now the government was on the offensive. A further convoy came in by road from Kabul to Jalalabad and a counter-attack at the end of April led to the guerrillas being driven out of the outskirts of the city. Resistance losses were heavy, probably totaling several thousand men, because of the lack of air cover on the *mujahidin* side and of a lack of discipline and effective command among the Mahaz forces. The presence of Pakistani officers and Arab fighters on the *mujahidin* side was insufficient to transform a guerrilla force into a regular army. The massacre of seventy soldiers and mutilation of their bodies by Khales's men during the capture of a frontier post also stiffened the government troops.[19]

This notable setback was to have a number of consequences. First, there was a certain distancing by the United States, and later the morale of those *mujahidin* who no longer believed in a military victory began to suffer. As Ismail Khan admitted, 'The battle of Jalalabad lost

---

[18] A charge which Masud denied, while attacking Pakistan's strategy (according to an interview in October 1991).

[19] *Les Nouvelles d'Afghanistan*, 43, June 1989.

us the credit won in ten years of fighting.'[20] In consequence the strategies of the parties began to lean towards a coup d'état, as the prospect of a military overthrow of the regime receded.

During the two years which followed the defeat at Jalalabad, the situation appeared to ossify, and in some areas the resistance even lost ground. The capture of Khost on 31 March 1991 was an unusual military success for the opposition, but this was a town which had been completely surrounded since the beginning of the war and was not of great strategic significance, although its capture did facilitate the journey to Pakistan. During this period, as the fighting became less intense, Masud was the only dynamic element; in both 1990 and 1991 he launched a spring offensive, and its success, though limited, allowed him to extend his influence in the north. On 11 April 1990 he took Dasht-i Archi, and in June 1991 at Khwaja Ghar he inflicted a defeat on the government militias, who withdrew towards Mazar-i Sharif. Masud strengthened the security of his supply routes on the Pakistani frontier with the capture on 15 July 1991 of Zibak, and on 21 July of Ishkashem in the province of Badakhshan.

Generally, the military stagnation aggravated the tensions between the commanders and the leaderships in exile, whose shortcomings were the subject of lively criticism. The establishment of parties based in the country and the setting up of *shuras* by the commanders were both expressions of this difference of views. *Shuras* set up by commanders with assistance from the Pakistanis and the Americans were an attempt to bypass the party leaderships as the levels of aid diminished.[21] Two *shuras* involving the commanders took place in

---

[20] Interview, autumn 1989.

[21] In 1987 a bid to coordinate the commanders, taken at the initiative of Ismail Khan, took place with the aim of coordination at grassroots level to distance the commanders from the political intrigues of Peshawar. From 12 to 23 July 1987 commanders from all over Afghanistan and from all the parties went to Sholgar in Ghor province. Several thousand *mujahidin* attended, and around 1,200 commanders were represented, coming principally from Herat, Badghis, Ghor, Faryab, Farah, Helmand, Kandahar, Uruzgan, Wardak, Logar and Kabul. Among the leading commanders were *mullah* Naqibullah, Dr Fazlullah and Amanullah (from Hezb-i Islami in Helmand). Decisions taken related to improved coordination of the commanders (through radio contacts, joint training and strategic bases, and the common administration of justice) as well as to the rejection of any cease-fire or compromise with the government. The second meeting, set for six months later, failed to take place due to the opposition of the various headquarters in Peshawar.

Paktya, one from 7 to 9 May and another from 22 to 25 June 1990. A third meeting presided over by Masud was convened between 9 and 13 October at Shah Salim on the Badakhshan border. Among the major commanders attending were *mawlawi* Haqqani, Qari Baba, Abdul Haq, Amin Wardak, Sayyed Hasan *jaglan* and *mullah* Malang, acting as a representative of Ismail Khan. The main points on the agenda were military coordination, the free movement of guerrilla groups and the administrative division of Afghanistan into nine districts. Masud even paid his first visit to Pakistan since 1979 and in Islamabad met the army chief-of-staff General Beg and the head of the ISI, Lieutenant-General Asad Durrani—it appears that these meetings had no outcome. This initiative was undertaken with American support, but failed because of the divisions between the participants; in fact the plan lacked coherence because of the desire of some commanders for military cooperation while others, especially in Hezb-i Islami (Khales), wanted greater autonomy. In this context it was easy for the party leaderships in exile to connive at the failure of any such initiatives, which could have challenged their monopoly of representation.

This challenge to the parties also paved the way for the emergence of a local movement in the province of Kunar. Other than in the Nuristani regions, which followed their own line, the Kunar valley at the start of the war was largely Hezb-i Islami territory.[22] The *amir-welayati* (provincial commander) of Hezb-i Islami was Jamil ur-Rahman, whose real name was *mawlawi* Husein.[23] He was at that time an *alem* and a former student of the *madrasa* of Panj Pir, which was renowned for its fundamentalist teaching. The geographical position of Kunar and Jamil ur-Rahman's background meant that in the early years he benefited from Arab aid. This had been a significant factor from 1985 as the result of the involvement of Arab militants in the camps of the Bajaur Agency (in Pakistan), where refugees

---

[22] In the first phase of the rebellion before Hezb-i Islami took charge the *khans* were active. In the Pesh valley the revolt was led by Samiullah Safi, born in 1940 in Murchel, a notable (son of Sultan Mohammad Khan) who was a former schoolteacher and a member of the Wolesi Jirga from 1969 to 1973.

[23] Born around 1939 in Pesh, Jamil ur-Rahman, who was from the Safi tribe, became a member of the Islamist movement before the war and took part in the rising of 1975. He later joined Hezb-i Islami at the beginning of the war, and took part in the rising of July 1978.

from Kunar were present in large numbers. Many volunteers, in particular Egyptians, fought under Jamil ur-Rahman, who received money directly from King Fahd of Saudi Arabia. Jamil ur-Rahman left Hezb-i Islami in 1986 or 1987, when—with Arab aid broadly guaranteeing his independence—he headed the Jamaat-i Dawaat-i al-Quran wa-Sunna-yi Afghanistan (Society for the preaching of the Quran and the Sunna in Afghanistan). This party was ideologically close to the Ahl-i Hadith.[24]

The evacuation of Soviet troops and the militias in 1988 left the field free for Jamil ur-Rahman, who adopted an expansionist strategy, either crushing or buying off the other commanders in Kunar. At the end of 1989 he and his only serious competitor Hezb-i Islami reached an agreement providing for the election of a *shura*,[25] which in practice met in the early days of March 1990. However, rivalries quickly re-emerged and in January 1991 Jamil ur-Rahman proclaimed the establishment of an Islamic emirate of Kunar. The emirate was constituted as a government of fourteen ministers in the framework of a Central Council (Shura-yi Markazi), elected by an Executive Council (Shura-yi Ejray). All the ethnic groups of the province and the various political parties were represented, especially the Daulat-i Enqelab-i Islami-i Afghanistan Nuristani.[26] In the spring of 1991 Hezb-i Islami lost its main bases, and its leader *mawlawi* Faqer Muhammad found himself encircled by Jamil ur-Rahman's troops. Jamil ur-Rahman, who was himself absent in Saudi Arabia, sent an order to spare the life of *mawlawi* Faqer Muhammad, who was sent to Peshawar. At this moment in early 1991 the virtual elimination of Hezb-i Islami from Kunar prompted Hekmatyar to launch an offensive involving several hundred men, in cooperation with Hezb-i Islami (Khales) and Harakat-i Enqelab. In August the provincial capital, Asadabad, was captured and sacked (the offices of the humanitarian organisations were not spared) and some fifty Arabs were killed. After losing the battle Jamil ur-Rahman fled to Bajaur in Pakistan.

---

[24] There was never any collective *takfir* towards the population, as B. Rubin contends in *The Fragmentation of Afghanistan*, New Haven, CT: Yale University Press, 1995, p. 86.

[25] Hezb-i Islami always supported general elections, a point on which it differed from the other six parties of the provisional government.

[26] See the article by Paul Castella, 'Convoitises régionales sur l'Afghanistan. L'exemple du Kunar', *Les Nouvelles d'Afghanistan*, 55, 1, 1992.

Pakistan observed these developments attentively, and went as far as to send the Bajauri Scouts to re-open the Nawa pass, at one point closed because of the fighting. The presence of this unit at Jamil ur-Rahman's side was viewed in different ways. Some saw it as a signal that the ISI had dropped Hekmatyar, but in fact the recapture of Asadabad by Hezb-i Islami could not have been carried out without the tacit approval of the Pakistani intelligence services. In the following weeks the governor of the North West Frontier Province mediated between the vanquished Jamil ur-Rahman and Hezb-i Islami. On 30 August 1991, during these negotiations, Jamil ur-Rahman was assassinated by a twenty-four-year old Egyptian journalist, Abdullah Rumi, who immediately committed suicide.[27] Jamil ur-Rahman's successor, *mawlawi* Samiullah, remained in Pakistan.

This conflict may be interpreted in two complementary ways. First, it could be seen as the liquidation of a dissident Hezb-i Islami commander. Jamil ur-Rahman was not typical of a commander belonging to this party—his links with the fundamentalist network of the *madrasa* Panj Pir provided him with an opportunity to remain autonomous which he seized after the Soviet withdrawal—and this tends to confirm the general responsibility of the *ulema* for splits in Hezb-i Islami. The other interpretation lies in the context of the Gulf War. As it happened, Hezb-i Islami had adopted an explicitly pro-Iraqi and anti-American position, as had the majority within the Muslim Brotherhood. The struggle between Jamil ur-Rahman and Hezb-i Islami therefore set pro-Saudis and pro-Iraqis against each other.

In contrast to the fragmentation observed among the Sunnis, several Shi'ite movements merged in 1990 in the Hezb-i Wahdat (Party of Unity). This development, an augury of the impending regionalisation and ethnicisation of the parties, is analysed in the following chapters.

---

[27] Jamil ur-Rahman's assassin was close to the Muslim Brotherhood and especially to Abdullah Azzam. He had from some months been a journalist with *Al-Bunian-i Makhtus*, after previously working for the magazine *Jihad*. He left no indication of the reasons for his action.

Part IV. THE TALIBAN

In the period after 1992 both the actors concerned and the ideological positions they adopted were substantially different from those of the preceding era, to the extent that there are good reasons to speak of a second Afghan war. The conflict became politicised—not depoliticised as is sometimes claimed.[1] The crucial distinction was that between depoliticisation and demobilisation. After the fall of the Kabul regime religious duty could no longer be adduced as a justification for the war, and the spirit of *jihad*, the basis of popular solidarity, gradually dissipated. This development had been in evidence since the Soviet withdrawal. The distancing of the *mujahidin* from the people found expression in the language employed: the term *jang-i dakheli* (civil war) was now in use, and *jihad* was no longer mentioned. *Mujahidin* of all parties were accused of oppressing civilians, kidnapping and looting. Brigandage was also targeted at humanitarian aid operations, and attacks on convoys and hostage-taking became more frequent.

The aggravated rivalry between the parties—whose behaviour, far from being irrational, resulted from the fight for survival—discredited them in the popular view. In addition to the demobilisation of the population, this rivalry had two further consequences. First, the political forces became territorially based, controlling areas which showed a tendency to political homogeneity. Secondly, only those groups which had been able to put in place organised systems capable of taking control of resources were able to survive. These groups were the educated class in the north and the *ulema* in the south and in the Harzarajat. The process of concentration of resources therefore had both a communal and a social dimension.

The political actors, driven by competition, were obliged to develop strategies to mobilise their supporters, since the unchallengeable and essentially apolitical language of the *jihad* was no longer available. Some of the parties opted deliberately to appeal to communal solidarity, an opportunity presented to them as the result of regionalisation, while others were involuntarily obliged to follow suit.

[1] Olivier Roy, 'Afghanistan. Le retour des vieux démons', *Esprit*, October 1989.

The conflict was therefore open to interpretation on three different levels. It could be seen as being between ethnic groups; or between ideological tendencies (which might be communist, fundamentalist or Islamist); or between social groups—in particular the *ulema* and the educated class. The claim of legitimacy for one or other of these ways of reading the conflict was part of the strategy of the actors themselves, since it had its impact on the parties' policies and therefore in the end also on political loyalties. At first these lines of divisions did not coincide, which gave the war its particular character. For example, the educated individuals who dominated the north were either Jombesh communists or Jamiyat Islamists. The Hazara *ulema* of Hezb-i Wahdat were opposed to the Pushtun *ulema* of the Taliban, and the 'ethnic' parties, Hezb-i Wahdat and Jombesh, were controlled respectively by Shi'ite fundamentalist *ulema* and by educated communists. However, as the conflict developed, the various divisions were gradually drawn into line with each other, ultimately creating a single confrontation between a rural and fundamentalist Pushtun movement and an educated and Islamist Tajik opposition. As a prelude to the detailed examination of the issues of ethnicity and the confrontation between the *ulema* and the educated class, we now analyse the mechanism which led to the elimination of the majority of the actors and the coming into existence of a quasi-monopoly, to the benefit of the Taliban.

7. Competition and the Impetus towards Monopoly (1992–2001)

In the 1990s three basic constraints governed the pattern of rivalry between political groups. First, the confrontation took place within a closed and unchanging geographical area. In the modern world frontiers are more permanent than states, sometimes preceding them and generally surviving their demise. No one in Afghanistan or in the neighbouring countries sought to challenge them. The possibility that some part of Afghanistan's territory might be annexed by neighbouring countries, which had arisen repeatedly since the beginning of the war, was never likely to became actual. There was no internal frontier, either administrative or communal, which could conveniently have served as a basis for partition. In addition, the state constituted a potential resource—for international recognition, access to aid and established legitimacy—and became a principal objective of the struggle, even for those parties which were against its reconstruction. Competition between actors was therefore acted out within the framework of the concentration of resources. This process of coalescence through competition, with the difference that the frontiers of the state were defined and the process was much swifter, recalled the theories of Norbert Elias concerning the formation of the European states.[2]

Secondly, the war changed in nature. Guerrilla warfare to some extent disappeared, to be succeeded by more conventional conflicts. Operations, sometimes with air support, often involved tens of thousands of men. Their aim was to eradicate the enemy and capture the towns, where wealth and population were concentrated. Forces were increasingly territorialised, and recognisable front lines made their appearance. To some extent these conflicts remained geographically

[2] Norbert Elias, *op. cit.*

235

limited, in contrast to the period of the Soviet occupation, and outside the war zones the process of reconstruction went ahead. The actors who survived were therefore those whose level of organisation enabled them to accumulate resources. Commanders and parties which were too small or organised on the patrimonial model were eliminated, since they were unable to compete with large organisations. A particular phenomenon was that the figure of the commander as an autonomous power gradually disappeared from the scene.

Thirdly, it is impossible to ignore the role played by neighbouring states, which intervened on a large scale in the conflict through their Afghan proxies. Such proxies were Jombesh, which acted for Uzebkistan; Hezb-i Wahdat, which served the purposes of Iran; and Hezb-i Islami, and later the Taliban, which acted for Pakistan. Meanwhile, Jamiyat-i Islami developed its relations with India, Iran, Russia and the western countries. Relations between outside states and their Afghan clients were based on mutual instrumentalisation. The three regional powers had their own divergent interests, and rarely exerted any pressure towards a peaceful solution. However, their intervention altered the balance of power, and influenced the movement towards the concentration of resources. For example, Rashid Dostum was able to return to Mazar-i Sharif in 1997 thanks to help from Uzbekistan, and after the fall of Kabul in 1996 the survival of Masud depended largely on Russian, Iranian and western aid. However, although all the Afghan actors benefited from external assistance, Pakistan was the only state to have invested, first in Hezb-i Islami and then in the Taliban, to an extent which was in the end crucial in precipitating the transition towards the concentration of resources. Without the support of Pakistan the presidential coalition around Rabbani would probably have prevailed in 1992. Pakistan's logistical assistance played a key role in all the Taliban's military operations; For example, the counter-attack which led to the capture of Herat in 1995 would not have been possible without its material support. In addition a significant section of the Taliban fighters— about a third during the offensive in the spring of 1999—were foreign fundamentalists, either Pakistani or having passed through Pakistan.

The process of centralisation took place in several phases. The collapse of the state in 1992 created a fluid situation which accelerated the competition for resources and their accumulation in fewer hands.

Between 1992 and 1995 the political distribution on the ground was dramatically simplified through the process of regionalisation of forces. The rise of the Taliban brought with it a polarisation between it and the other parties, which were unable to do more than delay their own decline.

The collapse of the state

In August 1991 the attempted coup against Gorbachev irreversibly destabilised the Kabul regime, which could no longer rely on Russian aid.[3] Yeltsin was all the more anxious to distance himself from the Soviet legacy because of the support he derived from the *afghantsy* (veterans of the Afghan war): men such as Alexander Rutskoy, who opposed all support for Najibullah's regime. Inside Afghanistan perceptions also changed. The diplomatic efforts of the UN ceased to be relevant, and within the government many began to anticipate the post-Najibullah period. The royalists, Hezb-i Islami and Jamiyat-i Islami all increased their contacts with the communists. Competition between rivals got under way, to see who could profit most from the change of regime.

In the end Najibullah fell victim to the growing autonomy of the militias, which had become the principal military force in the north: ironically this was a development he himself had fostered when he was the head of the KHAD. The immediate reason for conflict was his encouragement of the Pushtuns, a strategy aimed at sidelining Karmal's supporters, who were mainly Persian-speakers. At the end of February the appointment of a Pushtun to a command in the province of Balkh provided the pretext for a revolt. Mumin, the commander of the base at Hayratan near the Amu Darya, refused to obey the government's orders. The garrison at Mazar-i Sharif, and then the north-west provinces, rose in a rebellion headed by Rashid Dostum, who declared himself the leader of a new party, the Jombesh-i Melli (National Movement). It quickly became apparent that Rashid Dostum was in collusion with Masud and the Hezb-i Wahdat to overthrow the regime.

On 18 March 1992 the *mujahidin* entered Mazar-i Sharif without a fight, and on the same day Najibullah announced that if a neutral

---

[3] In September 1991 the Soviet government announced that from 1 January 1992 it would deliver no more arms to the Kabul regime.

government could be installed he would resign. With the backing of the rebels, Masud then began his advance on the capital, where Rashid Dostum's militia, already installed, would give him crucial support. On 24 March 1992 Hezb-i Watan split up, and power devolved into the hands of a number of party officials: Farid Mazdak (deputy Defence Minister), Abdul Wakil (formerly Foreign Minister), Nabi Azimi (head of the Kabul garrison) and Rashid Dostum (head of the northern militias, who remained in Mazar-i Sharif). On 14 April Masud took Charikar without a fight, then Jabal ul-Seraj and Bagram air base. The road to Kabul was now open.

The following day, 15 April, Najibullah attempted to flee to India, but was prevented by Dostum's militia, who were in control of the airport. He took refuge in the UN offices, which were close to the French embassy.[4] On 16 April he was stripped of his power, and a council composed of members of Hezb-i Watan was set up to cover the interim period. On the same day the Interior Minister Gholam Faruq, Yaqubi the director of the WAD, and his deputy General Baqi were all killed by unknown assailants.

As the old regime collapsed the race to Kabul gathered speed. On 17 April Wakil, the former Foreign Minister, held a meeting with Masud at Charikar to discuss the transfer of power. On 17 and 18 April government aircraft bombed Hezb-i Islami to the south of Kabul, aiming to slow its advance. On 18 April Masud surrounded Kabul to block the approach of Hezb-i Islami, which was coming closer to the capital in spite of a rearguard action by Dostum's militiamen. On 22 April Benon Sevan met Masud at Charikar, but it was by then too late to agree on a transitional government. On 23 April the *mujahidin* entered the capital without a fight, but several hours later there were clashes between Hezb-i Islami and other groups, while in Peshawar the parties attempted to reach agreement on the formula on which a new government could be based.

On 24 April the Peshawar accords,[5] agreed by the seven parties, provided for the setting-up of an interim government of fifty-one

---

[4] Najibullah's family was already in India, which said it would accept him as a refugee without granting him political asylum. Though he had several opportunities to leave Afghanistan, he remained until he was murdered by the Taliban after the fall of Kabul in September 1996.

[5] The text of these accords can be found in an appendix to A. Saeed's article 'Afghanistan, Peshawar and After', *Regional Studies*, (Islamabad) 11 (2), 1993, pp. 103–58.

members under the leadership of Mujaddidi, to hold power for a period of two months; after which Rabbani would head a leadership council for a further four months. The Prime Minister-designate was Hekmatyar (Hezb-i Islami), while the Defence portfolio was assigned to Masud (Jamiyat-i Islami), Foreign Affairs to Gaylani (Mahaz), Justice to Muhammad Nabi (Harakat-i Enqelab), Education to *mawlawi* Khales (Hezb-i Islami Khales), and the Ministry of the Interior to Sayyaf (Ettehad). The Shi'ites rejected the agreement because their demand for a quarter of the ministerial positions was not met. On 28 April power was transferred from the former government to the interim council. Mujaddidi became president of the Islamic Republic of Afghanistan whose new black, white and green flag bore at its centre the *shahadat*, the Muslim profession of faith. The new regime was recognised by Pakistan on the same day, followed by the European Economic Community and the United States. The following day, 29 April, Masud entered the capital with an army of several thousand men and a hundred tanks.

During this transitional period the real loser was Hezb-i Islami. Under pressure from the other parties it rapidly lost its vantage points. On 29 April it was dislodged from the Ministry of the Interior that had been handed to it by the Khalqis. On 1 May an inter-party organisation, the Committee for the Security of Kabul, put in place a force of 1,600 men, ostensibly to prevent inter-party conflict and banditry but in reality to block any offensive moves on the part of Hekmatyar. On 2 May 1992 Hekmatyar demanded the withdrawal of Dostum's men, who were—with justification—accused of looting. Dostum's refusal gave Hekmatyar the pretext to launch the first bombardments of Kabul, which by 1996 would claim 40,000 lives and were to destroy much of the capital, which till then had been intact.[6] Meanwhile, on 5 May the parties formed a government of thirty-two members, not in conformity with the Peshawar accords, in which Hezb-i Islami was not represented. On 7 May Masud, who still held the Defence portfolio and had been appointed a general, held a press conference in which he violently criticised Hekmatyar.

---

[6] US Committee for Refugees, *World Refugee Survey*, 1997, pp. 124–5. Hezb-i Islami, though it in fact initiated these clashes, was only one of the groups which in due course bombed Kabul, though it bombed more systematically due to its inability to enter the city.

An attempt by commander *mawlawi* Haqqani to reconcile the two adversaries failed.

At the same time, relations between the parties worsened. Dostum, named as a four-star general by Mujaddidi, did not withdraw from Kabul, where he continued to hold strategic positions, namely Bala Hisar fort, the airport and a number of ministries. In addition, on 21 June Mujaddidi asked for the extension of his mandate, although the basis for his argument for this was dubious, and his request was refused by the other leaders. In the end he returned to the provisions of the Peshawar accords and stepped down as planned on 29 June, handing over to Rabbani. However, Rabbani breached the letter of the accords and hung on after December. The absence of consultation between the parties, the antagonism between the commanders, and the failure to include the Sh'ites all conspired to set the scene for a new phase of the civil war.

The regionalisation of the forces (1992–1995)

During the 1980s parties such as Hezb-i Islami (Khales), Jamiyat-i Islami and Ettehad enlarged their geographical base, but after the Soviet withdrawal a contrary phenomenon was in evidence. Regionalisation accelerated after the fall of Kabul, when the headquarters of the various parties were transferred to Afghanistan, since the scene was set by the capture of the towns for a significant concentration of resources. Distribution on the ground take increasingly the character of political regions, each of which was dominated by a single actor, whether a party, a commander or a coalition of commanders. In some instances there was instability, as in Kunduz, or even anarchy, the situation in Kandahar, but clashes were localised and involved only limited forces. No organisation was truly represented at the national level, since party discipline was generally less strong than local solidarity. For example, Masud and Ismail Khan belonged theoretically to the same party, but for the most part behaved as autonomous or even competing powers. Finally, the southern regions were more fragmented than those of the north.

The situation in Kabul developed in a very different way from the provinces. At the provincial level a new political distribution emerged after the entry of the *mujahidin* into the towns, between 17 and 22 April. In Herat, Ismail Khan controlled the local administration at the head of a coalition of commanders. Those militias which were still represented in the town were dissolved some months later. Civil order was consolidated, and the process of reconstruction was embarked on with some success, helped by the return of refugees from Iran. In Kandahar the town was partitioned between commanders of different parties—Mahaz, Jebhe and Jamiyat-i Islami—who took concerted action to expel Hezb-i Islami from the urban area. Afterwards the situation degenerated into anarchy, which prevailed till the arrival of the Taliban. In the north the town of Mazar-i Sharif was partitioned between Hezb-i Wahdat, Jombesh and Jamiyat-i Islami, an unstable situation which continued until the alliance between Jombesh and Jamiyat collapsed in January 1994. Jamiyat, which was militarily much reduced, was later driven out of the town. In Jalalabad, Hezb-i Islami (Khales) established itself in a position of strength. *haji* Qadir, the governor of the town, avoided becoming involved in national affairs, probably because of his involvement in drug trafficking, together with the internal tensions within the tribal coalition from which he drew his support. Harakat-i Enqelab was dominant in Ghazni. Hezb-i Islami succeeded in keeping strongpoints only in Laghman and Charasiab, south of Kabul. Hezb-i Wahdat controlled most of Hazarajat.

Between 1992 and 1994 the capital was the objective of most of the fighting. With the exception of Ismail Khan, all the actors of national importance maintained a military presence there with the intention of influencing future developments. Two alliances came into being, of which the dominant one supported the government constructed by Rabbani and Masud around Jamiyat-i Islami. The other, in the minority, grouped together opposition figures, with Hezb-i Islami as its rallying point. The two alliances were differently structured since only the one built around Jamiyat-i Islami was capable of governing, largely as the result of its dominant position in Kabul. The advantage possessed by Jamiyat-i Islami, in addition to its strength on the ground, was its acceptability in the eyes of the other parties except for Hezb-i Islami, which was thus fated to remain in opposition. Hezb-i Islami was used by other movements which allied themselves to it if they were unable to find a place within the governing coalition, or to strengthen their bargaining positions, but left as soon as they were able, since its hegemonic ambitions meant that nobody wished to see Hezb-i Islami actually achieve power. The other major opposition was that between Hezb-i Wahdat and Ettehad due to the latter's extreme anti-Shi'ite position.

In addition to the hostility of Hezb-i Islami, a further basic factor holding back the reconstruction of the state consisted of the policies of Jombesh and Hezb-i Wahdat, each of which aimed to prevent any coalition achieving sufficient power to reconstitute a central authority. For differing reasons each of these two parties feared political stabilisation. On the one hand, the former communists of Jombesh knew that they lacked the legitimacy that would have enabled them to survive beyond the end of the war. On the other hand, Hezb-i Wahdat demanded recognition for an autonomous entity in Hazarajat, and therefore a *de facto* federalism. This rejection of a unitary state arose from the desire for political emancipation by a minority which for a century had been a pariah in Afghan history, as well as from the fear of domination by the anti-Shi'ite fundamentalists of Ettehad and Hezb-i Islami (Khales).

Without going into the detailed chronology of the events of 1992–4, three phases may be distinguished. The first saw the formation of a coalition between Jombesh-i Melli, Jamiyat-i Islami and Hezb-i Wahdat. The common interest of these three actors was to forestall the settlement plan taking shape under the auspices of the UN. For Masud control of the capital enabled him to oust Hekmatyar and ensure that Jamiyat-i Islami would play a central role in any new balance of power. In Dostum's estimation Najibullah's disappearance would allow him to take power in the northwest provinces and win a place in the new political system. Meanwhile, Hezb-i Wahdat was taking the opportunity to gain a foothold in Kabul where there was a substantial Hazara community.

The breakup of this first alliance came in the autumn of 1992, when Masud launched an operation in Kabul to disarm Hezb-i Wahdat, whose substantial depredations against the population served as a pretext for Masud to break an alliance which prevented him from bringing the Sunni parties into government. As soon as Hezb-i Wahdat ceased to be in the coalition, support for the government was forthcoming from Harakat-i Enqelab, which had hitherto been undecided, as well as from Ettehad, which at this point broke its links with Hezb-i Islami. On 11 February 1993 Jamiyat and Ettehad launched a joint assault on Hezb-i Wahdat's headquarters, sited in the Polytechnic School in the suburb of Afshar. Hezb-i Wahdat's forces retreated, and the area was looted for twenty-four hours, with many civilians being murdered.

In the spring, as the result of pressure from Pakistan, Saudi Arabia and Iran, the parties reached a further agreement, which was signed on 7 March 1993. Rabbani was to remain President till June 1994 and Hekmatyar regained the position of Prime Minister. However, this agreement did not outlive the launch of assaults against the government by Hezb-i Wahdat, as well as an attack on Rabbani as he went to meet Hekmatyar. In April there was a major onslaught by Hekmatyar on government positions at the very moment when the parties were negotiating a new accord, ratified on 18 May, which officially installed Rabbani as Minister of Defence in place of Masud. For the rest of the year military activity was less intense, though increasing pressure was put on Hekmatyar by the successes of Ismail Khan in the south, where he took Helmand, and of Masud in the Shamali plain. However, the growing imbalance in favour of the government unsettled Rashid Dostum, who concluded during a visit to the capital in July that the government's increasing power would reduce its need to rely on his militia.

The third phase began in January 1994 with a change of allegiance of Jombesh-i Melli from the government to the opposition side. For some months the position of neutrality adopted by Jombesh in confrontations between Hezb-i Islami and Jamiyat-i Islami in the vicinity of Kabul had foreshadowed this reversal. In addition Jombesh had been involved in fighting in the autumn with Ettehad in Kunduz and with Ismail Khan in Badghis—clashes that had exposed the lack of consistency in Jamiyat-i Islami's policy. Attacks were in fact launched on Dustom at precisely the moment when Masud needed his aircraft around Kabul to assist in an offensive against Hezb-i Islami. In the end Jombesh's decision was prompted by the attitude of Hezb-i Wahdat, which in the autumn moved closer to Masud and even had the use of Masud's helicopters to move its headquarters to Kabul. The prospect began to loom of a real marginalisation of Hezb-i Islami in the vicinity of Kabul, which negated all justification for the presence of Dostum's men inside the capital.

On the opposition side Hezb-i Islami failed entirely to halt its marginalisation. In the summer of 1992 the offensive by Dostum and Masud came close to sweeping Hezb-i Islami from the south of Kabul, but it was temporarily rescued by the ceasefire imposed by Pakistan on an indecisive Rabbani; it then bombarded Kabul, hoping to weaken the government coalition. The rockets fired at the capital had no military objective, but were intended solely to prevent a return to normality which could have included the installation of an effective government.

To break out of its isolation Hezb-i Islami attempted to reach agreements with other parties. The first alliance was with Ettehad, which had been on bad terms with Hezb-i Islami during the war, and was purely a matter of expediency; Ettehad had launched more attacks against the Shi'ites, their primary enemy, than against Masud's forces. Although its bombardments were destabilising for the governing coalition as a whole, its links with Jamiyat-i Islami were never completely broken. Hezb-i Islami and Ettehad also had different objectives with each in effect fighting its separate war. For Ettehad the main priority was to dislodge Hezb-i Wahdat, in order to take its place in the governing coalition; it was under no illusions as to Hezb-i Islami's ability to take power, and did not wish to remain in the opposition. The second alliance, between Hezb-i Islami and Hezb-i Wahdat, was even more temporary and was never formalised; it could appropriately be viewed not as a political agreement between the two parties but as a cease-fire with some logistical cooperation. This alliance had no long-term future since the Shi'ites retained a significant enmity against Hezb-i Islami. A third alliance, between Hezb-i Islami and Jombesh, resulted from the rapprochement between Hezb-i Wahdat and Masud in the autumn of 1993 which precipitated Jombesh's defection. This alliance was also informal and ideologically incongruous, and lasted until the point was reached when Hezb-i Islami, which had been politically isolated for some months, lost its military and political power.

The sapping of Hezb-i Islami's strength in Kabul prompted a shift in Pakistani policy, and in an unexpected way resulted in a radical upset in the war. Hekmatyar's failure at Kabul was also a failure for the Pakistani intelligence services whose head, Lieutenant-General Naved Nasir, had been appointed by Nawaz Sharif. After the deposition of Nawaz Sharif by President Ghulam Ishaq Khan in 1993, Naved Nasir was dismissed along with several dozen other officers, and General Nasrullah Babar,[7] Benazir Bhutto's new Minister of the Interior, took charge of Pakistan's Afghan policy. At this stage, though Hezb-i Islami no longer enjoyed the status of a privileged ally, Nasrullah Babar had not yet clearly formulated his Afghan policy. In an interview in the *Frontier Post* on 30 April 1994, for example, he said he was in favour of the return of the king, but in fact the primary objective of the Pakistan government was to establish a land link to Turkmenistan in order to open up Central Asia to Pakistan's economic and political influence. In September 1994, at a ceremony attended by Nasrullah Babar as well as the Pakistani ambassador in Afghanistan and Ismail Khan, the governor of the town, a Pakistan consulate was opened in Herat. On the practical side the Pakistan government dispatched a convoy of thirty trucks to Turkmenistan in November. However, it was halted near Kandahar—at Ghar Killi in Takhta Pul—by several commanders who included notably *amir* Lalay and Sarkateb from the Hezb-i Islami.

Some months before Nasrullah had stationed a small military force, known as the Taliban, on the Afghan-Pakistani frontier to keep the road clear in the event of any commander presuming to obstruct the freedom of movement to Herat. The Taliban had their origin in the Jamiyat-i Taliban (Society of Taliban), a subsidiary of Harakat-i Enqelab, which came into being officially around 1990 but had earlier existed informally.[8] Since Harakat-i Enqelab was at that time in the process of collapse, a group of its commanders, and in particular Qari Baba and Rasul Akhundzada, gravitated towards Rabbani, while others moved closer to Ismail Khan. The Taliban had very close relations with the Pakistani Jamiyat-ul Ulema, which at that time supported the government of Benazir Bhutto, and this connection facilitated their link with Nasrullah Babar. In the spring of 1994, after training in ISI camps, the Taliban launched a successful attack on Spin Boldak, a frontier post on the Quetta-Kandahar road. It preached respect for Islamic morality to passing travellers, and obliged some to

---

[7] Nasrullah Babar, who is a Pushtun from the NWFP and a former governor of that province, had been in the 1970s the chief adviser on Afghan affairs to Zulfikar Ali Bhutto.

[8] The first attempt to make use of religious students may have been made as early as 1992–3 when General Durrani was head of the ISI. Benazir Bhutto's assumption of power had ended this experiment.

cut their hair. They also stood out against the extortion practised by the other parties.

The emergence of the Taliban coincided with a serious social crisis in southern Afghanistan. In Kandahar between 1992 and 1994 aimless quarrels between gangs broke out in the bazaar, while armed men openly smoked opium in the streets. No administration was in control of the town, and the schools were closed. Politics was in disrepute, to the profit of religious activists, since adherence to the *shariat* appeared preferable to the dissension (*fitna*) resulting from the strife between the various parties. In such a situation of moral and social crisis, allegiance to a charismatic person or movement enabled social relations to be rebuilt especially in a segmentary society where mobilisations around charismatic personalities were historically commonplace.[9] In this situation the Taliban appeared to present an alternative to disorder. Its programme was based on the restoration of order: freedom of movement and of trade, the end of banditry, a ban on drug use, and so on.[10]

The commandeering of the Pakistani convoy gave the Taliban the opportunity to mount a major operation aimed at Kandahar itself. On 5 November, after a number of clashes, it succeeded in occupying the town, and by the end of November entered the neighbouring provinces of Helmand and Zabul. At this point the Taliban were still regarded as allies by Rabbani's government, which may explain the attitude adopted by the Jamiyat commander Naqibullah, which in practice enabled it to take Kandahar. In January 1995 the Taliban made a deal with Ghaffur Akhundzada for the cession of Helmand, after which it found itself in contact with Ismail Khan's troops.[11] The movement then pressed on towards Kabul, sweeping aside commanders who had been in place since the beginning of the war—such as Amin Wardak, who fled to France, and Qari Baba, the leader

---

[9] For an anthropological analysis of charisma in politics in the Pakistani tribal zones, see Charles Lindholm, *Frontier Perspectives: Essays in Comparative Anthropology*, Oxford University Press, 1996, pp. 73 ff.

[10] This did not prevent the Taliban at that time from authorising the production of opium, justifying it with the sophistry that only its consumption is forbidden by the Quran.

[11] In 1994 the Taliban sent a mission to Herat to request Ismail Khan to apply Islamic law. A group of *ulema* from Herat went to Kandahar to reassure the Taliban that the *shariat* was highly respected in Herat.

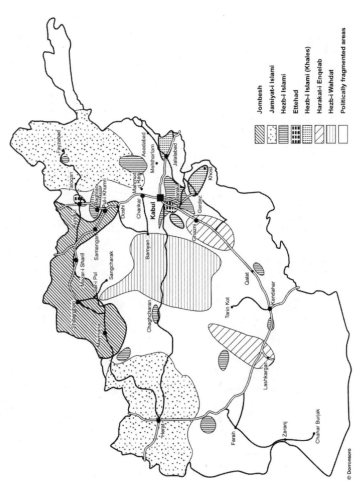

Simplified political map, 1992.

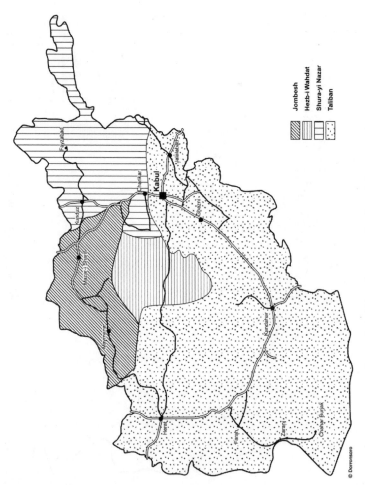

The regional distribution of political forces, 1996.

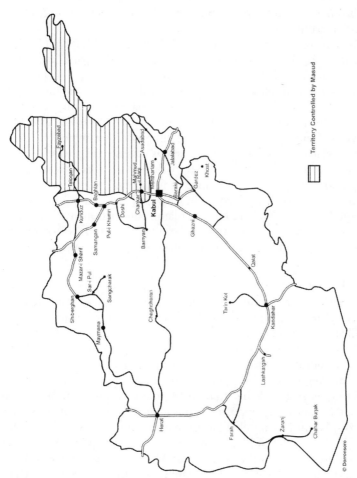

Territory controlled by Masud, March 2000.

of the *shura* at Ghazni, who rallied to Masud. The fall of Ghazni came at the end of January 1995 following a Hezb-i Islami offensive aimed at halting the Taliban's advance. During his resistance to this attack the governor, Qari Baba, actually made an alliance with the Taliban, at a point when government aircraft were also attacking Hezb-i Islami's positions.

In February 1995 the Taliban took Meydan Shahr, Pul-i Charkhi and most significantly Gulbuddin Hekmatyar's principal base at Charasiab, near Kabul. Within a few months its advance had brought about a major simplification of the political map, with the disappearance or marginalisation of the predominantly Pushtun parties—Mahaz, Jebhe, Ettehad, Harakat-i Enqelab and Hezb-i Islami. The town of Kandahar had been the only important stronghold belonging to Mahaz, for which Nangrahar was of less significance. Mahaz, the only party favouring the return of the king, was of only marginal importance in the overall balance of forces, and would not henceforth play any significant role. Similarly Harakat-i Enqelab was also merged into the Taliban. Hezb-i Islami, cut off from Pakistani aid, was reduced to a remnant, as was Ettehad. The regionalisation of forces was now complete and a new phase was set to begin.

Towards monopolisation

In due course it became clear that regionalisation was only an intermediate step in the process of the concentration of resources, as the Taliban, by reason of its demographic preponderance and the divisions among its adversaries, as well as its access to aid from Pakistan, came to dominate virtually the whole territory.

However, in Kabul itself, devastated as it was after three years of fighting, Masud made his strength felt, and a reunification of the city under his authority appeared a possibility. To the south of Kabul, Hezb-i Islami was in full flight before the Taliban advance. Inside the capital the Shi'ites of Hezb-i Wahdat were on the point of collapse, under pressure from the coalition of Masud's forces with Harakat-i Enqelab and Ettehad. In early March 1995 the government coalition's shelling of the Shi'ite areas was at its height, and the western part of the city was largely razed to the ground. Hoping to escape defeat, the Hezb-i Wahdat leader Mazari allowed the Taliban to enter the city, but on 19 March clashes broke out between the two groups. Mazari was taken prisoner but died in unexplained circumstances while being transferred to Kandahar.[12] Hezb-i Wahdat then split into two factions. One, under the leadership of Akbari, entered an alliance with the Rabbani government and established itself at Bamyan. The other, headed by Karim Khalili, allied itself with Dostum in June 1995. In southern Kabul, after a brief period of fraternisation, the president's men and the Taliban clashed when the Taliban rejected Masud's demand that it should disarm. Masud won back some territory, while the Taliban, which had suffered heavy losses, fell back towards the south. Masud was then in sole control of the capital, and pressed forward as far as Meydan Shahr, which became for some time the front line.

After pulling back from Kabul, the Taliban then faced a threat from the west, where Ismail Khan launched in early March an attack which carried him to within 200 km of Kandahar, the Taliban's principal stronghold. At the beginning of April 1995 Dostum launched a successful attack against the province of Badghis, north-west of Herat, as part of a pincer movement against Herat. However, the Taliban lost a battle at Shindand where fierce fighting left hundreds dead. Its only achievement during the spring of 1995 was in May on the Kabul front when it ousted Sayyaf from his base at Paghman.

In the summer Ismail Khan launched a new offensive aimed at Kandahar. In August he took Girishk, but the military situation underwent a spectacular reverse on 28 August when the Taliban recaptured the town and then the air base at Shindand. Ismail Khan's demoralised *mujahidin* fell back to the neighbourhood of Herat and in the ensuing chaos dispersed into small groups. On 4 September Ismail Khan relinquished his command to his deputy, Allauddin Khan, before crossing over the Iranian border. During the night the town was abandoned. On the following day, 5 September, Herat fell into the hands of the Taliban without a fight.

There were many reasons for Ismail Khan's collapse.[13] The principal factor, which was entirely fortuitous, was the death in early Sep-

---

[12] The helicopter taking Mazari to Kandahar stopped at the Baraki Barak hospital to drop off wounded men. According to a witness, Mazari was at that point unchained and did not appear to have been beaten. The Taliban version—that Mazari was killed at Ghazni while trying to escape—seems therefore to have some credibility.

[13] See Muhammad Zahir Azimi, *Taliban chegune amadand?* (The Taliban: how did it arrive?), no publisher, 1998. Muhammad Zahir, who formerly belonged to the

tember of an important commander Dr Nasir Ahmad Yar during the fighting for Girish. There were also the operations against Herat by Rashid Dostum's militias, aimed at helping the Taliban to victory. In addition Ismail Khan's forces were fragmented and out of control. The *mujahidin* sent by the Kabul government in the spring of 1995, most of them Panjshiris, were especially reluctant to accept Ismail Khan's authority. In addition, Ismail Khan's autonomous ambitions put him in opposition to Rabbani's government. For instance, shortly before the fall of Herat a commission sent out by Kabul failed to achieve a compromise, particularly over financial issues, with Herat refusing to pass money on to the central government in spite of the substantial revenues it derived from the customs post on the Turkmen frontier.[14] Another bone of contention was the nomination of governors to the western provinces, who were appointed by Ismail Khan without consultation with Kabul. Ismail Khan's attack on Dostum in the spring of 1994 ran counter to the interests of Masud, whose aim was above all to maintain his control over the capital. Similarly the meeting held at Herat in early August 1994 was the preliminary to a *shura* scheduled for November. Rabbani's authority was directly challenged when the meeting demanded the ending of his term of office. In the last resort Ismail Khan may have wished to present himself as a compromise candidate between the parties. It must be added that in more purely military terms the offensive against Herat was mainly the brainchild of the Pakistan intelligence services, from which originated the superior logistics and enhanced mobility which foreshadowed the later offensives in the north.

This defeat was a turning-point in the war. The Taliban was no longer trapped between Masud's forces and those of Ismail Khan, and was able to deploy its forces with greater ease. With its capture of Shindand the Taliban gained an air base of prime importance and also some ten aircraft. Also the road from Pakistan to Turkmenistan was

---

Rad, was the commander of Harakat-i Islami in Herat and worked with Ismail Khan throughout the war. Accusations of treason made at this time against Ismail Khan by Masud's associates were unfounded.

[14] One member of this commission, Delju Huseini, a Herati who had been a member of the Islamic movement before the war, had notoriously bad relations with Ismail Khan. This serves as an illustration of the antagonism between the Islamic networks before the war and the officials of the Emarat.

opened, which brought great economic and political benefits. Finally, on 8 September 1995, the capture of Herat sparked off an unprecedented crisis in Afghanistan's relations with Pakistan when the Pakistani embassy in Kabul was plundered. In December 1995 there was a further wave of incidents in Pakistan, when 65 bombs left 78 dead, for which the Pakistani government held Masud responsible.

The limits of Masud's strategy were exposed when the priority he gave to maintaining control over Kabul prevented him from pushing outward into the northwest,[15] while at the same time he was unable to secure a military victory in the south because of the Pushtuns' unwillingness to put themselves under the control of a predominantly Panjshiri army. Ismail Khan's strategy, which was predicated on a victory over Dostum, was probably in the end more fruitful, even though Jombesh could call on formidable military strength.[16] Lastly Masud could not have foreseen the Taliban's success, while his initial support for the movement, which was essentially verbal, was based on the antagonism between him and Hezb-i Islami. Another consequence of the advance of the Taliban was the defeat of the Rabbani government's Pushtun allies, and in particular Qari Baba in Ghazni. Masud also paid the price for his expansionist strategy, which led many commanders to group themselves together in opposition to him, including even some commanders within Jamiyat itself. Analyses suggesting that Masud was a good soldier but a bad politician are probably based on a misunderstanding of both the constraints which limited his freedom of action and the fluidity of the situation. Whatever the truth of the matter, Jamiyat-i Islami's position was seriously undermined. The internal balance of the party shifted, with Masud becoming the sole leader, while Rabbani was left with only regional support, principally in his own home province of Badakhshan.[17]

---

[15] In theory this would have been possible with the assistance of the Jamiyat based in Mazar-i Sharif, but it was militarily difficult and politically fraught, since earlier attempts by Masud to gain a foothold in this region had been badly received.

[16] During his visit to Kabul in June 1994 Ismail Khan made no secret of his refusal to make any contact with Dostum, although he agreed to meet Hekmatyar.

[17] Rabbani was no longer able to play the Jamiyat commanders off against each other as he had hitherto done, for instance by offering the post of Minister of Defence to Ismail Khan in 1992 while he was in Herat: an offer which Ismail refused (personal information from Stéphane Thiollier).

From then on Kabul became the Taliban's target. The first stage was the capture on 12 September 1996 of Jalalabad after a brief battle.[18] The Taliban takeover had in fact been negotiated with a group of local commanders a few months earlier; the city was by now difficult to defend and fell into the Taliban's hands on 26 September. In order to conserve his strength, Masud refrained from resistance, retreating in good order to Panjshir, easily defeating at the same time an attempt by the Taliban to pursue him. From this point on, conquest of the north was within the grasp of the Taliban, which already controlled around two-thirds of the country and the larger towns, with the exception of Mazar-i Sharif. The new balance of power obliged Jamiyat, Hezb-i Wahdat and Jombesh to form an alliance to counter the Taliban's thrust. However, this did not imply a political transformation since, far from being a homogeneous political grouping, the alliance brought together parties which were opposed to each other in every way—in their ideology, their constituency and their political ambitions.[19] Military coordination between them was largely in the realms of theory. This coalition underwent its first serious defeat with the capture of Mazar-i Sharif by the Taliban on 24 May 1997.[20] The Taliban took advantage of the treachery of the commander of Maymana, Malik, whose motive was vengeance for the death of his brother, assassinated by Dostum on 25 June 1996. Once within Mazar-i Sharif, however, the Taliban reneged on the agreements it had made with Malik, in particular its request for representation on an ethnic basis together with a decentralised system. Consequently Malik repudiated the terms of the alliance and inflicted serious losses on the Taliban, massacring 2–3,000 Taliban

[18] *Haji* Qadir, who led the Jalalabad *shura*, fell from power and retreated to Pakistan, where he organised two offensives against the Taliban at the end of 1996 and in February 1997. Pressure from Pakistan afterwards prevented him from continuing his operations.

[19] On 21 August 1997 the death in an air accident of Abdul Rahim Ghaffurzai, who had been designated Prime Minister a week earlier, was a further blow to the northern coalition. Ghaffurzai was a former representative at the UN under Najibullah and a member of the Muhammadzai clan. He would have been able to bring greater cohesion to the Northern Alliance and could have put them in touch with the Pushtuns.

[20] Ismail Khan, who had returned from Iran to fight the Taliban, was at this time taken prisoner. He later escaped after two years of detention.

prisoners.[21] In September a second Taliban attack would have been successful except for a massive delivery of Iranian aid. On this occasion it used Kunduz as its main base, and was joined there by the Pushtun commanders which enabled it to obstruct all attempts by Masud to reach Mazar-i Sharif.

Although Dostum retook Mazar-i Sharif in November, Malik's treason had weakened Jombesh. The decisive attack, which set the seal on the Taliban victory, began in the spring of 1998. The capture of Faryab province and then Samangan opened the way to Mazar-i Sharif, which fell in August 1998. In revenge for the massacres of the previous years, several thousand mainly Hazara civilians were killed and their bodies were left lying in the streets for days. In a further incident the murder of a number of Iranian diplomats stationed in Mazar-i Sharif led to the mobilisation of Iranian troops on the Afghan frontier. Another consequence of the capture of Mazar-i Sharif was the disappearance of Hezb-i Wahdat as a major military force in the north. Sporadic fighting broke out in May 1999, especially around Bamyan and Sar-i Pul, but a significant part of Hezb-i Wahdat joined up with the Taliban. Karim Khalili, however, stood by his alliance with Masud.

The confrontation between the Taliban and Masud had by this time become a clash between a centralised power that was steadily consolidating itself and a guerrilla force entrenched in the mountains. Masud's control extended over less than 10% of the population and none of the towns. It was difficult for him to enlarge his territory since he had at his disposal only some 6,000 men, which precluded operations of any size. The Taliban also had control in the air. However, Masud's organisational ability and tactical skill enabled him to hold out. As a result of underestimating him the Taliban failed to consolidate its summer offensive to the north of Kabul in 1999, when Masud counter-attacked brilliantly. Masud's predicament was the reason why he paid particular attention to the international dimensions of the conflict. For example, the recognition of the Rabbani government by the UN was one of the last cards available for him to play. Masud was also able to get help from the regional powers—Iran, Uzbekistan and Russia—to which a Taliban victory appeared

---

[21] Amnesty International, *Afghanistan: report of mass graves of Taliban militia*, 1997, AI index 11/11/97.

as a threat to the stability of Central Asia. Meanwhile the coup of 12 October 1999 against Nawaz Sharif and the return of Pakistan to military rule under General Pervez Musharraf brought no marked alteration in Pakistan's Afghan policy.

Finally, the elimination of the opposition was also being carried out outside Afghanistan, with assassinations of Afghan personalities who were either involved in the search for a negotiated solution or opposed to the Taliban. The leftists, the nationalists and the royalists were the first to be targeted.[22] In July 1999 the assassination in Quetta of Abdul Ahad Khan Karzai, a former diplomat and senator, coincided with a new bid by the royalists to implement a compromise solution involving the king. A member of Sebghatullah Mujaddidi's family was also attacked, and in addition Afghan women working in the refugee camps were threatened. Similarly, the fear of attack by the Taliban obliged the leftist feminist association RAWA (Revolutionary Association of Women in Afghanistan) to cancel planned demonstrations in Peshawar. Even commanders who had once enjoyed Pakistani support were eliminated. The massacre of the family of Abdul Haq in the spring of 1999 was a sign that the Taliban was determined to finish off the remaining commanders. In addition, Hekmatyar was refused a visa for Pakistan, in a clear signal of the Pakistan authorities' unquestioning support for the Taliban and the Taliban's rejection of any compromise.

---

[22] See Human Rights Commission of Pakistan, *State and Human rights in 1998*, Lahore, 1999, p. 293.

8. The Ethnicisation of the Conflict

As the result of regionalisation each of the parties was inevitably driven to recruit from a constituency which increasingly comprised a single ethnicity. Between 1994 and 1998 the political disposition on the ground and that of the major ethnic groups largely coincided. Hezb-i Wahdat was entirely Hazara, Jombesh was predominantly Uzbek, Jamiyat-i Islami was for the most part Tajik, and the Taliban drew its membership essentially from the Pushtuns. In this situation some parties used the rhetoric of community to mobilise support; the appeal to the *jihad* was no longer sufficient to guarantee support for a group. The situation of Hezb-i Islami exemplified this transformation. To offset its marginalisation Hekmatyar increasingly turned to the argument that Pushtun interests must be defended, an argument presented at first in less formal contexts but in due course more overtly, as in the party's daily newspaper *Shahadat*.

This appeal to community solidarity was logical in view of the much increased tension between communities manifested in massacres targeted against particular communities. The towns, and in particular the capital, had ceased to be ethnic melting-pots. In pre-war times inhabitants of different ethnic origins had made their homes in their own particular areas of Kabul, but the existence of the governing class and the effects of the urban way of life served to foster the emergence of a Kabuli identity. This tendency lost its momentum when the war began. In Mazar-i Sharif in the 1990s recurrent clashes had weakened the urban identity, so that relationships between ethnicities deteriorated. Even in Herat, which continued to typify the urban melting-pot where intercommunal tension was low, the situation in the outskirts of the town steadily worsened. The collapse of the state and of the educational system caused linguistic frontiers to become more marked than before. In Kandahar, for example, the Pushtuns spoke less Persian, while it became rare for Pushtu to be taught in the north. These processes were reinforced by the media; on the radio the ethnic affiliation of the leaders was, at least implicitly, presented as a factor explaining their political positions. Such leaders as Rabbani, who came from Badakhshan, and Masud, from Panjshir, began to be described as 'Tajik'.

Although the war certainly gave ethnic affiliation a political significance, this was a process with implicit limitations. Within the operations of the parties the ideology of ethno–nationalism never dominated, while local solidarities were always the determining factor. In any case two different processes, between which it is important to distinguish, were subsumed under the idea of ethnicisation. In the case of Hezb-i Wahdat and Jombesh-i Melli, although ethnic rhetoric was openly employed, the official party line remained ambiguous. Shi'ism and not Hazara nationalism remained the ideological foundation of Hezb-i Wahdat, while Jombesh maintained somewhat vaguely that its doors were open to all the 'northern communities'. On the other hand, neither Jamiyat nor the Taliban based its strategy on ethnic affiliation but set itself instead the goal of reunifying the country. Ethnicisation was therefore an unintended and counter-productive result of regionalisation, rather than a strategy of mobilisation.

Ethnicisation as a strategy

Although Hezb-i Wahdat and Jombesh claimed respectively to represent the Hazaras and the 'Turks', the ethnic strategies of these two parties were validated in two different ways. Hezb-i Wahdat was constituted as a movement for the unification of the Hazara parties, and reflected a strong popular demand for autonomy. However, for Jombesh ethnic mobilisation was largely a political stratagem by the Parchami communist functionaries wanting to survive the collapse of the regime.

Hezb-i Wahdat. The launching in 1990 of Hezb-i Wahdat (Party of Unity) was an event of critical importance not only for Hazarajat, whose political aspect it profoundly altered, but also for the Afghan political landscape as a whole. The ethnicisation of politics and the process of regionalisation were already implicit within it.

At the close of the 1980s popular discontent over the endless war between the Shi'ite parties prompted the notables and religious leaders to call for a general ceasefire. The palpable loss of confidence in the parties created a climate propitious to political change, but the crucial impetus came from Iran. The reason was that its leaders, not having taken part in the Geneva negotiations, feared marginalisation in the context of a Soviet-Pakistani agreement and had decided, to make every effort to create a Shi'ite front able to exert its influence in the field of politics. It was therefore no accident that the initial preparatory meeting was held at the precise moment when the Soviet withdrawal became a certainty, taking place at Panjao between 12 and 16 July 1988. At this meeting the decision was taken to set up a Hasta-yi Wahdat (Nucleus of Unity), whose task would be to prepare the way for the unification of the parties. On 1 September 1988 delegates meeting at Lal o Sarjangal issued a twelve-point declaration which ratified the union between Sepah and Nasr and specified Bamyan as seat of the future movement. Hezb-i Wahdat was officially inaugurated on 16 June 1990 in Teheran, with the participation of Shura, Nasr, Sepah and other smaller groups. Only Harakat-i Islami persisted in staying outside the new party.

Hezb-i Wahdat set up its headquarters at Bamyan. Its leadership consisted of representatives from Nasr, Sepah, Shura, Niru, Nehzat and Dawat, the parties which had united. This council was unelected, its members holding their positions *ex officio*. There was also a *shura* with a membership of several hundred, delegated by the parties, some of whom were elected by popular vote. With the exception of Sayyed Hasan *jaglan*, who took charge of military affairs, all the leading figures were *ulema*, notably the president Abdul Ali Mazari, a former Nasr leader; Muhammad Akbari, a former leader of Sepah; and Muhammad Karim Khalili, the movement's spokesman. Hazarajat was administratively divided according to the various pre-war provinces and districts. From 1988 onward the old regime's buildings were gradually rebuilt. In general the organisation recalled the early days of the Shura. In theory there was military service, and taxation was raised.

The creation of a Hazara party capable of overcoming partisan divisions and presenting a united front against the Pushtuns and the Sunnis in general was greeted in many places by a wave of nationalist fervour. There was no doubt that popular support sprang from the nationalist agenda rather than support for revolutionary Shi'ism. Notwithstanding its religious rhetoric, the formation of Hezb-i Wahdat was primarily an expression of the Hazara community, as was demonstrated by the failure of attempts to expand the movements to all the Shi'ites, in particular the Qizilbash. Hezb-i Wahdat never succeeded in enlarging its membership beyond its original constituency of Hazaras, run by clerics;[1] for example, Harakat-i Islami refused to become part of Hezb-i Wahdat because its leader *ayatollah* Mohseni was non-Hazara, as were many of its activists, and Harakat-i Islami's relations with Iran were difficult. After fruitless negotiations over a merger with Harakat-i Islami, Hezb-i Wahdat's leadership attempted to recruit Harakat's commanders individually. This strategy was of limited effectiveness, although it met with some success in Ghorband and Behsud, and the two parties contrived a *modus vivendi*. In addition Hezb-i Wahdat never really succeeded in recruiting cadres other than Hazara clerics.

Jombesh. Jombesh-i Melli (National Front) was established and developed very differently from all the parties previously discussed, since its basis was an alliance between the northern militias and the Parchami cadres who had supported Babrak Karmal. In fact Dostum remained close to Karmal up till his death in 1996. Fifteen years of war had given a distinctive political personality to the northwest provinces, where the policy of national reconciliation had met with some success. The region was structured on a framework of positions where the government was well represented, while its political and to some extent its economic centre was the town of Shibergan rather than Mazar-i Sharif. The region was the only one to offer a haven to which the militias and the members of Hezb-i Watan could withdraw after the collapse of the government.

The militias of Rashid Dostum and of Rasul Palawan at Maymana comprised the military basis of Jombesh.[2] The Ismailis, who con-

---

[1] However, some of the *khans'* sons, with little political background, had some success in joining Hezb-i Wahdat, where their technical abilities made them welcome.

[2] A list of the main leaders of Jombesh, with their ethnic affiliations is given by Esedullah Oguz in *Afghanistan*, Istanbul: Cep Kitaplari, 1999, p. 26.

trolled a crucial position on the road between Mazar-i Sharif and Kabul, also gave their support to Rashid Dostum, but were inclined to maintain their autonomy politically. In addition to the regional militias, groups which had been militarily defeated tended to rally to Jombesh. This was the case particularly with the militiamen of Herat after their expulsion by Ismail Khan at the end of 1992. Numerous *mujahidin*, in particular those from Hezb-i Islami, also joined. After the disappearance of Harakat-i Enqelab in the north-west, the *mujahidin* mainly regrouped into the two opposing parties, Hezb-i Islami and Jamiyat-i Islami. This polarisation encouraged Hezb-i Islami's commanders to join Jombesh, although in Kabul these two parties were in opposition. This was probably due more to the disintegration of Hezb-i Islami in the north than to a strategy of infiltration prompted by Hekmatyar. Some Harakat-i Enqelab commanders, especially in the province of Samangan, rallied to Jombesh for financial reasons. For example *raïs* Abdul Rahman, who was appointed governor of Faryab in 1992 without real power, was a former Harakat-i Enqelab commander. A splinter group such as that of Azad Beg, who proclaimed his allegiance to Uzbek nationalism, also saw fit to join Jombesh, although it had probably been created originally by the Pakistan secret services to destabilise Soviet Uzbekistan. Jombesh also attracted figures 'independent' of the parties, in a direct continuation of the policy of National Reconciliation, particularly after the fall of the Kabul government. Finally, in certain instances when offers of membership failed, Jombesh undertook political assassinations, like that of the responsible Jamiyat-i Islami figure in Almar, Afizullah Fateh, while he was negotiating with Rasul Palawan at Maymana in 1992.

Jombesh was an amalgam between the state administration and the militias. The militia commanders were integrated into the army: Rashid Dostum was a general, although he had no formal military training. Within Jombesh any boundary between the regular army and the militia lost its meaning, since the militia leaders were in the midst of regular army officers and organised their men on the same lines. Jombesh commanders were also established locally and in the countryside. In practice the militia chiefs retained close links with their villages of origin, where they had built up a clientele. There was a sense of distance from the towns as a result of the militia commanders' local roots. This was naturally more true of *mujahidin* recruits such as Rasul Palawan than of Dostum himself, who regarded Shibergan as his base more than he did his native village.

From the ideological point of view Jombesh was formally organised as an Islamic movement. However, the attitude of the party officials left little doubt about their real beliefs: their acceptance of Islam was entirely pragmatic and tactical, within the continuation of the policy of National Reconciliation. Their alliance with the Ismailis was another measure of the sincerity of their affiliation to an Islamic ideology. In reality Jombesh's Islam was non-political, and was restricted to law and to religious ritual. In the government *madrasas* the *mullahs* wore western dress—suits and overcoats—and Soviet Islam inspired the approach of the official clergy. In these *madrasas* future *ulema*, entirely identified with officialdom, were under the strict control of the authorities.

Although official announcements avoided all reference to any particular ethnic group, propaganda emphasised the 'Turkish' personality of Rashid Dostum, the party's principal leader, and Dostum's travels in Uzbekistan and Turkey were represented as the result of ethnic solidarity.[3] Was such nationalism behind Uzbekistan's support for Jombesh? Uzbekistan's support is explained rather, in terms of the search for a reliable ally to guard its southern frontier and not as ethnic solidarity between Uzbeks, which seems to have been a marginal factor. The construction of an Uzbek nationalism such as Jombesh envisaged was certainly not encouraged by Uzbekistan, which would not have considered any challenge to its frontiers with Afghanistan. In practice, however, part of the armaments received by Jombesh's forces came from the Uzbek army's arsenal; the frontier was relatively open and trade was lively. In addition Turkmenistan had opened a new road to Andkhoy. Dostum's aircraft sometimes made use of the airbase at Termez, but Uzbekistan's assistance had its limits: for example fuel deliveries were not adequate.

In any case, ethno-nationalist mobilisation clashed with the complexity of communal affiliations, whence the ambiguous expression

---

[3] In 1992 Rashid Dostum began a series of trips to Turkey which would put him in touch with various Turkish politicians, such as the parliamentary deputy Ayvaz Gökdemir, a former *ülkücü* (ultra-nationalist) then supporting Tansu Ciller, as well as officials of the regime. See Esedullah Oguz, *op. cit.*, p. 28.

'Peoples of the North' found in some Jombesh documents. For example, because of the presence of a Turkmen minority it was the broader 'Turkish' rather than the 'Uzbek' aspect on which stress was laid. In addition Tajiks and Hazaras were represented in Dostum's militias, and this, added to the alliance with the Ismailis, necessitated a degree of rhetorical prudence. The region of Turkestan, from Faryab to Balkh, had never been politically unified, although the attempt at secession made in 1888 by Ishaq Khan, governor of Turkestan, seems to have been welcomed by the population.[4] Ethnic distribution on the ground in northern Afghanistan was extremely complex, and did not lend itself to nationalist mobilisation.[5] In essence the northwest provinces of Faryab, Jozjan and Sar-i Pul might be seen as predominantly Uzbek, with strong Turkmen minorities in Andkhoy and along the frontier as far as the province of Kunduz. Pockets of Uzbek population were also found in the eastern provinces of Takhar and Badakhshan. However the idea of an Uzbek identity as such was less of a mobilising force than the multiple tribal identities of peoples of widely different origins and characters, making sense only in relation to a contrasting overall identity. For example, Turkish and Mongol groups pronounced themselves to be Uzbeks when in contention with Tajik or Pushtun neighbours.

For the Jombesh functionaries the problem was therefore to initiate nationalist mobilisation in a context where only local identities existed. The intention was to move from communal solidarity, based on *qowms*, to a more abstract loyalty oriented towards a 'macroethnicity' identified with Jombesh's para-statal apparatus. This transition required both an ideological framework and methods of mobilisation. In the urban context the party continued to mobilise using methods reminiscent of those of Hezb-i Demokratik-i Khalq-i Afghanistan. Although the subject-matter might have changed, the style of propaganda was still that of the former regime, especially as its officials had mostly continued to carry out their functions. Jombesh systematically used nationalist symbolism: in Shibergan the street-

---

[4] Jonathan Lee, 'The History of Maymana in Northwestern Afghanistan, 1731–1893', *Iran* 35, 1987. Ishaq had a Pushtun father and an Armenian mother, but he had been able to enlist the support of the northern population by promising independence for Turkestan.

[5] Pierre Centlivres, 'L'histoire récente de l'Afghanistan et la configuration ethnique des provinces du nord-est', *Studia Iranica* (Paris) 5 (2), pp. 255–68.

names were changed to demonstrate affiliation to 'Northern Afghanistan'. The Pushtun village of Pushtun Kot was re-named Imam Saheb, a sign of rejection of the Pushtun presence in the north. The new street-names referred to Uzbek personalities or reverted to historical nomenclature, as in Khorasan. In education Central Asian languages—Uzbek and Turkmen—were adopted, which posed the problem of converting to the Cyrillic alphabet, to open the door to Uzbek and Turkmen literature. Pushtun was abandoned.

To strengthen its position Jombesh attempted to enlist the Uzbek and Turkmen regions in northern Afghanistan to boost its 'ethnic sphere' and strengthen its control over the frontiers, especially in the province of Kunduz. In this region the commanders were affiliated mainly to Hezb-i Islami, and to a limited extent to Jamiyat-i Islami.[6] Political activities such as the forging of alliances and transfer of allegiance from one party to another were undertaken for local community reasons connected with the village or the clan, without reference to any solidarity to a 'macro-ethnicity'. From 1992 relations with Jombesh were established on the basis of material considerations such as gifts of petrol, vehicles and money; the commanders maintained their link not for ideological reasons but rather to bolster their local power with the help of a powerful ally. What led to the emergence of an ethnic ideology was the reaction of other parties in the province who were unsettled by the ascendancy of Jombesh. From this point of view the clashes of the autumn of 1993—when Jombesh's new recruits, rapidly reinforced by Dostum's forces who arrived from Mazar-i Sharif, clashed with the commanders of the provincial *shura*—solidified the communal boundaries. The attacks mounted by the other parties and the looting which followed created tensions between the Turkmen communities on the one hand and the Pushtuns and Tajiks on the other, which justified their affiliation to Jombesh after the fact. The Turkmen commanders were in any case not taken in by this blackmail, which drove them somewhat against their will into the arms of Jombesh, with which they had few ideological affinities. Thus ethnically motivated enlistments to Jombesh apparently concealed other processes more complex than nationalist fervour.

---

[6] In Imam Saheb Hezb-i Islami sought Uzbek rather than Pushtun recruits. Allegiance was based here on social rather than communal proximity.

Jombesh's nationalist mobilisation nevertheless ran up against a series of obstacles. First, it was not able to draw on popular demands as strong as those of the Hazaras. Even among its own functionaries, Jombesh's nationalist rhetoric was a matter of expediency since the majority were former Parchamis who were unlikely to have been Uzbek nationalists by conviction. However, with the passing of years tensions appeared, since ethnic affiliation became a determinant of access to power. Secondly, even within Jombesh the motivating force of the *qowms* continued to be stronger than either the language of nationalism or party solidarity. The assassination of Rasul Palawan, the Jombesh leader at Maymana, mobilised the solidarity of his *qowm*, rather than strengthening Dostum, who has ordered it, so that Rasul Palawan's brother Malik entered an alliance with the Taliban which led to the first fall of Mazar-i Sharif in 1997.

Ethnicisation as an unintended consequence

In contrast to Hezb-i Wahdat and Jombesh, the influence of the Taliban and Jamiyat-i Islami was never intended to be limited to a single geographical region or community. At the outset these two movements sought to restore a central state, but political developments restricted them to recruitment in practice from a single ethnic community, with consequences for their activities.

Jamiyat-i Islami. Although it was the most firmly entrenched party at the point of the Soviet withdrawal, Jamiyat saw itself progressively driven back into the northeast quarter of the country. Its decline began with the agreement between Masud and Jombesh, which had the effect in the northwest of marginalising Jamiyat, led by *mawlawi* Alam in Mazar-i Sharif. In 1994 the arrival of the Taliban in the south led to Jamiyat's loss of its Pushtun commanders, and the loss of Herat in 1995 completed the regionalisation of the party. In addition the establishment of Hazara and Uzbek nationalist parties meant that in reaction some Tajiks were liable to identify themselves politically with Jamiyat.

On the other hand, a number of factors militated in practice against Jamiyat's slide towards Tajik nationalism. The preponderance of Tajiks within Jamiyat did not lead to a neglect of local identities in favour of a Tajik identity, which continued to be elusive. The leaders themselves rejected ethnicisation and turned instead to identities which were either more local or broader. During the war Ismail Khan refused to admit his ethnic identity precisely to avoid the interpretation of his actions in this light.[7] Until the fall of Kabul, Rabbani relied during his presidency on a clientele based on a province rather than on an ethnic group, and surrounded himself with Badakhshis rather than with Tajiks in the wider sense. Masud regarded himself more as a Panjshiri than as a Tajik, and the war reinforced the identity of the inhabitants of the Panjshir valley to the point where it virtually became an ethnicity.

Further, the creation of a coherent political region was never possible, and indeed would not have responded to a demand, as in the case of Hazarajat, since the complexity of the distribution of ethnicities in fact made the formulation of a demand for a Tajik territory impossible. The Tajiks, in the event of a demand for a federal structure, would not have been able to lay claim to a homogeneous and viable territory. In any case the principal leaders of Jamiyat-i Islami refused to contemplate a federal state; rather, despite the Tajik presence, most of the larger towns tended to favour attachment to the Afghan state rather than to any ethnic loyalty. In the last resort Jamiyat was constructed by Islamist networks established in the pre-war period on a political rather than a communal basis. What was seen in the end was a reinforcement of local solidarities, which guaranteed both loyalty and access to resources, rather than a Tajik ethnonationalism. The effectiveness of these networks was balanced by a progessive exclusivity of Jamiyat-i Islami which, at any rate in Kabul, seemed increasingly to be in the hands of the Panjshiri *qowm*.

The Taliban. The initial success of the Taliban was astonishing, but after the south of Afghanistan had fallen into its hands it encountered structured organisations that controlled mainly non-Pushtun populations, for example in Herat. As a result it recruited only among the Pushtuns, and although it never identified itself as such, it was seen

---

[7] In fact Ismail Khan, like his deputy Allauddin, was a Persian-speaker from the region of Shindand, but having lived in a Pushtun environment he spoke both languages fluently.

by many as enabling a return to the traditional Pushtun domination of Afghanistan's national territory.

In this sense the Taliban is sometimes described as a 'tribal' or 'nationalist' Pushtun movement, two concepts which were not always distinguished from each other. However, it was a movement dominated by a group of religious individuals, who established their authority with no reference to tribal institutions, which in any case barely existed in the region of Kandahar where the movement had its base. Taliban law was greatly at variance with tribal customs. The hypothesis that it was a tribal movement cannot be sustained, since neither tribes nor clans were represented in their own right within it.

In addition the Taliban movement was founded on a fundamentalist ideology opposed to all nationalist pretensions. Its official goal was the reunification of all Afghans under an Islamic government. It rejected all national or tribal justifications and took satisfaction in drawing attention to the presence within the movement of non-Pushtuns such as *mullah* Ghaysuddin Agha, who was a member of the *shura* of Kabul and came originally from Badakhshan. On two occasions ideological tendencies alien to the Taliban attempted to appeal to a putative Pushtun solidarity in an attempt to make use of the movement, and its failure is in itself informative. Former communists believed at one point that they could insinuate themselves into the Taliban movement on the basis of Pushtun solidarity. At first the Taliban accepted them since their officers were particularly important for a relatively unstructured movement without military experts other than some Pakistani officers. After the capture of Kabul, however, most of the former communists were ousted or even physically eliminated. Also, the royalists wanted to make use of the Taliban to put the king or his heir back on the throne, making their appeal to the origins of the Afghan dynasty in Kandahar. Here again harsh disillusionment followed since the religious and charismatic nature of the Taliban was incompatible with the royalist project.

Within the movement local solidarities were a stronger mobilising force than affiliation to a Pushtun ethnicity as such. For example, *mullah* Omar is from Tarin Kot in the province of Uruzgan, and a strong representation of his countrymen was to be observed in positions of authority, e.g. *mullah* Abbas. In addition, *mullah* Omar was a Ghilzai Pushtun Hottak, a group which Pierre Centlivres has established was over-represented in the Taliban government.[8] Other solidarity networks existed, such as that between *mujahidin* who had previously served under the same commander, such as *mawlawi* Jalaluddin Haqqani, formerly of Hezb-i Islami (Khales). On a more personal level the ministers and the governors surrounded themselves with members of their own families—e.g. *mullah* Muhammad Abbas and his family in the Ministry of Health.

Still, the Taliban retained a distinct Pushtun sensibility, especially in cultural affairs, tending to reject the Persian culture which was the basis of the training of *ulema* in pre-war times. Teaching in the *madrasas* of the North-West Frontier Province was traditionally carried out in Pushtu and Arabic. The Pushtuns had also continued to nurture the desire once more to achieve domination within Afghanistan's national territory. This attitude did not necessarily demonstrate the existence of a nascent—or re-nascent—nationalism, but rather the wish to perpetuate an ethnic hierarchy dominated by Pushtuns. Further, the Taliban did at some points employ ethnic arguments to mobilise support. For instance, in 1995 as Ismail Khan advanced towards Kandahar, it appealed to Pushtun solidarity against a Tajik aggressor. Similarly in the north its preference for alliances with Pushtun minorities gave credence, with hindsight, to the ethnic prejudices of both sides. The Taliban was also led by confrontation and suspicion to institute discriminatory practices, for example against the Panjshiris of Kabul who were suspected of assisting Masud.

The challenge to the ethnic hierarchy

The civil war and the collapse of the state undermined the informal ethnic hierarchy according to which relations between groups had been organised. Such political transformations had as their consequence that the pre-war ethnic hierarchy no longer appeared 'natural', i.e. it was not accepted by all sides. The Pushtuns had in fact lost the leverage of the state, which had once given them a considerable advantage, while the other communities armed themselves for the struggle against the Soviets and in the process acquired their autonomy. Several groups underwent a change of status during the war, in particular the Hazaras and the Uzbeks who in the past had often

---

[8] Personal information, March 1999.

been mistrusted and excluded from the army and political authority. These changes had tangible effects on relations between ethnicities examples were a ban on Pushtun nomads from pasturing their flocks in Hazara territory, and pressure on Pushtun minorities in the north due to competition for land. There was an asymmetry between ethnicities and regions which should not be overlooked. The Pushtun south was ethnically homogeneous, and tensions were therefore centred on the north. In these provinces the Pushtun minorities were often subjected to pressure by their neighbours and therefore generally supported the Taliban. In particular the tensions arising from this challenge to the position of communities caused a number of massacres. Few of these explicitly targeted an ethnic group, and the majority were directed against the Hazaras. On 11 February 1993 Sayyaf and Masud's troops launched an attack on the Shi'ite party Hezb-i Wahdat, which lost control of Afshar, a district west of Kabul. The victorious troops were given their head, and perhaps as many as 2–300 civilians were massacred by Sayyaf and Masud's men in an episode which continued till 14 February. Witnesses claim the *mujahidin* went into houses and carried out various atrocities, including rapes, killings and the mutilation of bodies.[9] In 1998 during the second capture of Mazar-i Sharif the Taliban massacred hundreds of Hazara civilians. Witnesses agree on the facts: the Taliban took the town and during the following three days slaughtered the Hazaras, going into houses to uncover and kill men of fighting age. There were probably several hundred victims. The bodies were left in the streets for several days, after which the Taliban made members of the public pick up the bodies and bury them in the common graves used the year before for the bodies of Taliban prisoners massacred by Malik's forces after the first capture of the town in 1997.[10] On the evidence of eye-witnesses, the executions were carried out on the basis of ethnic and religious affiliation, since in the north Hazaras were not easily distinguishable. It is possible that Pakistani fundamentalists—who are also supposed to have been responsible for the death of the Iranians who were in Mazar-i Sharif—may have played a role

---

[9] See Etienne Gille, 'Crimes à Afchar', *Les Nouvelles d'Afghanistan*, no. 60, 1993, p. ii.

[10] Eye-witness accounts collected in Mazar-i Sharif, April 2000, and in Pakistan in 1999.

in these killings. This would explain why the Shi'ite Hazaras, who did not bear the main responsibility for the massacres of 1997, should have been the sole targets. Nothing on a similar scale took place in relation to the Uzbeks.[11] There were to be no further massacres on this scale, but various operations in Hazarajat were notable for their brutality, including on several occasions the killing of civilians and in particular old men. In June 2001 the Taliban took and destroyed the town of Yakaolang, Hezb-i Wahdat's fief in the heart of Hazarajat.[12]

How does one explain such massacres? The first point to emphasise is that they cannot be accounted for by a desire to exterminate a particular group or carry out ethnic cleansing of the kind seen in the Balkans. There was in fact no ethnic cleansing on a major scale in Afghanistan in the 1990s, although local minority groups were the victims of pressure from neighbours who coveted their lands. The survivors of victim groups were able later to return to the same spot, since there was no systematic attempt at the transfer of populations.[13] For example, after the clashes in Bamyan, the Hazaras returned to their villages, and similarly there was no flight of Hazaras after the massacres in Mazar-i Sharif.[14]

The Taliban rebuilt a centralised authority at a local level, exploiting its alliances with local solidarity networks, a circumstance which militated against the politicisation of identity construction on the base of local ethnicities. In November 1998 Muhammad Akbari joined up with the Taliban, on the grounds of its recognition by the Shi'ite *ulema*; the Taliban in turn recognised them as legitimate *ulema*, with the aim of making use of them as arms of the central state.[15] In Bamyan

---

[11] However, the Uzbek village of Zari (Balkh) suffered a massacre after being retaken by the Taliban in May 2001.

[12] 'Afghanistan, Paying for the Taliban's Crimes: Abuses Against Ethnic Pushtuns in Northern Afghanistan', *Human Rights Watch*, April 2002, vol. 14, no. 2.

[13] Nevertheless mention might be made of at least two places, the Bangi valley (Takhar) and Robatak (Samangan), where Pushtun or Gujjara populations moved in after the eviction of Hazaras, Tajiks or Uzbeks.

[14] The Taliban took responsibility for a number of war crimes at Bamyan, including cutting the throats of several dozen old men, and the summary execution of dozens of civilians.

[15] This was in striking contrast to the Pakistani Deobandis, who were violently anti-Shi'ite.

the Taliban made a local alliance with the Tajiks in order to over-come the Hazaras. Their standpoint was in practice a return to the pre-war ethnic hierarchy, which was incompatible with ethnic cleansing. There was no wish to put a halt to multi-ethnic coexistence, but such tolerance was only made possible because the communities stood in a hierarchical relationship, a situation which offers a brutal explanation of the massacres to which the Hazaras were subjected. The Hazaras were not recognised as equal interlocutors, since this would have breached the ethnic hierarchy. The massacres can there-fore be seen as in essence part of a move towards internal reconquest, and were not without echoes of the campaigns conducted by Abdul Rahman Khan at the close of the nineteenth century.

In contrast, as developments that followed the fall of the Taliban confirmed, the parties in the north—Jombesh, Hezb-i Wahdat and Jamiyat-i Islami—tended in the direction of driving the Pushtuns out of the north. The conflicts brought about a transformation of national feeling, by way of a new connection between national identity and communal affiliation. In exile the only Afghan national identity acknowledged by the Pakistani government and the humanitarian aid agencies manifested itself paradoxically to the detriment of regional and tribal identities.[16] Exposure to a quite different way of life also gave rise to a feeling of common identity between exiled Afghans, who at least shared similar interests if not the same opinions. In the same sense the presence of hundreds of thousands of Pushtuns in Pakistan often gave rise to tensions between the newly-arrived population and the host country, which tended to reinforce the feeling of being Afghan to the detriment of a trans-border Push-tun identity. Although 70% of the refugees came from the Afghan provinces bordering Pakistan, there was no general integration be-tween the local population and the refugees.[17] The settlement in the frontier regions of several hundred thousand Afghans with Pakistani identity cards had not up to that point resulted in assimilation.

[16] Pierre Centlivres, Micheline Centlivres-Demont, *Afghanistan Info*, 29, March 1991.

[17] Richard English, 'The Economic Impact of Afghan Refugee Settlement on the Tribal Areas of North-West Pakistan', UNHCR, unpublished, 1989, p. 35.

9. The Clerical State

The Taliban regime can be interpreted in several different ways.[1] The hypothesis defended here is that its power was of a religious or, more precisely, a clerical nature. A comparison with revolutionary Iran in terms of three key factors will help to illuminate the unique nature of the Afghan situation. These factors are (1) the identity of the actors; (2) the institutional model adopted; and (3) the plan of social organisation.

(1) While in Afghanistan it was a group of *ulema* which took power, the political actors who emerged from the revolution in Iran were much more varied. The Iranian clergy had been largely inactive during the twentieth century except at certain moments of crisis, and were far from unanimous in their backing for Khomeini.[2] The urban population, who were the major agents of the revolution, did not regard Khomeini solely or even principally as a cleric. A further element of difference here was that the relationship between the *ulema* and the Islamists was different in Iran and Afghanistan. In Iran the *ulema* and the Islamists acted in collaboration, while in Afghanistan the opposition between these two groups was deepening. In the Iranian revolution also the mobilisation of urban groups was a crucial factor, in contrast to the rural origins of the Taliban's rank and file.

(2) As for the institutional model, although the Iranian regime is authoritarian and the constitutional principle of the *wilayat al-faqih* placed serious restrictions on the freedom of the administration, the government nevertheless emerged from contested elections. In con-

---

[1] See in particular William Maley (ed.), *op. cit.*

[2] On these issues see Farhad Khosrokhavar, *L'utopie sacrifiée. Sociologie de la révolution iranienne*, Paris: Presses de la Fondation nationale des sciences politiques, 1993; and Paul Vieille, 'L'orientalisme est théoriquement spécifique? A propos des interprétations de la révolution iranienne', *Peuples méditerranéens* 50, Jan.–March 1990, pp. 149–61.

trast to the situation in Afghanistan, Iranian political life was complex, with opportunities for the exercise of liberty.

(3) Although religious puritanism was a consideration in both countries, the social models in the two cases were very different. The Iranian revolution was primarily a phenomenon of modernisation, while the aims of the Taliban were reactionary. We consider these issues further in relation to the Afghan case by means of a sociological study of the personnel of the revolutionary movements, an examination of state structures, and an analysis of the puritanical order imposed by the regime.

The party functionaries

The Taliban was not a political party in the classic sense, since the movement had no clear structure and soon became indistinguishable from the state.[3] The social origin of its officials showed a high level of uniformity, and this consistency of membership was the source of the movement's unity. The party functionaries were generally Pushtuns, poor and of rural origin, with no education except what they had received in the *madrasas*. Brought up during the war—*mullah* Omar was born around 1961—they had fought as members of various parties, but had seldom held positions of responsibility since they had little in the way of education, religious charisma or notability to recommend them. The new ruling class was therefore entirely alien to the bourgeois and urban world from which Afghan élites had hitherto emerged. Their status as 'outsiders' partly explained their coherence as a group.

Their rise to power, the result of a collective mobilisation, enabled them to occupy positions of prestige and authority out of proportion to what they could have expected within the Afghan society of the 1970s, when the prestige of the *ulema* had been in decline. *Mullah* Omar himself, the son of a poor family, did not complete the studies which would conventionally have given him the right to the title of *alem*. His position as head of the Taliban represented a new departure in the political and religious field. Under the Taliban the

---

[3] Membership of the movement was signified by the fact of having fought in Taliban groups or of carrying out administrative duties. This is the conclusion from the decrees of *mullah* Omar, where he calls for the expulsion of corrupt members of the movement (Decree 49, *Gazette* 788).

great families lost most of the prestige on which they relied both as *ulema* and as brotherhood leaders.[4] They were not absorbed into the Taliban, although the *ulema* linked to the Mujaddidi family in the Ghazni region did join it after having already installed locally a fairly similar fundamentalist political system themselves. The ousting of the dominant families was the result of a twofold process. Although the heirs of these families combined religious knowledge as *ulema* with hereditary charisma as *pirs*, they were too implicated in political manoeuvres, corruption and the associated violence to appear as a credible alternative. An instance of this phenomenon was the erosion of the legitimacy of the two great family networks, the Gaylani and the Mujaddidi, both directly linked to political parties whose influence was waning and which were notorious for their nepotism. Subsequently, without competent officials and lacking support from Pakistan, these parties were unable to play a significant role on the ground.

Positions of authority were held entirely by *ulema* belonging to the closed circle of 'historic' Taliban—those who had joined in the early days. The social homogeneity of the Taliban leadership and the unchallenged authority of *mullah* Omar may explain why there were never internecine armed clashes or moves towards defection as a result of internal tensions, even after resounding defeats such as that at Mazar-i Sharif in 1997. In this the Taliban differed from all other Afghan parties. However the opacity of its administration has meant that it is difficult to analyse its internal decision mechanisms.[5] For instance, there was never any serious basis for the supposition of hostility between *mullah* Omar and *mullah* Rabbani, to which attention was once regularly drawn. There were probably some disagreements between leaders who were keen to achieve international recognition, such as that between *mullah* Abdul Muttawakil (Minister for Foreign Affairs) and *mullah* Muhammad Abbas Istanekzai (Minister of Health), on the one hand, and certain commanders, including

---

[4] In addition, *ulema* who emerged from the government *madrasas,* who if they were politicised were in general modernisers and Islamists, tended to take the side of Masud's opposition, where they were not given positions of authority within his organisation.

[5] An informant in Kabul in 2000, who was himself a judge and an *alem*, verified that information on the workings of the Taliban government was unavailable except to a few hundred Taliban *ulema*.

Dadullah, on the other. However, *mullah* Omar continued to be the unchallenged arbiter.

Although the Taliban movement was coherent it was not monolithic, and the networks of which it consisted may be differentiated, in the first instance geographically. Under more detailed analysis three groups of *ulema* can be distinguished: first, those from the region of Kandahar, who were directly aware of *mullah* Omar; secondly, the *ulema* of Ghazni and Logar, south of Kabul, who were historically close to the Mujaddidi family and enlisted in 1995 and 1996; and finally the *ulema* in the east of the country, such as *mawlawi* Haqqani. The significance of local solidarities, sometimes of tribal, has already been examined. The existence of separate networks did not imply ideological differences, and there is nothing to suggest irreconcilable tensions. The reality was that access to the resources of the administration was shared, an outcome achieved through compromise.

The key experience shared by the group was the education of its members in the Pakistani *madrasas* in the 1980s.[6] Most of the *ulema* at the level of the leadership had emerged from the *madrasas* of the North–West Frontier Province and Baluchistan, for example the Dar ul-Ulum Haqqania *madrasa* at Akora Khattak in NWFP.[7] From this *madrasa* came *haji* Ahmad Jan, Minister of Mines, *mawlawi* Qalamuddin, head of the religious police, and *mawlawi* Arefullah Aref, deputy Minister of Finance. One of the few former commanders to become a leader of the movement, *mawlawi* Haqqani from Hezb-i Islami (Khales), spent several years at the *madrasa* Dar ul-Ulum Haqqaniya, first as a student and then as a teacher. An address by *mullah* Omar was read from the platform at the ceremony marking the

---

[6] When considering the following facts one must bear in mind that membership of the Taliban was different in 2001 from what it had been on its first appearance in 1994. The Taliban was at first made up of a few hundred theology students, but their numbers were substantially boosted by the membership of *mujahidin* from the former parties, and from the government itself, as well as by the recruitment of young men with no prior experience at a time when many of the Taliban 'old guard' had been killed in the fighting of recent years. In addition, the opportunistic adherence of former officials complicates the analysis. Finally, Pakistani nationals sometimes played a significant role in the expansion of the movement, although the leadership was undisputedly Afghan and stable from 1994 onwards.

[7] Kamal Matinuddin, *The Afghan Phenomenon: Afghanistan 1994–1997*, Oxford University Press, 1999, p. 17.

graduation as *ulema* of Afghan and Pakistani students at this *madrasa*. Also three close advisers of *mullah* Omar were graduates of the *madrasa* Jamiyat ul-Ulum ul-Islamiyah, so that it was no surprise when he sent a message of support after the assassination of two of its teachers in November 1997.

The numbers of Afghans at the Pakistani *madrasas* was a phenomenon related to two considerations: first, religious institutions in Pakistan were anyway increasing in size and numbers, and secondly the substantial influx of Afghan refugees meant that more Afghans were available as students. From the 1960s both the number of *madrasas* in Pakistan and the number of students (*taliban*) had expanded dramatically. Between 1960 and 1983 the number of *taliban* increased tenfold, from 7,500 to 78,500, and of teachers from 321 to 2,217.[8] There was no slackening in this increase, which was much more rapid than that of the population. In 1988 there were 1,320 *madrasas* in Punjab, but by 1997 there were 2,512 with 220,000 students.[9] In Karachi there were twenty-nine *madrasas* which educated an average of 2,000 students each year.[10] The acceleration in the 1980s was partly a consequence of the policy of Islamisation undertaken by the regime of Zia ul-Haq (1977–88). Two particularly important measures taken by Zia were the recognition of diplomas from the *madrasas* by the universities and the introduction of obligatory *zakat*, of which part was given to the *madrasas*.[11] Zia also encouraged *madrasas* to open in the NWFP in order to sustain the Afghan *jihad*, which explains a larger increase in the number in this province than the national average.

The *madrasas* were attached to different religious tendencies: Deobandi, Barelwi and Ahl-i Hadith. The teaching of the Deobandi and Barelwi *madrasas* was generally very conservative. One of the fundamental texts, the *Dars-i Nizamiyya*, dates from the eighteenth century, and Aristotle's logic was still taught. Some Deobandi *madrasas* exerted their influence on the national scale, in particular the Jamiyat al-Ulum al-Islamiyah, founded by Yusuf Binari at Binari Town close to Karachi, which had 8,000 students, including those at its twelve affiliated mosques. Though fewer students are at present

[8] Jamal Malik, *op. cit.*, p. 178.
[9] *The News International*, 28 May 1997.
[10] *The Herald*, December 1997.
[11] However, some *madrasas* refused the *zakat* to preserve their independence.

taken by the *madrasa* Dar al–Uum Haqqaniyah at Akora Khattak in the Peshawar district, founded in 1947 and now run by *maulana* Sami al–Haq, in the past it produced a third of the Deobandi *ulema* in Pakistan. Other *madrasas*, attached to the Ahl–i Hadith tendency or linked to Jamaat–i Islami, displayed aspects of a more modernising tendency, for example in their teaching of information technology and English. Jamaat–i Islami opened a significant number of *madrasas*; especially in NWFP, where its forty-one, including nineteen set up after the Soviet invasion, made up more than a third of the new foundations in this province. Elsewhere Saudi Arabia financed the construction of the Jamiyat Imam Bukhari *madrasa* at Peshawar, which was opened in June 1999 at a ceremony addressed by a representative of the Saudi Ministry of Religious Affairs, Muhammad Abdul Rahman.[12] It was in the Ahl–i Hadith tradition and headed by an official of the Jamaat al-Dawa lil-Quran wa lil-Sunna, a movement which before the arrival of the Taliban had a presence in Afghanistan in the province of Kunar.

What was the position of Afghan students in these *madrasas*? When the war began, the proportion of Afghan students rose markedly. After 1982 some 9% of the students of religion in NWFP were Afghans.[13] For example Afghans made up the vast majority of the 750 students of the Jamiyat Imam Bukhari *madrasa* mentioned above. In the 1960s, 15 per cent of the students at the *madrasa* Dar ul-Ulum Haqqaniyah were Afghans, but by 1985 this proportion had risen to 60 per cent.[14] Afghan students mainly attended Deobandi *madrasas*, since these were in the majority in the frontier region and since the Afghan *ulema* had historic links with the *madrasa* Dar al-Ulum Deoband in India, though the links between this institution and the Pakistani *madrasas* which claimed to follow the same teaching had weakened. Under the generic term 'Deobandi' there are in fact movements of sometimes quite varied tendencies, and neither the coherence of this school of thought nor the level of education of its *ulema* should be over-estimated.[15] Education at these *madrasas* had

---

[12] *The News International*, 25 June 1999.
[13] Jamal Malik, *op. cit.*, p. 206.
[14] Jamal Malik, *op. cit.*, p. 207.
[15] Concerning the penetration of the reformist movements in Afghanistan and Central Asia, see the special issue of *La lettre d'Asie centrale* 2, autumn 1994.

two major consequences for their Afghan graduates: the cementing of strong solidarities, emerging from a shared experience and a common world view; and (an issue to which we return) the appearance of transnational networks.

State structures

The idea that the Taliban was not interested in the state and left it to decay can be dismissed. Between 1996 and 2001 it gradually reconstructed various institutions, especially the administrative structure and the judicial system. Still, Taliban ideology limited the remit of the state to security, justice and the observation of religious regulations. It intervened little in economic matters, since there were few taxes and little investment, or in the social sphere, which was largely reduced almost entirely to the action of religious charities. Analysis of state structures under the Taliban begins with the position of the *ulema*, and continues with the administration and finally the judiciary.

The position of the ulema in state institutions. The legitimacy of the new Afghan state was based neither on nationalist ideology nor on popular sovereignty. In particular, the Taliban rejected political parties and the idea of democratically contested elections as a foundation for political legitimacy. This is a theme common to many Islamic or fundamentalist movements, which take issue with the idea that it is not within the scope of a majority of electors to alter the law of God. The *shariat*, interpreted by the *ulema*, was seen as the only legitimate source of law, while religious scholars dominated the judiciary, the executive and legislative activity, with distinctions drawn in practice between these three functions. The members of *shuras* were mostly *ulema*, since religious qualification was preferred to technical expertise or being socially representative as a criterion for membership. In addition, several of *mullah* Omar's decrees tended to reinforce the special role of the *ulema*, in particular the preservation of 'Muslim heritage' through religious education. The *ulema* maintained vigilance over morals and identified transgressors, for whom reform was compulsory.

For the individual, religious affiliation was a determining factor in political status. This was tantamount to a return to the form of legitimation of the Afghan state at the time of its establishment at the end of the nineteenth century, before nationalist ideology came into play. A consequence was that non-Muslims, which meant in practice some thousands of Hindus, were obliged, at least in theory, to wear distinctive marks and were subjected to the status of *dhimmi* (those under protection), a provision which rested on a 1924 amendment to the 1923 constitution.[16] As for the Shi'ites, the Ismailis and the Twelver Shi'ites faced different situations. The Ismailis were not regarded as Muslims, and were subjected to forcible conversion to the Sunni creed. Many were driven into exile, but they were not numerically important. In contrast, despite some localised incidents, mainstream Shi'ites were not forcibly converted and were able, for example, to observe *ashura* in public in Kabul, including self-flagellation, which was nevertheless criticised by many Sunnis.

Mullah Omar was the cornerstone of the political structure, since he brought together the legislative, executive and judicial powers. His decrees, signed '*amir al-mu'minin mujahid mullah* Muhammad Omar Akhund', covered all issues, including the status of women, the treatment of prisoners, the obligation to say prayers, and the appointment of administrative officials and judges. The authority of the various *shuras*, including the government in Kabul, did not exceed what was delegated to them, and their power was entirely advisory.

The charismatic authority of *mullah* Omar did not arise from the depth of his religious knowledge but was seen as a gift from God, and his dreams were interpreted by his disciples as signs of the divine will.[17] Accounts of him convey the stereotypical image of a man of religion with an inclination towards mysticism. He was said to be

---

[16] This measure, which the Taliban promulgated, was later abandoned.

[17] For a biography of *mullah* Omar see Kamal Matinuddin, *op. cit.*, p. 223. He was born in 1961 in the village of Naudeh (in the district of Panjwai, Kandahar province). His father afterwards lived at Dehrwut (in the district of Tarin Kot, Uruzgan province), where he was the *mullah* of a small mosque. *Mullah* Omar fought as a member of various parties (Harakat-i Enqelab, Hezb-i Islami (Khales) with Nik Mohammad and Jamiyat-i Islami) and was wounded a number of times. He speaks Persian and had studied theology, but did not officially hold the title of *alem*. After the Soviet withdrawal he continued to live in Nashke Nakhud, in the village of Sinsegar in the district of Maywand, Kandahar province, rather than move to Pakistan, in contrast to many other future officials of the movement. There have been very few interviews with *mullah* Omar; however see 'L'Islam au bout du fusil … Entretien avec Mohammad Omar', *Politique internationale* 74, winter 1996–7, pp. 135–43.

humble and soft-spoken, and to derive his authority from an ability to listen, from lack of personal ambition, and from the rigour of his application of the *shariat*. His election as *amir al-mu'minin* (commander of the faithful) in Kandahar in April 1996 by an assembly of 1,527 *ulema* from Afghanistan, Pakistan and Iran was the first step in the 'routinisation' of his charisma. At the moment of his election the cloak of the Prophet was displayed at a public gathering in Kandahar. This cloak was a relic preserved at a *zariat* in Kandahar and had last been displayed in 1935 during a cholera epidemic. This ceremonial, reflecting the ritual previously used by Abdul Rahman Khan, was an indication that the *amir* was regarded as God-sent rather than elected in the usual sense. *Mullah* Omar, incidentally, had been criticised by the Gaylani and the Mujaddidi who correctly perceived him as challenging the established religious hierarchy.[18] Official recognition by the body of *ulema* enabled a link to be established between the charisma of the leader and the governmental institution.

Administrative structures. Mullah Omar did not personally head the government in Kabul, which he delegated to his faithful followers while himself remaining in Kandahar. However, his keeping a deliberate distance from the capital and from the government institutions did not detract from his absolute authority. The structures of power evolved after the capture of Kandahar. In the initial phases *mullah* Omar was supported by *shuras*—advisory councils—whose membership was made public on a number of occasions, but once the Taliban had strengthened its grip, following the capture of Kabul in 1996, the failure to distinguish between the structures of the state and the Taliban movement became more marked.

A number of phases may be distinguished as a simplified account of events will show. In the first place, *mullah* Omar was backed up by a ten-strong *shura* mainly concerned with military activities. After the capture of Herat the *shura* was expanded in size, rising from thirty members in 1995 to 100 at the time of the capture of Kabul.[19] The *shura* then established in the capital progressively became the

---

[18] This appellation had, already been applied to *mullah* Omar, see *The News International*, 27 January 1995. Rabbani had also received it from the Shura Ahl-i Hal wa Hakd in 1994, as had Jamil ur-Rahman in Kunar, from a local religious assembly.

[19] According to the *Frontier Post* of 24 February 1995, the *shura* of Kandahar included *mawlawi* Muhammad Rabbani, *mawlawi* Esanullah, *mawlawi* Abbas, *mawlawi*

effective government of the country, led by *mullah* Rabbani, who was known as the Raïs-i Shura-yi Sarparast (director of the council of guardianship). Another *shura* continued to function in Kandahar with some ten *ulema* who made up *mullah* Omar's immediate entourage. Some members of this *shura* were also members of the *shura* of Kabul. The consolidation of the military situation and the seizure of the capital created the opportunity for more elaborate formal structures to be set up. In October 1997 Afghanistan was renamed the Islamic Emirate of Afghanistan, and the administrative divisions which had existed under Daud were mostly re-established.[20]

At the beginning the Taliban did not have sufficient numbers to occupy the countryside in depth and controlled only the towns and the principal roads. The outcome was basically the establishment of a limited level of control. For instance, in Logar and Ghazni *ulema* from Kandahar took over the posts of district officials (*uluswal*) while the rest of the administration remained in place. Later the Taliban did set up a local administrative system. In the towns, especially Kandahar, each of the various sectors was placed under the authority of a commander responsible for security and respect for 'Islamic morals'. There were also local *shuras* which provided liaison between the Taliban and the population, and looked after the details of everyday life such as the organisation of the bazaar and the supervision of traffic. These councils were in principle elected by villagers. The guardians of the bazaars were elected in an analogous way.[21] Similarly the local *mullah* was normally chosen by the inhabitants rather than by the *uluswal*.[22] In practice the *mullahs* had a decisive influence over these councils, tending to exclude the *khans* and the educated class.

Muhammad, *mawlawi* Pasaband, *mawlawi* Muhammad Hasan, *mawlawi* Nuruddin, *mawlawi* Walik Ahmad, *mawlawi* Shir Muhammad Malang, *mawlawi* Abd al-Rahman, *mawlawi* Abd al-Hakim, *mawlawi* Sardar Ahmad, *haji* Muhammad Ghaus and Masum Afghani. The *shura* of Kabul included *mullah* Muhammad Rabbani, *mullah* Muhammad Hasan, *mullah* Muhammad Ghaus, *mullah* Seyyed Ghaysuddin Agha, *mullah* Ghazil Muhammad and *mullah* Abdul Razaq.

[20] See decree no. 12 of 7 March 1996, Official *Gazette* no. 783, 1997, p. 21, which sets up the same ministries which existed under Daud. The original date of this decree is given as 1375/12/16, but it is noteworthy that from 1999 the Taliban applied the lunar Islamic calendar (under which 1999 coincided broadly with 1419) abolishing the solar calendar where 1999 was equivalent to 1378.

[21] Decree no. 1981 of 20 March 1995 (1374/12/29).

[22] Undated decree, Ministry of Justice, Kabul.

To avoid rivalry between communities, the Taliban administrative system was organised on the principle of a rapid rotation of officials, and their appointment in principle outside their home regions, except in Kandahar. The provincial governors (the *walis*) were generally changed over within a few months, and brought their own teams of officials, often drawn from their own *qowm*, together with their own equipment, including vehicles. This avoided the establishment of strong regional powers, and prevented internal struggles from developing into armed clashes. Rotation became less rapid as the regime became more stable, but the principle of appointing governors from outside any given province remained the rule. The same considerations resulted in the efficient and swift collection of weapons, since the authorities gave the appearance of being external to local conflicts. Apparently the Taliban used fragmentation as a means of conflict management, and situated itself in the position of a referee. Retribution against former party activists was not pursued on condition that they refrained from further political activity; this meant an escape from the cycle of vendetta.

The principal ministers, who took up office one by one, were able only with difficulty to carry out their responsibilities since some 100,000 educated Afghans had fled the country, creating a crucial lack of officials. A further difficulty was the lack of money, resulting from the war and from the effects of the international embargo imposed in 1999. After a cut in staff of 40% in April 2000, 130,000 staff were employed by the regime. The reduction in staff numbers was concentrated in Kabul, with women particularly affected. With a personnel and an outlook which scarcely fitted it for government, the Taliban made the discovery that it was in practice dependent on humanitarian aid. Although there were moments of strain, especially when the NGOs temporarily withdrew in 1998, NGO activity was perceived by the authorities as vital. The reality was that in 1998 the NGOs spent $113 million in Afghanistan, and provided work for around 25,000 Afghans.[23] One of *mullah* Omar's edicts decreed five years' imprisonment for anyone attacking foreigners working in Afghanistan.

In some parts of the country humanitarian aid was essential to stave off famine and avert a further popular exodus. In the district of

[23] United Nations, *Afghanistan Outlook*, December 2000.

Bamyan, in Bamyan province, around a quarter of the income of the population in 2000 was derived from humanitarian programmes.[24] This was an exceptional situation, but the drought in 2001 caused malnutrition and even famine. There was a general deterioration in relations between the NGOs and the Taliban, who seem to have wanted to increase the level of participation of Islamic NGOs.

The judiciary. In theory at least the judicial system was independent of the executive. The *qadis* did not answer to the provincial governors (the *walis*) or to the district officials (*uluswal*), although all ultimately fell under the authority of *mullah* Omar. There were judges in all districts and three levels of jurisdiction were in place in each province.[25] In principle no punishment or sentence of imprisonment could take effect without the sanction of a *qadi*.[26] An edict was published by *mullah* Omar which decreed that detainees should not be beaten—torture had been widespread under all Afghan regimes—and that their money should not be taken.[27] However, the conditions of prisoners were not improved while the Taliban was in power, and ill-treatment remained widespread, especially when the secret police were involved.

All laws were subject to the approval of a *shura* of *ulema* which scrutinised their conformity with the *shariat* and with Hanafi jurisprudence. The existing constitution, as well as a section of the criminal and civil law, was declared to be in conflict with the *shariat* and was consequently abolished. Over criminal law and personal rights Hanafi jurisprudence was applied, especially in the case of punishments such as amputation and stoning. An examination of juridical texts issued by the Taliban shows that these generally followed the precedent of the most traditionalist Afghan *ulema*, with no notable

---

[24] This estimate is based on the reports of the NGO Solidarité Afghanistan.

[25] Decree no. 105 of 10 September 1999 (1419/5/18), which distinguished between the lower courts (*eptedai*), then the court of appeal (*morafea*) and finally the higher court (*tahmiz*).

[26] See in particular the decrees of *mullah* Omar no. 4265 of 4 March 1999 (1419/11/16) and no. 234 of 29 January 1999 (1419/10/11), available at the Ministry of Justice, Kabul.

[27] Decree no. 141 of 27 April 1997 (1376/6/7), available at the Ministry of Justice, Kabul.

innovations. Most of the measures promulgated derived from the *hadith* collected by Ismail al-Bukhari (who died *circa* 870), which served as the basis of Islamic law in Afghanistan. There was therefore little novelty except for the re-adoption of certain punishments and other judicial measures which had fallen into disuse in Afghanistan and in the majority of other Muslim countries. Thus amputations for theft became frequent, although this practice had been abolished in the 1950s. A number of women were stoned for adultery in spite of the disapproval of many of the *ulema*. The practice had been abolished before the war and been infrequent since, with only one reported case in Badakhshan.

Finally, the judgements of the *qadis* frequently went against tribal customs, particularly with the outlawing of vendettas. In a case of murder, the relatives of the victims were invited themselves to kill the murderers, although a financial settlement was also provided for. In all cases vendetta was forbidden.

The social backlash: the puritan order and social resistance

The intention of the Taliban was to institute a moral order such as it imagined had existed before the modernist reforms of the 1950s. It also largely readopted the measures taken in 1929 by Habibullah Kalakani, who prohibited the wearing of European clothes, banned the cutting of beards, and forbade women to move about without the permission of their *wali* (male representative).[28] Although the media apparently discovered these measures only in 1996, they were not radically new since most of the commanders had already implemented them during the war, including such measures as bans on music and cigarettes and the compulsory wearing of beards. Such fundamentalist parties as Ettehad and Hezb-i Islami (Khales) were perfectly in sympathy with this aspect of Taliban policy.

On this basis the religious police, *al-Amr bil-Ma'ruf wal-Nahi 'an al-Munkar*, became a feature of the mechanism of social control.[29]

---

[28] On the measures adopted in 1929 see Muhammad Naser Kemal, *op. cit.*, p. 152. For comparison with the Taliban, see for example decree no. 3409 of 25 December 1996 (1375/10/4), Official *Gazette* no. 783, 1997, p. 9.

[29] The name refers to a verse in the Quran (*sura* 3, verse 104) which enjoins the 'enforcement of virtue and the suppression of vice'.

This institution was organised at the national level with the status of a ministry, and was especially active in Kabul, although a force probably numbering no more than 2–3,000 was unable to control the population. It was to some extent a re-invention of a former institution, the *muhtaseb*, whose members were appointed by the local *qadi*, with the responsibility of preventing petty crime, checking weights and measures in the markets, and maintaining public morality through such matters as attendance at the mosque. Under Nadir Shah the *muhtaseb* had the power to demand the recitation of prayers from passers-by, whipping them if they did not know the words. The Taliban reintroduced this practice, and in addition made absence from daily prayers punishable by up to ten days' imprisonment.

In daily life the implementation of the *shariat* implied a degree of puritanism hitherto unknown in Afghan society, as well as an intrusive police presence.[30] Personal appearance was regulated. The beard was to be of a precise length—a fist's width below the chin—and those failing to comply were jailed until their beards reached the appropriate length. In contrast, hair was to be kept short. As a general rule all entertainment was forbidden. The festival of *Nawruz*, the New Year, on 21 March, customarily marked by parties and picnics, was declared unlawful because of its non-Muslim origin. Similarly music-making was banned. To this end houses were searched, usually as the result of a denunciation, and those in contravention were arrested and sometimes beaten. This brought radical change to the atmosphere of a town such as Kandahar. Those caught selling audio cassettes were liable to several days in prison and a lashing. The ownership of pigeons and other birds was no longer allowed as a hobby. Pictures of living beings were forbidden,[31] so that decorative designs on lorries were erased, while television and the cinema were prohibited. In common with the rest of the press, the Taliban newspaper *Zarb-i Mu'minin* (The Onslaught of the Faithful) strictly adhered to this prohibition. School textbooks were censored to ensure the removal of pictures of people and animals.

Although fundamentalism had been increasing in Afghanistan for twenty years, the Taliban regime, because of its radicalism, clashed

---

[30] See Peter Marsden, *The Taliban: war, religion and the new order in Afghanistan*, London: Zed Books, 1998.

[31] The sole exception to this rule seems to have been identity photographs for official documents.

286

the people had no way of giving direct expression to their discontent, since all demonstrations were ruthlessly suppressed. In early
December 1998, medical students protesting at the lack of resources
at the University of Jalalabad were brutally dispersed by the *Qita-i
Muntazeri* (Forces of Intervention), with the deaths of two demonstrators. Sometimes the Taliban was obliged to withdraw minor measures. For example, after the ban on *Nawruz* celebrations at Mazar-i
Sharif, it made a number of concession in the light of popular dissatisfaction. A further consideration was that there were no independent media or other independent organisations which could act as a
channel for discontent.

In such a situation, where open protest had become impossible,
the only alternatives were exile, for those who had the financial means
to leave, or oblique forms of popular resistance. In a city such as Kabul
discontent with the agents of the Taliban system was clearly evident,
with remarks sometimes being made even in their presence when
they were unable to understand Persian.[32] Dissidence was also expressed through humour and through pressing aspects of physical
appearance to the limit of legality. In the towns the beard might be
worn a little short, with haircuts longish and romantic. Such popular
inertia and resistance meant that the regulations were far from being
applied to the letter. Music was still heard in private and even in
shared taxis once out of town, while birds were bought and sold in
spite of the ban. Books were sold under the counter in a trade which
was illegal in theory but tolerated in practice. Prostitution flourished
in spite of official puritanism since many women, especially widows,
were unable to carry on working. Street children were, and still are,
also easy prey.

Resistance to the regime was not unanimous. The degree of dissidence varied in different social groups and communities. The Taliban
enjoyed a certain level of support in the Pushtun countryside, where
the moral code was largely that of the local people, and because the
Taliban regime was a guarantee of security. Another factor was that
the *ulema* gave unstinting support to the new regime, which had spec-

---

[32] On this kind of phenomena see in particular James Scott, *Domination and the Arts
of Resistance*, New Haven and London: Yale University Press, 1990. See also
Michel de Certeau, *L'invention du quotidien*, Paris: Gallimard, 1990.

tacularly enhanced their prosperity and raised their social standing. A further issue was that the rise of the Taliban gave expression to the desire of rural people to avenge themselves on the towns. Many young unemployed peasants from the south had joined the Taliban both to earn a living and to obtain social status. Finally, some members of the merchant class had been favourable to the Taliban from the start. The early operations on the Pakistan frontier in 1994 had been partly financed by Kandahari merchants whose aim was to secure freedom of movement. In this sphere the Taliban's attitude was permissive; roads were kept open, while controls and taxes on trade were minimal. The bazaars were also rebuilt, particularly in Kandahar.

As a general rule, however, the non-Pushtun population and the Shi'ites were opposed to the new authorities. Communal affiliation was not a determining factor; membership of the educated class was more prescriptive of a person's attitude to the Taliban than his ethnic origin. To illustrate in practice the diversity of reactions towards the regime, we now examine in detail the circumstances of three very disparate social groups—men of religion, the educated class and women.

The official role of the Ulema. The transformation of the *ulema* into state officials had already been a long-term trend in most Muslim societies, for example in Turkey and Pakistan. For more than a century the Afghan state had attempted to gain control of the *ulema* by bringing them into the administration. Paradoxically the Taliban regime, which was infested with *ulema*, succeeded in divesting them of their autonomy. The great majority of the *ulema* willingly came over to the new regime, which provided them with a highly effective means of exerting influence over Afghan society. The process of 'officialisation' took place by way of the establishment of an administrative hierarchy, so that *ulema* were ranked on a salary scale according to their qualifications. The *madrasas*, in common with all teaching institutions, were henceforth controlled by the Ministry of Education.

Another issue was that the role played by the *mullahs* in the administrative process reinforced their relationship with the state apparatus. In particular, they were entrusted with the evaluation of those taxes which were obligatory on the citizens (*ushr* and *zakat*);[33] they appropriated part of the revenue for their own needs, forwarding the rest

[33] See decree no. 32, Official *Gazette* 788 and Official *Gazette* 789, p. 42.

to the Ministry of Finance. Clearly such responsibilities placed a village *mullah* in the position of a representative of the state, playing a role which had hitherto been the prerogative of functionaries or local notables. The only circumstance which in theory allowed relative autonomy to the religious establishment in its relations with the authorities was the election of the *mullah* by the local community. Still, although events observed in Wardak and Kabul might lead to contrary conclusions, continuity tended to prevail. The available choices were restricted, and the identification of the *mullahs* with the machinery of state was not in reality called into question by this procedure.

Therefore, in contrast to the previous situation the *ulema* wielded an authority which depended on their relationship with the state. This was a total reversal, since the *ulema* had been bastions of opposition to the state throughout most of the twentieth century, especially to measures of modernisation. However, under the Taliban they were assimilated to the state and therefore subject to criticism on the grounds of their inefficiency and sometimes their corruption.

The alienation of the educated class from the state. Discontent was concentrated in the towns, especially Kabul, since the Taliban, in common with rural Pushtuns in general, particularly detested the urban culture which it saw as anti-Islamic; in the town, they believed, they were in danger of assimilation and therefore loss of identity.[34] The Taliban's seizure of power was among other things a class struggle, in which the urban bourgeoisie were for the moment the losers.

The urban élites, who valued modernity and their personal liberties whatever their communal affiliation, were unanimously critical of the Taliban. Although their social influence was significant, they were numerically in the minority and were politically marginalised after the fall of Kabul in 1996. The privileged triangular relationship which had existed between the state, the process of modernisation and the educated class disappeared with the clericalisation of the state. The educated class depended for its position on access to state-legitimised educational resources, while the state was at the same time been its main employer. In consequence the majority of the edu-

---

[34] Jon. W. Anderson, 'Social Structure and the Veil: comportment and interaction in Afghanistan', *Anthropos*, 77, 1982, p. 416.

cated class fled Afghanistan in successive waves.[35] Those who remained were obliged to find jobs outside state institutions in either
humanitarian organisations or private institutions.

It is difficult to estimate the number of educated individuals working for NGOs in Afghanistan under the Taliban, a total to which
may be added these doing similar work in Pakistan who frequently
return to Afghanistan. On the basis of figures provided by the NGOs
themselves, an initial estimate might be some 10,000, taking into account that job descriptions were relatively fluid and that many employees were over-qualified in relation to the positions they occupied.[36]
More than 250 NGOs were officially registered, which at least enabled enterprising educated individuals to find niches in the humanitarian sphere. The numbers were relatively limited, but the NGOs
were probably as significant an employer as the Afghan state itself for
the educated class. The state actually employed its officials only part-
time and paid extremely low salaries—less than $10 per month for a
teacher, including bonuses—and dismissed between a quarter and
half of its employees in 2000. Additionally, the most motivated and
highly qualified graduates tended to prefer working in NGOs, for
both financial and ideological reasons.

In fact parastatal organisations such as NGOs offered an organisational model and an ideological framework which were compatible
with the preconceptions of the Afghan educated class. The modernising role was thus transferred from the state to the NGOs, which
operated in a decentralised style, maintaining contact directly with
local circumstances. A further factor was that the NGOs constituted
a template for organisational modernity and bureaucratic rationality,
so that posts within them were much sought after by the educated.[37]

---

[35] Research at a number of private schools at Mazar-i Sharif in April 2000 revealed
that between one-third and half of the boys aged 8–12 who were asked about
their future said they wished to go abroad. Though without statistical validity,
these results probably show that emigration was the predominant goal for those
seeking education.

[36] This rough estimate is based on the 2001 handbook of organisations working in
Afghanistan produced by ACBAR, which serves as a coordinating body for the
NGOs and is available at the headquarters of ACBAR in Peshawar.

[37] The evidence suggests, however, that the relations between Afghan-educated individuals and expatriates were not without complications. The growing distance
between the expatriates and the Afghan population had ramifications. Issues

Consequently, because of their ethos, they became in practice a focus
of opposition to the Taliban government. The Taliban was not unaware of the situation, and the ambiguity of its attitude revealed the
two constraints under which it operated: there was its need to col-
laborate with the NGOs, but on the other hand it wished to keep
them under control, especially over issues relating to women's right
to work or education.

In the educational sector itself the evident deficiencies of the regime led the educated class to break free from the state. Educated
Afghans attached particular importance to schools, since education
provided a field for the transmission of their values and resources. At
the same time the *ulema*, themselves taught within the *madrasas*, displayed overt mistrust of the educational system. During the war fundamentalists frequently accused schoolteachers of being leftists, and
many schools were destroyed for this reason.

The state's dereliction of this key sector resulted in a proliferation
of private classes, and those for girls were conducted in secret. Although
there seem to be no figures relating to this phenomenon, it was of
real significance and showed a failure by the state to respond to an
urgent social demand which extended far beyond the educated class
itself. However, because of the lack of financial resources the level of
teaching was low. There was one exception: five Turco-Afghan schools
of a very good standard operated in Afghanistan. Though *mullah*
Omar had issued a decree that banned foreigners from running
schools and required strict monitoring of financial donations, these
schools were nevertheless tolerated, since their personnel were Turkish, and hence Muslim, and they were ideologically close to Fethul-
lah Gülen, a disciple of the Islamist Nurcu movement in Turkey.[38]
This movement's objective was to provide a basis of training for the
entire educational system—just as the schools funded by the western
countries had done in the past—and to produce an Islamist élite
open to ideas of modernity.

The confrontation between these two social groups was not confined to Afghan territory. The *ulema* and the educated class both

included the influential role of educated Afghans as intermediaries, as well as
tensions between 'locals' and 'expatriates'.

[38] Bayram Balci, *Missionnaires de l'islam en Asie centrale*, Paris: Maisonneuve et Larose,
2003.

operated transnational strategies for the mobilisation of support. Associations run by educated Afghans, not all of whom were necessarily favourable to Masud, opted for transnational strategies based on human rights, and were thus able to link up with a vibrant international network. In particular Afghan feminist groups, whose ability to organise inside the country had always been limited, succeeded in obtaining publicity for their cause.

Women. Why has the status of women become a central issue in the west's perception of Afghanistan? This question may well appear either naïve or provocative, since self-evidently the oppression Afghan women have suffered from the Taliban is a justification for international solidarity. Without wishing to ignore these arguments, one should place in perspective a number of other issues which may lead to some modification of this point of view. First, the degradation of women's status did not originate with the Taliban, but dates back to the fall of Kabul in 1992 or even to the beginning of the civil war. Nevertheless, western public opinion—or at least the media (a valid distinction)—was hardly interested in Afghan women before 1996. There was some study of the issue before the Soviet invasion, but Afghanistan was seen primarily as a 'traditional' society, living by time-honoured principles which were not conducive to critical analysis of the position of women. Further, following the Soviet invasion arguments relating to the liberation of women were appropriated by the Kabul regime, and these lessened their legitimacy in western eyes.

In this context the fall of Kabul came as a turning-point because of the visibility of the Taliban's actions in an urban environment relatively well covered by the media. However, revulsion towards the 'monstrous Taliban' did not lead to a better understanding of local issues. The veil was probably the clearest example of the perverse nature of media coverage. Before the Taliban the wearing of the *chador* (the Iranian-style veil) was widespread in the countryside, while the *burqa* was worn both in the towns and everywhere in the south of the country. Social pressures ensured the continuation of this practice, including in Panjshir, where Masud wished to present himself as more modernised. In Herat the *mujahidin* had already threatened to attack unveiled women in the towns. The *burqa* became obligatory from 1992 onwards.

The imposition of the *burqa* by the Taliban thus mainly affected the educated class, particularly in Kabul, where it had been in disuse for a generation. Despite the relative marginality of this question in comparison with such issues as economic difficulties, violence against the person and access to education and medical care, it nevertheless became basic in international campaigns of mobilisation, which for the first time included mass-circulation women's magazines. It was symptomatic that there was little media coverage of the report of 'Physicians for Human Rights' in 2001, a considerable modification of its report of 1998 which had caused a considerable stir.[39] This may have been because, counter-intuitively, it pointed out that the veil was not a central issue for most Afghan women, emphasising instead the obstacles which limited access to health care. The fall of the Taliban has led to the virtual disappearance from the media agenda of the issue of the veil, and indeed of Afghan women in general.[40] Thus the situation of Afghan women in its diversity and its development needs to be presented in a broader historical perspective.

Masculine domination and the diversity of women's situations. A number of social norms serve to legitimise the subservient position of women in Afghan society. The dominant values are male—namely activity, strength and independence. These are set in opposition to such feminine characteristics as physical weakness; susceptibility to influence, especially from magical spirits; and impurity, connected with menstruation. The differentiation of tasks by gender is extremely marked, with a clear separation between men's and women's spheres of activity.[41] Inequality is difficult to challenge since it is seen as originating in biology or the 'natural' order, and inextricably linked to the religious principle by way of interpretations of the Quran which 'confirm' the weakness of women. Boys are celebrated from birth, while the birth of a girl is perceived as a problem. The

---

[39] Physicians for Human Rights, *The Taliban's War on Women: a health and human rights crisis in Afghanistan*, Boston, MA, 1998, p. 27.

[40] In captions to newspaper pictures the *burqa* was once more being described as a 'traditional veil'.

[41] Many points of similarity may be observed with Kabyle society; see Pierre Bourdieu, *Le sens pratique*, Paris: Editions de Minuit, 1980.

hyper-mortality of female infants is a result of the lower level of care accorded to them by their mothers. However, the marriage of boys is an expensive matter, which symmetrically entails the fact that girl children may bring substantial sums to their families. For instance, the dowry of young women of the Turkmen community, who weave carpets, may be the equivalent of several years' income.

This inferiority, which is socially constructed and interiorised by both sexes, has legal implications. In tribal custom, especially among the Pushtuns, women have no inheritance and under Islamic law their inheritance is half that of men. Marriage is arranged in almost all cases, including among the bourgeoisie, and in most cases is an expression of family strategies and economic interests. A further factor is that polygamy is a legitimate practice, although, being for the rich only, it is relatively rare, involving only some 5% of marriages. Consequently the 'couple' is not a basic element in social life, and for a woman her husband is not necessarily the most important man. Despite relatively egalitarian legislation from the 1960s, divorce is practised solely at the man's initiative, but the importance of the dowry and the risks of conflict between family groups act in general as a barrier.

Women have very restricted access to public space, since they are the repository of the honour of the group.[42] In this matter—where the dictates of honour often run counter to Islamic law—Afghanistan resembles the pattern of Mediterranean societies, as in southern Italy and Spain. Women's behaviour is monitored by the men of the household, their husbands or brothers, a social obligation which is a source of psychological tensions to individuals of both sexes. What is prohibited is not merely adultery in the strict sense—although this would in theory entail the death penalty—but any act that allows the slightest suspicion to fall upon a woman and therefore on the family honour. This is a system very different from that of the *shariat* which demands proof of individual culpability. Another issue is that the women do not necessarily perform only a passive role in the

---

[42] In the view of some authors the veil, rather than providing protection for women, safeguards men against feminine sexuality, which is unconsciously perceived as uncontrollable and anti-social. On this issue see Inger W. Boesen, 'Women, Honour and Love: some aspects of the Pushtun woman's life in eastern Afghanistan,' *Afghanistan Journal*, no. 2, 1980.

protection of the honour of the group. They also play an important role in the vendetta as bearers of the memory of the insult. A man who refuses to take vengeance runs the risk of being openly despised within his own house.

Children or older people may serve as intermediaries for women in the public sphere, in the transmission of news, making purchases and so on.[43] A woman exercises a certain degree of economic autonomy over the disposal of her own property, but employs a representative (*wakil*) to manage her affairs. In general women's freedom of movement is very restricted, except among nomadic groups where they go unveiled, a special status which they would lose if they become sedentarised. There are noticeably few women in the bazaars, and many have never been outside their villages except for brief visits to their relatives or to *ziarats*. Contact with strangers is not generally feasible, and guests do not normally meet women. Children serve at table and the guest is received in a special room which is only an ante-chamber to the truly private areas where only relatives in whose presence the women are not obliged to be veiled are permitted to enter.

Finally, there is the issue of the specific influence of Islam in the pre-war period. Rather than the 'Middle Ages' with which it is fashionable to draw comparisons when discussing Afghanistan, rural France of the nineteenth century may provide a more meaningful parallel.[44] Which religion is in play is not crucial, so that Catholicism could in reality serve as well as Islam as a justification for classifying women as inferior in terms of either biology or religion.

Other than in the these general aspects, women are not in any case a homogeneous group, and three principal dichotomies can be observed. First, they live in markedly different circumstances in the town and in the country. In the villages women make up communities which work and seek their entertainment together. When the men have left for the fields they are often alone in the village and

---

[43] Women do not pray at the mosque but, in principle at least, do so at home. A woman does not therefore have access to the basic location for village sociability. Meetings at the well or work jointly undertaken are their main opportunities for social exchange.

[44] Eugen Weber, *Peasants into Frenchmen: The modernization of rural France 1870–1914*, Stanford University Press, 1976, esp. chapter 11.

enjoy great freedom of movement.[45] In the towns women are much less free to move about; they are easily confined to the house and have no independent economic activities and hence no separate source of income. The wearing of the *burqa*—apparently introduced during the nineteenth century—is a symbol both of social superiority and of a stricter seclusion.

Secondly, age and especially maternity is one decisive factors in a woman's situation within the family. The young wife is transferred from the authority of her father to that of her mother, and falls under the domination of her mother-in law, for whom she in effect becomes an assistant or even a servant. Only if she bears male children is she gradually able to acquire some degree of authority. As she grows older she comes to occupy a position of power and influence within the household, since she often chooses wives for her sons and, although usually illiterate, she plays a decisive role in the management of goods and in financial decisions. In some cases the sons will ally themselves with her against their father, especially if he is persuaded by his children to divide up the land.[46] Finally, as an older woman she is more easily able to speak in public, sometimes with considerable authority.

Thirdly, the status of women differs from one community to another. The main distinction is that between the Pushtuns, situated mainly in the south, and the rest. Among the Pushtuns the code of manners and honour is extremely strict, and the separation between men and women is especially rigid.[47] In the Uzbek, Turkmen and Hazara communities, mostly in the north of Afghanistan, relations between men and women follow more flexible rules.[48] Among the

---

[45] See Michelle Robin, 'La société des femmes dans un village afghan', *Communautés*, no. 79, January–March 1987, pp. 95–101.

[46] On this issue see Cherry Lindholm, 'The Swat Pukhtun Family as a Political Training Group' in Charles Lindholm (ed.), *Frontier Perspectives: Essays in comparative anthropology*, Oxford University Press, 1996, pp. 17–27. The author analyses the structures of Pushtun families, bringing out in particular the often violent nature of family relationships.

[47] Jon W. Anderson, 'Social Structure and the Veil: comportment and interaction in Afghanistan', *Anthropos* 77, 1982. The author particularly stresses the point—not well grasped in the west—that the veil is 'reciprocal' and acts as an organising principle in the avoidance behaviour of both men and women outside the family circle.

[48] Among the Aymaqs of central Afghanistan relations between men and women are relatively egalitarian. See Bernard Dupaigne, 'La femme dans l'économie

Uzbeks nocturnal visits by a fiancé to his future bride are accepted. Among the Hazaras women go outside the house without difficulty and are able to speak to guests. A traveller may thus take tea with a couple, the wife participating in the conversation on an equal footing with the husband, which would be wholly unthinkable among the rural Pushtuns. Women's economic situations or, to be more precise, their occupations also vary according to the community in question. For example, Nuristani women cultivate crops, while the men devote themselves more exclusively to pasturage. In areas where weaving is a significant activity, especially in the north, it is the women who weave carpets.

Apprenticeship to modernity. The status of women is a symbolic issue which arouses political and religious passions and becomes a kind of testing-point for the authorities. Amanullah's government (1919–29) was the first to attempt to modernise or westernise it, especially through such dramatic measures as the unveiling of women at court, and the establishment in 1921 of the first school for girls. In the same year the reaffirmation of the abolition of slavery, a measure which had already been proclaimed at the beginning of the century, set free hundreds of women who had been kept as concubines in Kabul.[49]

Some decades later, between 1953 and 1963, Daud reintroduced a similar reformist project when he decreed—or, more precisely, allowed—the unveiling of women. This was pushed through in the face of protests from conservatives, who mobilised forcefully against it. His initial measures were followed by others, particularly in education. In 1960 co-education was established in higher education. Female students and scholarship-holders were still very few, with only 7% of the scholarships in higher education allocated to women in 1970, but from then onwards a trend towards modernisation was firmly established. The obligation placed on both boys and girls to wear uniform at secondary schools in effect introduced western dress.

It was a decisive factor that these decisions were taken mainly by the political authorities, with no significant support from the popu-

---

rurale' in *La femme afghane à travers l'histoire de l'Afghanistan*, Actes du colloque Unesco, Paris 11 December 1998, p. 22.

[49] Aman-i Afghan, Kabul, Dalwa 18, 1299/7 February 1921, quoted in 'Afghan Women and Women in Islam: parallels and divergences' in *La femme afghane à travers l'histoire*, Actes du colloque Unesco, Paris, 11 December 1988, p. 45.

lation, and this factor determined the direction of future developments. In the countryside women did not openly challenge the patriarchal order. Although some established values, such as arranged marriages, were challenged by the traditional Pushtun women's songs (*landais*), these also celebrated the dominant code of behaviour, particularly honour and virility. Reforms were initiated from above, and their failure to take root explains why women remained largely excluded from the public sphere, even in bourgeois circles. There were no women's associations—leaving out of account for the moment the feminist movement—which could have lobbied effectively for legislation, and few women were members of political movements. Only the Maoist groups and the communists, with certain exceptions, took notice of issues relating to women.[50] Even in the towns the presence of women in public was frowned on. As late as the 1970s a women's demonstration was attacked by men who threw acid over the demonstrators.

In contrast to the communist regimes in China and the Soviet Union, which at certain points envisaged the abolition of the conventional family, the communist regime in Afghanistan showed no wish, or was not able, to intrude into private life. It adopted progressive policies concerning women, but also took traditional values into account, recognising in particular the role of the *shariat* as complementary to state law. The continuity between the communist regime in Kabul and previous projects of modernisation was marked. The regime maintained the proportion of women members of the party at around 15% although many of these were the wives or daughters of militants since many marriages took place within the party. In addition, there were women members of the party militias, especially in Kabul and in some of the northern towns. The most marked changes were in public education, especially at the middle and lower levels. In Kabul half of the holders of public teaching posts were women, as were the majority of the staff of the Ministries of Education and Health. Similarly, 55% of the students were girls.[51]

---

[50] In Herat in the spring of 1989 an informant recalled the agitation of the Maoist groups in favour of women, and the unenthusiastic response to these efforts from the highly conservative local population.

[51] See Micheline Centlivres-Demont, 'Les femmes afghanes aujourd'hui', *Afghanistan Info*, Neuchâtel, no. 23, November 1998, pp. 17–18.

Finally, especially in Kabul where the regime was relatively well established and able to guarantee a degree of security, the wives of the middle class carried on the modernising tendencies of previous regimes. For instance, dress codes showed the beginnings of a break with traditional practices, although these innovations were mostly restricted to the modern areas of the capital and to a lesser extent of Jalalabad and Mazar-i Sharif. This process of modernisation contrasted with the situation in the countryside, where the *mujahidin* imposed an order of a kind that was much more conservative or even fundamentalist.

The confrontation with fundamentalism. The *mujahidin's* prohibition of women's participation in public activities became stricter. The resistance parties had generally not called on women to mobilise, although there were some women's groups, particularly within Harakat-i Islami and Hezb-i Islami. The collapse of the structures of the state brought education more or less to a halt, while opposition from fundamentalists, including those among the population at large, considerably restricted the educational opportunities for girls. In some areas the commanders who controlled the countryside continued to permit education for girls, for example in Herat and in a large part of the north, but this happened less in the Pushtun regions.

Women were a majority among the refugees (28% of women against 25% of men were refugees).[52] The seclusion to which refugee women were subject was even stricter than that prevailing in the villages, because of their exile in an unknown situation, where they were under the sway of the rigid conceptions of honour of the tribal Pushtuns among whom they found themselves. Because of overcrowding, it was difficult in the camps to protect private space. On the other hand, the health conditions were an improvement, so that infant mortality fell substantially to a level even lower than that among the rural Pakistani population. The Islamist parties attempted to improve the education of girls in the refugee camps, although they were separated from the boys, while at the same time the fundamentalist movements continued to discourage the education of girls. Women's lack of political influence, without recognised representation, obstructed

[52] Micheline Centlivres-Demont, *op. cit.*, p. 18.

them from struggling for recognition of their rights when the Kabul regime fell and movements of the most fundamentalist type gradually took hold of the reins of power.

The arrival of the *mujahidin* in 1992 inaugurated a range of restrictions, from the wearing of the veil to the ban on women appearing on television. In August 1995 Afghan women were refused authorisation by Rabbani's government to go to the fourth World Women's Conference in Beijing, which was viewed as un-Islamic. The representation of women in those areas of the administration still functioning fell markedly. The practices of different political groups varied, but the fundamentalist influence was universally felt. Some commanders had a more open attitude regarding women's education and kept the secondary schools open, for example in Herat and in the north. The former communist militias in the north, which remained in power till 1998, altered few features of the day-to-day operation of the administration. Other commanders ordered the girls' schools to be definitively shut and insisted on the strict application of the *shariat*. Finally, in some regions insecurity and fighting reached such a pitch that the schools were shut anyway, while widespread violence had particular consequences for women: for example, at the time of the capture of Jalalabad in 1992, the nomadic tribes carried women off and enacted 'marriages' which were no more than enforced prostitution. In Kabul all the armed groups, especially Dostum's militias, were guilty of rapes and kidnapping, leading sometimes to the suicide of young girls who had been dishonoured. The very few women who dared to dress in the western style in the modern part of Kabul were harassed by the *mujahidin*. All this was a new departure, and a contrast, since Afghan women had seldom before been threatened with deliberate acts of violence, and certainly not with rape.

In this respect the Taliban's victory represented the triumph of the most fundamentalist tendency. The status it imposed on women was above all a rejection of urban and bourgeois culture, which stood opposed to the idea of women held by the rural and fundamentalist Pushtuns. Its earliest victims were educated women, who were mainly in Kabul and numbered around 165,000.[53] Aggression against women

[53] See Carol Leduc, 'The Impact of Conflict on Women's Lives post-1992' in *La*

was one of the major factors which led to the reluctance of the urban bourgeoisie to cooperate with the regime and their flight into exile. The situation was different in the towns, in which the religious police were especially strict, from the countryside where daily life was little changed. Outside the towns women continued to wear the *chador*—a veil over the head—rather than the *burqa*. For country women, who for practical or other reasons did not have access to schools or paid work, the principal effect of the arrival of the Taliban was an end to insecurity.

Taliban legislation installed the *shariat* as the basis of both civil and criminal law, and the status of women declined, especially in the towns. However, in some cases the measures put in place by the Taliban were more benign than the tribal customs normally enforced among the Pushtuns. For instance, a decree issued by *mullah* Omar[54] forbade the frequent tribal practice of obliging a widow to marry a brother of her deceased husband, as well as outlawing the 'gift' of a woman as a compensation for a killing.[55] These measures marked an advance over Pushtun tribal law, but a step backwards compared to the positive legal situation before the war.

The separation of the sexes, which was already the rule in many situations, was carried to the extreme. Women were obliged to sit at the back in buses, where they were henceforth separated from the men by a screen, while the fare collector had to be under ten years old.[56] The Taliban also required the inhabitants of Kabul to paint over windows to a height of 1.80 metres and forbade women to wash clothes at the riverside. Women were also obliged to wear the *burqa*, while white socks and noisy heels were banned. They were officially allowed out only in the company of a *mahram*, a male member of their family who acted as their representative and protector—although groups of unaccompanied women were in fact to be seen in

---

femme afghane à travers l'histoire de l'Afghanistan, Actes du colloque Unesco, Paris, 11 December 1998, p. 63.

[54] Decree no. 103, 10 September 1999 (1419/5/18).

[55] See especially Pierre Centlivres, who sets out in detail the contradictions between Taliban law and tribal custom regarding the rights of women. Pierre Centlivres, 'Le mouvement Taliban et la condition féminine', *Afghanistan Info*, March 1999, pp. 11–14.

[56] See Choong-Uyun Paik, *Final Report on the Situation of Human Rights in Afghanistan*, United Nations, 1997 (www.reliefweb.int).

the bazaar in Kabul during the Taliban regime. The Taliban also banned women from working outside the home, particularly in international organisations, a measure which had been in place in Jalalabad since 1994, though an exception was made for hospitals. The major defeat for women was their dismissal from all state administrative posts and their exclusion from the universities, where they had achieved virtually equal status during the war.

The issue of education and access to health care reveals the inability of the Taliban to include women in the educational and health services. The Taliban was not formally opposed in principle to the education of women, but wanted to set up an 'Islamic' system whose details were never clarified, although it was to be based on the separation of men and women. While there had sometimes been provision on a local basis, women had no access to education after the age of ten or twelve. Their use of hospital services was not forbidden in principle, contrary to what has sometimes been alleged, but was strictly supervised. In principle, women were to be examined only by women. In this area the crucial obstacles were economic, and were also related to the attitudes of male family members. There were significant differences between regions in the way these measures were applied.

The radicalisation of the Taliban

The installation of the Taliban government should have effectively removed the barriers to its international recognition, thus depriving the opposition of the last element of leverage it might have had.[57] The Taliban earnestly desired such a development, which would have entrenched its regime. The United States was initially in favour. The capture of Kabul in 1996 was described as a 'positive step' by the State Department, which however gradually shifted its position after the appointment of Madeleine Albright as Secretary of State, and as a result of the influence of campaigns for women's rights. Oil companies, especially UNOCAL, also attempted to engage positively with the Taliban up to 1998–9 in the hope of exploiting Afghanistan as a channel for the export of Turkmenistan's energy resources. Initially

[57] Only Saudi Arabia, Pakistan and the United Arab Emirates recognised the Taliban regime.

Zalmay Khalilzad, who was close to Paul Wolfowitz and a consul-
tant to UNOCAL, gave his blessing to a dialogue with the Taliban,
but he later fell in with the majority view and declared himself in
favour of their destabilisation.[58] Finally, the split with the United
States was precipitated more by the presence of radical groups on
Afghan soil rather than human rights violations or drugs.

The Taliban had inherited the networks and training camps
which had been established in the 1980s, when collaboration between Islamic movements and the Afghan parties had been actively
encouraged by the United States.[59] The majority of the Afghan factions, including those which belonged to the Northern Alliance, were
at that time in contact with groups based in Peshawar which provided financial assistance and a flow of volunteers for the Afghan *jihad*.
For thousands of militants, who afterwards returned to their own
countries, their stay in Afghanistan was a significant or even decisive
experience. The militants were progressively radicalised, and dozens
of the splinter groups based in Peshawar took up increasingly anti-
western positions towards the end of the 1980s. In due course the
Gulf War offered the pretext for an open break with the United
States, especially over the presence of its troops in Saudi Arabia.

The fall of Kabul in 1992 deprived the commitment of foreign
militants of much of its point, but also opened the door to various
organisations to install themselves on Afghan territory, particularly
in the east, thus enabling them to escape the influence of Pakistan. In
particular, some Pakistanis set up camps in Afghanistan to train their
mujahidin for service in Kashmir.[60] This applied particularly to Hezb
ul-Mujahidin, the military wing of Jamaat-i Islami, and to Harakat
ul-Ansar, which was still known by this name after it officially re-
entitled itself Harakat ul-Mujahidin. The Harakat ul-Ansar militants,
led by *mawlawi* Jabbar in Afghanistan and Qari Fazlur Rahman
Khalil in Pakistan, came mainly from the Punjab and underwent a
six-month military course, usually at Darwanta near Jalalabad, in a
camp initially set up by Hekmatyar for the Arabs, and then closed by
the Taliban after the capture of Khost in September 1996.[61] Camps

---

[58] See, in particular, *Washington Quarterly*, winter 2000.
[59] On this issue, see John Cooley, *Unholy Wars*, London: Pluto Press, 2002.
[60] Since these training camps were therefore outside Pakistan's territory, this in theory at least, exempted them from India's strictures.
[61] *The News International*, 23 August, 1988.

were also maintained at Muzafarabad and near Khost by two splinter groups of Harakat ul-Ansar, namely Jamiyat ul-Mujahidin, led by Mufti Bashir, and Harakat Jihad Islami, led by Qari Saif ul-Islam Akhtar. However, the origins of the Pakistani fundamentalists and their evolution had little to do with the Afghan crisis, and Afghanistan's role must be seen in perspective, although Zia ul-Haq's policy of establishing *madrasas* was an indirect consequence of the Soviet invasion. In particular, sectarian violence between Shi'ites and Sunnis was neither a result of war in Afghanistan nor a by-product of the success of the Taliban.

The Pakistani *madrasas* were directly linked to the Afghan conflict through the participation of their *taliban* in the *jihad*, which was the natural extension of their teaching. While the volunteers were mainly Afghans, there were also Pakistanis: the majority of these were Pushtuns from the NWFP and Baluchistan, but there were also Sindhis and Muhajirs. In September 1994 when Kandahar was captured, the first *taliban* were the product of *madrasas* throughout NWFP and Baluchistan.[62] According to the Deputy Chief of the Citizens' Police Liaison Committee of Karachi, between 600 and 700 *taliban* were sent to Afghanistan in May 1997.[63] By the end, during the offensive of August 1999, Pakistani and Afghan *taliban* came in their thousands—perhaps as many as 5,000—to reinforce *mullah* Omar's troops.

The presence of these militants in Afghanistan gave rise to problems both with their countries of origins and with the United States. During a journey to Egypt in November 1993, for example, it was significant that Rabbani signed an extradition agreement with the Egyptian government, committing himself to the expulsion of extremist groups. The perpetrators of various anti-American incidents had been trained in the Afghan camps, including Ramzi Yusuf, one of those who carried out the 1993 attack on the World Trade Centre, and Mir Aimal Kainsi, a Pakistani national who was accused of machine-gunning offices belonging to the CIA in January 1994.[64]

---

[62] The *madrasas* included, among others, Maulana Nur Muhammad Saqib, at Katcha Garhi Camp, Zia ul-Madaris at Peshawar, Hashmia Madrasa at Bara, and Dar ul-Ulum Haqqaniya at Akora. See *The News International*, 11 December 1994.

[63] Owais Tohid, *The Herald*, December 1997.

[64] He was later arrested in Pakistan, in June 1997, and was extradited to the United States.

In response to such criticisms Pakistan decided at this point to deport *jihadi* fighters from Pakistan to Afghanistan, a move whose principal long-term effect was to displace the problem and to place these groups still further beyond control. Pakistan was able to escape inclusion in the State Department's 1994 list of countries supporting terrorism, which would have led to the cutting off of international financial aid essential for Pakistan's economic survival.

After the fall of Kabul to the Taliban, various foreign but non-Pakistani radical groups, whose numbers had dropped after the fall of Kabul in 1992, returned to Afghanistan. These included in particular the militants of the Uzbek Islamic Movement, numbering 2,000, and around 3,000 Arabs of various origins who set up bases with the Taliban's consent.[65] The foreign fighters were organised by Osama Bin Laden, who had come to wage the *jihad* in Afghanistan at the beginning of the 1980s, and had been Abdullah Azzam's deputy when the latter had been the head of the Maktab-i Khidamat-i Mujahidin (Mujahidin Services Office). In contrast to Abdullah Azzam, Bin Laden expressed a desire immediately to expand his field of action to include the United States, perhaps under the influence of the Egyptian radical Ayman al-Zawahiri. In 1987 he declared himself independent of Abdullah Azzam's group, and established Al-Qa'ida (The Base). Azzam was assassinated in 1989.[66]

Bin Laden, the heir to a large family fortune, employed both his organising ability and his money to develop his group, and above all to seek a safe haven from which he could launch his global *jihad*. In order to carry on his struggle, he had set up a network which was basically Arab but was also genuinely transnational—a rare event—and had for some years been looking for a base. After a failed attempt to establish himself in Sudan in 1989, he returned there in 1992 and developing a civil engineering business in parallel to his clandestine activity. In spite of his good relations with Hasan Turabi, he was expelled from Sudan in 1996 in response to pressure from the United

---

[65] Anthony Davies, 'Foreign fighters step up activity in Afghan civil war', *Jane's Intelligence Review*, vol. 13, no. 8, August 1, 2001.

[66] Rohan Gunaratna in *Inside Al-Qaida*, London: Hurst, 2002, p. 25, pursues the theory that Azzam was assassinated on Bin Laden's instructions, but the weakness of this theory is that it is founded on the evidence of renegades. For a more reliable account of the relations between Bin Laden and Azzam see Stephen Engelberg, 'Holy Warriors', *New York Times*, 14 January 2001.

States, and subsequently based himself once more in Afghanistan, where he took advantage of the absence of an organised state and of the Taliban's blunt political style. The process of convergence between two movements which were very different in their origins and their membership was never easy. Personal relationships later came into existence between Bin Laden and *mullah* Omar:[67] Bin Laden's marriage to *mullah* Omar's daughter cemented the ties between the two movements.

The *"fatwa"* of 23 February 1998, signed by various Al-Qa'ida officials including Bin Laden himself, conveys an idea of his view of the world and of his objectives. His grievances were precise and political; namely the presence of American forces in Saudi Arabia, the destruction of Iraq by the sanctions, and the occupation of Palestine. There followed an appeal to launch indiscriminate attacks against the Americans, in the name of *jihad*.[68] In most respects, Bin Laden's claims do not differ greatly from those of the Arab nationalists.

More broadly, Bin Laden's religious rhetoric is a response to American financial, military and cultural domination that has been perceived by Muslim populations, and particularly by the Arabs, as a threat to their identity, opening the way to the adoption of a religious vocabulary by opposition movements[69]. The Middle East, by reason of its proximity to Europe and its richness in crucial commodities, falls within what might be called the exploitable hinterland of the Western powers. In the event, after the fall of the Soviet Union, the United States and its allies, especially Turkey and Israel, enjoyed unchallenged hegemony. However, the United States has been incapable of fulfilling the role of an arbiter in the Middle East,

[67] It is unlikely that financial considerations came much into play. Actually Bin Laden's financial resources were certainly less than the profits from smuggling across the Pakistani frontier, especially opium.

[68] For a translation and a commentary on the text, see Magnus Ranstorp, "Interpreting the Broader Context and Meaning of Bin-Laden's *Fatwa*," *"Studies in Conflict and Terrorism,"* 21, 1998, pp. 321–330.

[69] François Burgat rightly lays stress on the affirmation of identity by contemporary Islamic movements, which have often taken up the programmes of nationalist and Marxist movements. See François Burgat, *L'islamisme au Maghreb*, Paris, Karthala, 1988; and, in relation to Turkey, Günter Seufert, *Politischer Islam in der Türkei: Islamismus als symbolische Repräsentation einer sich modernisierenden Muslimischen Gesellschaft*, Istanbul, Franz Steiner Verlag, 1997.

especially in the Israeli–Palestinian conflict. In addition, the US has supported authoritarian regimes, often unpopular, such as those in Egypt and Saudi Arabia. The Gulf War of 1991 resulted in the emasculation of the only Arab country which had the ability to formulate an independent policy, while ending the alliance between the United States and the fundamentalist movements, which had come into being in Afghanistan during the 1980s.[70] Following the Gulf War, and in breach of the initial agreements, the United States kept its forces in Saudi Arabia, which provided a *casus belli* for the Islamic movements, and foremost among them that of Bin Laden. The chronology testifies to the expansion of anti-American actions after the Gulf War. The first attack on the World Trade centre took place in 1993.[71]

Bin Laden's originality is to plan and act at a global level. This was a striking departure from the practices of other radical groups, for example the Egyptians, whose membership and objectives were local. Bin Laden's strategic innovation, which seems unlikely now to cease with his death or even with the destruction of Al-Qa'ida, was to strike directly at the United States, and at its embassies and warships, even before 11 September 2001. In an interview in 1998, Bin Laden developed these arguments and elaborated on his opinion of his adversary.[72] A crucial issue, which offers a partial explanation of his strategic decisions, was his perception of the United States as a morally weak power, which was unable to accept military losses in a conflict. This view was based directly on events in Somalia, where Al-Qa'ida appears to have played a part in the attacks on the Americans, which led to the withdrawal of American forces after the humiliating incident on 3 October 1993 when 18 American soldiers were killed. It is likely that the plan to target the World Trade Centre was already in gestation by this time. However it was in Africa that Bin Laden would strike his first truly spectacular blow against the Americans.

---

[70] John K. Cooley, *Unholy Wars: Afghanistan, American and International Terrorism*, London, Pluto Press, 2002 (1999).

[71] The reader should not leap to the conclusion that anti-American operations multiplied in this period. In fact, in the 1990s, the number of attacks registered as 'terrorist' by the State Department fell by 29 per cent in relation to the 1980s. During the Clinton presidency, in spite of alarmist language, the number of dead averaged 14 per year. Andrew J. Bacevich, *American Empire*, Harvard University Press, 2002, p. 118.

[72] The interview was conducted with an ABC reporter. See www.pbs.org/wgbh/pages/frontline/.

On 7 August 1998, eight years after the entry of US troops into Saudi Arabia, the US embassies in Nairobi and Dar es-Salaam came under simultaneous attack, resulting in the deaths of 247 people, including twelve Americans. On 20 August US missiles struck a number of camps in Afghanistan as well as a pharmaceutical factory in Sudan. The military value of this response was doubtful: twenty people died in Afghanistan, but none of them was from the Al-Qa'ida leadership, and the attack in Sudan, based on faulty intelligence, destroyed only a genuine pharmaceutical plant.

US strategy, as it was deployed up till 2001, was not aimed at the overthrow of the Taliban but at the maintenance of sufficient pressure on them to bring about the expulsion of Bin Laden. However, the 1998 missile attacks had a political result which was actually the reverse of the US objective, namely that Bin Laden became a popular figure in Pakistan and the Gulf, in the eyes of Afghan and Pakistani fundamentalists, and more generally to anyone with anti-American views. Posters of Bin Laden went on sale in shops in Peshawar, where they were openly displayed, while the given name Osama became unprecedentedly popular in the frontier provinces. However, as has been seen, it was on the Pakistani fundamentalist movements that the Taliban relied, especially for the organisation of large-scale offensives. This, no doubt, is why Prince Turki, then the head of the Saudi secret services, who had a relatively encouraging reception when he visited Kandahar in June 1998 to ask for Bin Laden's expulsion, saw his initiative turned down at the end of the summer.

The United States had two viable strategic options after the attacks in Africa. The first was to combat the Taliban by supporting Masud while putting pressure on Pakistan. However, its relations with Masud had never been good, and it did not want to confront Pakistan. The second option was to recognise the Taliban and speed up the reconstruction of the Afghan state, which would have strengthened the hand of those who opposed the presence of radical factions within the Taliban. However, this was a strategy which required time, and was not politically acceptable at home given the growing wave of anti-Taliban opinion in the US media. In fact the United States chose a third option, namely to put increasing pressure on the Taliban. In the event this strategy failed, since diplomatic isolation only increased its radicalisation while at the same time, thanks to assistance from Pakistan, its ability to act on the ground was undiminished. The 'rational' approach of the Americans failed probably because of their misunderstanding of the ideological constraints under which the Taliban operated, as well as the virulent mistrust inspired in general by US policies. In addition, the Taliban believed at this point that it was invulnerable, both because a US intervention was very unlikely and because it was convinced that it could withstand an American invasion, just as it had fought off the Soviets.

With no convincing military option, the United States then took the decision to place its faith once more in the sanctions embodied the UN Security Council's resolution 1267, unanimously adopted by the Council on 15 October 1999, which had been reinforced by resolution 1333 on 19 December 2000. Specifically, these sanctions provided for an embargo on the importation of weapons into Afghanistan, the reduction of the size of foreign diplomatic missions in Kabul, and the closure of Taliban offices abroad. Another measure froze Taliban financial resources abroad, while the airline Ariana was no longer permitted to fly outside Afghanistan's frontiers. These sanctions achieved only a marginal economic effect, without the depth of those which had inflicted grave damage on Iraq in the 1990s. In fact Afghanistan's infrastructure had already been largely destroyed, while for political reasons it was difficult to halt the work of NGOs in a country on the verge of famine because of a drought of historic proportions. 'Smart' sanctions were particularly difficult to apply because of the scale of illicit cross-border trafficking. Nevertheless, the report issued by the UN on the effects of the sanctions demonstrates that the population believed they were more comprehensive than they were in reality.[73]

On the Taliban side the attitude of the west was not seen as a preliminary to negotiation, as the US government would have wished it to be, but rather as an existential threat. After the closure in January 2001 of its office in New York, the Taliban was no longer even recognised as an interlocutor, which in practice brought to a halt the peace talks set up by F. Vendrell within the framework of the UN's mediating role. Contacts with US representatives in Pakistan continued to the end, but remained unofficial.

---

[73] United Nations, *Vulnerability and Humanitarian Impact of UN Security Council Sanctions in Afghanistan*, prepared by the Office of the humanitarian coordinator for Afghanistan, Islamabad, Pakistan, 16 September, 2000.

The position of the Taliban concerning Bin Laden's extradition remained virtually unchanged, and was also supported by the government of Pakistan before 11 September 2001.[74] The Taliban put forward compromise proposals, having ruled out both the option of bringing Bin Laden to justice in Afghanistan, and that of his direct extradition to the United States. One suggestion was that after an initial hearing by *ulema* from Afghanistan, Saudi Arabia and a third country, Bin Laden could be deported to a Muslim country. The Minister of Foreign Affairs, *mullah* Abdul Muttawakil, made a further suggestion, proposing a mechanism whereby he would be placed under surveillance by the Organisation of the Islamic Conference. It appears that the foreign Minister had additionally proposed that recognition might be extended to the Taliban government in exchange for Bin Laden's expulsion. Whether because *mullah* Omar did not back this suggestion, or because the United States rejected it, this proposal came to nothing. The impasse reflected Bin Laden's growing influence over the regime, the nationalist response to the US attacks of 1998, and the importance to the Taliban of transnational solidarities, at a time when the war was not yet over.

In addition to its support for fundamentalist movements, there was a further issue which caused problems for the Taliban. This was that Afghanistan had become the world's leading producer of opium, overtaking Burma. According to the UN Drug Control Programme, half the world's heroin was produced in Afghanistan, while 80% of the heroin consumed in Europe was of Afghan origin.[75] In its approach to this issue the Taliban displayed unaccustomed efficiency, dramatically cutting down opium production. This was a demonstration of the degree of control it exercised in the countryside, but worsened the situation of the rural population who were already affected by the drought. However, these measures brought the Taliban no benefit in terms of diplomacy, since the United States was interested only in Bin Laden.

By 2001, following the renewal of the sanctions in December 2000, the radicalisation of the regime was undeniable. In this context the destruction of the Buddhas of Bamyan was symbolic of a defini-

[74] See in particular the interview with President Musharraf in the *Washington Times*, 21 March 2001.
[75] *The Economist Intelligence Unit*, 1999, p. 34.

tive break with the international community. The act was evidently
political, since previous decrees of *mullah* Omar, issued in July 1999,
had offered protection to works of art in general and specifically to
the Buddhas. Following the decree of 26 February 2001 ordering
their destruction, they were finally dynamited in March after repeated attempts to dissuade the Taliban from the destruction of a
unique monument.[76]

Relations with the NGOs also worsened in 2001 as a result of the
overall deterioration of the situation. The policy of religious conversion implemented by some organisations such as 'Shelter Now' was
the cause of a further crisis. The practice of carrying out conversions
under the cover of humanitarian action was condemned by the
majority of the NGOs because of its intrinsic dishonesty and its
exploitation of the inferior economic status of the population. The
increasing presence of Protestant Christian preachers in a Muslim
country represented a return to a nineteenth-century practice, leading
probably to similar results.[77] In the case of Afghanistan the security
of the great majority of NGOs whose operations were above-board
was put at risk by these organisations. As another consequence the
Islamic NGOs came to play an increasing role, whether they were of
fundamentalist inclination such as the Rasheed Trust, or non-funda-
mentalist such as Fetullahci and the Canadian Relief Foundation.

After the UN vote to re-impose sanctions Pakistan was the last
ally left to the Taliban, and its support largely accounts for the continued offensive capacity of the regime up to the summer of 2001.
However, questions began to be asked about the rationale for Pakistani assistance. The installation of a Taliban government in Kabul
had been intended to open up Central Asia to Pakistan's economic
and political influence, but in practice the outcome had been the reverse, with the result that Pakistan found itself faced by hostility from
the Central Asian countries, except for Turkmenistan. The undisguised presence of Taliban *mujahidin* in Tajikistan fighting alongside
the Islamist opposition, and the links between the Uzbek Islamic
Movement and the Taliban, were seen as part of a deliberate bid to
destabilise Central Asia.[78] After the capture of Kabul in September

---

[76] See Pierre Centlivres, *Les Bouddhas d'Afghanistan*, Paris: Favre, 2001.

[77] This presence was reinforced after 11 September 2001; see *Time*, 4 August 2003.

[78] The Taliban commander in Uzbekistan, Namangani, was put in charge of military
operations in the north of the country during the war against the United States.

1996 Russia and the countries of Central Asia immediately organised a summit meeting on security issues, whose tone was clearly hostile to Pakistan. During a further summit in 1997 accusations were made against Pakistan over its Afghan policy, in spite of the mollifying remarks of Nawaz Sharif. Finally, the offensives of 1999 and 2000 aroused protests from the regional powers and the UN against both Pakistan and the Taliban.

In reaction to Pakistani policies some states developed a strategy of containment of both Afghanistan and Pakistan. Iran represented no political threat due to its broadly conservative position, but took the decision to make economic overtures to Central Asia. The construction of a railway from Sarakhs in Turkmenistan to the Iranian port of Bandar Abbas, together with the development of the port, offered Turkmenistan an alternative outlet to that offered by Afghanistan. Turkmenistan and Iran also established a free trade zone at Sarakhs, and in 1999 India signed an agreement with Iran to permit the transit of goods from central Asia.

Finally, Pakistan lacked the resources to provide sufficient aid for Afghanistan, particularly for the infrastructural repairs required for the transport of goods to Central Asia. Even the section of road from Kandahar to the Pakistani frontier was in bad repair, and was thus a considerable obstacle to trade with Quetta. The National Highway Authority, charged with the rebuilding of the road to Turkmenistan, failed to produce any practical results, despite negotiations begun in December 1996; while the so-called 'Afghan Trade Cell', established in July 1997,[79] was never allowed a budget sufficient to make any real impact on cross-border trade.

[79] This was the successor to the 'Afghan Trade Development Cell' set up within the Ministry of the Interior by Nasrullah Babar.

Part V. THE AMERICAN INVASION AND THE RETURN TO FRAGMENTATION

Perhaps as a result of the absence of TV stations—banned by the Taliban—the attacks of 11 September 2001 were not immediately seen in Afghanistan as a major event, and the displays of emotion seen elsewhere did not occur. The population, especially in the countryside, were preoccupied with another and more immediate problem—the drought. Much of the country was free of conflict, with fighting localised in a few provinces. Although the Taliban was internationally ostracised after its destruction of the Buddhas of Bamyan, it was nevertheless in control of most of Afghanistan, with the result that journeys between the large towns could be undertaken without hindrance. Certainly the regime had become more radicalised, but Bin Laden's role in domestic Afghan politics was minimal. Real ideological differences separated him from the Taliban, and he was regarded with distrust and hostility by some members of *mullah* Omar's circle who suspected, not without justification, that he would not hesitate to sacrifice them in the interests of his wider strategy.[1] In spite of potentially grave consequences, *mullah* Omar refused to yield to American pressure to expel Bin Laden. For Afghanistan the '9/11' phenomenon really began with the American bombing and the rapid sequence of events which led to the Taliban's downfall.

During the American intervention and throughout the following months the debate hinged on two questions. Would an anti-American guerrilla movement emerge after the military defeat of the Taliban? And would a return to political fragmentation be a more probable outcome than the re-establishment of a state? According to the most widely-held theory, stabilisation would rapidly ensue. For example, Olivier Roy argued, 'It is unlikely that a Taliban resistance will come

---

[1] Hence the intelligence passed on a little before 11 September 2001 by the Taliban Minister for Foreign Affairs, Mottawakil, concerning a planned attack in the United States.

into being', and that the Taliban's defeat would 'signal the probable disappearance of the radical Islamists in Afghanistan'.[2] The opposition represented a viable alternative which would preclude a return to civil war, and the end of the war was at hand: 'There is no longer an Afghan issue, except on the symbolic level.'[3] According to other interpretations, which took a different line, a 'strong fundamentalist tendency' would continue,[4] while it was presumed that 'the American intervention would result in a return to the political fragmentation of the 1990s, with a possible return to civil war'.[5] These two analyses also led to contradictory positions over the success of Bin Laden's strategy. In the first case he was viewed as having lost the battle: 'The military campaign of October and November 2001 has considerably weakened the transnational Islamic networks.'[6] But in the second case, 'because of the triangular nature of the conflict, the defeat of the Taliban will not in itself guarantee the victory of the United States.'[7]

Developments on the ground have disproved the first of these hypotheses. The collapse of the Taliban regime in the event gave rise to a resurgence of locally-based power centres, independent in practice of the Kabul government, although lip-service might be paid to it. International aid and the presence of foreign troops have not so far led to reconstruction of the state. The government, subject to strong internal divisions, exercises no authority outside the capital and is unable to control recurrent clashes between warlords. The policy of liberal modernisation supported by the UN faces strong resistance, even inside the new regime, and the continued existence of a strong fundamentalist tendency is manifest. Able to fall back on sanctuary within Pakistan, the neo-Taliban continue to control the Pushtun territories, while at the same time US troops carry out military operations against an openly antagonistic Pushtun population, inflicting

---

[2] Mariam Abou Zahab and Olivier Roy, *Réseaux islamiques*, Paris: Autrement, 2002, p. 70 and p. 68 (published in 2004 as *Islamic Networks: the Afghan and Pakistani Connection*, London: Hurst).

[3] Olivier Roy, *Les illusions du 11 septembre*, Paris: Seuil, p. 32.

[4] Interview with Pierre Centlivres, *Le Monde*, September 2001.

[5] Gilles Dorronsoro, 'Après les Taliban. Fragmentation politique, hiérarchie communautaire et classes sociales en Afghanistan', *Cultures et Conflits*, January 2002.

[6] Mariam Abou Zahab and Olivier Roy, *op. cit.*, p. 71.

[7] Gilles Dorronsoro, *op. cit.*, p. 1.

a concomitant burden of 'collateral damage'. An American with-drawal would unleash chaos, and probably lead to the recapture of Kandahar by *mullah* Omar. Finally, Al-Qa'ida has discovered a real social base as well as sanctuary on the Afghanistan–Pakistan frontier, where Bin Laden's popularity remains undiminished, confirming the largely illusory character of the US victory in the autumn of 2001.

10. 'A Splendid Little War'?*

Bin Laden's strategy, which was both audacious and logical, has so far been successful. The evidence militates against any account based on 'religious fanaticism'. Other massacres in recent history, whether comparable or even larger in scale, have not led to the presumption of irrationality in those responsible. Leaving aside moral considerations, the attacks of 11 September 2001 were a strategic operation, executed with great economy of means; and it is historically rare for a small group to achieve such a massive impact on the international situation. The attacks employed few men and little money but struck a devastating political and economic blow. They left 3,000 dead, resulted in direct and indirect costs of several hundred billion dollars, and last but not least brought about a significant and probably lasting restriction of personal liberty in the United States. One of the most unsettling effects of this strategy has been its 'ratchet effect', where the perception of threat rules out a return to the pre-11 September situation.

The objective of Al-Qa'ida was radically to change popular perceptions, in order to make the distinction between Muslims and non-Muslims a central element in political mobilisation, leading in turn to a diminution of western influence in the Islamic world. This was a strategic tactic similar to that of some anti-colonial struggles, where radicalisation was achieved through the politicisation of religious and communal identities. Seen from this standpoint, it was necessary that the attack should be spectacular and cruel in order to inflame anti-Muslim sentiments in western opinion. The growing gap between western and Muslim views suggests this aspect of the strategy has been effective. The wild statements persistently uttered by those American personalities who present the conflict as a confrontation between

* A phrase used in a letter from John Milton Hay to President Theodore Roosevelt of the Spanish-American war of 1898.

Islam and the Judaeo-Christian camp tend to reinforce the accepted perception of a clash between adversaries. The situation of Muslims in the United States has been undermined by programmes of surveillance, which are resented as harassment. Another factor is that visits by Muslims to the United States have become more problematic.[8]

Furthermore, the attacks guaranteed Bin Laden a global audience as well as access to media which have permitted him to exploit symbols relating to Islamic legitimacy, such as his cave and his Quranic quotations. This scenario ensured that a myth would spring up, and that there would be regular 'reappearances'. Bin Laden's death, whenever it takes place, might never be proved for certain. In any case he did not address himself to the western public but exclusively to Muslims, who were unaware of the American message. Clumsy attempts to censor Al-Jazeera during the US military operations, as well as the mobilisation of the media industry and of communication consultants, changed nothing. The reality of American domination led to resistance. The refusal to subscribe to any form of negotiation reinforces the integrity of Bin Laden's message, which served as a symbolic rejection of the present balance of power between the West and the Islamic world.

In consequence Muslim views took a different slant on the events of 11 September, in which Bin Laden was seldom seen as responsible for the attacks, while paradoxically he was admired at the same time for his boldness in opposing the United States. An opinion poll conducted in Pakistan showed that half of those questioned believed Mossad was responsible for the attacks.[9] Further, widespread credence has been given in the Middle East, even among educated and westernised sections of society, to rumours—which it is scarcely necessary to say are false—that Jews in New York did not go to work on the day of the attacks.[10] Bin Laden's popularity is startling, even in

---

[8] The number of Arab students in the United States went down by a third between 1999 and 2002 (Report on human development in the Arab world, October 2003, cited in *Le Monde*, 23 October 2003).

[9] Of the persons asked 12% said Bin Laden was responsible for the attacks; 24% saw them as an action which was part of the *jihad*; 48 % thought that Mossad was responsible; and only 6% of the population thought that Bin Laden was a 'terrorist'. Gallup International, quoted by www.tns-sofres.com, 17 October 2001.

[10] The phenomenal success in Europe of a book denying that a plane crashed on the Pentagon shows that this kind of fantasy is not exclusively Middle Eastern.

the light of the diplomatic and psychological errors made by the United States. In a survey carried out in Indonesia, Morocco and Pakistan and among the Palestinians, Bin Laden was nominated as one of three personalities who would be trusted to 'do the right thing'.[11]

In addition to such political and symbolic issues, Bin Laden's aim was to lead the United States into a prolonged deployment of its military force in various parts of the Middle East, and thus to transform a cultural and economic hegemony into direct military domination, which would be both more costly and more liable to provoke resistance. Bin Laden, convinced that the United States was politically fragile, hoped for an American invasion of Afghanistan which would draw it into a trap. Faced with this challenge, what was the American response?

The strategy of the United States

Far from opening a debate in the United States on the country's hegemony and the resistance to which it gave rise, 11 September was the signal for a firmer commitment to imperialist policy.[12] From this moment the goal of the United States was global military hegemony, arrogating to itself a unique position in international relations based on what it saw as its exceptional status.[13] America's political and military doctrine thus represented an open break with international law. A central provision of the UN Charter, the restriction of the use of force to self-defence, was in effect flouted by the adoption of a doc-

---

Similarly, a majority of Americans, no doubt influenced by the ambiguous language adopted by their government, believe that Iraq was implicated in the attacks of 11 September.

[11] Pew Global Attitudes Project, consultable at www.people-press.org, quoted in *International Herald Tribune*, 4 June 2003.

[12] See in particular the analyses by Andrew J. Bacevich, *American Empire*, Harvard University Press, 2002. It could also be asked whether the increasing militarisation of American politics is not primarily a reflection of the relative decline of the United States in the international scene. On this issue see Charles Kupchan, *The End of the American Era: US Foreign Policy and the Geopolitics of the Twenty-First Century*, New York: Random House, 2002.

[13] *The National Security Strategy of the United States of America*, Washington, DC: the White House, September 2002. The central concept was to deter any possible future challenge.

trine of preventive action. This development had in fact already begun to take shape under President Clinton, but had not hitherto been proclaimed in so clear and coherent a fashion. In practice the American doctrine implied that states on the perimeter of the West would enjoy only limited sovereignty.[14] For instance, on 6 November 2002 a missile fired by a CIA plane hit a vehicle in Yemen, killing six persons suspected of participation in the attacks on the USS *Cole* in 2000.

Although this hegemonic project attracted a wide consensus among American élites, the specific policies of the Bush administration attracted opposition. In the event, the United States distanced itself from its traditional allies, especially its NATO partners, since it came to view them as militarily insignificant and politically untrustworthy. Alliances were perceived as constraints and, especially under the influence of the Defense Secretary Donald Rumsfeld, military doctrine prioritised the mobility of forces and relatively light operations. This unilateralist posture was widely rejected abroad, so that the United States found itself diplomatically isolated, as was to be seen some months later in the Iraq crisis.[15]

The result of the attacks of 11 September had been to impose a new international agenda, where the issue of 'terrorism' took a central position. Semantically, the expression 'the war against terror' was in itself odd, since terrorism is not an adversary as such but a method of action. However, the slogan has many advantages. In fact, the linkage between a doctrine of preventive action and a fluid definition of the enemy permitted the legitimation as defensive of all kinds of steps, even those—such as the measures taken against Iraq—which were most overtly hegemonic. In the name of these new priorities the United States continues to extend its military involvement throughout the world—in Central Asia, in the Caucasus and in the Middle East.

Although the license to characterise movements as 'terrorist' has its advantages, the drawing up of lists of countries and organisations

---

[14] Which did not deter the United States from acting to reinforce their internal strength, especially for the repression of dissident movements.

[15] A major problem for the United States was precisely the increasing impossibility of reconciling its image with that of the 'benevolent empire', to quote Robert Kagan's expression, and with the overt antagonism of which it was the object around the world.

may rebound dangerously through the creation of common interests between previously disparate groups.[16] In fact Al-Qa'ida is the antithesis of regionally based movements such as Hezbollah and Hamas, whose objectives are limited and negotiable. While these groups strongly denounce Bin Laden, as for example in the declarations of Shaikh Fadlallah, the construction of lists of terrorist organisations creates in practice a degree of solidarity between such organisations. Instead of playing on the essentially contradictory interests of such movements in order to target those which directly threaten the western countries, the strategy of the 'war against terror', by promoting a degree of cooperation between networks, actually increases the risks of bringing into being an anti-American front.

Even before the redefinition of American strategy in the months that followed the attacks of 11 September, the first priority was the elimination of Bin Laden, who was soon seen as the instigator of the attacks. To deal with the Afghan aspect of the problem, the United States was able to call upon a range of capabilities and alliances. However NATO, in spite of a historic declaration of solidarity based on Article 5 of its founding treaty, was completely ignored by the United States, a move which upset various sensibilities. Britain and certain other countries offered some marginal assistance, but the war remained in essence an American affair.

In the weeks following 11 September, the United States moved with great efficiency to put in place the necessary diplomatic and military preparations. Afghanistan is a landlocked country, and there were political difficulties in basing a significant number of troops in Pakistan, or even in Central Asia. In any case, the United States was quick to rule out a land operation of any significant size. In fact the Kosovo conflict was adopted as the strategic model, with the corresponding strategy of air strikes combined with the mobilisation of local allies. The vast air power of the United States and the employment of Special Forces to coordinate operations on the ground were therefore much in evidence. The number of troops committed never exceeded 50,000, and losses were limited to a handful, often the victims of 'friendly fire'.

At first the United States brought its logistical capability into play to set up bases in Afghanistan's immediate neighbourhood. On 5 Octo-

---

[16] In December 2001, the State Department published a list of thirty-nine organisations viewed as terrorist.

ber a first contingent of 1,000 men arrived at Khanabad in Uzbekistan. At the same time, although the US presence at the Jacobabad
base remained separate and limited, Pakistan's military cooperation
was confirmed, and its army attempted to close the frontier to prevent the flight of Al-Qa'ida militants. A further factor was that Iran,
which had been on the point of recognising the Taliban regime,
hastily entered an agreement on the possible recovery of US pilots.
Aircraft-carriers were deployed in the Indian Ocean and extra resources were given to the CIA.[17] In particular, the Egyptian, Jordanian and Algerian intelligence services received subventions from
the United States, and the task of interrogating suspects was delegated to them, often with the use of torture.

On the diplomatic level the international isolation of the Taliban
was completed within a few weeks. At the end of September Saudi
Arabia broke off relations with Kabul, shortly after the United Arab
Emirates had taken the same step. Pakistan offered a channel for negotiations up till the outbreak of war, when the Afghan ambassador
in Islamabad was arrested and handed over to the United States.
Within a few weeks the United States was militarily ready to attack
the Afghan regime. However, the complexity of the situation dictated that its strategy was developed with caution.

The initial strategic issue was relatively easy to formulate, but its
resolution was highly complex. The war in Afghanistan, the first
conflict of its kind, was exceptional because of the confrontation of
three protagonists of different kinds. These were a state (the United
States), a quasi-state unrecognised internationally (the Taliban), and a
transnational movement (Al-Qa'ida). In addition, the Bin Laden
networks were active in the south and east of the country, where the
Taliban had a real power-base, while the opposition, which was militarily weak, was based in the north. Theoretically, the only effective
stratagem for the elimination of the radical networks would be to
make an alliance with the Taliban, which was in undisputed control
of the terrain, as its eradication of opium production in eastern and
southern Afghanistan had demonstrated. However, the Taliban was
difficult to talk to, and time was short. A variation on this approach
would be to destabilise the Taliban from within and retrieve the
so-called 'moderate' elements, in other words those who would
agree to an alliance with the United States.

[17] Robert Woodward, *Bush at War*, New York: Simon and Schuster, 2002, p. 77.

The second possibility was to use the Northern Alliance to overcome the regime by military means, but it was politically divided and militarily weak and could provide no access to the south, since Masud's troops would never fight in Kandahar, and therefore was not a means of overcoming Al-Qa'ida. In addition a northern victory would involve the rejection of the Pushtuns. According to Charles Tenet, head of the CIA, there would be opposition from the Pushtuns if the Northern Alliance took power.[18]

American strategy was largely improvised and led to clashes between the State Department and the Pentagon. The first option was preferred by the State Department, which wanted to make use of Pakistan's assistance; while the second was the choice of the Pentagon, which wanted more rapid results. The first strategy, which would have had the advantage of avoiding the fragmentation of the country, did not pay off quickly enough, and the second, though militarily viable in the short run, opened the way to fragmentation.

Up to the end of September the United States, in parallel with the expansion of its military capacity, opted to negotiate through Pakistan in the hope of persuading Bin Laden to give himself up to the United States. To this end a delegation of Pakistani religious figures together with Mahmood Ahmed, the director of the ISI, paid a fruitless visit to Kandahar on 17 September. A second visit on 28 September was equally unproductive, as were numerous subsequent contacts. The situation nevertheless remained fluid since on 20 September the Afghan *ulema*, after a meeting in Kabul, declared that Bin Laden should leave of his own accord. Pakistan's President Musharraf afterwards asked for Mahmood Ahmed's resignation, replacing him with Lieutenant-General Ehsanul Haq, whose brief was to counter pro-Taliban elements within the ISI. Two elements played their part in this failure. One of these was the ambiguous part played by the Pakistani *ulema*, who rather tended to support the position of *mullah* Omar.[19] The other factor was the political situation within the United States, which was such that the American government preferred to give the Taliban an ultimatum rather than negotiate, hence the refusal to provide any kind of proof of Bin Laden's implication.

---

[18] Woodward, *op. cit.*, p. 123.
[19] *The Nation*, 1 October 2001.

In the last week of September there was a significant shift in the position of the United States, which abandoned the search for a diplomatic solution and by the same token changed its objectives. On 20 September the Secretary of State Colin Powell again said that he did not exclude a dialogue with the Taliban if it dismantled the radical camps and networks within Afghanistan,[20] and added that the aim of the US administration was to put pressure on the Taliban rather than eliminate it entirely.[21] Some days later Condoleezza Rice, the National Security Advisor, issued a contradictory declaration: from now on the goal was to be to overturn the Afghan regime.[22]

On 7 October the initial bombing raids took place and 'Operation Enduring Freedom' was under way. During the first weeks of the war, however, the United States continued to look for a 'Pakistani' solution to the conflict, that is to say the replacement of the Afghan regime by allies of Pakistan.

The failure of the Pakistani solution

The initial American plan, proposed by the State Department, was to take place in two stages: first the overthrow of the Taliban by subversive measures and the liquidation of the radical networks by commando operations; then the installation of a pro-Pakistan regime in Kabul. Under this plan the Northern Alliance was to be largely ignored in order not to upset Pakistan. This was the reason for the relatively superficial nature of the initial bombing, which irritated the Northern Alliance. To the great displeasure of India in particular the United States largely relied on Pakistan, while its strategy was predicated on the idea that only Pakistan could destabilise the Taliban, to whose rise to power it had so greatly contributed. The military side of the operation consisted of putting troops in position around Afghanistan to facilitate in-depth raids, while relatively light bombing was used to destroy certain symbolic targets in the aim of sowing panic among the Taliban. According to this proposal, the United States would not clash with the Afghans but would operate directly against the Al-Qa'ida network.

---

[20] *The Statesman*, 21 September, 2001.
[21] Woodward, *op. cit.*, p. 124.
[22] *The Times*, 24 September, 2001.

In an attempt to sow division among the Taliban, the United States and Pakistan on a number of occasions proposed the inclusion of 'moderate' Taliban in the future government. This was explicitly mooted during a joint press conference conducted by President Musharraf and Colin Powell at the end of September. In early October Powell once more took up the same idea, and expressed his opposition to the proposal that the Northern Alliance should take Kabul in order to avoid a setback for the Pakistanis.[23] Western diplomats were thus working towards the establishment of a coalition government, in spite of the complete opposition of the Northern Alliance to Taliban participation. An initial attempt was organised by Gaylani, with Pakistani support, but it did not succeed in attracting any of the acknowledged leaders or apparently even any significant tribal chieftains. At the end of September Karzai held a meeting with tribal leaders at Quetta and suggested setting up a *loya jirga* with the participation of a section of the Taliban.[24] Finally, on 1 October negotiations between the royalists and the Northern Alliance produced a compromise, but excluded the Taliban. With the capture some weeks later of Kabul by the Northern Alliance, this compromise solution became irrelevant.

While diplomatic exchanges gathered pace, Pakistan made a bid to destabilise the Taliban. The CIA distributed $70 million in the south to bring over the tribes, while infiltration of Taliban-held territory intensified.[25] However, this strategy soon failed. Attempts to destabilise the eastern region of Afghanistan were inconclusive. The Taliban appointed as commander-in-chief Jalaluddin Haqqani, who had substantial influence in the eastern provinces. In October a short-lived revolt in Khost was rapidly crushed. The tribal chiefs and commanders sent to persuade the Pushtun tribes to change sides had no success. Abdul Haq was arrested and executed by the Taliban. Hamid Karzai, the future President of the provisional government, was rescued from a perilous situation after a clandestine excursion to the Kandahar region.

The reality was that the American operations on Afghan soil had revealed an unsophisticated but courageous adversary, who did not

---

[23] Woodward, *op. cit.*, p. 192.
[24] *The News*, 29 September, 2001.
[25] Woodward, *op. cit.*, p. 317.

give ground and whose morale at that point was excellent. An attack on 29 October against the buildings used before 11 September by *mullah* Omar collapsed, and the US troops found themselves in a trap: US spokesmen conceded that some thirty had been wounded. The mystique attached by the western media to Special Forces operations should not obscure the fact that they require a different environment from that of southern Afghanistan, where there were few military targets and western intelligence was exiguous.

The issue is: could the American approach have been effective? The US–Pakistani strategy was based on the conviction that the Taliban was a transitory phenomenon, with neither a local basis nor an ideology. Viewed in this way, the *ulema* were taken to be a marginal force, who could be dislodged with the help of the *khans*. This was particularly unrealistic, since it presumed rapid and efficient cooperation between the tribal chiefs, virtually a contradiction in terms. In addition the strategy had been impeded by the US bombing, which came too soon; this was the view taken by Abdul Haq in the last interview he gave before his death, when he denounced the bombing for having hampered his approaches to tribal leaders, who were obliged to support the *jihad*. Eye-witnesses report there were large-scale mobilisations by the *mullahs* in the mosques, which considerably reduced the scope for the activities of non-religious élites.[26] Before the tribal leaders could change sides it would be necessary at the very least to wait for the fall of the Taliban.[27]

All that this crisis achieved was to illustrate the rapid changes in the Taliban movement over the space of a few years, something that it had hitherto found difficulty in seeing. The politicisation of the movement, which was already apparent, had gathered pace. The professionalisation of its leadership was partly due to the involvement of foreigners, but was also related to an intake of relatively well-educated younger men. Outdoing even Bin Laden's still at communication, the Taliban's representatives played the media game well, although media coverage was highly unfavourable towards it—a measure of the success of American efforts to prevent its message from getting out. In contrast to the practice of Saddam Hussein in 1991, the Taliban showed its civilian casualties and exploited them.

[26] Various personal reports communicated in Peshawar in November 2001.
[27] Gilles Dorronsoro, 'Après les Taliban. Fragmentation politique, hiérarchies communautaires et classes sociales en Afghanistan', *Cultures et Conflits*, January 2002.

The fall of the Taliban

By early November 2001, almost a month after the start of the bombing, there was no observable result on the ground. To get results before the beginning of Ramadan, and avoid the impression of dragging its feet, the United States adjusted its strategy towards giving greater support to the Northern Alliance.[28] There were few practical obstacles to this option, and the United States faced no particular difficulty in establishing a home territory for the opposition in northern Afghanistan, although the Taliban put up an honourable fight at Mazar and in Kunduz.

Special forces were already on the ground with the Northern Alliance, but the essential change in early November was the use of air power. Extraordinary firepower was deployed by the B-51 bombers, which operated in conjunction with Stealth B-1s flying from Diego Garcia and from the United States itself. In addition four 15,000-pound (7,000 kilo) 'Daisy Cutter' bombs were dropped. Fragmentation bombs were also dropped, which continue to cause frequent casualties. By the end of December 12,000 bombs had been dropped on Afghanistan, of which 6,700 were so-called precision weapons.

On 9 November forces led by Dostum, Muhammad Atta and Ustad Mohaqqeq took Mazar-i Sharif. The entire northeast collapsed rapidly, with the fall of Maimana on 11 November and Herat the following day. On the same day the Shura-yi Nazar attacked Kabul, taking the city in spite of warnings from Pakistan. Jalalabad fell the day after Kabul. On 22 November Pakistan closed its Kabul embassy. In the north the resistance was especially strong in Kunduz because of the presence of foreign fighters, especially Arabs and Pakistanis, who had no avenue of retreat. Some of these were evacuated to Pakistan by air, with US approval, in a nocturnal operation lasting two weeks. On 9 December Kandahar fell after one last apocalyptic speech from *mullah* Omar.

In the shorter term this remarkable series of successes was not fully carried through to victory. Due to its unwillingness to commit

[28] At a meeting in Uzbekistan on 30 October 2001, General Tommy Franks, the commander-in-chief of CENTCOM, is reported to have promised that US air power would henceforth be placed at the service of the Northern Alliance. See Michael Kranish, 'Turning the Tide', *Boston Globe*, 31 December, 2001.

ground forces, the United States was unable to capitalise on its successes and decapitate Al-Qa'ida and the Taliban movement. In late November US ground troops first arrived in Afghanistan in significant numbers, but were put to guard prisoners. When Kandahar fell, *mullah* Omar was able to flee to Uruzgan after negotiations between Afghan *ulema* and pro-US commanders. Undoubtedly it was the militias who let him go, and American inaction at this juncture was later seen to have been a grave error. Another factor was that even after the campaign to capture Bin Laden had been launched, the Americans were unable to mount a decisive attack on the Tora Bora caves to which his retinue had retreated. The Special Forces failed to seal off the mountain complex, leaving operations on the ground to Afghan commanders who were at odds with each other. The US officer in charge is reported to have refused offers of surrender from Al-Qa'ida militants,[29] while the final assault was not a success since most of the Taliban fighters had bribed the Afghan commanders to allow them to escape to Pakistan. The Pakistan government closed the frontier, with the deployment of 40,000 men, but although several hundred fighters were captured as they crossed over, no senior Taliban official was detained. Nevertheless Bin Laden, who had been wounded, is reported still to have been in this region around 16 December, after which he went to the frontier.

No account was kept of civilian casualties, which the US army refuses in principle to estimate, but they were probably amounted to several thousand. Enemy military losses also went unrecorded.[30] However, a number of war crimes were committed by allies of the United States. For example, on 25 November hundreds of Taliban prisoners were killed in the prison at Mazar-i Sharif, after a revolt in which a CIA agent who had been interrogating prisoners was killed. Apparently many prisoners were summarily executed once they had been recaptured. The most serious incident concerned the deaths of Taliban and foreign prisoners who were suffocated inside containers. According to a meticulous inquiry,[31] around 3,000 Taliban prisoners

---

[29] Renaud Girard, *Le Figaro*, 19 June 2002.

[30] By comparison the Iraq conflict of 2003 caused between 5,000 and 10,000 civilian deaths and 30,000 wounded, in a campaign also described as 'surgical'.

[31] See the account given by Jamie Doran in his filmed documentary, *Massacre at Mazar*, with witness statements concerning the participation of American

were massacred by Northern Alliance forces, an atrocity which by some accounts was perpetrated in the presence of American soldiers. Despite the gravity of these reports and the known locations of communal graves, the UN declined to carry out an inquiry in order not to embarrass the Afghan and US governments.

The campaign lasted nine weeks. The loss of the north, which had always been likely and had probably been foreseen by the Taliban, deteriorated into a rout, with each defeat contributing to the panic. The Taliban's error was to have chosen to wage a conventional war rather than making preparations for the inevitable transition to guerrilla warfare, a course of action it took anyway some months later.

Although the Taliban was never solely the instrument of Pakistan's ISI (Inter Service Intelligence) it was in fact highly dependent upon them for its military strategy. The Taliban's principal vulnerability was military, resulting from the command of its troops by a coalition of commanders, a situation that reflected historic realities and sprang indirectly from the controlling influence of the Pakistanis. As a result of the ferocity of the US bombing the Taliban's military structure collapsed. Such disintegrations were not peculiar to the Taliban but had been a recurrent factor in Afghan movements in defeat. For example, Dostum's troops had scattered in 1997 and 1998, as had those of Ismail Khan in 1995. Masud alone had been able to retreat in good order after the loss of Kabul in 1996, thanks to the favourable terrain and his resolute professionalism. Another issue was that the foreign fighters, who numbered several thousand and were better organised, had never succeeded in organising the Afghans, whose relations with the 'Arabs' had always been difficult. It was the collapse of the military apparatus which brought about the collapse of the Taliban regime in the Pushtun region rather than any political or social challenge, which was made impossible by the relative breakdown of society.

The defeat of the Taliban was not therefore the result of a suicidal strategy, founded on the idea of sacrifice but, as in the case of Iraq in

---

soldiers in the torture and execution of the prisoners, and also Jamie Doran, 'Afghanistan's secret graves. A drive to death in the desert', *Le Monde Diplomatique*, September 2002. See also the report of Physicians for Human Rights, *www.phrusa.org/research/afghanistan/report_graves.html*. The United Nations halted the inquiry even though Dostum had killed or imprisoned a number of witnesses.

1991, stemmed from an insufficient understanding of the balance of power. The Taliban was probably also hampered by its high level of political centralisation,[32] while *mullah* Omar overestimated the level of his popular support, and the degree of resistance his men would show to the bombing.

---

[32] In particular, there was no split between the 'hardliners' and the 'moderates', which demonstrated the cohesion of the networks of *ulema* which provided the structure of the movement.

11. The Return to Political Fragmentation

The accords of 5 December 2001, signed at Schloss Petersberg in the German city of Bonn, paved the way for the establishment of the Afghanistan Interim Authority. The composition of this body was a triumph for the Northern Alliance leadership, Shura-yi Nazar, which obtained three key ministries—Defence, the Interior and Foreign Affairs—as well as control of the secret services. Meanwhile the presidency went to Hamid Karzai, a Pushtun, whose appointment was intended by the negotiators to endow the Interim Authority with legitimacy in Pushtun eyes. However, the remainder of the groups making up the Northern Alliance, other than Shura-yi Nazar itself, were united in condemning what they saw as the Interim Authority's unbalanced membership. In particular *haji* Abdul Qadir walked out of the conference in protest at the inadequate representation accorded to the Pushtuns. A further issue was that Dostum, Ismail Khan and Sayyaf roundly condemned the monopoly over power enjoyed by the Panjshiri membership of Shura-yi Nazar.

The issue of an international buffer force was bitterly contested. Shura-yi Nazar initially opposed the presence of any foreign force in Kabul, and objected *a fortiori* to the demilitarisation of the city. A compromise was reached in due course providing for an international force of limited size, and Shura-yi Nazar retained its troops in the capital. The negotiators accepted this formula because of Shura-yi Nazar's entrenchment within the city and because of the potential threat it represented to the future government. For these reasons an agreement seemed preferable to the risk of immediate destabilisation.

From the institutional standpoint the Bonn accords provided for the convening of a *Loya Jirga* within six months of the Interim Authority being established on 22 December. In the first stage of this process some 400 district assemblies selected representatives, and in the second stage the chosen representatives gathered in provincial centres, under the scrutiny of foreign observers, for a secret ballot to elect the actual delegates to the *loya jirga*. To the 1,501 delegates elected by this process 450 more were added to represent women, nomads, refugees and 'civil society', a term that included the religious and intellectual establishment. Some observers criticised the method by which the delegates were appointed, which was open to undue influence from the commanders.[1]

The role of the *loya jirga*, inaugurated by the former king Zahir Shah on 11 June 2002, was the transfer of the interim administration's authority to the Afghanistan Transitional Authority. There was inevitably some confusion, but the positions of the various delegates gravitated towards the exclusion of former 'commanders' and to support for Zahir Shah. However, the crucial decisions, and in particular the choice of Hamid Karzai, had already been taken by the Americans, at whose behest Zahir Shah was obliged to step aside. Actually, a majority of the delegates appeared to be prepared to cast their votes for Zahir Shah, a development which would have blocked the election of the Americans' candidate. For his part the king let it be known that he was ready to assume any responsibility which the Loya Jirga might wish to confer upon him, but in spite of this, shortly after the Loya Jirga opened, the US envoy Zalmay Khalilzad publicly denied that Zahir Shah intended to put himself forward, and confirmed that he would give his support to Hamid Karzai. Some hours later Zahir Shah fell into line with the US position at a press conference, where the only diplomatic observers present were Americans, and irrevocably renounced anything other than a ceremonial role.

In the two years which followed the formation of the Transitional Authority a new constitution was meant to be adopted, a national assembly elected, and a government appointed. However, it would be possible to hold elections only if peace was restored to the coun-

---

[1] 'Despite the best efforts of the Special Independent Commission for the Convening of the Emergency Loya Jirga (Special Commission) and the United Nations, warlords have infiltrated and manipulated the process for selecting the meeting's delegates, and will attend the meeting in large numbers or act through proxies.' Human Rights Watch Briefing Paper, *Afghanistan: Return of the Warlords*, June 2002, p. 2. During the deliberations the secret services attempted to influence some of the delegates.

try, and if the state institutions were rebuilt—goals which are still far from being achieved.

The reconstruction of the state

On the face of things, the US intervention had the effect of restoring the political situation of the later 1990s in the sense that the Taliban became once more the dominant political element in the Pushtun regions. The Kabul government has no power outside the capital, and little effective progress is being made towards the construction of a central state. However, the presence of the western forces has made a major difference. Control of the capital is no longer the objective of armed groups, while the survival of the government is guaranteed by the foreign support it receives. The current situation is marked by two opposing tendencies: on the one hand the impetus towards the reconstruction of the state, together with attempts to bring the regional forces under control, and on the other the resurgence of a Taliban guerrilla force, now well entrenched in the Pushtun areas.

The distribution of political power in the provinces. The immediate result of the US invasion was the demolition of the still tenuous political base established by the Taliban. In the south and east the results of US action have tended towards fragmentation. As events have unfolded, the United States has not been willing to commit a significant number of troops and as a substitute has opted to finance local militias, a policy inimical to any move towards centralisation. Mounting insecurity and the re-emergence of opium production have been the two immediate consequences of the erosion of central authority. Unofficial 'checkpoints' have re-appeared on some roads. The level of insecurity remains high even in Kabul, where the international forces are stationed.

At the time of writing no open challenge is mounted against the Kabul government other than by the Taliban (an issue still to be considered), and there are no armed clashes in the capital itself. However, the regional authorities are able to protect their autonomy against encroachments, whether by the central authority or by rivals. One of the first announcements by the *shura* of Jalalabad was its rejection of any Northern Alliance presence within the city; similarly, at the moment when the Taliban fell, the Pushtun tribes in Kandahar rejected external interference, which heralded a brief outbreak of conflict against Ismail Khan in the Farah province. There are today five significant regional authorities, together with dozens of smaller groups.

In the north the fall of the Taliban opened the way for the Northern Alliance parties to reoccupy the positions they held in the 1990s. The regional authorities are based in the principal towns. Thus Jombesh is based in Shibergan; Jamiat-i Islami, locally led by Muhammad Atta, is established in Mazar-i Sharif; Ismail Khan holds Herat; and Kabul serves as the base of Shura-yi Nazar. Finally Hezb-i Wahdat, lacking control over a town, has established itself in the village of Bamyan, although it also maintains some armed forces inside Mazar-i Sharif. The degree of regional coherence in the north should not be exaggerated: the seizure of Mazar-i Sharif by a number of parties— Jombesh, Jamiat, and Hezb-i Wahdat—provides a clue to the instability of the region, in which fighting is endemic. In Hazarajat tension runs high between different tendencies within Hezb-i Wahdat. The Panjshir valley itself is divided between various rival commanders, as humanitarian aid workers based there are aware.

In the east and south the political balance is more complex. The towns are politically less homogeneous and do not exercise control over the countryside. In practice the balance of power often depends on relationships between tribes. For example, three factions vie for control of Kandahar. Gul Agha Shirzai,[2] has recovered his position as governor but is challenged both by *mullah* Naqibullah, a former Jamiat-i Islami commander who has some support from Shura-yi Nazar, and by Ahmad Wali Karzai, the President's brother. These factional struggles are reinforced by the tribal oppositions between the Barakzai (the tribe of Gul Agha Shirzai), the Alikozai (that of *mullah* Naqibullah), and the Popolzai (that of Hamid Karzai). In the east the degree of fragmentation is still greater. For example, the *shura* of Jalalabad is divided into a number of factions and exercises no authority further than a few kilometres from the town.

A divided government. The fragmentation of political factions might almost have been of benefit to a central government seeking to extend

---

[2] Gul Agha Shirzai was formerly governor of Kandahar, while his father *haji* Abdul Latif was a powerful commander.

its influence, but for the fact that the government was itself split between the presidency and Shura-yi Nazar. The government,[3] whose membership was announced on 24 June 2002, was dominated by Shura-yi Nazar, which retained the portfolios of Defence and Foreign Affairs and the headship of the secret police. Muhammad Qasim Fahim, who had been both vice-president and Minister of Defence in the Interim Administration, retained those portfolios. After long negotiations one of Karzai's associates, Taj Muhammad, took the post of Minister of the Interior after his predecessor Yunus Qanuni had reluctantly agreed to accept the education portfolio combined with a position as special adviser on national security. The Ministry of Finance, headed by Ashraf Ghani, was the other significant ministry which eluded Shura-yi Nazar.

Political conflict within the government broke out during 2002 as various attempts were made to subvert it. It was not always clear who was responsible for them, but they served to underline the absence of trust and collaboration between the presidency and Shura-yi Nazar. In February 2002 the assassination of the Minister for Civil Aviation, Abdul Rahman,[4] was the first event to spark off a crisis.

---

[3] President, Hamid Karzai; vice-presidents, Muhammad Fahim, Karim Khalili, Abdul Qadir; Minister of Education and special adviser for security, Yunus Qanuni; Minister of Defence, Muhammad Fahim; Minister for Foreign Affairs, Abdullah Abdullah; Minister of Finance, Ashraf Ghani; Minister of the Interior, Taj Muhammad Wardak; Minister for Planning, Muhammad Mohaqiq; Minister of Communications, Masum Stanakzai; Minister for Frontiers, Arif Nurzai; Minister for Refugees, Inayatullah Nazeri; Minister of Mines, Juma M. Muhammadi; Minister for Light Industry, Muhammad Alem Razm; Minister of Public Health, Dr Sohaila Siddiqi; Minister of Commerce, Sayyed Mustafa Kasemi; Minister of Agriculture, Sayyed Hussain Anwari; Minister of Justice, Abbas Karimi; Minister for Information and Culture, Saïd Makhdum Rahim; Minister for Reconstruction, Muhammad Fahim Farhang; Minister of Mosques and the Hajj, Muhammad Amin Naziryar; Minister for Urban Affairs, Yusuf Pashtun; Minister for Public Works, Abdul Qadir; Minister for Social Affairs, Nour Muhammad Karkin; Minister for Water and Electricity, Ahmad Shakar Karkar; Minister for Irrigation and the Environment, Ahmad Yusuf Nuristani; Minister for Martyrs and the Handicapped, Abdullah Wardak; Minister for Higher Education, Sharif Faez; Minister for Civil Aviation and Tourism, Mirwais Saddiq; Minister of Transport, Sayyed Muhammad Ali Jawad; Minister for Rural Development, Hanif Asmar; president of the Supreme Court, *shaikh haji* Shinwari.

[4] Abdul Rahman was from Nuristan and had occupied the same positions under the presidency of Rabbani (1992–6), but then left Shura-yi Nazar in order to support Karzai.

Abdul Rahman lost his life in an incident at Kabul airport, possibly at the hands of pilgrims enraged by having to wait to set off on the *hajj*. Hamid Karzai accused Shura-yi Nazar directly of responsibility for the killing. A number of officials were arrested, but later released. Tensions within the government were also revealed by a further incident. In August 2002 Shura-yi Nazar supporters demonstrated against the removal of a Shura-yi Nazar member, Abdul Hafiz Mansur, as head of the state radio and television organisation, to be replaced by Makhdum, a long-time exile in the United States and an associate of Karzai. Mansur had banned television broadcasts of singing or dancing by women, and his replacement was an indication of Karzai's determination to appoint ministers who were ideologically more liberal and closer to him politically. Finally the assassination in Kabul on 6 July 2002 of *haji* Abdul Qadir, Vice-President and Minister for Public Works, has never been satisfactorily explained.

The centralisation process and peripheral autonomy. The history of Afghanistan in the twentieth century has demonstrated that it is possible for some part of the resources necessary for the formation of a state to be derived from external aid. In 2002 the situation was such that it was once more in the interest of external powers to establish a central authority in Afghanistan. In January 2002, as UN sanctions were about to be lifted, an international aid conference was held in Tokyo where $4.4 billion in donations and $1.4 billion in loans were promised; however, these figures were not high *per capita* compared to other conflicts, such as that in Bosnia.[5] A further issue was that only a modest proportion of these funds (16%) was given directly to the Afghan government, with a priority set on emergency aid, which left only 29% to be used for reconstruction. Finally, international aid was subject to the vagaries of global politics, and as the Iraqi situation evolved, US priorities increasingly lay elsewhere. The US budget for 2004 provided only a minimal appropriation for Afghanistan by comparison with that for Iraq. For the year 2004 Congress was asked to approve $1.2 billion of civilian aid, of which

---

[5] The sum envisaged for Afghanistan was $42 per annum per inhabitant for the period 2002–6 as against $326 for Bosnia in the period 1996–9. See *Analysis of Aid Flow to Afghanistan*, www.af.

$400 million were funds remaining from the 2003 appropriation. By comparison $11 billion were earmarked for military operations in Afghanistan.

The part played by international aid was all the more significant because of the Kabul government's inability to mobilise resources of its own. The economic state of the country scarcely permitted taxes to be levied on agriculture, while the most profitable sectors were already either taxed by local authorities or, as in the case of opium and smuggling, illegal. Customs duties were a major source of revenue for powerful regional organisations such as those of Dostum and Ismail Khan—this issue had been a cause of contention between the commanders and Kabul since 1992. Arguing that customs duties had in the past been made over by Kabul to the frontier provinces, the governors refused to pass them to the treasury, although the surpluses were large, at least in the case of Herat, because of the redirection of the transit routes to Iran. In the north customs duties were simply shared out among the leading commanders, Muhammad Atta and Dostum, together with Muhaqqiq, who represented Hezb-i Wahdat. Lastly Afghanistan had once more become the world's leading opium producer, a development from which some groups, including in particular the *shura* of Jalalabad, Jombesh and the commanders of the north-east, were able to derive profit. In some areas opium again became the principal crop, especially in Badakhshan, where some peasants seem to have abandoned their traditional cultivation of wheat.

External funding of development is a phenomenon reminiscent of the 1960s and 1970s, although the political context has become more problematic. The international organisations and the NGOs continue to play important roles in public administration, with all the negative results for the government that such a situation may involve. The impact of humanitarian aid on the process of strengthening the central government is also mixed because of the tendency of the NGOs to replicate the functions of the state, sometimes with the effect of undermining them, especially when they by-pass the government to conclude agreements directly with local authorities. A further issue is that the NGOs attract the best-educated staff away from the government because of the higher salaries they are able to offer. Finally, the high level of corruption in the government remains such that it discourages investment by Afghans abroad and militates against the logical use of resources.

Despite such obstacles, the reconstruction of the state apparatus has hitherto made some headway through the incorporation of local power-brokers who emerged when the Taliban collapsed. These recognised the Kabul government which was in turn obliged to do business with them. Karzai gave official positions to most of the major commanders, thus effectively legalising their power. In some instances such commanders, or their proxies, were given ministerial posts, *haji* Qadir became Vice-President and Minister for Public Works, while Karim Khalili, the leader of Hezb-i Wahdat, was also made Vice-President. Mirwais Siddiq, one of Ismail Khan's sons, was appointed Minister of Civil Aviation, and Ahmad Shaker Kargar, an associate of Dostum, was made Minister for Social Affairs.

In further instances of the same phenomenon, Ismail Khan was appointed governor of Herat, Gul Agha governor of Kandahar and Din Muhammad governor of Jalalabad. Centralisation of administrative and military authority had the effect of enabling commanders to extend their control over regions comprising several provinces, as was shown by Dostum's appointment of governors in Jozjan and Faryab after the fall of the Taliban. Similarly, the province of Ghor was in practice run from Herat. In general, governors appointed heads of districts (*uluswal*) without reference to Kabul. However, armed groups were brought nominally under the authority of the Ministry of Defence. Amalgamation of units mirrored the pattern of distribution of the militias. For example, the 7th and 8th corps in Mazar-i Sharif and Shiberghan could not be merged, as had previously been customary, because of the rivalry between Rashid Dostum and Muhammad Atta, each of whom was appointed a general.

In 2003, in reaction to the increasing strength of the regional power brokers in 2002, the government strove in various ways to assert its authority. In February 2003 Ali Ahmad Jalali, the new Minister of the Interior, moved to appoint two new governors in Jozjan and Faryab as soon as he had taken office, but the resulting outbreak of violence revealed the fragility of the local political equilibrium. Events in Khost also underlined the complexity of local factors and illustrated the difficulties facing the central authority as it attempted to identify locally acceptable candidates for office. At the time of the

Bonn conference Padshah Khan, a leader of the Jadran tribe who had supported Karzai, had been appointed governor of Paktia, at Gardez. His brother Amanullah Khan was given the Ministry for Frontiers, while his other brother Kamal was appointed governor of the province of Khost. However, in spite of attempting to impose himself by force in the spring of 2002, Padshah Khan was unable to make good his position as governor of Gardez because of opposition from a local rival, and at the same time his own relations with government deteriorated. In June 2002, during the *Loya Jirga*, Padshah Khan actually supported the king, thus opposing Karzai and Shura-yi Nazar.[6] In the end an alternative governor was appointed.

The outward symbol of the reconstruction of the state was the rebuilding of national armed forces. However, fusion of the regional militias was difficult to achieve, owing to the absence of any mechanism which would guarantee the neutrality of a future army. The Ministry of Defence was viewed as the fief of the Panjshiris, who almost entirely made up the garrison in Kabul and for that reason were not able to present themselves as the credible nucleus of a national army. The appointment in September 2003 of officers who did not belong to Shura-yi Nazar brought no immediate or decisive results. A salient feature of the agreement between the Afghan Ministry of Defence and the UN Assistance Mission in Afghanistan was its provision for the demobilisation of the militias, beginning in October 2003, in the context of the 'Afghanistan New Beginnings Program' announced by Karzai in April 2003. The United States earmarked $60 million to be used for this purpose during 2004. The mandate of ISAF (International Security Assistance Force) was extended to the provinces, but there are still at present insufficient forces to curb commanders who do not keep their promises by military means. Incidents continue to be frequent, in spite of the establishment in May 2002 of a Security Commission for northern Afghanistan.

Overall, little progress has been made up to the present in the formation of a national army. Ten battalions, comprising around 6,000

---

[6] Padshah Khan's collaboration with the United States came to an end following the supply of false intelligence which led to the bombing of a mosque in December 2001 and then to an attack on a convoy of officials on their way to support Karzai in Kabul.

soldiers, had been formed by the spring of 2003, but the soldiers receive only around $17 a month, and desertions run at 30–50%, especially when men are posted outside their home provinces.[7] Absenteeism and even criminality are common in most units.

The drive to reconstruct the state has therefore clashed with the efforts of the regional powers to remain autonomous. The real obstacle, however, has been the re-emergence of the Taliban movement, which has obstructed all efforts at pacification.

The new guerrilla movement

'Had the Taliban been an organic outgrowth of the Afghan society, they would have survived much longer, and a campaign of harassment of the new power holders would have begun immediately.'[8] By the winter of 2002–3 there was no longer any question that the Taliban had re-formed, an issue over which in the summer of 2002 there remained some doubt. In Kandahar, in March 2003, the United States deployed more than 1,000 men with strong air support in a single operation against a Taliban guerrilla force which was already beginning to carry out daily operations against the US forces and their Afghan allies.

After some months of reorganisation, the Taliban had resumed its leading role in the Pushtun provinces. As far as can be ascertained, there had been no significant change of personnel among the movement's activists, except for the replacement of those lost during the war. At the head of the movement there seems to have been no challenge to *mullah* Omar's leadership. Most of his former charisma had probably dissipated by the time of the Taliban regime's military collapse, but he remains the leader of a disciplined group. The role of his associates also continues to be significant. These include *mullah* Baradar, from the same district as *mullah* Omar; Akhtar Muhammad Osmani, the former military governor of Kandahar; and *mullah* Abdul Razak, the former Minister of the Interior. Meanwhile the prestige enjoyed by Jalaluddin Haqqani continues to boost the guerrillas in the east of the country.

---

[7] International Crisis Group, *Disarmament and Reintegration in Afghanistan*, Asia Report 65, September 2003, p. 5.
[8] William Maley, *The Afghan Wars*, London: Palgrave, 2002, p. 267.

The alliance with Hekmatyar has entailed further radicalisation among the Taliban and more stress on ideology.[9] In particular its co-operation with Hekmatyar after his return to Afghanistan, when the CIA made its attempt to assassinate him, won the Taliban supporters in the towns, especially Kabul. Training camps for foreign recruits once more appeared on the frontier, in the region of Asadabad, taking the form of small mobile teams of some twenty individuals.

The Taliban seems to have changed its strategy after a period of some months during which guerrilla actions were limited to ineffectual mortar attacks against US positions. Taliban military operations became more effective, especially its ambushes, although by mid-2003 western losses since the beginning of the war had not exceeded fifty men. Another factor was the adoption by the guerrillas of new tactics, hitherto unseen in Afghanistan. In June 2003 four German soldiers were killed near Kabul in a suicide attack, probably organised by Al-Qa'ida, or perhaps by Hekmatyar's network. However, the Taliban has generally avoided direct confrontation with western forces and is digging in for a long-term struggle, for which it possesses the necessary economic resources and manpower. The availability to it of a refuge inside Pakistan, an issue discussed in further detail below, has helped them replenish their arms supplies and elude their pursuers.

The aim of the Taliban is to prevent the reconstruction of the central state. Afghan government troops have therefore become a priority target, along with the UN and the NGOs. The Taliban now maintains guerrilla forces several hundred strong in a number of locations in the south and has the ability to seize government positions of moderate size. Following the hit-and-run operations of 2002 the new trend is to base groups of fighters inside Afghanistan. In Ghazni the Taliban is able to move freely within the town, though without arms, and has killed a UN employee in a daylight attack. Only US air power has so far hindered the Taliban from starting the process of reconquest with the capture of small towns.

There is uncertainty over the ability of the Taliban to extend beyond the Pushtun regions, despite its efforts to give the conflict a reli-

---

[9] The assassination in cold blood in April 2003 of an ICRC representative illustrates this issue. The likelihood of such incidents occurring was heightened because of the increasing integration of humanitarian aid workers into the western strategic deployment.

gious dimension, Afghanistan is today the scene of a veritable propaganda battle.[10] Taliban tracts denouncing the occupiers and their allies, couched in primarily religious and nationalistic terms, are distributed, even in Kabul. In one such pamphlet American soldiers are pictured body-searching a young woman.

The Taliban is now an acknowledged force in the south, to the extent that in the province of Zabul, where it enjoys overwhelming support from the population, the government has negotiated a ceasefire. The new governor of the province, Hafizullah Tukhi, initiated talks in the summer of 2003. It seems likely that Hamid Karzai intends to put pressure on Shura-yi Nazar by leaving open the door for the rehabilitation of the Taliban. Alternatively these events may also be interpreted in military terms, as a consequence of the government's inability to overcome the guerrillas, who have forces of several hundred fighters in some districts, for example in Dayshopan, while the western military presence remains insufficiently strong.

The western forces number around 13,000, of whom 8,000 are American, and 5,000 men of the International Security Assistance Force (ISAF) stationed in Kabul (March 2004). In addition, logistical support for the US troops involves more than 50,000 troops in the surrounding region, particularly in Central Asia. The cost to the United States of these operations is around $1 billion each month. Because of the restricted size of its forces, it relies on air power and embarks on few large-scale ground operations, whose risky nature was illustrated by the fate of 'Operation Anaconda', launched near Gardez on 1 March, 2002, which was intended to dislodge Taliban and Al-Qa'ida fighters from a mountainous region with numerous caves. The Americans lost two Chinook helicopters as the result of poor planning and the under-estimation of their adversary; fifty soldiers were wounded, and if they had not worn body-armour the number would have been much higher. The guerrillas appear to have withdrawn into Pakistan territory with no significant losses. From the spring of 2003 the increase in infiltration by the Taliban

---

[10] Nor are US efforts on an insignificant scale. In April 2002 US aircraft dropped 10,000 Afghani banknotes in the Spin Boldak and Shaman areas. Pamphlets were attached or dropped separately showing a woman begin beaten by the Taliban. The effect of other leaflets depicting *mullah* Omar as a dog was probably ambiguous when distributed by non-Muslim forces.

prompted the Americans to step up the number of hunt-and-destroy missions, in which they provided air support for Afghan troops. However, the Taliban avoided contact with the Americans where possible and could always disappear into the population if the pressure became too strong. In this sense the initiative remains with the guerrillas, who have learned the importance of mobility in the face of foreign forces whose intelligence-gathering is still, after two years in the country, surprisingly poor.

The US forces are unwelcome, especially in the Pushtun areas, where the civilians have complained of harrassment. Regularly and predictably, military operations result in civilian casualties, which are all the more resented since the United States neither acknowledges them nor pays compensation. For instance, forty-two Afghans died and 118 were wounded on the night of 30 June–1 July 2002 when four villages near Kakrakai in the province of Uruzgan were bombed during a marriage ceremony. In early July the military authorities acknowledged that B-52s and AC-130s took part in the attack and claimed that the planes retaliated after being targeted. An internal report by the UN contradicted this allegation, stressing the subsequent appearance of US troops at the scene to remove traces of the bombing. The treatment of prisoners of war also does not measure up to international standards. In a communiqué on 28 January, 2003 the World Organisation Against Torture stated that Taliban detained by the Americans had been subjected to torture in CIA interrogation centres, particularly at Bagram air base in Afghanistan and on the island of Diego Garcia.[11] A further point is the continuing uncertainty over the status of more than 600 prisoners detained at Guantanamo Bay in contravention of international law, pending a decision by the US Supreme Court.

In early 2002 both the UN and the Karzai government appealed for further US forces to be sent to Afghanistan. According to F. Vendrell, deputy to the UN envoy Lakhdar Brahimi, 30,000 troops would be necessary to guarantee security in the major towns alone. For

---

[11] The WOAT report was based principally on an article in the *Washington Post* for 26 December 2002, 'U.S. decries abuse but defends interrogations'. Prisoners in these detention centres are said to have been subjected to physical and psychological torture. Three detainees are said to have died at Bagram airbase following ill-treatment.

months this request went unanswered, owing to a shortage of available troops and to a lack of commitment on the part of the United States.

From the autumn of 2002, however, the US government became increasingly conscious of the resurgence of the Taliban and of the generally deteriorating situation. There were two indications that its position had changed. First, it backed ISAF's transfer to NATO control in the autumn of 2003, and then endorsed the extension of its mandate to cover areas outside Kabul, giving it the capacity to intervene in any of the major towns. Second, at the end of September 2003 the United States appointed Zalmay Khalilzad as its ambassador in Kabul, replacing Robert Finn. With Khalilzad's appoint came an increased willingness to give higher priority to the reconstruction of the state. In particular the US administration wished to put advisers into all the ministries, in the same way as its advisers already led Afghan military units. In addition the United States put pressure on Shura-yi Nazar to relinquish its control over the Ministry of Defence, to pave the way for the re-formation of a national army. Finally, the objective of waging an efficient counter-insurgency campaign led to the formation of Provincial Reconstruction Teams (PRA). These units of fifty to 100 men, situated in a dozen key provinces including in particularly Gardez, Bamyan and Kunduz, were given the task of coordinating military operations with the humanitarian effort. This plan was completely rejected by the NGOs working in Afghanistan, which preferred to be dissociated from the military, fearing for their security if they were not.

Ethnicity, social groups and ideologies

Two significant changes have taken place in the social balance of power in Afghanistan. First, there has been a shift of power away from a group of religious figures and towards new and more diverse élites. Second, in parallel, the religious hierarchy has been overthrown.

The consequences of the lack of an accepted ethnic hierarchy from the outset of the war have already been analysed. The fall of the Taliban led to a new imbalance in representation in the national institutions. The Uzbeks are able up to a point to regard themselves as represented by Dostum, while the Hazaras are represented by Hezb-i Wahdat and the Persian-speakers of the northeast by Jamiyat-i

Islami.[12] However, the Pushtuns, the most numerous ethnic community, have unquestionably been marginalised by the new regime. The ethnic cleansing to which they have been subjected in the north has been tolerated or even connived at by the two principal backers of the government, Jamiyat-i Islami and Jombesh, while Hamid Karzai has had neither the will nor the ability to interfere.[13] The provinces most concerned have been Faryab, Jozjan, Badghis, Kunduz, Baghlan and Takhar. In February 2002 some 20,000 people fled from northern Afghanistan because of ethnic persecution. At Dast-i Arshi, where the Pushtuns fell victim to aggression by the Uzbeks, they fled *en masse*. There are today several tens of thousands of Pushtun refugees in the south of the country. A further issue is that there is an increasingly direct correspondence between ethnicity and political affiliation, particularly in the north. After the fall of the Taliban the Uzbek commanders joined up with Jombesh so as to be able to resist the pressure of Shura-yi Nazar, a fact which explains Jombesh's recent appearance in the province of Takhar, especially at Taloqan, Masud's former base.

The balance between social groups has also been upset. The *ulema* no longer occupy a significant position in national politics, as was demonstrated by their virtual absence from the interim government formed in December 2001. On the other hand, their exclusion from politics has enabled them to resume their earlier position as critics of the government. Still, the elections planned for 2005 could bring a return to power by the *ulema* in some areas. However, in this context Hezb-i Wahdat is a regional exception within Hazarajat. The Shi'ite *ulema* never left the political arena in Hazarajat, both because they form part of the Northern Alliance and because there is no alternative to them. A further point is that, in the absence of trained personnel, the *ulema* continue to play a significant role in the fields of primary education and justice. Finally, the disappearance of the Taliban government may permit the religious families to return, espe-

---

[12] Pierre Centlivres and Micheline Centlivres-Demont remark on 'having heard with surprise a mythical tale of Masud being of Pushtun descent, an indication that he may be accepted by some Pushtuns as a national hero and martyr who is above ethnicity' (personal information, April 2003). An imaginary genealogy of this kind could also be interpreted as a sign of the downgrading of the Pushtuns.

[13] *Afghanistan: Monthly Review,* April 2003.

cially the Gaylani, who are attempting to rebuild their networks of clients, partly for political purposes.

As for the educated class, impoverishment or exile was their only prospect under the Taliban, since the prospects for employment offered by the NGOs were limited. It is evident today that this situation has been reversed. Political figures at the national level are mostly university graduates or have at least been educated to secondary level. Foreign aid has led to the development of bureaucracies, such as those within the NGOs, the Afghan state and international organisations, which are able to offer employment. The reopening of the girls' schools and jobs in NGOs have opened up employment opportunities to workless Afghans. In addition, other opportunities for modern kinds of activity have emerged in the major towns, especially Kabul itself.

However, the élites display only minimal coherence in their social and ideological position, and distinctions based on social origins remain marked. The current President himself, Hamid Karzai, a typical product of the traditional élites, is the son of a distinguished Pushtun family from Kandahar, related to the royal family, which includes a large number of high officials.[14] This family enjoys the support of the Popolzai of the Kandahar region, but it was his exile in the United States which enabled Karzai to gain the backing of the US government and therefore achieve his present position. Karzai tends to rely on the support of men who have had similar careers. Thus Ashraf Ghani, the Minister of Finance, is a former employee of the World Bank. In contrast, the officials of Jamiyat-i Islami or Ettehad derive their legitimacy from their participation in the *jihad*. Various factions have emerged since the fall of the Taliban, mostly from the erstwhile parties in Peshawar.

The end of the Taliban did not automatically imply the end of the fundamentalist tendency, which continues to flourish even within the present government. Opposition to the west is not a monopoly of the armed opposition, and there is strong resistance to the liberalising measures initiated by the UN and the NGOs. A campaign of intimidation has been waged against the Minister for Women's Affairs, Dr Sima Samar, who was accused of blasphemy in June 2002, and

[14] For biographies of members of the Karzai family see Ludwig Adamec, *Who's Who in Afghanistain*, Graz: Akademische Druck- und Verlagsanstalt, 1987.

later acquitted. The head of the Afghan Supreme Court, *mawlawi* Shinwari, follows an interpretation of the Quran close to that of the Taliban. In September 2003 the council of *ulema* banned women from working in the NGOs. This had previously been authorised by *mawlawi* Shinwari although he declared that they should be separated from men in the workplace. For example, he ruled that women should not be permitted to make journeys of longer than three hours, or travel abroad, unless accompanied by a male member of their family.

Finally, marked regional distinctions, which had been to some extent suppressed by the Taliban, have re-appeared and seem set to persist even after the hypothetical construction of the state. The provinces stand in opposition to Kabul, where the insulating effect resulting from the presence of the humanitarian organisations has led to an accelerated process of westernisation among a section of the younger people. However, even in the capital the *burqa* generally continues to be worn, except in only a few areas. At the same time everyday customs have been little changed in the Pushtun south, where few girls go to school and a return to customary law is in evidence. Hazarajat is dominated by Hezb-i Wahdat, whose officials are all men of religion, and whose ideology is clerical and fundamentalist. Herat, under the authority of Ismail Khan, is in an intermediate position. Strict rules are maintained and women are obliged to wear the *burqa*, which they have always done, even during the Soviet occupation, but on the other hand girls are permitted to go to school.

12. The Policy of Pakistan

Only a decade after the fall of the Soviet Union, the United States set up military bases in Central Asia, thus radically altering the parameters of regional security. Russia has been dislodged from its position of regional supremacy, and the United States is now able to exert direct influence over the internal political balance of the Central Asian states. In Uzbekistan the presence of US troops is primarily of internal significance, allowing all opposition to be suppressed in the name of the war against terrorism. Elsewhere the United States has denounced Iran as part of the 'Axis of Evil', openly encouraging the overthrow of the current regime. A consequence of the invasion of Iraq was that both of Iran's immediate neighbours were occupied by US troops. This situation explains the extreme caution of the Iranian government, which refrains from significant interference in Afghanistan. In any case Iran no longer has a local proxy, since Hezb-i Wahdat has opted to cooperate with the United States.

Ultimately the position of Pakistan will be decisive for the future of Afghanistan. The United States needed Pakistan's help, primarily to seal the frontier during its military operations, but also for logistical reasons.[1] Although Pakistan is a nuclear power, it has been unable to resist the demands of the United States because of its parlous financial position. The Americans have neatly saved Pakistan's face by presenting its acquiescence as a negotiated agreement. Pakistan's change of direction was disclosed by President Musharraf in a major speech on 19 September 2001,[2] in which he justified Pakistan's alignment with the United States and its abandonment of the Taliban on the grounds of national interest and of the necessity of preventing the installation of an anti-Pakistan government in Kabul. He backed up

---

[1] These were the use by the US forces of the bases at Dalbandin (in Baluchistan), Jalalabad and Pasni.

[2] The full text in English is given in *The News*, 20 September 2001.

his position with a Quranic text which endorses the principle of tactical alliance with non-Muslims.

At first glance Pakistan had succeeded in a démarche similar to that which it had employed at the time of the Soviet invasion; Musharraf's government used an international crisis to re-establish its credibility. Following Pakistan's humiliation at Kargil in 1998, the military coup and the international economic sanctions triggered by the nuclear tests, relations between Washington and Islamabad were at their lowest ebb. However, the diplomatic détente did not signify a return to the 'golden age' of the 1980s. The objective of the United States was to ward off the collapse of Musharraf's government by affording him the scope to suppress radical movements within his territory. However, the level of US economic aid was limited, amounting to around $6 billion,[3] while Pakistan continued in reality to suffer from a degree of diplomatic isolation. Above all, Pakistan could not count on US support over the Kashmir issue. In the last resort the pro-Indian orientation of the United States was based on a real long-term commitment, the result of a pro-Indian pressure group active in the US Congress, at a moment when Pakistan had lost much of its support there.[4]

The abrupt realignment of Pakistani policy resulted in a confrontation with the religious movements, hitherto instrumentalised by the state. There follows an analysis of pro-Taliban mobilisation, and of developments in human and economic movements between the two countries.

Trial of strength with the pro-Taliban movements

'Pro-Taliban forces in Pakistan foresee an Iraq-like invasion of Afghanistan led by the United States, Russia and their allies. Neither Iran nor Pakistan would be in a position to support Islamic warriors when the doomsday arrives. Perhaps, realizing such an eventuality, the religious groups in Pakistan and their leadership are engaged in "necessary homework" to save their friends in Afghanistan.' (Shaikh Akram, 'A Storm is Brewing', *Viewpoint*, May 2001, p. 15)

---

[3] In the same period Turkey and Argentina, each with a much smaller population, had credit facilities with the IMF of over $30 billion and $22 billion respectively.
[4] Arthur G. Rubinoff, 'Changing Perceptions of India in the US Congress', *Asian Affairs*, 4–11, 2001.

As this quotation demonstrates, the Pakistani state's abandonment of the Taliban was foreseen by some fundamentalist movements which never had any illusions concerning the permanence of its support. Although public opinion in Pakistan was flatly opposed to American intervention, pro-Taliban mobilisation at the national level in fact remained relatively low. The attacks of 11 September were viewed as terrorism by 64% of Pakistanis, while 24% saw them as justifiable in terms of the *jihad*. On the other hand, Bin Laden was well regarded, with 82% seeing him as a *mujahid*, while to 6% he was a terrorist. Only 3% of Pakistanis declared themselves pro-American as against 83% who took the side of the Taliban; 75% were opposed to the use of Pakistani air bases by the United States. Nevertheless, Musharraf's position enjoyed the sympathy of much of the population: 51% were favourable to cooperation with the United States, no doubt hoping not to be isolated in the confrontation with India, as against 41% who actively disapproved.[5]

Popular support for the Taliban only rarely went as far as active participation, and mobilisation in favour of it was geographically restricted and on a limited scale. This can be explained in a number of ways. At the international level there was no pro-Taliban mobilisation comparable to that seen in favour of Iraq at the time of the Gulf War, probably because Arab solidarity did not apply. At the same time, poor coordination between the parties opposed to the American intervention, together with the lack of support from the two major national parties, the PPP (Pakistan People's Party) and the PML (Pakistani Muslim League), deprived the pro-Taliban movement of active supporters. Those parties which did actively protest, Jamaat-i Islami and Jamiyat-i Ulema, were relatively unpopular. Also there was a tough government clamp-down. After a purge of the army ridding Musharraf of potential opposition, leading fundamentalist figures were placed under house arrest and the police did not hesitate to open fire on demonstrators, killing fifteen. The government took prudent steps to forestall escalation, notably by outlawing the use of mosque loudspeakers for political statements.

Support for the Taliban took different forms, including street demonstrations, humanitarian aid and the dispatch of volunteers to

[5] Figures taken from a Gallup poll, in www.sofres.com, 17 October 2001.

Afghanistan. Islamic humanitarian organisations attempted to supplant the western NGOs whose relations with the Taliban staggered from one crisis to another. For instance, Islamic Relief gave $3 million to the Taliban government, while the Rasheed Trust made a bid to replace the World Food Program, which had withdrawn from Afghanistan in June 2001. In a related phenomenon the various fundamentalist and Islamist organisations regularly demonstrated after Friday prayers and launched strike appeals in the bazaars, with varying degrees of success.

The most significant level of mobilisation was seen in the tribal zones on the Afghanistan-Pakistan frontier, where the Pushtun population was committed to Bin Laden's cause and that of the Taliban, due to both ethnic and religious solidarity. At the end of October armed tribesmen mounted a five-day blockade of the Karakorum highway linking Pakistan and China. A further development was the organisation by fundamentalist movements of the transfer of volunteers to Afghanistan.[6] In November it was estimated that there were thousands of fighters waiting at the Bajaur Agency, where the inhabitants provided them with food. Afghan refugees fleeing from the bombing were being welcomed in the same spirit as the *muhajjirin* of the early 1980s at the time of the Soviet invasion.

The level of mobilisation might have appeared as a setback for the pro-Taliban parties, but these groups, which had previously done badly at the polls, made major advances in the elections of November 2002, especially in the provinces bordering Afghanistan. In the NWFP the election was won by Muttahida Majlis-i Amal (MMA), a union of six pro-Taliban parties including Jamiyat-i Ulema and Jamaat-i Islami, which set the scene for a rampant 'Talibanisation' of the province.[7] The emergence of provincial administrations which overtly supported the Taliban contributed to establishing the frontier regions as a haven for the guerillas, who embarked on an undisguised propaganda campaign and were able to make preparations for the military operations they intended to carry out inside Afghanistan. Entire quarters of Quetta fell under *de facto* Taliban control.

---

[6] *The News,* 2 November, 2001.

[7] The expression is not too strong: the authorities clamped down on musicians, male journalists were banned from covering women's sporting events, and in broader terms there was a 'shariatisation' of the law.

Despite the authoritarianism of President Musharraf's government there was little it could do directly against movements which remained within the law and enjoyed parliamentary representation. The most radical fringe groups had always been the particular object of repression, a tendency which increased in the wake of the attack against the Indian parliament on 12 December 2001. In January 2002 a wide-ranging operation against jihadist movements resulted in thousands of arrests, while hundreds of the offices of such movements were closed down across Pakistan. Several armed groups were proscribed, including Lashkar-i Taiba and Jaish-i Muhammad, those accused by India of responsibility for the attack on its parliament, and two Pakistani movements implicated in sectarian conflict, namely the Sunni movement Sipah-i Sihaba Pakistan (SSP) and the Shi'ite Tehreek-i Jafria Pakistan, were also banned. A pro-Taliban organisation which had dispatched thousands of volunteers to Afghanistan, Tehreek-i Nifaz-i Shariat Muhammado (TNSM), was dissolved.

After the American intervention, the ensuing political crisis prompted President Musharraf to re-emphasise two policies he had mooted at the time of his seizure of power. These were the extension of state control over the religious institutions, and the re-imposition of government authority in the frontier regions. On 18 August 2001 the government promulgated the Pakistan Madrassah Education Board Ordinance, which was in effect a first step towards the integration of the *madrasas* into the educational system, but which encountered stiff resistance from the *ulema*.[8] However, little changed in the period following 11 September, since the government did not have the funds to finance profound changes in the educational system. In Punjab alone there were more than a quarter of a million students in the *madrasas,* most from poor families.[9] The trial of strength between the government and the religious movements exacerbated the existing polarisation between social groups, in which the modern urban class, which was antipathetic to the *ulema*, found itself in opposition to the population at large, over whom the *ulema* still exercised substantial influence, especially in the frontier provinces.

[8] Another factor was that the American administration earmarked 100 million dollars to extend surveillance over *madrasa* students, which was an indication of a US intention to take a direct hand in intelligence operations in Pakistan.

[9] *Herald*, November 2001, p. 50.

In parallel, there was also a movement to weaken the autonomy of the Tribal Areas, although it was only with great difficulty that control could be maintained over heavily-armed tribesmen who depended for their economic survival on contraband. After the fall of the Taliban the Pakistan army was able for the first time to enter the FATA (Federally Administered Tribal Areas),[10] and specifically occupied the Mohmand Agency. However, the army undertook not to interfere in the contraband trade, and the sale of firearms was allowed to continue. In May 2002 the arrival of a small US force at Miram Shah was regarded as a provocation, especially when the troops searched a *madrasa*, while joint Afghan-Pakistani operations met with little success. Islamabad's lack of control was clear, even though it seemed beyond doubt that Bin Laden had taken refuge in the FATA.

A final factor was that even within Pakistan government circles policy towards Afghanistan continued to be a subject for debate. At the behest of the Northern Alliance, backed by Russia and India, Pakistan had been entirely excluded from negotiations on the future of Afghanistan. The hope of an Afghan-Pakistani alliance against India faded, as Pakistan saw a pro-Indian and anti-Pakistan government re-established in Kabul. Meanwhile diplomatic relations between Pakistan and Afghanistan were less than warm, and the lack of an agreed frontier line was an additional source of friction. At this point some elements in Pakistan toyed with the idea of destabilising the Afghan government, to open the way for the return to power of a pro-Pakistan faction, though for the time being the presence of American troops precluded open Pakistani support for the armed Afghan opposition. For its part the Afghan government wanted the United States to put pressure on Pakistan to dismantle the guerrilla groups, but the options for the United States were limited from the moment when it became apparent that any political alternative to the regime of General Musharraf in Pakistan would be to its disadvantage. The continuing arrests of Al-Qa'ida militants in Pakistan, together with occasional military operations, allowed Pakistan for

---

[10] The NWFP proper is distinct from the FATA (Federally Administered Tribal Agencies) which are administered by a political agent appointed by Islamabad, on the British model of 'indirect rule'. There are seven Tribal Agencies (South Waziristan, North Waziristan, Mohmand, Kurram, Orakzai, Bajaur and Khyber) as well as five Frontier Regions in the interior of the NWFP.

the time being to make some response to Washington's demands without prejudicing the possibility of it intervening in Afghanistan in future.

Commercial and human movements

One of the results of twenty-five years of war has been the opening up of Afghanistan, especially as a result of two socio-economic phenomena, namely the Afghan refugee communities and cross-border trade.

During the war cross-border trade, previously limited, developed to a striking extent, especially in the 1990s when the Afghan state ceased to exist as such, while the intensity of the fighting diminished. The development of towns close to the frontier, such as Jalalabad and Khost, can be explained by the suppression of the checkpoints on Afghan roads, of which there were more than fifty between Kandahar and the Pakistan frontier. Smuggling was especially profitable, since the thirty-year Afghan Transit Trade Agreement (ATTA) signed in 1965 permitted Afghanistan, as a land-locked country, to import goods in sealed containers through the port of Karachi. This mechanism allowed goods to be illegally re-exported to the Pakistani tribal areas. Far from being locally restricted, trade between Pakistan and Afghanistan therefore brought wider networks into play, especially involving the Gulf countries, where merchant families were based.[11]

Pakistan, which was losing considerable sums in customs duties, attempted on a number of occasions to renegotiate the ATTA. Since 1995, when the 1965 accords came to an end, it has striven to restrict the flow of Afghan imports through Karachi, but these attempts have resulted in the re-routing of trade channels, so that goods now come to Herat by way of Iran before, as previously, entering Pakistan as contraband. Customs duties from the Herat region have correspondingly increased, while those from Kandahar and Nangrahar have shrunk. About three-quarters of Afghanistan's commerce now passes through Iran.

[11] Afghanistan's exports were diverse. Wood for the construction industry was a constant export, contributing to Afghanistan's deforestation. However, vehicles and electronic items brought from Asia by way of Dubai made up the bulk of the goods involved. For 1997, the World Bank estimated that the volume of smuggling, excluding the drugs trade, amounted to 2.5 billion dollars. See Ahmed Rashid, *Nation*, 21 January 1998.

The second significant element in Afghanistan's relationship with Pakistan has been the return of the refugees. By the end of the 1990s more than 3 million Afghans were registered as refugees in Pakistan. A large proportion of these were settled in NWFP and Baluchistan, where their presence was initially accepted by Pakistan, although requests for their return to Afghanistan were heard increasingly as time went on. However, many refugees spontaneously returned to Afghanistan.[12] By the time of the Taliban's fall only some 1.2 million remained out of an original 3 million. Their return was largely due to the improvement of Afghanistan's internal security. However, the figures must be treated with caution because of the phenomenon of 'simulated return' undertaken to obtain UNHCR grants. It is evident today that hundreds of thousands of Afghan refugees, of whom many now have Pakistani citizenship, do not intend to return permanently to Afghanistan.

---

[12] Iran put very real pressure on the refugees to go back to Afghanistan, but several hundred thousand remain in Iran.

Conclusion

The Afghan war is not over, and there is no indication that a rapid pacification of the country can be expected. A generation of Afghans including many well into adulthood have experienced nothing but war. As a result of such traumas of the most profound kind the pre-war society has largely ceased to exist.

A primary consequence of the war has been abrupt and rapid politicisation. Rebellion undertaken in the name of the *jihad* fell progressively under the control of increasingly sophisticated organisations. In different regions the new political élites were either *ulema* or members of the educated class, the two groups which alone could organise themselves sufficiently. Political struggles were therefore linked to the confrontation between these two social groups, the educated class and the *ulema*, a phenomenon which has explosively expanded the diversity of ideological and social positions found within political Islam. While antagonism between the two groups became entrenched as the 1990s went on, ideological differences on certain issues became more flexible. The Islamists largely renounced their modernising project and toughened their attitude on social issues, at the same time as traditionalist movements such as the Taliban became more radical as a result of their contact with transnational organisations such as Al-Qa'ida, and embarked on an abortive plan to set up a fundamentalist state. Here the Taliban demonstrated that fundamentalists are not necessarily unaware of ideas relating to the state. This in turn means that any notion that such a movement must necessarily be committed solely to re-Islamisation from below should at least be qualified.

In the French edition of this book which appeared in 2000 the author stressed the unique nature of the Taliban regime, which did not seem to offer a model adaptable to other circumstances by reason of the very unusual conditions necessary for a religiously motivated group to be in a position to impose a new kind of political structure.

However, the Taliban model had then, and still has today, an ideological impact in Pakistan and in the Gulf, although it is highly unlikely that the *ulema* could exercise similar influence in a more differentiated society, such as that of Pakistan. The persistence of a strong fundamentalist strain after the fall of the Taliban regime demonstrates in any case the resistance of a substantial section of Afghan society to the liberal model presented under the auspices of international assistance.

From the 1990s onwards one aspect of this accelerated politicisation, namely ethnicisation, has taken on a growing importance. The redefinition of national feeling through its attachment to ethnic identities has been another major result of the war. Without a recognised ethnic hierarchy, and in the absence of mechanisms capable of guaranteeing the equitable representation of different groups within institutions, the present situation is characterised by the marginalisation of the Pushtuns, the numerically most significant ethnic group. In this sense, the present situation could lead to mass slaughter, particularly in the north, where the position of Pushtun population groups which are locally in the minority could become especially perilous if international forces are withdrawn.

The re-establishment of the state has been the key issue in Afghanistan since the Soviet withdrawal and the victory of the *mujahidin* in 1992. The Afghan government exists solely as a consequence of international military and financial aid, the continuation of which depends on considerations beyond the control of the Afghans themselves. Afghanistan's subjection to international intervention, resulting from the position of the Taliban as an anomaly within the international order, has led to an experiment in social engineering with effects that are sometimes unpredictable. The need to buttress the central authority could easily generate an authoritarian regime, and constitutional plans at present under consideration are not reassuring on this point. Another issue is that there is nothing to indicate that this nascent state could survive the discontinuation of international aid, while much will ultimately depend on the capacity of the United States to oversee the process of reconstruction over the long-term.

Having exploited the Afghan resistance to weaken the Soviet Union with some success, the United States subsequently had no coherent policy for Afghanistan. Only the existence of its radical movements obliged the United States once again to become involved, but this involvement was concerned solely with security considerations. Even in this context the outcome has not necessarily been positive for the Americans. The radical militants are today able to seek refuge in a region on the Afghan-Pakistani border in which they can move unhindered. In addition—and this is a key point—they are not under the control of any state since this zone largely falls outside both Pakistani and Afghan control. A further issue is that the continued presence of US forces in Afghanistan entails the disadvantage that the Americans present a permanent target for small groups of fighters. The presence of these forces perpetuates the link between the Afghan crisis and a more global confrontation. The dynamic resulting from this interaction of heterogeneous actors—states, networks, transnational organisations and parties—has effects which are largely unpredictable.

In any case, there is nothing to suggest that even with its overwhelming technological superiority the United States will in the short term achieve the stabilisation of Afghanistan. The guerrilla movements, though regional, have the capacity to survive for years, placing their faith in an eventual disengagement by the United States. Failure in Afghanistan would have significant consequences for America as a power, and thus the issues involved in this interminable war extend far beyond the destiny of Afghanistan itself.

Select Bibliography

Abadi, Basir Ahmad Daulat, *Hazâb va jarayânât-i siâsi-yi Afghanistan* (Parts and political events in Afghanistan), Tehran: Moallef, 1982.

Adamec, Ludwig W., *Who's Who of Afghanistan*, Graz: Akademische Druck- und Verlagstanstalt, 1975.

———, *A Biographical Dictionary of Contemporary Afghanistan*, Graz: Akademische Druck- und Verlagsanstalt, 1987.

———, *Historical Dictionary of Afghanistan*, Metuchen: Scarecrow Press, 1991.

———, 'Afghanistan', *Les Temps Modernes*, July–August 1980 (special issue).

AFRANE (Amitié Franco-Afghane), *La femme afghane à travers l'histoire de l'Afghanistan*, Actes du colloque Unesco, Paris, 11 December 1998.

Ahmad, Qeyamuddin, *The Wahabi Movement in India*, Islamabad: National Book Foundation, 1979.

Ahmed, Akbar S., *Millennium and Charisma among Pathans: a Critical Essay in Social Anthropology*, London: Routledge and Kegan Paul, 1976.

———, *Pukhtun Economy and Society*, London: Routledge and Kegan Paul, 1980.

———, 'The impact of Afghan refugees on ethnicity and politics in Baluchistan', *Central Survey* 9 (3), 1980.

———, and D. Hart (eds), *Islam in Tribal Societies*, London: Routledge and Kegan Paul, 1984.

Allan, P., and A. Stahel, 'Tribal guerilla warfare against a colonial power', *Journal of Conflict Resolution* 27 (4), December 1983.

Amstutz, J. B., *The First Five Years of Soviet Occupation*, Washington, DC: National Defense University Press, 1986.

Anderson, Jon W., 'Tribe and community among the Ghilzai Pashtuns', *Anthropos* 70, 1975.

———, 'There are no Khans anymore: economic development and social change in tribal Afghanistan', *Middle East Journal* 32, 1978.

———, 'Social structure and the veil: comportment and interaction in Afghanistan', *Anthropos*, 77, 1982.

Arjomand, Saïd Amir, *The Turban for the Crown*, Oxford University Press, 1989.

Arnold, Anthony, *Afghanistan: the Soviet Invasion in Perspective*, Stanford, CA: Hoover Institute Press, 1981.

————, *Afghanistan's Two-Party Communism*, Stanford, CA: Hoover Institute Press, 1983.

————, *The Fateful Pebble: Afghanistan's Role in the Fall of the Soviet Empire*, CA: Presidio, 1993.

Aziz, Abdullah, *Essai sur les catégories dirigeantes de l'Afghanistan 1945–1963*, Frankfurt-am-Main: Peter Lang, 1987.

Azoy, Whitney, *Buzkashi—So that his Name Shall Rise*, Philadelphia: University of Pennsylvania Press, 1982.

Bahadur, Kalim, *The Jama'at-i-Islami of Pakistan*, Lahore: Progressive Books, 1978.

Baitemann, Olga, 'NGOs and the Afghan War: the politicisation of humanitarian aid', *Third World Quarterly* 12 (1), January 1990.

Balleau-Lajoinie, *La condition des femmes en Afghanistan*, Paris: Editions Sociales, 1980.

Barry, Mike, *Afghanistan*, Paris: Seuil, 1971.

————, 'Répression et guerre soviétiques', *Les Temps modernes*, July–August 1980.

Barry, Mike, *Le royaume de l'insolence*, Paris: Flammarion, 1984.

————, 'L'Afghanistan entre Marx et le Coran', *Politique internationale* 31, spring 1986.

————, 'La deuxième mort de l'Afghanistan', *Politique Internationale* 50, 1991.

Barth, Fredrik, *Political Leadership among Swat Pathans*, London: Athlone Press, 1959.

————, 'Pathan Identity and its Maintenance' in F. Barth (ed.), *Ethnic Groups and Boundaries: The Social Organisation of Culture Difference*, Bergen, Oslo: Universitätsforlaget; London, Geo. Allen and Unwin, 1969.

————, *The Last Wali of Swat*, Oslo: Norwegian Universities Press, 1985.

Bennigsen, Alexandre, and Chantal Lemercier-Quelquejay, 'L'expérience soviétique en pays musulman. Les leçons du passé et l'Afghanistan', *Politique étrangère* 4, 1980.

————, *Le soufi et le commissaire*, Paris: Seuil, 1986.

Broxup, Marie, 'The Soviets in Afghanistan: anatomy of a takeover', *Central Asian Survey* 1 (4), 1983.

Canfield, Robert L., *Hazara Integration into the Afghan Nation: Some Changing Relations between the Hazaras and the Afghans Officials*, New York: Asian Society, 1972, Occasional Paper no. 3.

———— and M. N. Saharani (eds), *Revolutions and Rebellions in Afghanistan*, Berkeley: University of California Press, 1984.

Carré, Olivier, *Mystique et politique*, Paris: Editions du Cerf, Presses Sc-Po, 1984.

———, *L'Islam laïque ou le retour à la grande tradition*, Paris: Armand Colin, 1993.

Centlivres, Pierre, *Un bazar d'Asie centrale*, Wiesbaden: Ludwig Riechert, 1972.

———, *Paysannerie et pouvoir en Afghanistan. De la fin de la monarchie à l'intervention soviétique*, Geneva: Institut universitaire de hautes études internationales (Occasional Papers), 1985.

———, 'Les tulipes rouges d'Afghanistan. Ancêtres, maîtres spirituels et martyrs dans une société musulmane' in J. Hamard, R. Kaehr and F. Sabelli (eds), *Les ancêtres sont parmi nous*, Neuchâtel: Musée d'ethnographie, 1988.

———, 'Les trois pôles de l'identité afghane au Pakistan', *L'Homme* 8/4 (108), 1988.

Centlivres, Pierre et al., *Afghanistan, la colonisation impossible*, Paris, Les Editions du Cerf, 1984.

Centlivres, P., and Micheline Centlivres-Demont,, *Et si l'on parlait de l'Afghanistan?*, Neuchâtel, Editions de l'Institut d'ethnologie, Paris, Editions de la Maison des sciences de l'homme, 1988.

Centlivres, P., and Micheline Centlivres-Demont, 'Hommes d'influence et hommes de partis. L'organisation politique dans les villages de réfugiés afghans au Pakistan' in Erwin Grötzbach (ed.), *Neue Beiträge zur Afghanistanforschung*, Liestal: Bibliotheca Afghanica, 1988.

Centlivres Demont, Micheline, 'Types d'occupation et relations interethniques dans le Nord-Est de l'Afghanistan', *Studia Iranica* 5 (2), 1976, pp. 69–77.

———, 'Les réfugiés afghans au Pakistan. Gestion, enjeux, perspectives' in R. Bocco and D. Mohammad-Reza (eds), *Moyen-Orient. Migrations, démocratisation, médiations*, Geneva: Institut Universitaire des Hautes Etudes Internationales, 1994.

———, 'Les femmes dans le conflit Afghan', *Société suisse, Moyen Orient et Culture Islamique*, no. 2, May 1996, pp. 16–18.

Chishti, Nighat Mehroze, *Constitutional Development in Afghanistan*, Karachi: Royal Book Company, 1998.

Daoud, Zemaray, *L'Etat monarchique dans la formation afghane*, Bern-Frankfurt/Main: Peter Lang, 1982.

Digard, Jean-Pierre (ed.), *Le fait ethnique en Iran et en Afghanistan*, Paris: Editions du CNRS, 1988.

Dikshit, P., '1993: Afghanistan policy', *Strategic Analysis* XVI (8), November 1993.

Dorronsoro, Gilles, 'L'aide humanitaire en Afghanistan', *Cultures et conflits*, autumn 1993.

———, 'La politique de pacification en Afghanistan' in Gérard Chaliand (ed.), *Stratégies de la guérilla*, Paris: Payot, 1994.

———, 'Politique et ethnicité. Les Tâdjiks d'Afghanistan', *CEMOTI* 18, 1994.

———, 'Afghanistan. Des réseaux de solidarités aux espaces régionaux' in François Jean and Jean-Christophe Rufin (eds), *Economie des guerres civiles*, Paris: Hachette, 1996.

———, 'Les oulémas afghans', *Archives des sciences sociales des religions*, November 2001.

———, 'Pakistan and the Taliban: State Policy, Religious Networks and Political Connections' in Christophe Jaffrelot (ed.), *Pakistan: Nationalism without a Nation?*, Delhi: Manohar, 2002.

Duprée, Louis, 'Mahmud Tarzi: the forgotten nationalist', *American Universities Field Staff Report* VIII (1), January 1964.

———, 'Afghanistan under the Khalq', *Problems of Communism*, July–August 1979.

———, *Afghanistan*, Princeton University Press, 1980 (1st edition 1973).

———, 'Tribal Warfare in Afghanistan and Pakistan: a Reflection of the Segmentary Lineage System' in A. S. Ahmed and David Hart (eds), *Islam in Tribal Societies*, London: Routledge and Kegan Paul, 1984.

Duprée, Nancy Hatch, 'Femmes d'Afghanistan' (special report), *Les Nouvelles d'Afghanistan*, no. 29–30, Paris, 1986.

———, 'Afghanistan: Women Society and Development', *Journal of Developing Societies*, 8 (1), 1992, pp. 30–42.

Edwards, David Busby, 'Charismatic leadership and political process in Afghanistan', *Central Asian Survey* 5 (3–4), 1986.

———, 'The Evolution of Shi'i Political Dissent in Afghanistan' in J. R. I. Cole and N. R. Keddie (eds), *Shi'ism and Social Protest*, New Haven: Yale University Press, 1986.

———, 'Summoning Muslims: print, politics, and religious ideology in Afghanistan', *Journal of Asian Studies* 52 (3), 1993.

Elphinstone, Mountstuart, *An Account of the Kingdom of Caubul*, Oxford University Press, 1972 (1st edition 1815).

Etienne, Gilbert, *L'Afghanistan ou les aléas de la coopération*, Paris: PUF, 1972.

Farhang, Mir Muhammad Sediq, *Afghanistan dar panj qarn-i akhir* (L'Afghanistan dans les cinq derniers siècles), Peshawar: Derarshesh, 1988.

Ferdinand, Klaus, 'Nomad expansion and commerce in central Afghanistan', *Folk* (4), 1962.

Gaborieau, Marc, 'Typologie des spécialistes religieux chez les musulmans du sous-continent indien. Les limites de l'islamisation', *Archives des sciences sociales des religions* 55 (1), 1983, pp. 29–51.

———, 'Le néo-fondamentalisme au Pakistan: Maududi et la Jama'at-islami' in Olivier Carré (ed.), *Radicalismes islamiques*, Paris: L'Harmattan, 1986.

Gellner, Ernest, *Saints of the Atlas*, London: Weidenfeld and Nicolson, 1969.

Gentelle, Pierre, 'L'Afghanistan et l'aide internationale', *Tiers-monde*, 80, 1979.

Ghani, Ashraf, 'Islam and state building in a tribal society: Afghanistan 1880–1901', *Modern Asian Studies*, 12 (2), 1978.

————, 'Disputes in a court of Sharia, Kunar Valley, Afghanistan', *International Journal of Middle Eastern Studies*, 15, 1983.

Gregorian, Vartan, 'Mahmud Tarzi and the Saraj-al-Akhbar: ideology of nationalism and modernisation in Afghanistan', *Middle East Journal*, 21 (3), 1967, pp. 345–68.

————, *The Emergence of Modern Afghanistan*, Stanford University Press, 1969.

Hauner, Milan, 'One man against the Empire: the Faqir of Ipi and the British in Central Asia on the eve of and during the second world war', *Journal of Contemporary History*, 16 (1), 1981.

Lobato, Chantal, 'Femmes afghanes, femmes musulmanes. Islam, le grand malentendu', *Autrement*, no. 95, Paris, 1987.

————, 'Kaboul 1980–1986. Un islam officiel pour légitimer le pouvoir communiste', *Central Asian Survey*, 7 (2–3), 1988.

Lorentz, J. H., 'Afghan aid: The role of private voluntary organizations', *Journal of South Asian and Middle East Studies*, XI (1–2), autumn-winter 1987.

Majrouh, Sayd Bahodine, 'Petite anthologie de la poésie féminine', *Pashto Quarterly*, Kabul, 1, 3, spring, 1978.

Maley, William (ed.), *Fundamentalism reborn? Afghanistan and the Taliban*, London: Hurst, 1998.

Malik, Jamal, *Colonization of Islam: Dissolution of Traditional Institutions in Pakistan*, Lahore: Vanguard Books, 1996.

Marsden, Peter, *The Taliban: War, Religion and the New Order in Afghanistan*, London: Zed Books, 1998.

Marwat, Dr Fazal-ur-Rahim, *The Evolution and Growth of Communism in Afghanistan, 1917–1979*, Karachi: Royal Book Company, 1997.

Matinuddin, Kamal, *The Afghan Phenomenon: Afghanistan 1994–1997*, Karachi: Oxford University Press, 1999.

Metcalf, Barbara Daly, *Islamic Revival in British India: Deoband 1860–1900*, Princeton University Press, 1982.

Newell, Richard S., 'The government of Muhammad Mussa Shafiq: the last chapter of Afghan liberalism', *Central Asian Survey*, July, 1982.

Poullada, Leon, *Reform and Rebellion in Afghanistan 1919–1929: King Amanullah's Failure to Transform a Tribal Society*, Ithaca, NY: Cornell University Press, 1973.

Roy, Olivier, 'Afghanistan. La guerre des paysans', *Révoltes logiques*, 13, 1981.

362 Select Bibliography

————, 'Intellectuels et ulémas dans la résistance afghane', *Peuples méditerranéens*, 21, 1982.

————, 'Sufism in the Afghan resistance', *Central Asian Survey*, 2 (4), 1983.

————, *L'Afghanistan, Islam et modernité politique*, Paris: Esprit-Seuil, 1985.

————, 'Le double code afghan. Marxisme et tribalisme', *Revue française de science politique*, 35 (5), December 1985.

————, 'Etat et société en Afghanistan', *Revue française de science politique*, 36 (6), December 1986.

————, *L'échec de l'Islam politique*, Paris: Esprit-Seuil, 1992.

————, 'La guerre d'Afghanistan. De la guerre idéologique à la guerre ethnique', *L'Homme et la société*, 107–108, 1993.

Rubin, B. R., 'Lineage of the State in Afghanistan', *Asian Survey*, XXVIII (11), 1988.

————, 'The old regime in Afghanistan: recruitment and training of a state elite', *Central Afghan Survey*, 10 (3), 1991.

————, 'Political elites in Afghanistan: rentier state building, rentier state wrecking', *International Journal of Middle East Studies*, 24, 1992.

————, *The Fragmentation of Afghanistan*, New Haven, London: Yale University Press, 1995.

Shalinsky, Audrey, 'Ethnic reactions to the current regime in Afghanistan: A case study', *Central Asian Survey*, 3 (4), 1984.

Sivan, E., 'Ibn Taymiyya, father of the Islamic revolution', *Encounter*, May 1983.

Sliwinski, Marek, 'Afghanistan 1978–1987: War, demography and society', *Central Asian Survey* (Incidental Papers Series), 1988.

Stahel, Albert A., 'Simulation of Guerilla Warfare' in J. Halin (ed.), *Simulationstechnik*, Springer Verlag, 1987.

Tapper, Nancy, *Bartered Brides: Politics, Gender and Marriage in an Afghan Tribal Society*, Cambridge University Press, 1991.

Tapper, Richard, 'Holier than You: Islam in Three Tribal Societies' in Akbar S. Ahmed, David M. Hart (eds), *Islam in Tribal Societies*, London: Routledge and Kegan Paul, 1984.

———— (ed.), *The Conflict of Tribe and State in Iran and Afghanistan*, London: Croom Helm, 1983.

Yousaf, Mohammad, *The Silent Soldier*, Lahore: Jang Publishers, 1991.

JOURNALS

Afghanistan Info, Comité suisse de soutien au peuple afghan, Neuchâtel, 1980.
Les Nouvelles d'Afghanistan, AFRANE (Amitié franco-afghane), Paris, 1980.

Index